Library of
Davidson College

The Politics of Chile:
A Sociogeographical Assessment

Other Titles in This Series

Brazil: Foreign Relations of a Future World Power, Ronald Schneider

Mexico's Economy: A Political Analysis with Forecasts to 1990, Robert E. Looney

The Future of Brazil, edited by William H. Overholt

Technological Progress in Latin America: The Prospects for Overcoming Dependency, edited by James H. Street and Dilmus D. James

Westview Special Studies on Latin America

The Politics of Chile:
A Sociogeographical Assessment
César Caviedes

Chile's road to socialism, points out the author, was not a linear one. In the last twenty years political parties of an astonishingly wide range of opinions participated in the administration of the country, and their successes and failures have been clearly reflected in the shifting preferences of the voting population. Political ideas did not always receive nationwide acceptance; disobedience, dissent, and confrontation with the government or party officials in Santiago were frequent; and the struggle between centralism and provincial aspirations was a continuing fact of Chilean political life.

Dr. Caviedes focuses clearly on the main protagonists of Chilean politics—the politicians and the voters—and interprets the changing fortunes of the different political parties, both historically and within the context of existing local social, political, and economic conditions. He provides a province-by-province analysis of twenty presidential and congressional elections, demonstrating the variegated character of the voters throughout the country and exploring as well the relevant links with the international political scene.

César Caviedes, a native of Valparaiso, Chile, is associate professor of geography at the University of Regina, Saskatchewan. He conducted graduate studies in Italy and the German Federal Republic, and participated in research activities at the University of Wisconsin-Milwaukee. Dr. Caviedes was one of the founders of the Revista Geográfica de Valparaíso and has worked as a contributing editor of the *Handbook of Latin American Studies* and of *Geospectrum*.

Salvador Allende, Baltazar Castro, Jorge Alessandri
Eduardo Frei
Carlos Ibañez del Campo, Eduardo Cruz Coke, Gabriel Gonzalez
Radomiro Tomic, Arturo Alessandri
Carlos Altamirano, J. Antonio Rios, Pedro Aguirre Cerda

Photocollage by A.V. Services, University of Regina

The Politics of Chile:
A Sociogeographical Assessment
César Caviedes

Westview Press / Boulder, Colorado

Westview Special Studies on Latin America

All rights reserved. No part of this publication may be reproduced or transmitted in any form or by any means, electronic or mechanical, including photocopy, recording, or any information storage and retrieval system, without permission in writing from the publisher.

Copyright © 1979 by Westview Press, Inc.

Published in 1979 in the United States of America by
  Westview Press, Inc.
  5500 Central Avenue
  Boulder, Colorado 80301
  Frederick A. Praeger, Publisher

Caviedes, César.
  The politics of Chile.
  (Westview special studies in Latin America)
  Bibliography: p.
  Includes index.
  1. Chile—Politics and government—1920- 2. Elections—Chile. 3. Social classes—Chile. I. Title.
JL2631.C37   301.5'92'0983   78-23843
ISBN 0-89158-365-3

Printed and bound in the United States of America

Contents

List of Tables and Figures ix
Preface xi

Introduction 1

1. Land and State 7

   The Socioeconomic Landscapes of Chile. 7
   The Organization of the Chilean State. 31

2. Electoral Practices, Voters, Parties, and Politicians 45

   The Electoral Process 46
   Apportionment. 51
   Political Parties 56
   Politicians 68

3. The Social Texture 79

   Aristocracy. 79
   Entrepreneurial Bourgeoisie 91
   The Middle Class. 107
   The Urban Working Class 123
   The Peasantry 135

4. Forty Years of Democratic Life 157

   Prelude: 1924-1932. 157
   The Emergence of Socialism: 1932-1941 159
   The Golden Years of the Bourgeoisie: 1942-1952. 173
   Political Messianism: 1952-1964. 189
   Ideology and Polarization: 1964-1973 219

5. The Regionalization of Politics 275
   The Leftist North 276
   The Radical-Liberal *Norte Chico* 280
   The Capricious Metropolitan Area. 282
   The "Traditionalism" of the Agrarian Provinces 287
   Concepción-Arauco: The Leftist Enclave 289
   Political Regionalism in *La Frontera* 290
   The Center-Right Tendencies of the
      Provinces of Modern Colonization. 291
   Conservative and Radical Chiloé 292
   Socialist Magallanes. 294
   National Survey. 295

Notes. 301
Bibliography 325
Index. 347

Tables and Figures

Table

1. Apportionment and Number of Citizens Represented by a Deputy 52
2. Number of Citizens Represented by a Senator in 1930 and 1970 54
3. Geographical Location of Landed Estates and Political Representation of the Landowner Class 84
4. Representation of Aristocratic Families in the Executive Power and in the Congress of Chile (1810-1953) 87
5. Typology of Chilean Workers Based on Their Sociopolitical Awareness 126
6. Average Vote and Standard Deviations of the Major Parties Congressional Elections, 1932-1973 277
7. Average Vote and Standard Deviations of Presidential Coalitions, 1932-1973 278

Figure

1. Provinces and regions of Chile 9
2. The congressional elections of 1937 164
3. The presidential election of 1938 167
4. The congressional elections of 1941 170
5. The presidential election of 1942 175
6. The congressional elections of 1945 179
7. The presidential election of 1946 183
8. The congressional elections of 1949 187
9. The presidential election of 1952 192
10. The congressional elections of 1953 196
11. The congressional elections of 1957 201

Figure

12. The presidential election of 1958 207
13. The congressional elections of 1961 211
14. The presidential election of 1964 225
15. The congressional elections of 1965 234
16. The congressional elections of 1969 245
17. The presidential election of 1970 255
18. The congressional elections of 1973 269

Preface

Politics for a Chilean has always been a fact of life. Political decisions at the national or local level have influenced education, affected social and economic status, and shaped personalities. During the period covered by this book, I was born, educated, employed, and enfranchised in this highly politicized country. For me, politics became an ingredient of life that I certainly missed when I first left my native country. But in the view from outside I could observe clearly the highs and lows of the Chilean soul and became aware of the many misguided and often downright false ideas disseminated by so-called experts on Chile.

As a university teacher and a geographer I had enviable opportunities to deal with the intelligentsia as well as with the simple people of the country: the miners of the North, the peasants of Middle Chile, and the shepherds of Magallanes. Prolonged contacts with all of them offered me insight into their aspirations and disenchantments not only in life but also in politics. As I came to know them better, I realized that their political responses were not so much prompted by ideological stimuli as by personal perceptions of their place in society and by the influence of their environment. Politics in Chile should therefore be understood in the sociogeographical context of the protagonists: the voters and the politicians. Along these lines, Doctor Ricardo Cruz Coke produced with great intuition his pioneer work *Geografía electoral de Chile* in the early 1950s. Recent and significant changes in social relations, electoral procedures, and political conditions have, however, made an updating both desirable and necessary.

Further, the traumatic onslaught on democracy in Chile and the ensuing emotionalism that it caused showed the need for a study on the sociogeographical background of Chilean politics before the numerous mythmakers, both at home and abroad, could embark on a distortion of the past. The 1973 paralysis of the country's political institutions and civic traditions offered the possibility of analyzing Chile's recent past in a fashion that resembles the "instant freeze" technique used in cytological studies. For this reason, the past tense has been used most of the time in the discussion of institutions and processes. I hope that, in the near future, we shall be able to use the present tense again.

In order to offer new insights into Chilean politics, emphasis has been placed on the behavior of social groups and the regional variations of political responses rather than on ideologies. Political and social figures have been directly referred to by name since politics, I believe, is more a product of people than the result of incorporeal doctrines. Moreover, numerous references have been made to the importance of the family name in the career of Chilean politicians.

This book owes its completion to the contribution of several persons. Christiana Donauer-Caviedes, my wife, has worked over the different stages of this study with great dedication and organizational talent. Professor Sam E. Stewart, University of Regina, and Miss Marcia Stewart read the manuscript and made valuable suggestions that I gratefully acknowledge here. The illustrations were drawn by Guillermo Lagos and James G. Ursaki, who sacrificed many well-deserved weekend rest hours.

I have profited very much from my past association and continued friendship with the staff of the *Handbook of Latin American Studies*, Library of the Congress, Washington, D.C. A great deal of the information contained in this book is derived from the library's bibliographic facilities.

Finally, I must not leave unmentioned the positive and encouraging attitudes of the editorial personnel of Westview Press, who made the production of this book a most enjoyable experience.

C.C.

The Politics of Chile:
A Sociogeographical Assessment

Introduction

Voting in a democratic, pluralistic state is the exercise of a civic right whereby an individual, without coercion, expresses his preference for a certain candidate, issue, or ideology. Therefore, the study of electoral behavior is actually an investigation into individual preferences, which, for the purpose of collective decisions, are dealt with in an aggregate form. Up to the present, ecological and statistical analyses of Chile's politics have been carried out with little regard for the personal motivations of the voters or for the geographical setting of the society. In explaining political reactions great emphasis has been placed on ideology, historical experiences, and socioeconomic conditions. However, this approach fails to stress the importance of the act of voting as a sovereign expression of individuality. Since decisions on political matters are ruled not only by an ideology or by the political significance of an issue, but also by the social experiences of an individual and by local situations, these factors warrant consideration.

There is no doubt that Chilean society has been highly politicized, particularly during the twentieth century, and that this process molded a very distinct mentality. After decades of exposure to a wide array of social doctrines, Chileans developed a very tolerant, yet skeptical, attitude toward ideologies. Although they recognized that the political schemes offered by many parties were oriented toward satisfying the justified desires for social change expressed by the most needy sectors of the population, they were also aware of the severe complications involved in the implementation of those ideologies; for the realization of utopias depends on people and not on the quality of the political ideas per se. Thus, dissent and pluralism were accepted and doctrinairism was abhorred. It was difficult for any party to stay in power very long, since as soon as it reached the executive, it came under heavy attack from the opposition. The ensuing electoral wearing and withdrawal of popular support were acknowledged by the party in power, and the rules of democratic determination were usually respected.

In dealing with the politics of the country, special traits of the Chilean political mentality have to be recognized and taken into account. Outstanding among these is the Chileans' propensity to mythicize. Wine, women, family life, landscapes, political institutions, just to name a few, are thought to be better in Chile than anywhere else in the world, and this has to be so because Chileans want it to be so. Similarly, the political myth is rooted in the wish of the people for an archetype or an illusory order of things, and emotions rather than rationality feed and support these beliefs--cold reality is often rejected.

The popular devotion that vested personalities such as Diego Portales, José M. Balmaceda, and Salvador Allende, who met tragic ends, with attributes they may never have possessed while alive is an expression of this idealism. The mythical images projected were usually not based on the personal charisma of the statesmen, but emanated from the fervent wishes of their admirers. Taking advantage of their people's fable, the party propaganda machines generated the short-lived myth of the impeccable statesman and model citizen, the *Augenblicksgott*. And much too frequently the Chilean voter fell into the trap that he so willingly helped to set.

The ordinary Chilean voter, unlike the political activist, longs for a superior leader or for one that he believes is superior. As Tomás Moulian observed so correctly, when people cast their votes they are motivated not so much by an ideology as by the desire to find a solution to the socioeconomic problems that affect their society. In the belief that the "superior man" will bring about the necessary structural changes, they vest a political leader with the civic attributes of honesty, integrity, and austerity, which they sense as necessary for the fulfillment of such a task. Another expectation that greatly influences the process of selecting a candidate is the longing for "a man with a firm hand." Politicians who in the past advocated drastic socioeconomic changes and promised to abrogate venality in public affairs were usually more attractive to the electorate than those who advocated stability and moderation.

Introduction 3

Under these premises it is no wonder that the Chilean electorate has nurtured messianic expectations most of the time. The political messiah has been envisioned as the civic leader who would bring not so much a social revolution as an improvement of economic conditions that would guarantee a more comfortable life for all Chileans. As messianic expectations have flourished in Israel in difficult times, hopes for a political savior in Chile have reached their highest level in periods of social unrest and economic decay. The success of the presidential campaigns of Carlos Ibañez del Campo (1952), Jorge Alessandri (1958), Eduardo Frei (1964), and Salvador Allende (1970) was due not only to the ideological positions of the contenders, but also to a great extent to the discontent of the moment and the messianic expectations of the voters.

The continuous search for a messiah explains yet another trait of the Chilean voter, namely his inconsistency. Although this inconsistency becomes evident from electoral results, only a few political analysts have reported on it. A close observer of Chilean society must have noticed that in the last several decades the habit of changing political views from one election to another was widespread, acceptable, and even regarded as a sign of political maturity. A "change of colors" (Chileans use the descriptive term *cambiar de camiseta*) was seen not as a superficiality or inconsistency but as an expression of the voter's continuous search for a candidate or party that responded better to his evolving political views and fulfilled his expectations for a political messiah.

As in other countries in Latin America, national politics have been centralized in the capital city. This has led to an abnormal dependence of the provinces on the politics developed in Santiago and to the emergence of strong anticentralist feelings. So far, the influence of this response on the electoral behavior has gone unadverted. The increasing dominance of a political establishment based in Santiago in the past provoked rebellious attitudes in the North, the South, and the depressed areas of Chile. So the regional factor played an important role, and there was no uniform political reaction from the electorate as a whole. Social and economic conditions and media exposure, different in each of the provinces, helped to mold political behavior of the most varied nature, on which a geographical analysis can shed some light. The impact of local conditions on electoral responses was naturally most decisive in municipal elections, much more so than in congressional and presidential elections. This does not exclude but rather complements the role played by party organization in the shaping of political opinions, since party systems and political competition extended countrywide.

Research on electoral geography can be conducted only in countries where institutional stability and political pluralism exist. Both were present in Chile between 1932 and 1973. Clearly defined voting regulations and supervision of the electoral proceedings by responsible organizations prevented interference from the parties in power. With a steady extension of the franchise, elections were under these circumstances a true gauge of the changing moods of large sectors of the population and not the farce that exists in totalitarian regimes. In Chile everybody was free to choose and vote for the political group of his liking. Thus, the political affairs were characterized by a sustained dynamism as each party and each politician strove to maintain their appeal to their clientele and as each voter had the conviction that he was a coveted electoral subject, entitled to be kept informed about the political developments in the country.

A note on the election maps in this book: To those familiar with the shape of Chile (Figure 1), the representation of the electoral results in Figures 2 to 18 will be unusual. Area cartograms of congressional elections were drawn in proportion to the number of deputies per province according to the apportionment of 1931, which was maintained, with only slight variations, until the congressional elections of 1973. The area of the provinces was calculated by using the province of Maule (75,730 inhabitants in 1930, and 3 deputies) as scaling factor 1. In this type of representation the weight of the electoral unit in the Congress (its number of deputies) rather than its number of voters is the determining factor.

In presidential elections the areas of electoral units (provinces or districts) are proportionate to the total number of voters, again calculated by using the province of Maule as scaling factor 1. The cartograms of presidential elections clearly depict in which electoral unit a candidate obtained a plurality and how important that particular unit was in relation to the national electorate.

Both types of cartograms show the winning party or candidate and the percentage range by which the winning margin was held.

Introduction 5

Cartography of electoral results has not yet solved the problem of representing on the same map second and third places. Nevertheless, these cartograms serve the purpose of illustrating the geographical areas in which a party or a candidate was dominant at a certain point in time.

1
Land and State

The Socioeconomic Landscapes of Chile

The name Chile is thought to be derived from an Aymara word that means "where the land ends." The inhabitants of the Peruvian highlands could not have been more accurate when referring to the remoteness of that country, as the word describes graphically the position of Chile at the southwestern edge of South America and, in the Aymara perception, "beyond the deserts and beyond the mountains." Confinement and isolation, although negative in economic terms, were by no means inhibiting factors in the development of Chilean society. On the contrary, they promoted great racial homogeneity and a strong sense of national identification. Destructive regionalism was impeded and a remarkable spirit of adventure and enterprise was stimulated.

The 2,630-mile-long country extends from tropical (18°S) into subantarctic (56°S) latitudes. The term tropic, however, is highly misleading in the case of Chile. Because of peculiar macroclimatic conditions (chiefly the cooling effect of the Peruvian current), the stereotypic image of tropical landscapes and people that so frequently accompanies the notion of Latin America is to be found nowhere in the country. Landscapes and temperate people stand in contradiction to those commonplaces about Latin America. Thus, uniqueness both in racial and in geographical terms is the prominent peculiarity of a people whose political attitudes and social reactions are quite different from those of their neighbors. The reader is therefore advised to be prepared to reexamine many preconceptions, or even misconceptions, of Chile as just another Latin American country.

A certain simplicity in the arrangement of the physical landscapes has permitted the classical regionalization of the country into: 1) the North, 2) the transitional belt of the *Norte Chico,* 3) Middle Chile, 4) Southern Chile, and 5) the Far South.[1] There is no question but these units are outlined by peculiar landforms, by climate, and by demographic and economic features.

The North is a desert that has a concentrated urban population dependent on the extractive industries of mining and fishing. To the south, at about 27°S, there begins the transition into a more temperate and humid region, the *Norte Chico.* A blend of mining and intensive agriculture constitutes the economic activities in the river oases that become more numerous as one moves further south. Middle Chile stretches from 33°S, where the Central Valley begins, down to the margins of the Bío-Bío River at 37°S. This regional unit, also referred to as "mediterranean Chile," "cradle of the nation," or "subtropical Iberochilean region,"[2] is the heartland of the country, containing 73 percent of the population, most of Chile's manufacturing industries, and the most valuable agricultural land.

Southern Chile is a semihumid, less densely populated, extensive agricultural belt that extends from the Bío-Bío River into the northern part of the island of Chiloé at about 43°S. Racially this is a highly variegated region. The indigenous Mapuches, a mestizo population, and descendants of European colonists are all well represented in the provinces known under the historical-geographical name of *La Frontera,* a fringe of land between the Bío-Bío and Toltén rivers. Further south lies a forested, lake-dotted region, the Lake District, which was opened up only around 1850 when European colonists were granted land. Today descendants of the colonists constitute an elite superimposed on the mestizo population. Far to the south, where continental Chile splits into countless islands, channels, and sounds, is the province of Chiloé, the most rural and depressed area of the country.

The Far South encompasses the remote and sparsely colonized province of Aysén and the southernmost province of Magallanes. In the latter, settlements and activities (oil extraction and sheep raising) exist chiefly along both sides of the natural corridor of the Strait of Magellan. The rest is inhospitable land, covered by ice fields and rain forests, continuously battered by the bitter westerlies.

Twenty-five provinces have served as units of administration policymaking, and economic development (Figure 1). The major

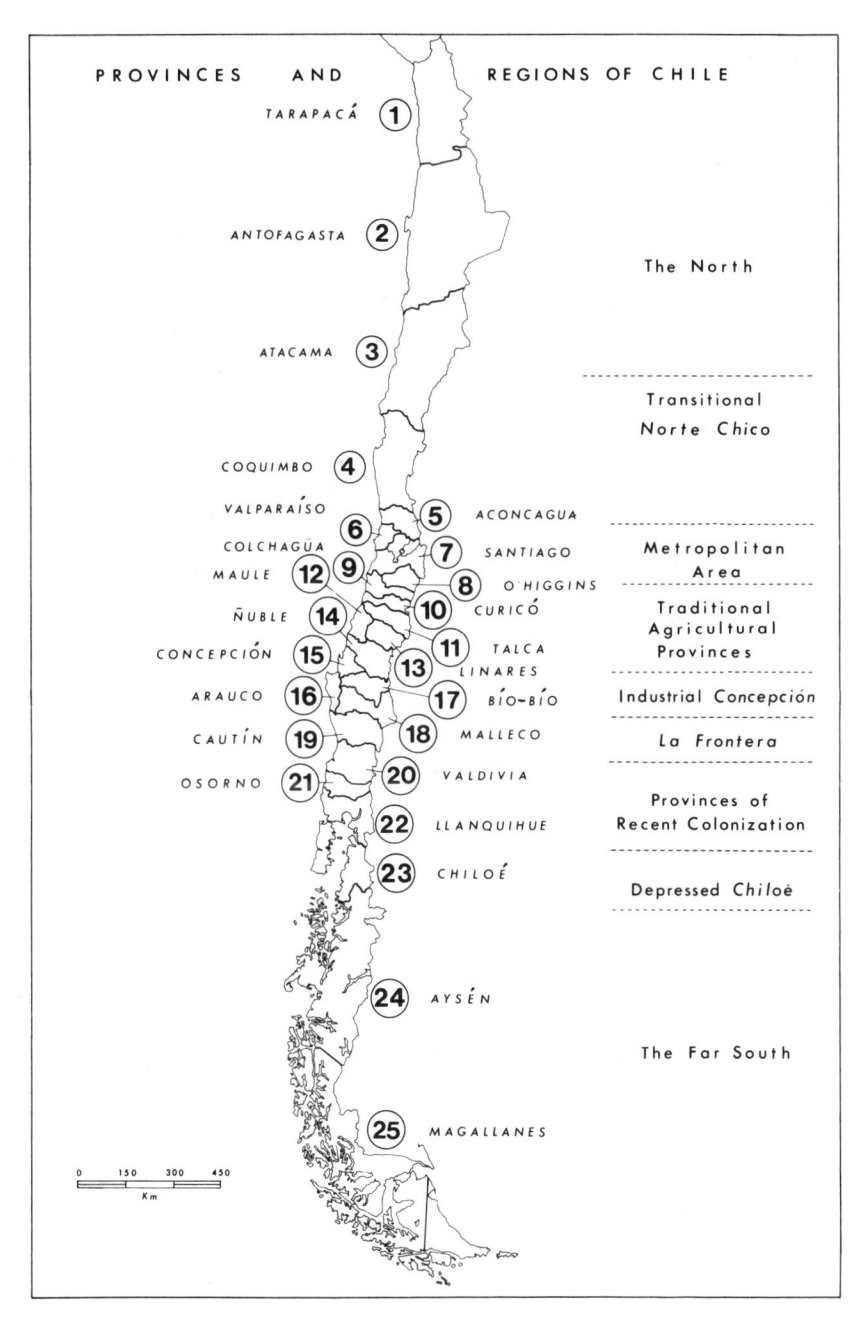

Figure 1.—Provinces and regions of Chile.

regions as well as the provinces, though they may be useful for a synthetical geographical analysis, are somewhat inadequate for socioeconomic characterization and differentiation of the country into homogeneous cells. For example, the conventional regionalization includes the whole province of Atacama in the North, thereby overlooking the fact that the southern segment of that province has a pronounced agricultural component in its economy that makes it more similar to the agricultural-mining *Norte Chico*. This may explain why the political behavior of the province of Atacama at election time will often differ considerably from the electoral responses of the North and will be closer to that of Coquimbo, a typical province of the *Norte Chico*. Another flaw in Chile's regionalization is the persistent reference to Concepción and *La Frontera* as a unit, ignoring completely the striking economic and social differences between Concepción and its neighboring provinces. Indeed, an attempt to find a political analogy between Concepción and its natural region can be a frustrating and fruitless enterprise.

It then becomes evident that a socioeconomic or a sociopolitical analysis of the country, especially when aimed at the interpretation of political reactions, cannot be conducted on the basis of the classical regionalization. Moreover, the *provincia* units, which must be respected because of the customary format of demographic data and electoral returns, are frequently so artificially outlined that a certain sociogeographical typology may in some cases embrace several provincial units, while in others (e.g., Atacama) it may describe the heterogeneous reality of one province insufficiently.[3]

In a pioneer work on the social characterization of Chile, Armand Mattelart and Manuel Garretón[4] proposed a typological scheme of the Chilean population based on socioeconomic variables at municipal levels. Leaning on that information, Mattelart drew up a picture of the socioeconomic characteristics of the country that is more suitable for a regional analysis of its politics.[5] It will be shown in the following chapters that in the electoral results, the geographically conditioned social landscapes (which are not demarcated by natural or political boundaries) are expressed more accurately than administrative areas.

The North

The North blends better than any other region in Chile the

natural with the economic, social, and political elements to produce a homogeneous unit. Administratively, it encompasses the provinces of Tarapacá (1), Antofagasta (2), and Atacama (3), all of them located in the most arid environment of South America (numbers refer to provinces in Figure 1). The position of the North in relation to the heartland of Chile, as well as to the demographic cores of Bolivia and Peru (countries to which these territories belonged in the nineteenth century), warrants the designation of a "peripheral zone"[6] and also explains the region's dependence on the exterior for economic development.

The population is concentrated mainly in isolated coastal cities that principally function to provide services to the mining settlements of the hinterland and to the fishing and manufacturing industries of the coast itself. Manufacturing industries, services, and communications have attracted migrants to the larger cities and mining towns, where a highly organized proletariat has come into existence. Unlike their correlates in the central part of Chile, members of the working class (miners, industrial workers, transportation workers, and servicemen) enjoy a standard of living and levels of education equal to those of the most favored urban workers of the metropolitan area, and this places them above the laborers of the industrial province of Concepción.

Census data from 1970 reveal that in the North more workers own cars, radios, television sets, and modern housing facilities than in other parts of the country, with the sole exception of the province of Magallanes.[7] Brian Berry has placed the northern provinces on the same socioeconomic level as the most developed provinces of the country,[8] and Mattelart and Garretón have ranked them among the top provinces on their socioeconomic scales. Bähr and Golte also assign to the provinces of the North a high position in their ranking of the provinces.[9]

Thus, the advanced urban development of this region, the growing industrialization, and the extractive industries have combined to create a "resource frontier" contingent on certain population growth poles—the cities of Arica (87,750), Iquique (64,500), Antofagasta (125,090), and Calama (67,900). In all these centers a highly urbanized society has developed with acceptable educational levels, housing, information services, and urban amenities that cannot be found in rural Chile. A very enlightening, positive result of urbanization in this part of the country, as Mattelart illustrates, is that those municipalities of the provinces of Tarapacá and Antofagasta which are cataloged as rural, show their socioeconomic scores at lower levels, similar to those found in the rural municipalities of agricultural Middle Chile.[10] It has become common to view the North as being economically dominated by the mining activities. This gross generalization is contradicted by statistical data on the labor force. If the labor employed in the different sectors of economic activities is used as a measure, Tarapacá and Antofagasta emerge as the most diversified provinces of the country; i.e., their labor is spread over the different activities more evenly than anywhere else in the country.[11] Hence a diversified economy, added to the positive aspects of urbanization, has created a progressive and dynamic society of people whose preference for the political Left can be explained by the general theory of Kornhauser that urbanization and industrialization are situations that favor the radical vote.

The Transitional Norte Chico

The term "transitional" applies with all its vigor to this region of Chile, with the desert gradually vanishing and pluviosity and river density increasing as one moves south. By contrast with the more concentrated population pattern in the North, settlement becomes scattered as agriculture intensifies and mining exploitation spreads.[12]

Wherever in the *Norte Chico* mining activities develop on a large scale, the population tends to concentrate in urban settlements and to react politically in the same way as in the urban centers of the North. However, the structural conditions of the province of Coquimbo (4) and the northern areas of the province of Aconcagua (5) are by no means comparable to those of the provinces of the North. All the socioeconomic indicators that rank the North in a high position place the *Norte Chico* provinces into relatively lower categories. As urbanization decreases, so do industrialization, educational levels, and standards of living. Poor housing, middle-to-low socioeconomic conditions, and poorly equipped dwellings indicate the change in social landscapes as compared with the North. The socioeconomic indicators of the province of Atacama (traditionally ascribed to the North) reveal the lower standard of living. In fact, even though that province is very similar to Antofagasta in terms of physical landscape and mining activities, a striking decrease of employment in services,

Land and State

trade, and manufacturing, coupled with a slight increase in agriculture, makes it more similar to Coquimbo than to its northern neighbor. This reveals, as suggested before, the beginning in southern Atacama of the transition into a different social and geographical landscape.

In Coquimbo and Aconcagua, the two provinces of the agricultural-mining *Norte Chico,* the importance of agrarian activities is underlined by the fact that in both provinces the levels of occupation in agriculture reach nearly 30 percent, a figure that relegates services and mining to secondary positions. Agricultural activities in these provinces are traditional and date back to the early times of Spanish settlement. In this the *Norte Chico* is very similar to the agricultural provinces of Middle Chile, where latifundia on irrigated land with rural tenants became the pillars of power of the landowner class. Moreover, the fortunes made by some enterprising individuals in mining ventures converted the *Norte Chico* into the "cradle of the Chilean bourgeoisie," and the coexistence of the two elements in that part of the country—the entrepreneurial bourgeoisie and the landowner class—paved the way for their ultimate union.

The archaic rural structure of the *Norte Chico* produces conditions similar to those in agricultural Middle Chile. Rural exodus from areas of large landed estates or from poverty-stricken minifundia areas has continuously drained population into the developing mining nuclei or into the principal cities on the coast, particularly the conurbation of La Serena-Coquimbo (129,120), where some manufacturing has been developed in the last decades. According to the established pattern that urbanization and mechanized mining raise socioeconomic levels, Armand Mattelart demonstrates that in the provinces of Atacama, Coquimbo, and Aconcagua standards of living and cultural levels are similar to those of larger cities only in the urban municipalities and in municipalities that contain large mining enterprises.[13] Conversely, as ruralism increases and agriculture becomes the primary activity, e.g., around the area of Combarbalá in the province of Coquimbo, sociocultural indicators drop abruptly to levels of economic, educational, and sanitary insufficiency.

The coexistence of traditional agricultural societies and modernized urban and mining agglomerations helps to explain why the provinces of the *Norte Chico* oscillate between progressive center-left parties and liberal-rightist parties and do not endorse the conservative wing of the Right or the revolutionary Left. However, in the last decades, as the politization of the country permeated the rural societies and dissatisfaction spread among peasants, these provinces showed an increasing preference for leftist parties.

The Metropolitan Area

Writer Benjamín Vicuña Mackena remarked that in the nineteenth century travellers used to indicate that they were on their way to Chile when, in fact, they were referring to the city of Santiago.[14] The historical implications of the use of Chile as a synonym for Santiago express the overwhelming influence the capital city and its surroundings have in the life of the country.

If the urban giant Santiago (2,730,900) constitutes the country's urban, industrial, and political center, it is no less true that around it an urban-industrial belt has developed that shares many of the socioeconomic characteristics of Greater Santiago. This area includes the entire province of Valparaíso (6), the southern part of the adjacent province of Aconcagua (5), and the northern portion of the province of O'Higgins (8), Santiago's neighbor to the south. The development of railroad and highway networks from Santiago to Valparaíso-Viña del Mar (444,250), Los Andes (23,600), San Felipe (25,100), and Rancagua (86,500), all urban centers of the adjacent provinces, has contributed to the expansion of manufacturing establishments and of urbanization within these provinces, so that the original rural landscapes are presently shrinking or are being restricted to the most remote parts of the metropolitan provinces. The high degree of communication between the city of Santiago and its metropolitan satellites strengthens the contention that the metropolitan area consists not only of Greater Santiago, but also of all the urban centers mentioned above and the intermediate rural zones.

To the same extent as urbanization and industrialization have radiated from Santiago into the neighboring provinces, the latter have become dependent upon the capital. The port city of Valparaíso was founded and developed as an outlet for Santiago, and as such it has never enjoyed a high degree of political or economic autonomy. The construction of railroads and fast highways into the capital city from Los Andes, San Felipe, and Rancagua brought about a further submission of these cities to the financial, cultural,

Land and State

and political domination of the capital. Some examples that underline this fact are that housekeepers from these cities do their major shopping in Santiago, that radio and television channels from the capital attract larger audiences than local stations, and that more than two-thirds of the newspapers sold in the provinces of Valparaíso, Aconcagua, and O'Higgins are printed in Santiago. To substantiate this further, the labor force employed in trade in the provinces of Aconcagua and O'Higgins is conspicuously low compared with that in Santiago or Valparaíso, suggesting a high dependence of those provinces on the commerce of Santiago and Valparaíso.

A few decades ago, there was an outcry in the city of Valparaíso when diplomatic missions, commercial institutions, governmental agencies, and trading establishments closed their doors and moved to Santiago. What the citizens of the port city failed to realize at that moment was that these developments were not an indication of the decline of Valparaíso (so prominent in the economic life of the country during the nineteenth century), but a consequence of its total assimilation into the metropolitan area.

The dominant role of this national center of growth is emphasized by its high levels of employment in the areas of social and personal services (29 percent), manufacturing (20 percent), and trading (14 percent). If one considers that those three activities supply jobs to nearly two-thirds of the active population, the conventional image of occupational diversification in an urban environment is totally dispelled. The metropolitan area of Middle Chile is in fact less diversified than other urban landscapes in the country: the North, industrial Concepción, and southernmost Magallanes.

A high percentage of labor in the areas of services, manufacturing, and trade points to the existence of a large salaried population. In fact, Santiago and Valparaíso have the highest national percentages (11 and 10 percent, respectively) of clerical personnel, and the second largest, after Concepción, of industrial workers (30 percent).

This large concentration of urban workers is partially the consequence of the continuous flow of immigrants into the industrial nuclei of the metropolitan area. Results from the 1970 census reveal that the provinces of Santiago and Valparaíso have the highest national percentages of inborn population (an average of

85 percent), but at the same time the largest number of natives from other provinces. In theory, the migrant inflow should satisfy the demand for labor in the industrialized metropolitan area, but, in practice, the saturated labor market causes the highest rates of unemployment in this part of the country, especially in Santiago.[15] The inevitable sequel is that unemployment or underemployment precipitates the formation of a large mass of urban marginals, *Lumpenproletariat*, whose existence becomes more than a visual blight in the slum areas that surround Santiago. Thus, although the province of Santiago as a whole ranks first in the socioeconomic classifications of Mattelart, Stöhr, Berry, Bähr, and Golte, it exhibits such startling contrasts in living standards that certain sectors of Greater Santiago could well be ranked at the lowest end of the scale because of the prevailing misery and backwardness. Certainly some of the elements of modernization (schooling, media exposure, house appliances) are available to those living in the poorest areas of Santiago, but the high rate of crime, familial disintegration, malnutrition, and alcoholism lowers the standard of living in those areas much below that in rural environments of similar levels and unleashes the anomic reactions that are common among many marginals of the larger Chilean cities.

One socioeconomic indicator that clearly reveals the poor living conditions of the urban proletariat in the province of Santiago is the quality of housing. The capital province has the highest percentage in the nation (20 percent) of families living in dilapidated houses (*conventillos*) or in shacks (*ranchos* or *chozas*), although in terms of house appliances this province ranks as high as the northern provinces or Magallanes.[16] The figures of the provincial total mask the most startling differences in socioeconomic standards, housing, and urban facilities that exist between municipalities like Providencia or Las Condes and Conchalí or Renca, all in the Third District. However, strong voting discrepancies between these and other electoral units reflect the social conditions that underlie the political behavior of the urban proletariat of Greater Santiago.

The socioeconomic situation of the province of Valparaíso is much better. There, although the percentage of labor in each industrial category is very similar to that of Santiago, the indicators for the standard of living, such as the quality of housing, employment levels, population dynamics, and economic development, place that province some points above Santiago.[17] In housing alone, poor quality dwellings drop to 10 percent compared with 20 in the province of Santiago. It appears, then, that in spite of the dependence of the province of Valparaíso on neighboring Santiago and the structural analogies between them both, Valparaíso enjoys somewhat higher living standards because it is not subject to the same demographic pressures or fluctuations of labor demands as Santiago. These socially more favorable conditions in Valparaíso are reflected in political spheres by more moderate and even conservative voter attitudes. In addition, media exposure is widespread (Santiago and Valparaíso rank in top positions in terms of the quantity of radios and television sets among low-salaried citizens). As a result, the population of these provinces is the best informed in the country, a positive point when political awareness is concerned.

The strong influence of the metropolitan area on all aspects of industry, culture, administration, and politics has had the natural result of concentrating the sources of power in that part of the country and has increased the socioeconomic gradient between the metropolis and the provincial peripheries.[18] Only the extreme zones of the country, the North and Magallanes, which developed as individual poles of growth, have escaped the strong centripetal forces of the metropolitan area, but they still depend on it politically and financially. All social groups that have held positions of power in the economy or politics, from capitalists to politicians and union leaders, established themselves in the capital city and made it compulsory for their dependents to undertake the pilgrimage to their seat of power. Such customs obviously strengthened the domination of that area over the rest of the country.

The Traditional Agricultural Provinces

The Basin of Santiago is the northernmost segment of the Central Valley of Chile. It is a fertile and intensively irrigated longitudinal depression in which the typical agricultural commodities of Chile (grain, fruits, vegetables, feed crops, and dairy products) attain their optimal levels. At about 38°S, where the quality of the soil and increased humidity have set limitations for some agricultural products,[19] land-tenure patterns are different and agriculture concentrates more on grains and dairy products, indicating the transition to a different agricultural realm.

The denomination "traditional agricultural provinces" stems from the area's early consolidation as a region of Spanish colonization based on granted landholdings (*estancias* or *haciendas*) where the rural society consisted of powerful landowners (*latifundistas*) and rural tenants (*inquilinos*). The ruralization of society led to the development of a particular attachment of the peasantry to the master of the countryside, resulting in a total dependence of the rural lower class on the latter and the formation of a landed oligarchy. Very little in these relationships changed in the course of the centuries, and after independence from Spanish rule the political power of the landowner class increased still further.

Industrialization and urbanization in Middle Chile, instead of exerting a modernizing effect on the rural society, did no more than alleviate the demographic pressures of the countryside. The rural migrants became independent urbanites, but the peasants continued in their traditional dependence. Since the modernization of the country had not changed social relations, nor resulted in the transfer of economic and political power, the rural society remained unaltered until the introduction of the agrarian reform, which undertook to transform land-tenure patterns in the traditional agricultural areas of Middle Chile before anywhere else.

During a great part of the twentieth century the establishment of a longitudinal network of communications expedited connections between the agrarian provinces of O'Higgins (8), Colchagua (9), Curicó (10), Talca (11), Linares (13), and Ñuble (14) and sped up the growth of urban nuclei along the central highway and the southern railroad (Ferrocarril Longitudinal Sur). Because of this these provinces have an average urban population of 45 percent—higher than that of any other rural province—and a moderate system of urban industrial centers has evolved along an axis of cities in the Central Valley: Rancagua (86,500), Curicó (59,620), Talca (94,450), Linares (37,950), and Chillán (87,560). In all of these centers manufacturing establishments have been opened—usually processing plants based on agricultural commodities—which have contributed to the creation of conditions necessary for the development of urban societies. Employment in services and manufacturing is slightly higher than in the *Norte Chico* and more similar to levels in the provinces of recent colonization. The cities of Rancagua and Talca have grown beyond the expected limits of agricultural cities, and the socioeconomic characteristics of their population differ little from those of larger cities like Santiago or Valparaíso. However, the overwhelming weight of agricultural activities (45 to 50 percent of the labor) and the ruralism associated with traditional land-tenure forms still have an important bearing on the socioeconomic characteristics of the provincial population. High levels of illiteracy, large family nuclei, high infant mortality, and loss of young people through migration continue to depress the socioeconomic levels of that rural population.

Mattelart and Stöhr[20] both distinguish traits in the overall development of O'Higgins (higher levels of education and better housing and home appliances) that place it at the top of the traditional agricultural provinces. The singularity of O'Higgins in this respect stems from its greater degree of urbanization and contiguity to Santiago, and from the importance of its mining activities, which account for a below-average employment in agriculture. In the other traditional agricultural provinces the percentage of agricultural laborers oscillates between 43 and 56 percent; in O'Higgins, however, it is 35 percent. The remarkable point here is that 30 percent of the population of Aconcagua, the agricultural province that borders on the northern edge of the metropolitan area and that also has a well-developed mining sector, is employed in agriculture. It is thus not a mere coincidence that the two provinces that serve as buffer zones to adjacent agricultural provinces and are overshadowed by the urban-industrial metropolitan area share some characteristics with the most developed area of the country. Further, the province of Talca, where the labor force employed in agricultural activities drops to 43 percent and that in manufacturing rises slightly, ranks higher than the rest of the agricultural provinces, except O'Higgins, by all socioeconomic indicators.

Strong emphasis has been placed here on the relationship between urban-industrial development with improved communication systems and higher overall development in the agricultural provinces of Middle Chile. The province of Maule confirms this. Located off the longitudinal communication network and occupying an area with serious limitations for the development of agriculture (soil erosion and lack of adequate irrigation facilities), this province has become the "sick man" of agricultural Middle

Chile. Maule is the province with the highest national rate of emigration (42 percent), serious housing quality problems, and scarcity of home appliances (radios, television sets, sewing machines, and refrigerators). These circumstances are in addition to land-tenure patterns in which the spread of minifundia reaches dangerous levels of agricultural inefficiency. Here the positive aspects of urbanism are almost absent. Apart from the population in the two languishing agricultural towns of Cauquenes (20,260) and Constitución (11,600), the rest (62 percent) is extremely ruralized and has a very low standard of living.

The negative effects of ruralization on the socioeconomic development become more evident at the southern edge of agricultural Middle Chile (37-38°S), where a belt of poor and backward rural municipalities surrounds the industrial province of Concepción and serves as a transition into the deprived agrarian provinces of La Frontera.[21]

Industrial Concepción

The city of Concepción was, along with La Serena and Santiago, a nucleus of Spanish colonization and its role as a population pole continued during the period of independent life. Originally Concepción was designed as a bridgehead for the penetration into uncolonized areas of the Bío-Bío River valley and the northern part of Araucanía. But although Concepción progressed in importance both in population and economic terms, the development of its hinterland did not keep pace and is still struggling at levels of underdevelopment. Hence, while Concepción stands out as an urban-industrial enclave and enjoys relatively high socioeconomic standards, it is in striking contrast with its depressed surroundings. Instead of radiating modernization into its hinterland, the sustained growth of Concepción has worked to the detriment of the population and of the region that it was expected to serve.[22]

The singular sociogeographic nature of the province of Concepción as a highly urbanized and industrial unit is also evident in its specialization in services (24 percent) and manufacturing (22 percent), which make it very similar to Santiago and Valparaíso. It differs, however, from the two principal provinces of the metropolitan area in its higher proportion of labor employed in agriculture (13 percent) and lower proportion in retail (10 percent). The higher proportion of employment in agricultural activities bears the implication of greater ruralism here than in Valparaíso or Santiago, and the lower employment in trade indicates Concepción's underdevelopment as a service center for its region, a fact that suggests the dissociation of this metropolis from its hinterland.

The industrial façade of Concepción is dominated by an urban-industrial corridor that stretches from the textile center of Tomé (29,600) through highly industrialized Talcahuano (147,990) and Concepción (161,010) into the coal mining districts of Coronel (37,315) and Lota (48,170). If the percentage of labor employed in mining is added to this figure, Concepción emerges as the province with the largest substratum of urban workers (41 percent).

Nevertheless, the large percentage of industrial activities in Concepción and the high urbanization of the province (81 percent) have not brought the same socioeconomic benefits to this region as they have to other parts of the country, such as the North and the metropolitan area. Per capita income ranks eighth in the country, and sanitary facilities and the number of physicians per capita are lower in Concepción than in these other areas; consequently, there is an unusually high rate of disease and infant mortality.[23] The quality of housing, although better than in the province of Santiago, is below that of Valparaíso, the North, and Magallanes; so is also the number of vehicles, radios, and television sets. These factors indicate the precarious living conditions that primarily beset the industrial proletariat; the middle or upper classes are not affected to the same extent. Another circumstance that contributes to the low socioeconomic level of the population of Concepción is that this province receives, after Santiago, the largest number of migrants (21 percent); they come mainly from the depressed buffer area that surrounds it. This inflow of population results in overburdened infrastructures, high unemployment, and low income levels, all of which spark anomic reactions both among the *Lumpenproletariat* and the numerous industrial workers. In this context, the traditional leftist preferences of Concepción must be associated with the structural faults the deprived sectors find in society. Further, the cultural indicators of Concepción, which make this province comparable to the metropolitan area, reveal acceptable levels of literacy and exposure to the media, two factors that lead to a highly developed sociopolitical awareness and militancy of its working class. These are the principal ways in which this province differs from the surrounding rural provinces.

La Frontera

The territory between the Laja–Bío-Bío River line and the Toltén River valley has been traditionally classified as a single regional unit because of the particular characteristics of the land opening and of its morphological and climatic features.[24] This ribbon of land was under the control of the Araucanians until the 1880s and was settled by Chileans and Europeans only during the last decades of the nineteenth century. In the early stages of colonization, the rolling topography, which gives way to the fluvial plains in the Central Valley, was clad in a deciduous forest that had to be cleared by the settlers.

In this newly opened colonization frontier, *La Frontera,* the cultural elements and land-tenure patterns imported from the Hispanic provinces of Middle Chile or from Central Europe were superimposed on an Indian substratum. The forcible imposition of foreign cultures and land-tenure patterns naturally resulted in dangerous imbalances between the autochthonous culture and the culture of the newcomers.

Although a grouping of the provinces of Bío-Bío (17), Malleco (18), and Cautín (19) in one region can be justified on historical and morphological grounds, the socioeconomic indicators of the population emphasize even more their individuality. The predominant economic activity continues to be agriculture, but with occupational levels below those of the traditional agricultural provinces (47 percent on the average). This can be explained by a movement of part of the labor force into industries related to forest exploitation: lumbering industries and paper mills. Correspondingly, 12 percent of the work force is employed in manufacturing as compared with 9 percent in the traditional agricultural provinces with the exception of O'Higgins.

The percentage of unspecified workers in all the *Frontera* provinces is also high (10 percent). Very likely the term "unspecified" is a euphemism here for unemployed. The occupational picture in all these provinces is similar: each employs 16 percent of its labor force in services and 7 percent in trade. Agriculture ranks first, although below the levels of the neighboring provinces to the north, and services and manufacturing are second at slightly higher levels.

The conjunction of agricultural activities and industries related to forest exploitation suggests a population of rural character; indeed the *Frontera* provinces have nearly 60 percent of their population living in places cataloged as rural by Chilean standards. With the exception of Temuco (110,300), the capital city of the province of Cautín, the urban centers of the region are of modest dimensions: Los Angeles (49,175) and Victoria (16,510). Connected with this rural character are great illiteracy, very poor housing quality, unsatisfactory urban facilities, and a shortage of physicians and hospital facilities. Infant mortality and morbidity are considerably higher than in the traditional agricultural provinces of Middle Chile. Also insufficient is the level of exposure to the media, as there are very few local newspapers or radio stations in any of the cities except Temuco. Most of the television sets and radios, as well as other household appliances and motor vehicles, are owned by the privileged sectors (4 to 8 percent) of the population.

Berry and Stöhr agree that the *Frontera* provinces have very low degrees of socioeconomic development, and the same picture emerges from Mattelart and Garretón's typification. The province of Bío-Bío is classified in the category of rural provinces with structural problems (number six on a scale of eight); Malleco and Cautín fall into number seven on this scale: "rural provinces with serious socioeconomic problems."[25]

Cultural backwardness and socioeconomic underdevelopment in *La Frontera* have been related, on the one hand, to the existence of rural marginals, generally of Indian background, whose illiteracy and low educational levels account for low living standards; on the other, the introduction of latifundia and the establishment of commercial relations with external centers of growth (Concepción or Santiago) explain the underdevelopment of the area in terms of internal dependence.[26] Donald MacPhail and his coresearchers find that the structural problems that beset *La Frontera* are very similar to those of the physical-cultural landscape of *La Montaña* (a plateau at the foot of the Andes between the provinces of Linares and Cautín), in which poor soils, minifundia, and low cultural levels have created a chronical underdevelopment situation.[27] Indeed, it is *La Frontera* and *La Montaña* that have Chile's most depressed rural proletariat, and it is from these regions that so many seek a better life for themselves in industrial Concepción or in Greater Santiago.

Yet the social tensions that have been brewing in the area for many decades (Ranquil in the upper reaches of the Bío-Bío River was the scene of a bloody peasant revolt in the mid-1930s) showed up in violent outbursts during the 1970s, accompanied by strong political militancy on the part of the Indians and the development of particular socioeconomic demands by rural marginals who sought to establish a new political and economic order based on the resources of the area and on a socialist economy.[28]

A socioeconomic characterization of *La Frontera* is not complete without outlining the case of the province of Arauco (16). Although the coastal strip of this province bases its economy on coal and thereby shares many of the social characteristics of the industrial society of Concepción, the interior of the province of Arauco is as remote, rural, and backward as are the provinces of *La Frontera*. In fact, this province is predominantly agricultural (43 percent), highly rural, and exhibits one of the lowest sociocultural levels in Chile: poor housing, insufficient education and hospital facilities, elevated infant mortality, and a high rate of emigration to the urban centers of the province of Concepción. In many respects, these indicators apply equally to the province of Maule, also in an outlying geographical position, but in the case of Arauco the natural environment is different and the mining component introduces significant structural differences into the population. The latter explains the political militancy of Arauco, which is very similar to that observed in neighboring Concepción, and the anomic reactions that underlie an endorsement of the Left.

The Agrarian Provinces of Recent Colonization

In the humid and forested areas between the Toltén River and the southern extreme of the Central Valley, the colonization by settlers of Spanish origin proceeded slowly from the turn of the nineteenth century, but received a strong impetus around 1850 when European families, particularly Germans, were granted land in that area.[29] The bridgehead into this frontier had been the city of Valdivia, an enclave of Spanish domination that had remained virtually isolated from the rest of the country during the colonial and most of the republican period. The new colonists settled in the fertile areas of the Central Valley, known as *Llanos de Osorno*, in the valley of the Valdivia River system, and on the margins of Llanquihue Lake.[30] From these main cores of colonization evolved the three provinces included in this complex, Valdivia (20), Osorno (21), and Llanquihue (22). The predominant activity in this area has always been agriculture. Nearly 41 percent of the active labor force is involved in agriculture, mainly in the cultivation of grain and sugar beets and in dairy farming. Unlike other agrarian provinces of the country, colonization was based on medium-sized landholdings (properties of twenty hectares or less comprise about 60 percent of the farmland) with the aim of expanding landownership and of increasing productivity. In the course of time, the tendency of concentrating land in the hands of a few, just as in Middle Chile, increased inexorably, especially in the forested foothills of the Andes where it occurred largely at the expense of Indian land.[31] This development was accompanied by the proliferation of rural tenants and servants, which reproduced many of the social conditions prevailing in the areas of latifundia in Middle Chile. In spite of the concentration of landownership, the medium-sized farms were maintained in many districts and helped to avert excessive ruralization. In fact, these provinces have in common a 51 percent proportion of rural population.

A rural society based on farmsteaders rather than on big landowners favored the development of urban service centers of greater dynamism here and not in the other agricultural provinces. Moreover, the urban origin of many European colonists—only 38 percent of the colonists had agrarian backgrounds[32]—helped to transform the cities of Valdivia (82,370), Osorno (68,815), and Puerto Montt (62,750) into active industrial centers. It is for these reasons that, compared with the provinces of *La Frontera* or with some of the traditional agricultural provinces, there is a higher percentage of employment (11 percent) in the manufacturing area and even higher levels of labor in services (19 percent). These two activities have contributed to the formation of an industrial proletariat, which, along with a relatively high number of medium-sized landholders, has lent to the provinces a more advanced socioeconomic image than that of other rural provinces in the country. Berry and Stöhr characterize them as provinces with low to medium socioeconomic levels of development and associate their relative well-being, in comparison with that of neighboring provinces, with the higher degree of urbanization and increased industrialization.[33] The socioeconomic indicators used by Mattelart and Garretón allowed them to establish a clear difference between the province of Osorno and the provinces of Valdivia and Llanquihue. Owing to higher levels of industrialization and income, better schooling and hospital facilities, Osorno ranks in a higher category (type five); Valdivia and Llanquihue fall into a lower category because of their poor housing, inadequate educational facilities, and greater morbidity. Nor should Valdivia and Llanquihue be categorized as similar, since Valdivia enjoys much higher levels of education, exposure to media, and industrialization than the province of Llanquihue.[34] Further, in the area of education and media access, Valdivia rates above even Osorno. The province of Llanquihue is in every respect the least developed of the three and, significantly, this coincides with both a drop in importance in the areas of service and manufacturing and a substantial increase in the number of agricultural laborers.

In general terms the provinces of recent colonization rate much higher than their neighboring provinces, a situation shown clearly by the larger proportion of inborn population and by the fact that the province of Osorno is the destination for many migrants from Llanquihue and Chiloé. On the political plane, the land-tenure structure and the emergence of industrial workers have created a preference for moderate progressive parties with an agrarian flavor and a rejection of both the extreme Right and Left.

Depressed Chiloé

When Chile gained independence in 1818, the island of Chiloé and adjacent isles constituted another enclave of the Spanish occupation in southern Chile. Chiloé was so remote and isolated from the Hispanic agricultural heartland of the country that the island continued to be, until 1826, a stronghold of loyalist resistance and a danger for the new Republic's territorial integrity.

Not only long years of Spanish rule, but ruralism and isolation as well gave the province of Chiloé the character of an internalized colony, which resulted in backwardness. A precarious equilibrium between resource development and fast population growth in the middle of the nineteenth century initiated a continuous flow of emigration that compounded the sociocultural problems of that extremely rural province. In 1970, with 77 percent of the population living in the countryside, Chiloé was the most rural province of Chile. At the turn of the century, the percentage had been 88. It is evident when one compares the national figures of 54 percent rural population at the beginning of the century and 25 percent in 1970 that Chiloé experienced little change in seventy years. Further, although in the early 1900s Chiloé was one of the moderately populated provinces, in 1970 it had become depopulated, along with Arauco and Maule. Because the traditional economic structure of Chiloé was unable to accommodate and provide satisfactory living standards to a poorly educated but energetic populace, emigration continued for decades to all the provinces of Chile's South and even to southern Argentina. *Chilotes* were the pioneers in the colonization and population of Magallanes, Llanquihue, and Aysén, and Argentina is indebted to them for the operation of its Patagonian oil fields and coal mines.[35] Yet the paradox remains that, with all their good working habits, the people of Chiloé, like the migrants of Italy's *Messogiorno*, used their labor talents to enrich other regions, whereas their home province remained in an underdeveloped stage and suffered from the departure of its most industrious elements.

The rural society of Chiloé fundamentally exploits the resources of the land and the sea; 64 percent of the active population is employed simultaneously in agricultural activities and fishing. *Chilotes* are basically a curious blend of small farmers and fishermen, both occupations carried out at subsistence levels or for intermediaries who maintain a profitable relationship with them.[36] Land-tenure patterns denote an excess of small-sized properties (66 percent of the holdings are twenty hectares or less), though there are a few large estates for grazing and lumber exploitation. Primarily it is the minifundia that render insufficient levels of production or only familial self-sufficiency. When the levels of production become higher, the necessary infrastructures for commercialization of agricultural products (transportation systems, roads, storage) are usually very primitive or are entirely absent, so that surpluses are virtually lost or must be sold at unnaturally low prices.[37]

Occupation in areas other than agriculture and fishing is extremely low. Personal and community services involve only 14 percent of the active labor force, and after Arauco (another province with serious socioeconomic problems) this percentage is the lowest in the country. Manufacturing and trading activities are both at a national low with 5 percent each. What these figures reveal is that an area like services, which in other provinces absorbs part of the active population (and thus masks unemployment), is underdeveloped in Chiloé, and that education and health and social services are inadequate at such a low percentage.

The shortage of personnel in many essential community services is manifest in the educational and welfare conditions of Chiloé. The province has the highest national percentage of illiterates in the population group over fifteen years of age (63 percent). Only 6 percent of that population group has attended high school and a scarce 0.3 percent has higher education. The sanitary aspect is even more depressing, since the availability of physicians and hospital facilities is among the lowest in the country. Nevertheless, Chiloé has a slightly lower morbidity rate, particularly in respiratory diseases, and a lower infant mortality rate as well as higher levels of nutrition than industrial Concepción and the rural provinces.[38] Housing, though not quite as poor as in other depressed provinces of the country, still leaves much to be desired: 38 percent of the dwellings have been cataloged as uninhabitable and the rate of occupancy per dwelling (six) is the highest in the country. Culturally, the province is still beset by traditional rural norms such as paternal authoritarianism, superstition, and conservatism, which are perpetuated from one generation to the next. The only escape is emigration, and this process actually contributes to the reinforcement of traditional usages, because it is the old and illiterate who stay behind.

A scheme that was proposed for the development of Chiloé clearly reveals the sore points in the socioeconomic situation of the island. In a first step toward industrialization, processing plants for the main products of the province—sea foods, dairy products, potatoes, and lumber—should be invigorated and expanded. The construction industry, which is the least developed in the whole of Chile, should be promoted by upgrading the urban road and sewage systems, which are deficient all over the island. And the critical shortage of educational and recreational facilities requires a long-range plan that would benefit construction and would eventually raise the cultural level of the population.[39] The numerous development committees, planners, and government officials that have visited the island and surveyed its structural deficiencies undoubtedly have had the best intentions. Yet so far all seem to have lacked either the power or interest to translate into action the numerous development projects that have been proposed. In the meantime, the steady drainage of Chiloé's most valuable elements continues, and nobody does anything about the stagnation of the island.

The Far South

In the continental zone of the province of Chiloé, a demographic desert begins that stretches to the southernmost tip of South America. Encompassing 30 percent of Chile's continental territories, the provinces of Aysén (24) and Magallanes (25) contain only 1.9 percent of the country's population. Since the Far South is mainly an inhospitable mountainous country, fragmented by glaciers into a myriad of islands exposed to the continuously blowing, moist westerlies, it is questionable whether the habitable areas (roughly 40 percent of the region), primarily located on the eastern slopes of the Andes,[40] can ever be settled, particularly with the communication system and development incentives remaining at their present precarious levels.

Settlement of the country's extreme South, which is concentrated in certain areas, namely on the shores of the Strait of Magellan and in some valleys on the eastern slopes of the Andes, was initially for strategical purposes; economic interests became important later. When access to the natural resources of the province of Magallanes was improved, the marginal areas were rapidly populated around the middle of the century. The more remote province of Aysén, however, had to await the turn of this century for its colonization to begin, and it developed, in socioeconomic terms, differently from Magallanes.

The province of Aysén is still a peripheral colonization area (1,684 inhabitants in 1920; 51,022 in 1970) where the people are clustered in small towns, the largest of which is Coyhaique with 16,069 inhabitants, and in a few villages and extremely isolated hamlets. The main activities of the areas serviced by these settlements are cattle and sheep raising.[41] It is this aspect of economic activities, added to the character of its colonization, that distinguishes Aysén from Magallanes. In Aysén 39 percent of the labor force is employed in agricultural and forestry activities, compared with 18 percent in Magallanes. Second place is occupied by services (22 percent) and third place by unspecified activities. This last element, which is very low in Magallanes, suggests a relatively high level of unemployment or underemployment in Aysén. Industrial activities, mainly lumber milling and dairy farming, are, at 8.6 percent, very low. Although these elements do not depict a very favorable employment situation, other economic indicators place Aysén in a more advantageous position than the depressed rural provinces. For one, Aysén enjoys a higher per-capita income than the provinces of *La Frontera,* Arauco, Chiloé, and Maule. In addition, housing, health conditions, and educational facilities are better than in these provinces. But on the cultural level, Aysén drops to one of the lowest in the nation.[42] Here the rurality and outlying location of the province play a role, but the fact that nearly 50 percent of Aysén's population are migrants from depressed areas, the provinces of Llanquihue and Chiloé, may partly explain the low cultural levels. Exposure to the media is also minimal. In short, the province of Aysén remains an isolated, insufficiently developed area where the interest of the Chilean state to maintain a boundary outpost against territorial expansionism from Argentina has been put above the creation of a regional unit, coherent and well-incorporated into the rest of the country.[43]

The overall development of the province of Magallanes, which ranks first by several socioeconomic and cultural indicators, has been completely different. The fact that it enjoys the highest employment in services (32 percent) in the nation reveals its strong orientation toward providing the infrastructure required by the primary and secondary sectors of the economy. One-sixth of the population is employed in the agricultural sector, which raises sheep exclusively. Magallanes has the largest sheep population in the country (42 percent) and is the leading exporter of lamb and wool. In industry the picture is dominated by oil fields on the eastern shores of the Strait of Magellan that supply about one-fifth of the country's demands for hydrocarbons. A sophisticated workers' elite, enjoying high living standards and above-average salaries, has been very beneficial for the population of the province. In or around Punta Arenas (61,850) all branches of the armed forces have their bases, a circumstance that greatly raises the percentage of employment, particularly in the area of services. In addition, with subsidized salaries for industrial workers and public employees, the community services (schools, welfare, and health services) are also above the national average. It follows that the province of Magallanes and most particularly its urban agglomerations, which host 92 percent of the province's population, have the best hospital attention, the lowest morbidity and infant mortality, and the highest level of school attendance for the population under fifteen years of age in Chile. Also in urban equipment and housing quality Magallanes ranks first, even ahead of the province of Santiago.[44] Perhaps the only structural disadvantage encountered in Magallanes is its isolation, which raises the cost of living and renders more difficult the availability of cultural amenities at higher levels. In spite of this, the exposure to the media, particularly radio and newspapers, is among the highest in the country. Magallanes has its radio receivers more evenly distributed among the social strata than any other province in the country.

All the socioeconomic elements mentioned above combine to form a homogeneous society without great social contrasts, and one in which a socialist perception of the community is highly developed. The European families who settled in the region during the nineteenth century and became rich as gold miners or operators of large sheep-raising *estancias* did create a bourgeois elite at that time in Magallanes, but their descendants have now moved into the more hospitable environments of Middle Chile or Buenos Aires. The case of many Chileans from the North, or even of many *Chilotes* who still choose to go and work and accumulate savings in Magallanes while they are young and productive, is no different. They hope later to retire to Middle Chile. Seen in this framework, the society of Magallanes still has that transient character that is so conspicuous in the communities of the northern frontiers of North America.

The Organization of the Chilean State

During the period considered in this book, the internal political life of Chile was organized according to the principles of the Constitution of 1925. This constitution had replaced the Constitution of 1833, the brainchild of the legendary statesman Diego Portales, which had been in force for almost a century and had called for a strong presidential regime.[45] The conservative authoritarianism of the Portales presidential concept, established by the charter of 1833, had been eroded during the years of the Liberal party rule by successive amendments to the constitution in 1861 and 1891, which had not only stripped the president of the Republic of many responsibilities, but had even made him the victim of the whims of Congress. Thus, in the course of a century, the Portalesian concept of the executive suffered such an upset that after the 1891 revolution the legislative power held unchallenged control of the state. The president had to submit to the dictates of the two Chambers and their powers of censure at any time. The cabinet had become so unstable that the administration of the Republic by the executive was a mere appearance. For example, between 1906 and 1919, there were thirty cabinet shuffles and twenty-one political combinations in ministerial positions. It was Arturo Alessandri, a clever statesman who had grown up and acquired his political skills during the halcyon years of the legislative power's strength (1891-1920), who finally brought forward a new constitution in 1925. More adapted to the social conditions of the twentieth century in Chile, this constitution was destined to restore the leadership of the president, which had been damaged so seriously after Parliament's successful attack on the executive in 1891.

The new constitution, the details of which will be analyzed in the following pages, was based on the Montesquieuian distinction of the three powers independent from, but responsible to, each other, with the executive dominating the whole state apparatus by virtue of its administrative functions. The law also provided a set of fundamental civil guarantees that were enforced throughout the country with little change or interruption from October 18, 1925, to September 11, 1973. One indication of the remarkable political maturity of the people was that, in spite of the inevitable shortcomings of this constitution, it was respected and accepted by all political parties in Chile, even by those who opposed a bourgeois state. There was universal consensus that no article of the constitution should be changed without the population as a whole being given an opportunity to express its opinion in a direct referendum. It speaks well of the civil education and the institutional respect of the Chilean people that in the course of the forty-seven years the Constitution of 1925 was operative, no government or organized political faction ever expressed serious constitutional contempt. When the course of events led to conflicts among the three powers, the issues were resolved by political ingenuity or institutional loopholes. Disregard of the fundamental charter that they themselves had subscribed to in 1925 would have been repugnant to the political sensibility of this extremely legalistic people.

Executive Power and Territorial Organization

Chileans think of their country as a territorial unit the operation of which lies entirely in the hands of the president who has been elected by the sovereign will of the people and who is therefore responsible in his actions to them. To provide for decentralization of authority and, at the same time, to ensure the presence of the executive power throughout the country, Chile was organized territorially into twenty-five provinces, each governed by an intendant appointed by the president of the Republic himself and responsible only to him. It is, perhaps, because of its strong dependence on a central power that Chile is different from other federalist countries where the citizens identify themselves and are more concerned with the politics of their own local unit than with the federal government and where administrative functions are shared by both local and federal governments. The unitarian and direct relationship Chileans have with their central government results in a vivid political awareness, combined with a desire to be kept informed about what is going on in the sphere of national politics.

To invest the president with legislative powers, the Constitution of 1925 authorized him to issue decree laws to implement specific points of bills already approved by the Chambers of the Congress and to issue decrees with the force of law in an emergency situation within legal areas not covered by bills that originated in the Congress.[46] In practice, these presidential decrees have seldom invaded areas that were the responsibility of the legislative power, but there have been instances when this constitutional right proved to be a point of contention. Other cases of disagreement between the two governmental bodies concerning the passage of laws have been resolved by a presidential veto, the power to reject a bill if

Congress cannot back it with more than two-thirds of its members. This procedure has worked to the advantage of presidents governing with a minority from their own party, as was the case, for instance, of Jorge Alessandri between 1958 and 1961.[47] The president can also speed up Congress's dispatching of bills (*proyectos de ley*) by assigning them different degrees of urgency, thus forcing the Chamber of Deputies and the Senate to study a bill proposal within a period of three to twenty days.

Another constitutional power granted to the president of the Republic and one considered a threat to civil liberties is that of restricting, on authorization by the Congress, the constitutional guarantees of freedom of speech, assembly, and press, for limited periods of time, if the internal order of the country is being disrupted by riots and contempt of authority. In addition to the legislative power and the constitutional authority over civil rights, the president of the Republic has the very important prerogative of appointing the chiefs-of-staff of the three military services and also the general of the national police force, thus ensuring their dependence on the political party in power. This provision entitled the president to nominate generals or admirals in his personal confidence; by choosing lower-ranking officers he could easily upset the order of promotion and force the superiors of the officers so chosen to submit to their code of honor and retire. In this way he could get rid of senior officers whose allegiance he did not trust. But, on the other hand, he could also provoke resentment, especially if the retired officers were respected and popular among the troops. Younger officers, however, were often sympathetic, because they could only profit from this method of thinning the upper ranks and increasing "the updraft of the chimney." These reshuffles created among the military a general sense of frustration and dependence on the politicians that reached dangerous proportions during the Allende years. In fact, the growing feeling of instability within the armed forces must be considered a contributing factor in the military coup of 1973.

It is also within the frame of reference of the president of the Republic to establish or suspend relations with foreign governments. In the past this often became a point of controversy in the internal politics of the country. Thus, in 1947 when Gabriel González Videla, who, ironically, had become president with the help of the Communist votes, yielded to the pressure of the

United States and broke diplomatic relations with the Soviet Union and with East European countries, he did not even consult his political allies first. Later, with Eduardo Frei as president, relations were resumed on the exclusive initiative of his Christian Democratic government. Once Salvador Allende was installed as president of the Republic, one of his first actions, without previous consultation with other parties or the Congress, was to take up relations again with Cuba and to initiate diplomatic ties with the People's Republic of China.[48] It may appear, today, as one of history's ironies that that country, which was the last to enter into diplomatic relations with the Chile of Allende, was also the only one to continue relations with the military regime that ousted President Allende. Although no approval from Congress was required for establishing or breaking diplomatic relations with a foreign nation, the president was at its mercy, however, when appointing an ambassador, because to represent the country abroad required the authorization of the upper Chamber. Many disagreements between the executive and the legislature on questions of international relations were settled in the person of an appointee.

What kind of people became presidents of the Republic? A model study by Gray and Kirwin[49] reveals that they were, by and large, well-educated individuals; two-thirds of them had attended university, especially the University of Chile, and nearly half of these held degrees in jurisprudence. Only 20 percent came from the ranks of the military, and not all of these gained access to the executive through military intervention. Many of the military people mentioned by the authors took over the presidency in periods of anarchy or in instances when the incumbent had resigned from office. The great majority of the elected presidents were familiar with national politics, either because they had previously had seats in the Congress, mostly as senators, or because they had held portfolios in former cabinets, a circumstance that has always proven beneficial for the country's administration. Also, since they knew most of the members of the Congress personally, they could use that knowledge to their advantage whenever confrontations occurred.

Ministers are the personal choice of the president, though approved by the party in power, and can be impeached only if they have violated the dictates of the constitution. The most influential is probably the minister of the interior, who, in case of the president's absence or impairment, acts as vice-president. Since he is in charge of the internal security, he is in direct command of the national police force (*Carabineros de Chile*) and of the Bureau of Investigation. He also controls the electoral register and the election mechanisms. All this makes him the strong man in the government, the one who enjoys the closest contact with the president, but also the favorite target of the opposition's attacks. In the recent past, the ministers José Tohá and Edmundo Pérez Zukovic, in the Allende and Frei administrations, respectively, were accused of repressive measures because they engaged police forces during periods of public unrest. Pérez Zukovic was murdered during the Allende years by elements of the subversive Organized Popular Vanguard, whom he had opposed while in office because of their terrorist activities; General Carlos Prats paid with his life, while in exile in Buenos Aires, for the differences he, as minister of the interior under Allende, had had with right-wing extremists.

The minister of finance has the difficult task of drawing up the state's budget and of designing the taxation schemes. As one author put it, "He has the ungrateful job of restraining the frequently too liberal expenses of the congressmen in order to please their electoral clientele."[50] In the course of the years, the state became the main employer in Chile, and a great portion of the national budget was destined to pay the salaries of the public administration, public corporations, and armed forces. Consequently, the debate on the budget has always been used by both the opposition and the government to bring each other into discredit. In the past it was a common practice of the opposition to overload the budget project with welfare-oriented expenditures, making its approval very complicated or even impossible for lack of funds. In retaliation, the government would use these incidents to denounce the opposition as squanderers and irresponsibles. These practices proved to be far from harmless. Discussions and delays of the budget law triggered the civil war that ousted President Balmaceda in 1891, and it was a similar situation that provoked, in January of 1924, the military's seven-year involvement in politics.

Another cabinet post that became quite important during the administration of Frei and Allende was that of the minister of agriculture. First, Hugo Trivelli under Frei and then Jacques Chonchol under Allende bore the responsibility of developing and carrying out the plans of the agrarian reform cautiously advanced during the last years of Jorge Alessandri's administration. The ministers of agriculture had not only to enforce the existing legislation, but they were also the last step in the proceedings of the Corporation of the Agrarian Reform, the professional organization in charge of determining which landholdings should be expropriated and administered by the state.

The other members of the cabinet are of lesser political relevance. The minister of foreign affairs, although second in the rank of ministers according to Decree no. 5802 of October 21, 1942, is not heard of much in domestic politics, even though all those appointed to the office have been nationally reputed and well-respected individuals. The minister of defense has little say in the direction of the armed forces, and his functions consist primarily of administering the logistic needs of the army, navy, and air force. The political importance of the minister of education is not much greater. Although he is in charge of the administration of all three branches of education, he cannot intervene directly in the affairs of the university, where political action has always been very intense.

Up to 1974, the executive power was directly represented in the provinces in the person of the intendant, whose role it was to supervise the functioning of the institutions of the central government within the province.[51] The prerogatives of this position were quite limited, as was also, in fact, its political relevance. In some provinces, however, the intendant had to be very knowledgeable about local politics, because it was he who was called upon to deal with possible confrontations between local promoters of unrest and the central government in Santiago. Each province was subdivided into departments, subdelegations, and districts, all under the authority of appointees who stood, like the intendants, in the president's confidence. In a few of the strategically important departments or subdelegations, such as the southern island of Navarino and Easter Island, these offices were held by the highest garrison officers. As in the case of the intendant, the influence of these representatives of the executive on local and national politics was small.

A more important role in Chilean politics was played by the municipal government of a commune (*comuna*). In some cases, the territory of a commune includes both a rural and an urban unit, while in others it is made up of a number of small villages and hamlets. Greater Santiago is subdivided into twelve communes, and Santiago itself is made up of two departments. The communes have a complete governing body and a particular set of prerogatives that make them almost administrative islands within the broader territory of the province. Within their limits there are particular bylaws for public works, licenses, industrial norms, and local taxes. Such political independence is a carry-over from the concept of an autonomous commune, introduced in 1891 under the auspices of the antipresidential conservative Senator Manuel J. Irarrázabal, who tried to strip the executive of its power of intervention in local politics and electoral processes.[52] However, the good intentions of the legislator worked to the benefit of the local patriarchs, mainly powerful landowners, who from then on dominated the rural communes of Chile almost unchallenged. The autonomy of the commune was severely curtailed by the Constitution of 1925, but certain powers were left with the municipal council that led to dangerous limitations of the basic rights of expression, as guaranteed by the constitution. For example, during the presidential campaign of 1970 the city council of Lota, completely in the hands of Allende supporters, passed a resolution that declared the candidate of the Right, Jorge Alessandri, persona non grata within the territory of the commune and denied him the right to address the people of the city.

Led by the mayor (*alcalde*), a municipal council with a variable number of aldermen (*regidores*) runs the affairs of the commune. The mayor is elected by the aldermen, a procedure that has prompted more than one bitter dispute in the microcosms of town politics. But in major cities such as Santiago, Valparaíso, Concepción, and Viña del Mar, with populations of over 100,000, the mayor is appointed by the president of the Republic. In the past this provision gave grounds for discontent, since no commune liked to have introduced into its local affairs a man in the chief-of-state's confidence. The composition of the municipal council was always a direct reflection of the local political currents, and these were rarely in keeping with the national currents in Santiago. In municipal politics greater significance was given to the personal respectability of the local politicians than to their ideology. The moral attributes of being a venerable teacher, a devoted leader of the community, a social-minded physician, or an honest businessman, were the assets that might well decide a person's election as alderman, rather than his rhetorical skills or his position within the hierarchy of a political party. It is this aspect of local politics that brought about the great differences in the popular vote during presidential or parliamentary elections and municipal elections.

The Legislative Power: The Chilean Congress

The first constitutional documents drafted by the Chilean separatists insisted on the establishment of a "Chamber of peoples' representatives" with similar privileges as the junta or the chief of state.[53] By this, the aristocracy tried to prevent future abuse on the part of the executive or a seizure of power by any faction from their own ranks.

From the early years of the Republic, the Chilean ruling classes envisaged the Congress as an institution generated by the sovereign will of the people. During the last century, however, the "people" encompassed only those few educated, socially prominent, and politically aware citizens whose affiliation in political parties gave them the possibility of participation in the affairs of the nation. This elitist concept changed radically with the electoral provisions and representation system of the more democratically oriented Constitution of 1925. The Congress continued to be structured into two Chambers, the Senate and the Chamber of Deputies, with 45 senators and 147 deputies respectively. With the introduction of constitutional amendments in October 1967, the appointment increased to 50 senators and 150 deputies. Senators are elected at a rate of 5 for each provincial grouping. Only the province of Santiago is allotted 5 senators of its own. A senator's term in office is eight years, but a special electoral mechanism foresees a partial rotation of the Senate every four years: at one time the odd-numbered provincial groupings have their elections, at another the even-numbered ones. The number of 147 deputies came from the provision of the 1925 constitution that for every 30,000 inhabitants or fraction over one-half thereof in a province, department, or subdelegation there must be a deputy. The minimum age for deputies is twenty-one, and for senators, thirty-five. This last requisite was provided by the fathers of the constitution probably to add a character of maturity, experience, and composure to the upper Chamber of the Congress.[54]

The constitution has endowed the two Chambers of Congress

with rights and duties that are neither parallel nor conflicting. They usually operate separately in the period of "ordinary legislature," from May 21 (in commemoration of the 1879 sea battle at Iquique) to September 18 (in celebration of the establishment of the first independent *cabildo* in 1810). This period can be extended upon request from the president and with the consent of Congress, or periods of "extraordinary sessions" can be called by the president of the Republic, the chairman of the Senate, or by a simple majority from either of the two Chambers. Special matters are dealt with by a meeting of the two Chambers at large, the *congreso pleno*. One of the matters that has to be decided by all congressmen meeting jointly is the proclamation of the president when, after a normal electoral contest, none of the candidates has obtained the absolute majority of at least 51 percent of all the votes cast. Such an important decision-making power of the *congreso pleno* has proven to be quite a sensitive point in Chilean politics, because, as expressed in the fundamental charter, Congress may proclaim as president of the Republic the candidate who received the second largest number of votes if he is supported by more congressmen than the first majority candidate. During the present century, Congress has never dared to proclaim the second candidate as president, respecting the results of the polls and establishing a principle that was customarily followed but could legally be set aside at any moment.[55]

Another very sensitive decision-making power of the *congreso pleno* is the initiation of the trial of the president of the Republic for constitutional infringements. The *congreso pleno* may, with cause, impeach him and ask for his resignation, if Congress agrees with at least a two-thirds majority of its members. Probably for fear of the reaction of those who elected the president, an instance of this kind has never occurred in the political history of the country; but it came dangerously close in 1973.

The *congreso pleno* also has the delicate political responsibility of granting extraordinary powers to the president of the Republic in case of an internal emergency. Even though it is clearly stated in the constitution that these powers are to be used only in extreme situations of widespread unrest or threat to the normal life of the Republic, it cannot be ruled out that a president, with enough backing from Congress, can run the country continuously under these restrictions of constitutionally established civil rights. It is to be understood that a situation like this, if agreed upon by Congress, can lead to constitutional dictatorship.

As to the power invested in each of the two Chambers, the Senate enjoys the most important decision-making and legislative powers. In the opinion of Weston Agor, its decision-making powers are the most significant of all because they influence directly the lawmaking processes, effecting delays, modifications, and even rejections of bills coming from the executive. The Senate can introduce additions and complements to bills that have been forwarded by the executive, so that the original spirit and purpose is distorted and they must be withdrawn. It is also within the discretion of the Senate to return to the executive or to the Chamber of Deputies bills that it does not approve, causing, of course, a delay in the discussion of the bills. Practices like these provide the Senate with a most effective obstructionist role in the political system.[56] Since the delays can be decided upon in special standing committees of the Senate where the majority may easily come from the opposition, it is often very difficult for a government to pass legislation that favors the interests of its electoral clientele.

It is also a common situation in Chilean politics that the opposition is in control of the Senate. This is caused by the fact that senators are elected for a period of eight years (presidents have terms of only six years) and that the upper Chamber's replacement every four years is only partial. In addition, the Chamber of Deputies, even if it favors the executive, does not have the constitutional power to make decisions or to force the Senate to adopt certain legislation. As a result, there has been in Chile's political history of the last forty years constant friction between the president of the Republic, his ministers, or even a government-friendly lower Chamber—and the mighty Senate. The latter exerted obstructionist policies in all the governments during the last decades, causing repeated complaints from the Right, Center, or Left, when each held the executive, about harassment from the Senate's opposition.[57] In spite of the negative effects of the Senate's deferring powers, there seems to be consensus among Chilean politicians that they are, in the long run, necessary for the operation of the state, because otherwise a delegation of full powers to either the executive or Congress could pave the road to dictatorship.

It is the Senate's right to indict and to pass political judgment on one, several, or all the ministers of the cabinet, if charges of constitutional wrongdoing, abuse of power, or misuse of fiscal funds, formulated by the Chamber of Deputies, are confirmed by an investigating committee of the Senate. Constitutional accusations have been used constantly by the opposition in Congress to disturb the operations of the president and his ministers, and to create unpleasant confrontations between the executive and the Senate. The people of Chile have recognized that in the past these accusations were often used as political vendettas and that they represented a gross misuse of valuable legislative time for matters of a most unconstructive nature. President Ibañez and his ministers, who had few sympathizers in the political establishment rooted in the Congress, were favorite targets of numerous constitutional accusations.[58] By no means more fortunate were President Frei aud President Allende, who lost some of their ministers through this kind of skirmish with the legislative power. The power to impeach makes it possible for the Senate to upset and even destroy a president's cabinet without giving it a chance to fight back, because, according to the constitution, the president of the Republic cannot dissolve Congress, although, as Prieur suggests, the amendments of January 1970 imply that the president may ask for authority to effect such disolution if he should find himself deadlocked in a dispute that might be resolved by a plebiscite.[59]

Also in the design of certain areas of international affairs the Senate has a decision-making and controlling power, for it must report on a government's nominee for a diplomatic appointment and assess international treaties signed by the government of Chile. Moreover, before January 1970, the president of the Republic could not plan an official visit abroad without the consent of the Senate. In 1967, President Frei accepted an invitation from the U.S. Government but could not go when the Senate refused to grant him permission to leave the country. On that occasion, the leftist and rightist senators joined forces to demonstrate who were the masters in the House. The 1970 constitutional amendments put an end to this abuse of power by the Senate; the president of the Republic is now free to travel abroad for a period of time not exceeding fifteen days, provided that he has been in office more than three months.[60] If it had not been for this change in the constitution, President Allende would never have been allowed to leave the country because, during the years of his administration the opposition was in control of the upper Chamber as customary.

Among the decision-making powers of the Senate, the right to review and approve the promotion of military officers in the top ranks is also of political importance. This brings the military under the control of Congress and counterbalances the president's right of appointing the chiefs-of-staff, thereby thinning out the upper ranks of the armed forces. Clearly, such a submission of their careers to the whims of political leaders and to those who happened to be the majority in Congress has never been accepted willingly by the military establishment in Chile.

In comparison with the prerogatives of the Senate, the powers left to the Chamber of Deputies appear disproportionately dwarfed. In the lawmaking process, the lower Chamber merely initiates legislation; final approval is in the hands of the Senate. Exclusive prerogatives of the Chamber of Deputies are those of introducing legislation on the raising of revenue and of reviewing and adding clauses to the budget law. More important in cases of political confrontations may be the Chamber of Deputies' right to lay and formulate charges leading to a constitutional accusation. Even so, such an accusation is judged in the end by the Senate. To be effective in this, the lower Chamber has to keep constant watch over the activities of the executive, and this wastes time that should be spent on more constructive work. Even though the activities of the executive are subject to the control of the Chamber of Deputies, the lower Chamber by itself cannot initiate any action against the president or a member of the cabinet. Scholars well acquainted with Chilean politics agree in their consideration of the lower Chamber as the best political forum for airing views on the way in which the business of the nation is conducted and on the proposals of structural changes presented by any party for the social and economic progress of the country. The same observers have often been delighted to see how many of the bills that were introduced in the lower Chamber in the form of motions signed by at least ten deputies from a minority group and therefore doomed to failure right from the start, were nevertheless forwarded to the Senate with the sole purpose of proving a certain political party's commitment to bring about structural changes and to test to what extent certain politicians, who had expressed a desire for change, were prepared to let deeds follow their words.

2
Electoral Practices, Voters, Parties, and Politicians

Democratic rule, institutional continuity, and a subdued personalism in politics made Chile the deviant case in Latin America. This uniqueness can be ascribed to a set of sociopolitical circumstances that developed very early in the history of republican Chile, at a time when other Latin American countries were still trying to find the form of organization most suitable to their national character. Very important for the early political stabilization of the country was the spirit of legitimacy that not only the ruling class, but also its competitors, were able to make their credo. The idea that the state, the parties, and the individuals were attached to each other by a set of binding rights and obligations from which none was excepted led to a stern obedience to the prescriptions of the constitution and assured a certain degree of fairness in the practice of politics. Chileans came to trust their parties and politicians as long as they did not show devious intentions of entrenching themselves in the executive or legislative body without the consent of the people as expressed at the polls. Each political party thus became the articulator of group demands and adjusted its political aims to the precepts of the constitution. Inasmuch as a party did not respond to the electorate's demands, which were in themselves inspired by parties and politicians, it paid by erosion of popularity and removal from power.

Under the constitutionally established rules of the game, parties and politicians engaged actively in catering to an electoral clientele that was difficult to satisfy. Ideology, electoral platforms, incorporation of new voters, and political brokerage established a system of continuous communication between the parties and their prospective supporters. Nevertheless, it would be fallacious to assume that the response of the electorate to a political stimulus was based on ideology and party propaganda alone. Behind each voter was the individual whose personal motivations, life experiences, and expectations played more than a secondary role in his political decision. This chapter will explore the peculiarities of the electoral system that the Chileans devised for themselves; it will focus on the development of the electorate as promoted by the parties of the country, and, finally, it will delineate a profile of the principal protagonists in the political drama: the politicians.

The Electoral Process

The Constitution of 1925, Article No. 7, established that "those entitled to vote must be Chilean citizens twenty-one years of age and over who can read and write and who are enrolled in the electoral register books." Physically or mentally impaired individuals unable to exercise the right to vote as a deliberate act and those who were being processed by a court of law or who had been convicted of a criminal offense were excluded. Although the formulation of the constitutionally based right to vote does not contain any other restrictive clauses, the regulatory bylaws of the *Ley General de Elecciones* of September 23, 1925, made no reference to women, and since nobody ever asked why no woman had cast a vote in congressional or presidential elections between 1925 and 1949, women were deprived of that right de facto for this additional twenty-four years. This is one of those situations that are so difficult to understand, a constitutional right never being challenged in Congress or in the courts probably from force of habit. Also, even though it is not explicitly stated in the constitution, military noncommissioned officers and the police troops also do not have a vote. The objective of this internal regulation has been to prevent any form of political participation and partiality from the armed forces. Moreover, officers who might want to exercise their right to vote, never can in practice, because on election day all the armed forces are on standby to maintain civil order and to ensure that correct procedures are followed at the polls.[1]

The constitution established that to be eligible to vote, Chilean citizens must be enrolled in the electoral register books, and a

Directorate of Electoral Registry was created as a department of the Ministry of the Interior. It is the task of this office to organize the voters in small units within which the electoral process can be conducted easily. These units are referred to as *mesas,* comprising up to 400 voters. A chairman, a secretary, and two supervisors are designated by the Directorate of Electoral Registry from among the citizens enrolled in each *mesa* to take on the responsibility for the smooth operation of the election within their respective units.

Notwithstanding the progress in electoral procedures, there existed practices that for many years distorted the true expression of political views. One of the most widespread in the years of the Parliamentary Republic (1891-1925) and most difficult to eradicate was that of vote buying.[2] It was used by parties with wealthy members who could readily afford to pay for a vote cast on behalf of one of their representatives. In urban districts, the transactions were usually initiated in information centers set up by individual candidates or by the parties during election campaigns for propaganda purposes. In the countryside, vote selling had to be viewed as just another form of the peasants' submission to the overall power of the landowners. On election day, those eligible to vote were assembled in front of the main building of the estate, and the name of the candidate for whom they were expected to vote was announced. This briefing was followed by a frugal breakfast consisting of beer, wine, and *empanadas*—a typical Chilean dish sure to raise the men's spirits. Once the feasting was over, the "voters" were loaded onto trucks and driven to the polls in the nearest village or town. In this way, each landowner knew exactly how many votes he was contributing to the candidate or party he supported.

Until 1958 voting irregularities were promoted by the balloting system itself. The ballots were supplied to the polls by the party or candidate and openly deposited inside the voting booth. It often happened that individuals who opposed a certain candidate or party would secretly take away that particular ballot from the booth, so that the next voter, if he did not insist on his right to ask the *mesa* president for the missing ballot, had to choose from the remaining candidates. This vicious practice was finally brought to an end by the introduction of the *cédula única,* the single official ballot, prepared and printed by the Directorate of Electoral

Registry.[3] In the single ballot, used for the first time in the presidential election of 1958, the names of all the candidates who registered with this office were included, individually in the case of presidential or complementary elections, and as party lists in the case of parliamentary and municipal elections. It was identified by a printed serial number to make sure that a person had actually cast his vote on the official ballot.

Presidential elections are held every six years, no later than two months before the expiration of the president's term in office. In the case of death or impairment of the president, elections must be held within three months after the office has become vacant. The Constitution of 1925 requires that parliamentary elections be held every four years. The whole Chamber of Deputies is to be elected at that time, whereas the Senate is only partially renewed every four years. Although not clearly specified in terms of time, congressional elections are normally never held in the same year as a presidential election. In the event of a president's premature withdrawal from office in the same year in which a congressional election is due, the latter is postponed to the next year. With these precautions, the fathers of the constitution tried to prevent a party's simultaneous conquest of the executive and legislative powers, paving the way for a dictatorial ruling of one political faction. The only time when presidential and congressional elections were held at the same time was on October 31, 1932, when all political parties agreed to end the seven years of political instability that had followed the resignation of Arturo Alessandri.

Municipal elections are to be held, under normal circumstances, every three years in the year following a general congressional election. But this rule in the past was frequently not followed. For instance, after the municipal elections of 1950, six years elapsed before the next municipal elections in 1956, and the aldermen elected in 1963 continued in office until 1967. Such extensions of terms were prompted by the awareness of the electorate and the political parties of the undue stress to which the country was exposed by continuous electoral campaigns. There were periods in which one electoral campaign was followed almost immediately by another, leading to a tremendous waste of funds and time. For example, campaigns were held in 1947, 1949, 1950, 1952, and 1953; and again in 1960, 1961, 1963, 1964, and 1965.

Since parties were considered a means of political expression, Chilean electoral regulations also allowed, after congressional approval, political alliances for electoral purposes. This was a common procedure when a party was trying to keep at least one of its representatives in Congress in order to survive. So it was not unusual for this party, anticipating not quite enough supporters in a given electoral district to have one representative elected, to get together with a second minority party in the same district. If the second party would agree to back the first party's candidate the first party would in return back the second party's candidate in another district where the second party was stronger. With these pacts, all the votes would be put to good use and none would be wasted on candidates who had little chance of winning. Pacts were generally arranged between parties of ideological affinity. Before the years of polarization (1964-1973), the Conservative and Liberal parties usually joined forces to take advantage of the conservative strength in rural areas with latifundia and of the liberal strength in bourgeois areas. The Radical party oscillated between the leftist Socialist party and the Liberal party, the strong anticlerical feelings of its supporters never permitting alliances with Christian candidates from the Conservative party or the Christian Democracy. The Socialist party established alliances with the Communist party and with microparties that had separated from the Socialist party.

Until 1962 electoral pacts were used in congressional and municipal elections mainly to take advantage of the *cifra repartidora* ("dividing number"). This was a formula destined to give "an effective proportionality in representation to all opinions and to all political parties."[4] The method, devised by Victor d'Hondt in Belgium, assigned seats to party lists, rather than to candidates directly, in proportion to the total number of votes received in the party's list. Once the dividing number was calculated, the total votes on each list divided by that number gave the number of seats to be attributed to that particular list. The candidates whose votes were higher than the dividing number were declared elected. If a list as a total had been allocated more than one seat, the second candidate or even the third was elected by the surplus of votes. However, the remarkable fact is that a second or third candidate could be elected with a number of personal votes that lay below the dividing number, whereas on other lists, candidates with higher personal votes were not elected for lack of surplus votes. Therefore, it was wise to put forward a strong candidate to head the list so that the overspill of votes created by his personal appeal could be divided among less popular candidates below him. Although this situation has been noted by several authors, none seem to have considered that this electoral method may have been responsible for the development of a particular breed of "itinerant politicians." They were well-known figures in the national political scene, nominated as candidates in places where the party strength was doubtful in order to ensure, with their personal overspill, the election of other less-known candidates. In the same way, a party could use the appeal of a very strong local personality to get a party functionary from Santiago elected, although that man may have been little known among the local voters.

Shortly before the presidential election of 1958, amendments to the electoral law prohibiting electoral pacts in municipal and deputies elections were passed by Congress. Four years later, a reform of Electoral Law No. 9334 prohibited the pacts in senatorial elections as well. Although this development might be seen as a sign of progress, it was, on the other hand, also responsible for the extreme polarization in Chilean politics between 1964 and 1973. Indeed, the prohibition did not prevent mini-parties from continuing, since the clause of representation in the Congress, as a condition for a party's legal existence, was still in effect. Thus, the Socialist Popular party of Raúl Ampuero, the Socialist faction led by Baltazar Castro, the Popular Independent Action (API) of Rafael Tarud, the Unified Movement of Popular Action (MAPU), the National Democratic party (PADENA), and the Socialist Democratic party of Fernando Luengo were able to last until 1973, because they all managed to keep at least one representative in Congress.[5] So, in 1970, the political spectrum of Chile was made up of five major parties and five minor satellites.

During the administration of President Allende, there was consensus among the political groups represented in Congress that the parliamentary elections of 1973 would be between the two mainstreams of *Allendismo* and anti-*Allendismo*, notwithstanding the fact that small parties still existed and enjoyed some popular support. The growing polarization between the government and the opposition sparked a revival, after ten years of rest, of the old electoral pacts. This time, a party with the right to enter into coalitions had to be registered at least eight months before the election date and was required to show popular support from more than 3 percent of the total voters. As before, the seats were distributed between the two lists that entered the electoral contest, the Democratic Confederation (CODE) and the Popular Unity (UP), according to the candidates that obtained the maximum number of personal votes. Excess votes from one candidate were transferred to another candidate on the list whose votes were insufficient to win a congressional seat.[6] That this system helped the coalition as well as the mini-parties is demonstrated by the fact that small factions, such as the Popular Independent Action, the Christian Left, the MAPU, the Socialist Popular Union, the Leftist Radical party, and the National Democratic party, were able to survive along with the traditional parties, and at the same time the strength of the coalition in which they were running increased. This return to a modality of the past clearly shows that there existed in Chilean politics a distinct awareness of the tendencies of the electorate and that the political establishment was skillful enough to adjust the rules of the game to the demands of the moment.

Apportionment

Related to the problem of political representation on a proportionate vote basis was the question of a balanced numerical representation. The distribution of seats in Congress was established by the constitution, Articles 37 and 40, at a rate of one deputy for every 30,000 inhabitants or each fraction of more than 15,000 inhabitants of a department or group of adjoining departments within each province, and five senators for each of the nine provincial groups established in Clause 5 of the Transitional Provisions of the constitution. The apportionment of both senators and deputies was based on the population figures of the 1930 census that followed the promulgation of the 1925 Constitution. The apportionment of deputies (Table 1) remained unchanged from 1932 until 1973, except for an increase of three deputies prior to the congressional elections of 1969. One of the new deputies was assigned to the province of Magallanes and two to the province of Aysén. With this, the number of deputies rose from 147—the figure established by the census of 1930—to 150 in 1969. However, in the almost forty years that lay between those two dates, the

Table 1

Apportionment and Number of Citizens Represented by a Deputy

Electoral unit	Population represented	Number of deputies	Number of deputies if reapportioned according to the 1970 census	Minimum number of votes required to elect a deputy (1973)
Tarapacá	43,682	4	6	9,595
Antofagasta	35,809	7	8	8,078
Atacama	76,163	2	5	19,439
Coquimbo	48,117	7	11	10,314
Aconcagua	53,607	3	5	16,515
Valparaíso	50,096	12	24	11,501
Santiago 1. District	110,659	18	38	7,782
Santiago 2. District	116,048	5	27	36,938
Santiago 3. District	116,149	5	27	73,143
Santiago 4. District	82,290	5	14	15,915
O'Higgins	51,143	6	10	8,221
Colchagua	41,974	4	6	5,459
Curicó	37,903	3	4	7,414
Talca	46,201	5	8	8,741
Maule	27,446	3	3	6,792
Linares	47,257	4	6	11,448
Ñuble 1.	44,056	5	7	8,419
Ñuble 2.	32,203	3	3	6,598
Concepción	70,902	9	21	16,999
Arauco	48,860	2	3	8,344
Bío-Bío	48,256	4	6	9,105
Malleco	29,343	6	6	5,647
Cautín	42,068	10	14	5,390
Valdivia	54,928	5	9	12,724
Osorno	42,891	3	5	12,124
Llanquihue	65,965	3	6	12,326
Chiloé	36,909	3	3	7,220
Aysén	25,541	2	2	3,918
Magallanes	44,122	2	2	13,956

population of the country had doubled, and some provinces like Santiago, Atacama, and Concepción had even tripled their population. Only Arauco and Maule showed little or no increase.

Obviously, the uneven regional growth in the course of forty years and nonadjusted apportionment resulted in cases of serious underrepresentation in some electoral units like the Second and Third districts of the province of Santiago, where the number of deputies was five times below what it should have been for such densely populated districts. If one compares a deputy from those districts with a deputy from a sparsely populated province like Aysén or Maule, it is clear that the former represents more than 165,000 citizens, whereas the latter represents fewer than 30,000. The other districts of Santiago and the provinces of Atacama, Concepción, and Llanquihue are also affected by such underrepresentation.[7] So it appears that in comparison with agricultural provinces (Colchagua, Curicó, Talca, Maule, Linares, Ñuble) or with the provinces of the extreme South (Chiloé, Aysén, and Magallanes), it is the industrial urban provinces that are most affected by the obsolete apportionment. In the rest of the provinces, according to the present population, the number of citizens represented by each deputy oscillates around the figure 50,000.

The inequitable apportionment is a question not only of underrepresentation, as in the case of Santiago, Concepción, and Atacama, but also of differential vote values, depending on the area in which a vote was cast, and this raises the question of discriminatory democracy. Since the value of representation changes for each deputy according to the population of the provinces, it follows that the minimum number of votes he needs to be elected changes also from one province to another. The fourth column of Table 1 reveals the remarkable differences in the popular support behind each deputy elected across the country in the congressional elections of 1973. Whereas in the Third District of Santiago the minimum number of votes required for the election of a deputy was 73,143, a deputy elected for Aysén needed only 3,918 votes. This means that a winning vote in Aysén was eighteen times greater than a winning vote in the Third District of Santiago, although, in comparative demographic terms, one voter from the province of Aysén was equivalent only to 0.05 of a voter from the Third District of Santiago. From the point of view of distributing the political efforts of a party, it required more effort to gather votes from the urban population than to conquer an electoral clientele in the agricultural provinces, in some of the mining provinces of the North, or in the extreme South.

The situation of electoral inequity changed slightly in the early 1960s. As mentioned by Cruz Coke, the number of votes that would elect a deputy in the agricultural provinces, where the Right used to be powerful, was less than in the urban industrialized provinces, where middle-class and leftist parties were stronger.[8] For the Right it became easier to elect deputies in the mining provinces of Tarapacá and Antofagasta or in the far South, and the Left, which had made great progress in the agricultural provinces of central Chile, found it also less difficult to elect deputies in that part of the country. The parties that suffered most from the new alignment of electoral forces were those that drew their clientele chiefly from urban centers.[9] A reapportionment of deputies, based on the 30,000 population rate, would give Santiago, Valparaíso, and Concepción, the three most industrialized and densely populated provinces, five, three, and four times more deputies respectively than they had in 1969 and 1973.

As the apportionment of deputies brings to light the underrepresentation and electoral disadvantages of the heavily populated provinces of Chile, especially Santiago, the same applies to the apportionment of senators (Table 2). The provincial groups of northern Chile are greatly favored because there a senator represents seven times fewer citizens than a senator of the province of Santiago. These mining provinces with a long leftist tradition have better representation in the Senate than groups of provinces from the central part of the country. The agrarian-industrial and mining provinces of Ñuble, Concepción, and Bío-Bío are also at a disadvantage in the same fashion, because there one vote has a value of only 0.39 when compared with a vote from one of the northern provinces. The provinces of recent colonization (Valdivia, Osorno, Llanquihue) and those of the extreme South (Chiloé, Aysén, and Magallanes), which were combined in the Senatorial Group No. 9, were comparatively underrepresented in the Senate until 1973. At

Table 2
Number of Citizens Represented by a Senator in 1930 and 1970

Senatorial district	Population represented by a senator in 1930	Population represented by a senator in 1970
1. Tarapacá-Antofagasta	59,476	85,079
2. Atacama-Coquimbo	52,825	97,829
3. Aconcagua-Valparaíso	94,386	176,395
4. Santiago	198,016	643,631
5. O'Higgins-Colchagua-Curicó	74,747	117,694
6. Talca-Linares-Maule	69,206	100,475
7. Ñuble-Concepción-Bío-Bío	124,960	229,176
8. Arauco-Malleco-Cautín	104,285	138,892
9. Valdivia-Llanquihue, Chiloé-Magallanes	95,136	204,031

that time, the latter were placed in the Senatorial Group No. 10, a move that was to the advantage of the numerous leftist voters of the province of Magallanes who previously had been outnumbered by the rightist voters of Chiloé, Llanquihue, Valdivia, and Osorno. In general, the advantages of the Left when electing senators in the North were balanced by losses in the extreme South of the country, whereas in the agricultural provinces of Middle Chile the representation was only slightly less than that from a mining province in the North. In the urban provinces of Valparaíso and Santiago, where the parties that identified with the aspirations of the middle class (Radical party and Christian Democracy) were relatively strong, candidates had to get high returns if they expected to be elected to Congress. The Radical party succeeded in this by alternately trying alliances with the Right and the Left, while the Christian Democrats had to rely almost exclusively on the appeal of their candidates. The Socialist and Communist parties also emphasized the personal qualities of their candidates when running for the senatorial seats in the provinces of Valparaíso and Santiago. During senatorial elections, the urban provinces were often the area in which the "heavyweights" of Chilean politics showed their "muscle." In accordance with this pattern, the last four presidents of the Republic were elected while holding seats in the Senate; Salvador Allende for the southernmost provinces; Eduardo Frei, Jorge Alessandri, and Carlos Ibañez del Campo for Santiago.

In spite of the politicians' awareness of the inequities of political representation in Congress, nothing convincing was done about it during the last forty years of independent political life. In fact, the 1969 reforms of the electoral law added only five senators to the provinces of Chiloé, Aysén, and Magallanes. As Ronald McDonald suggests, these minimal apportionment adjustments were made by the Chilean political establishment very much in accordance with the attitude of politicians in the central provinces. Favored by their location in the heart of the country, they would like to demonstrate to the distant provinces, if only by a gesture, that they also count in the political life of the nation.[10] It has always been clear to politicians and legislators in Chile that the present system of apportionment is highly discriminatory against urban provinces, especially Santiago, but no political party or established politician has dared to say that the capital province was entitled to more representatives. This, in the Chilean concept of regional balance, would mean that to the political dominance of Santiago a numerical element of superiority would be added. Although this aspect of the capital-province relationship has always existed and has played an important role in national politics, scholars dealing with the politics of Chile have underestimated the implications of this lack of proportion, probably because they considered the political life of Chile to be more monolithic than it actually has been.

Political Parties

By 1920, the forces that were to contend with each other in the political arena for the next fifty years were already finding their accommodation in the ideological and social trilogy of Right, Center, and Left. In Chile, more than in any other Latin American country, the grouping of the electorate formed around ideologies; movements around charismatic figures seldom survived for long. A good example of the latter is the *Ibañismo* of the early 1950s, which wore out so rapidly that in the municipal elections of 1956 it was completely disbanded. However, movements like these must not be confused with *Freísmo* or *Allendismo,* which were political movements based on doctrines devised and promoted by outstanding individuals. These appellations were synonyms for the global ideas of governmental action supported by the organized political groups backing Eduardo Frei and Salvador Allende.

The Chilean political spectrum has spanned from the fascist extreme-Right to the terrorist extreme-Left, covering intermediate shades such as nationalism, personalism, liberalism, social democracy, Christian democracy, populism, socialism, communism, anarchism, and the whole range of Marxist sects. In the past, an analyst of ideologies could have "travelled" from the Right to the Left without finding deep gaps between contiguous political groups; there was always a smooth transition from one ideological current to the next.

The Right, Center, and Left crystallized as individual blocks only when the emerging middle class was able to channel its political aspirations into parties that were not dominated by the patrician families of Chile. The gulf between centrist middle-class parties and traditional historic parties widened according to the degree in which parties like the Radical or Democratic responded to the social demands of the middle class and admitted their members into the directive cadres. In the political literature of the country, the designation "historical party" is given to parties such as the Conservative or Liberal, which appeared during the first half of the nineteenth century and monopolized the politics of the country during that century. Sometimes the Radical party is counted among them to emphasize the fact that it developed as a faction of the Liberal party of the past.

The Left developed from its origin as a vehicle of expression for workers' vindications into a conglomerate of Marxist currents led by the Socialist and Communist parties in which increasing numbers of middle-class individuals and accommodated intellectuals found their harbor. Even though, in practical politics, both the Center and the Left exhibit progressive sociopolitical views, they show ideological differences stemming from the Marxist dogmatism of the latter and the democratic postulates of the former. This is quite different from the doctrinaire position of the political Right, which advocates a return to the absolutism of the past and envisages social progress only through economic expansion and not through change of established socioeconomic structures.

The political figures and organization cadres of the Right, but not all electoral clientele (a point often overlooked by analysts of Chilean politics), come from the landowners, the entrepreneurial bourgeoisie, and the professionals of the upper middle class. The most prominent and archetypical element of the Right was the Conservative party, the political expression of the landed aristocracy and its epigones. Its doctrine reflected the Portalesian concept of the autocratic state, emphasized national independence from foreign ideologies, and endorsed the precepts of obedience and hierarchic order so emphasized by the traditional cadres of the Catholic church.[11] From 1920 onwards, modernizing winds swept several times over the stubborn traditionalism of the Conservative party. In the 1930s, the social insensitivity of party officials caused the defection of the progressive and younger elements who formed the National Falange, later known as the Christian Democracy. In the 1940s, doctrinaire disputes centered again around the social views of the party's executive and split the party in two: the Traditionalist Conservative party and the Doctrinary Conservative party operated separately until 1953, when segments of the "doctrinaries" joined the "traditionalists" to form the United Conservative party. The remaining elements of the doctrinary faction increased the ranks of the National Falange.[12] In 1966 the United Conservative party merged with the Liberal party and with other groups of similar political affinities to form a single rightist party called the National party.

The typical representatives of the entrepreneurial bourgeoisie (bankers, industrialists, brokers) felt more comfortable within the Liberal party, which had been formed in the nineteenth century in opposition to the Conservative party. An ideology of economic liberalism, secularism, and liberal democracy, imported from Europe, successfully challenged the autocracy of the Conservatives in 1861 and kept the Liberal party in government for nearly sixty years. The unyielding spirit of the Liberals tore the party apart in such a way that in the early 1920s there were four different factions of the former Liberal party. The most important of these were the Unified Liberal party (the mainstream of the historical Liberal party) and the Liberal Democratic party, made up of the supporters of the overthrown President José M. Balmaceda. In 1932, these two groups and other dispersed fragments finally found their place in a cohesive Liberal party and carried on independently until their union with the Conservatives in 1966. This amalgamation of the two rightist parties had been only a matter of time. Ideological differences of the previous century had long been resolved, and socially it was difficult to separate aristocrats of Conservative from those of Liberal tendencies.[13]

In 1931, an important branch of landowners from the southern provinces defected from the ranks of the Liberal party. They formed the Agrarian party with the purpose of promoting their demands for a corporate state in which the government would encourage and protect private enterprise, principally in the agrarian sector. This doctrine was also supported by agrarian entrepreneurs of nonaristocratic background, especially in the recently colonized provinces, who added to the party program a high measure of nationalism.[14] In 1951, when fourteen years of Radical rule were nearing an end, most of the Agrarians backed the presidential candidacy of Carlos Ibañez del Campo under the name of the Agrarian Labor party, which initially leaned toward the center of Chile's political spectrum. Those who disliked the populist flavor of *Ibañismo* created an independent movement called the Partido Nacional. In 1966, the last remnants of this faction joined with the

Conservatives and Liberals to form the rightist union of the same name, the National party.[15] The Agrarian Labor party did not survive the erosion of Ibañez del Campo's administration and its ranks disintegrated into the Christian Democracy, the Radical party, and the PADENA during the late 1950s.

Although the existence of a "center" in recent Chilean politics is questioned by leftist scholars, there certainly was one in the tempestuous 1920s and it continued to exist and play a capital role in the country's politics until the ideological polarization of the 1960s. The appearance and development of the political center is attributable to two basic factors: on the one side, the political emergence of the middle class as an active social force; on the other, the defection of progressive and farsighted politicians from the originally so-called historical parties. In this perspective, centrist parties may be considered modernizations of previously existing parties, following the social exigencies of the present time to fill the middle ground that was left by the withdrawal of oligarchic parties into conservative positions and the exclusive dedication of the socialist parties to organized labor. The Christian Democratic party is a good example of this trend; it branched off from the Conservatives because of that party's callous attitude to social injustice in Chile. Concern for the deprived classes of the country became very intense among young Catholics, who were motivated by the social content of the encyclicals *Rerum novarum* and *Quadragesimo anno*. Between 1935 and 1938 their concern was not shared, or even understood, by the Conservatives, and the younger elements became increasingly militant in an open defiance of the tradition-bound cadres of the party. Finally, unbearable tension resulted in the formation of a new party, the National Falange, which began its political life with seven young deputies and one minister of state.[16]

Social justice according to the principles of Christian humanism is the ideological platform of Christian Democracy; that is, integration of all individuals into the affairs of the nation, emphasis on communitarian organizations, rejection of capitalist exploitation and imperialist dependence, state intervention in the major areas of the country's economy, and respect for basic individual rights, which include the right to a decent life guaranteed by the state.[17]

Since realization of these aims would be stubbornly opposed by the oligarchic classes, the maximum cooperation of the populace and its government had to be secured by a national organization, the Popular Promotion. Once the popular basis had been integrated and the people made aware of their role in the molding of their future, a "revolution in freedom" could proceed.[18] At first these elaborate and intellectual postulates did not have a great impact on the popular masses. The Catholicism of their leaders and family ties with the traditional aristocracy made them look like disguised Conservatives or, as the leftist press referred to them, "the other side of the reactionaries." But as the years went by and one faction after another, the Radicals, *Ibañismo*, and the Right with Jorge Alessandri, gained the executive power and wore themselves out in the process, the Christian Democracy captured the hopes of a dissatisfied lower and middle class, increased its representation in the Congress, and finally, in 1964, succeeded in having Eduardo Frei elected president of the Republic.

However, power proved to be deleterious for the Christian Democracy too. With the allegations that the promised structural changes of Chilean society were not progressing at a satisfactory pace and that the party was too much under the control of conservative elements, a group of young and impatient militants abandoned the Christian Democracy in 1969 and created the MAPU (United Popular Action Movement). One year later they joined the Popular Unity to cooperate in the electoral campaign of Salvador Allende.[19]

No other political group portrays better the contradictions of the Chilean middle class than the Radical party. Internal dissension or political schizophrenia, as Federico Gil so aptly put it, retarded progress of the party from its uncertain beginnings in the 1860s to its virtual disappearance in the congressional elections of 1973. The roots of its troubles are to be found in its origin as the brainchild of rich miners, landowners, and intellectuals of the nineteenth century, whose endorsement of economic liberalism gave the party an undeniably bourgeois outlook.[20] But at the same time it also harbored many newcomers in politics, such as anticlerical intellectuals, freethinkers, and educated middle-class individuals, whose quest for social change and democracy were not met by the historical parties and, at the same time, conflicted with the bourgeois elements in the party. Thus, as the Radical party grew with the influx of an enlarging middle class, and as some of its leaders enriched themselves through politics, an internal alignment into a social-democratic and a liberal-democratic wing took place. Only the successful alliances formed by the party, obviously because they provided easy access to governmental jobs, kept it together and even led to a broadening of its base. After 1932, the Radical party became the symbol of patronage for public employees, and in political circles its members were known as masters of opportunism and compromise.[21]

To satisfy its heterogeneous members, the Radical party formulated a political ideology that blended socialism and individualism in the style of the European liberalism of the nineteenth century. In the field of economics, a mixture of state protectionism and financial laissez-faire was promoted, although after 1938, the Radical party involved the state actively in long-term industrial projects. With a good part of the electoral clientele coming from among teachers and public employees, the expansion of secular educational possibilities was strongly emphasized by the party. This secularism is another ideological remnant from the nineteenth century, when the patriarchs of radicalism passionately attacked the traditional alliance of the Conservative party with the hierarchy of the Catholic church and the church's monopoly in education. In the present century, the Freemasonry, to which the directors of the party belong almost without exception, has kept that old anticlerical spirit alive.[22]

As happened with all the Chilean parties with pluralistic support, the Radical party was plagued with defections. Factions began splitting off when the party first obtained access to the executive by having members of its ranks appointed ministers within rightist coalitions. They were then held responsible for antipopular policies backed by those governments.[23] It also became traditional for the highest administrative body of the party, the National Executive Council (CEN), to be controlled by the eldest and socioeconomically most influential members of the party, a situation that led to confrontations with the younger and more "radical" party members. The restive 1930s saw dispersion of the most militant elements into the Republican Union, the Social Republican party, and the Radical Socialist party. This was prompted by the determination of progressive elements not to enter into political alliances with rightist parties and not to collaborate with the liberal government of Arturo Alessandri, which the rest of the party had decided to support. In 1948, a group of Radicals who disagreed with the center-right policies of President González Videla left the party and created two factions, the Radical Democratic party and the Radical Doctrinary, neither of which fared well in the elections of 1949 and 1953 when radicalism was beginning to lose its popular appeal.[24] After a short regrouping for the presidential election of 1958, the Radical party was again on the decline as its political clientele joined either the Christian Democracy or the coalition of the Socialist and Communist parties (FRAP). During the 1964 presidential election, while the party's rightist segments endorsed the hopeless candidacy of Julio Durán, the leftists closed ranks with Salvador Allende. After that, what was left of the Radical party could no longer act as a first order political force; consequently it either drifted around the major parties of the Center and the Right under the name of Radical Democracy or united with the Popular Unity as the Radical Party of the Left. When the last congressional elections were held in March of 1973, the main branch of the Radical party had become a minority partner of the Popular Unity, and the rightist elements had aligned themselves with the Democratic Confederation. In total the last remnants of radicalism could barely rally 1 percent of the popular vote. This marked the sad demise of a party that in 1921, its most successful year, had carried one-third of the total electorate on its own.

A similar fate befell the Democratic party. After attracting strong support from among the working masses at the turn of the century, it fell into the same political vacuum that characterized the historic parties during the futile Parliamentary Republic years (1891-1925) and lost its credibility among the proletariat.[25] The doctrine of this predominantly urban party stressed the improvement of the socioeconomic conditions of the lower middle class, the artisans, and industrial workers through social legislation and gradual reform. Supported by the working class, the party was able to exert pressure on the political establishment, but soon its initial reformist objectives and political efficiency were overrun by the revolutionary fervor of some socialist militants (Recabarren was one of them), and the party not only lost cohesion, but many of its members turned to the Marxist parties.[26]

In 1934, a major scission occurred when one faction, the *Partido Democrático,* established liaisons with Socialists and Communists, and the other faction, the *Partido Demócrata,* moved towards the Center.[27] Neither of the two factions ever held more than 9 percent of the national vote, and until 1952 they acted as satellites of centrist and leftist political alliances. During that time, the proleftist Democrats won more votes than the centrist-oriented faction. Prior to the presidential election of 1951, the *Partido Democrático* and another new branch, the Democratic Party of the People, joined forces and backed the candidacy of Ibañez del Campo. When the forces of *Ibañismo* scattered in the mid-1950s, the remnants of the former branches of the Democrats gathered in a procentrist group known as the National Democratic party (PADENA); others drifted as the People's Democratic party or the Democratic Party of Chile into the emerging alliance of the Left, the Popular Action Front.[28] In the congressional elections of 1969, none of the offspring of the old Democratic party elected a candidate, and after the 1973 congressional elections this political party ceased to exist as an electoral force.

Since the Democratic Party of Chile and its many variants emphasized social progress through reform and not revolutionary change, they have been considered here primarily as a centrist political force. Moreover, because of their democratic views, they preferred alliances with moderate parties wherever possible, rather than with the Left. Association with the latter always resulted in an erosion of the already meager support of the salaried groups, whom the Democrats pampered as their electoral clientele.

The Left as a unitary and articulate movement, acting according to the rules of the game of Chilean politics, came into being only in the early 1930s. Before that, the activity of the leading figures of the Chilean Left was focused on the organization of the laboring class with sporadic incursions into Congress by using the Democratic party as a host. The social protest movements and unions were joined by intellectuals only during the turbulent six years from 1925 to 1931. Their input gave the necessary ideological coherence and doctrinary content that made possible the formation of parties with socialist orientations.

The first socialist group to organize on the pattern of Marxist ideology and to draw up a concrete strategy for political action was the Communist Party of Chile, founded in Iquique as the Socialist Labor party. In 1922, under the direction of Luis E. Recabarren, it adhered to the Third International, professed solidarity with the world's proletariat, and endorsed Stalinism.[29] The unconditional adherence to Moscow evinced by the Communist Party of Chile caused an immediate split of workers, intellectuals, and progressive middle-class elements into several Marxist dissident groups—the Socialist Marxist party, the New Public Action, the Socialist Revolutionary Alliance, the Unified Socialist party, and the Socialist Order. This fact can surely be considered indicative of how far back the doctrinary cleavages within Chilean Marxism started. While the Trotskyites rallied under the leadership of Manuel Hidalgo and separated from the Communist party, other Socialists with nationalistic leanings preferred to maintain their independence from international Marxism and, led by Eugenio Matte Hurtado, Carlos A. Martínez, Marmaduke Grove, Oscar Schnake, and Arturo Bianchi, founded the Socialist party in April of 1933.[30]

It is easy to understand that because of the varied nature of its components, the Socialist party was a volatile conglomerate of Marxists, whose only common characteristic was the fact that they shared the concepts of class struggle, dictatorship of the proletariat, and solidarity with the proletarians of Latin America; but they differed from each other (and thus gave great ideological flexibility to the party) regarding the pace and methods by which the social change in the country was to be achieved. These views not only made the Socialist party independent from Moscow's Communism, but they added a Latin American flavor to the movement, referred to at times as *socialismo criollo*. However, this orientation was not welcomed by the Communist party, which opposed the proselytist drives of the young Socialists since the foundation of the Socialist party. Their rebellious spirit was to create serious problems for the unity of the party in the near future. In 1939, as the Socialist party joined the government of the radical President Aguirre Cerda, some Socialists, rejecting such an alliance, broke away and created the Socialist Workers party, which then ran candidates in the congressional elections of 1941. The following year, this group was absorbed by the Communist party. Sharing the executive power with the Radicals caused further splits within the Socialist party. In 1944, a group of dissidents withdrew under the leadership of Marmaduke Grove to form the Authentic Socialist party. This party was active until the congressional elections of 1949, when it disappeared without much ado.[31] Nor could the rest of the Socialists avoid scission. As the Socialist party was actively competing with the Communist party for the support of organized labor, the radical President Gabriel González Videla outlawed the Communist party on grounds of internal security. This action led to divided opinions among the Socialists: one group, denouncing such an act as antidemocratic, formed a faction called the Popular Socialist party, while another, glad to be free from the competition of the Communists for the support of the working class, gathered under the banner of the Socialist Party of Chile. After that, violent exchanges by leaders and members of the two factions created a deep abyss between the two that was bridged only in July of 1957, when the National Congress of Socialist Unification brought them back together.[32]

Relations with the Communist party continued to be in jeopardy as a consequence of the Socialist party's criticism of the Soviet Union's intimidating policies vis-à-vis the revisionary policies of Marshal Tito in Yugoslavia. This notwithstanding, the two parties were reconciled in 1956 and formed the Popular Action Front (FRAP). A relative internal calm permitted a rejuvenation and expansion of the Socialist party during the 1960s. However, minor splits still occurred. The picturesque caudillo Baltazar Castro moved away from the party to form a socialist-populist party, the People's National Vanguard, whose main strength was in the province of O'Higgins. This party lasted only until 1973, when the term of Senator Baltazar Castro expired. Another defection from the Socialist party occurred in 1967 when the ungovernable Raúl Ampuero was expelled from the party because of quarrels over party leadership with Salvador Allende, Aniceto Rodríguez, and Carlos Altamirano. Ampuero organized his supporters in the Popular Socialist Union (USOPO) and continued within the Popular Unity coalition until 1973. The USOPO drew most of its support from the mine workers of the province of Antofagasta and from isolated pockets of middle-class Socialists of the provinces of Colchagua and Malleco.

The development of the Communist party in Chile from the 1930s until the showdown of 1973 was quite different. The rigid hierarchical structure of the party and the almost monastic discipline and obedience of the basic cells offered little opportunity for the infiltration of ideological currents that were opposed to the official line of the party. Moreover, ten years underground (1948-1958) gave an almost "mystical" strength to the party and reenforced its internal unity. After participating in the electoral contest of 1957 under the cover name of *Partido del Trabajo,* the Communist party became legal again in 1958 through Law No. 12927. Once more the party's officials avowed their allegiance to the Soviet Union and denounced all challenges to the Soviet leadership of international communism. These challenges were presented by the ideological split of Albania and the estrangement between the People's Republic of China and the Soviet Union.[33] And it was the conflict between the two giants of communism that had serious repercussions for the Communist party in Chile. In 1963, China sympathizers who were members of the party and prominent intellectual figures of Santiago's intelligentsia, promoted the dissemination of Chinese writings that aired China's viewpoint of the Soviet expansion in Asia. These Communists were quickly reprimanded by the central committee, and when they persisted in their pro-Chinese activities they were either expelled or forced to resign from the Communist party. Splinter groups that resulted from this conflict were referred to as *Pekinistas* in Chilean political jargon; they consisted of the Communist Revolutionary Movement and the *Espartaco* faction. After a relative short period of independence, these small groups joined forces with dissidents from the Socialist party, such as the Revolutionary Workers party and the Revolutionary Marxist Vanguard, to create the Movement of Support of the Anti-Imperialist Revolution.[34] Centered around urban intellectuals (especially university teachers), such movements had little contact with the working class and their activities were usually restricted to the skirmishes within university politics that were so common in the second half of the 1960s.

Nevertheless, these intellectuals were instrumental in spreading Marxist ideas among the younger generation. For instance, in 1964 at the University of Concepción, a group of young Communists from affluent families organized a highly militant group, the Leftist Revolutionary Movement (MIR), based on the principle that social and political change in Chile could be accomplished only through armed revolution, as in Cuba, and that under the existing circumstances, neither reform à la Frei nor the peaceful road to socialism as proposed by the Communist party was a feasible alternative.[35]

This ideological posture was followed in the case of the MIR by effective action. A mobilization of urban slum dwellers and of migrant rural workers was actively pursued with funds seized in armed robberies of banks. Thus, for the first time in Chile's political history, an economic-intellectual elite was able to put its socialist romanticism into action.

A reference to romantic socialist movements, as initiated by members of favored social classes, prompts a brief consideration of the National Socialist party of Chile, whose political action, though restricted to the 1930s and early 1940s, had tragic consequences for some of its members and coined a type of ideology that persisted in Chilean politics through the decades that followed. The political turbulence and social unrest in Chile during the 1930s and early 1940s led not only to Marxist activism among intellectuals and workers, but also to the intervention of the military in politics. When the democratic system was reestablished and Arturo Alessandri began his second term as president of the Republic, a handful of progovernment public figures under the leadership of Julio Schwarzenberg created a paramilitary organization named the *Milicia Republicana* (Republican Militia) for the purpose of preventing, by force if necessary, any attempts by Communists or the military to seize political power in the country.[36] This drive toward the formation of a "body of guards of republican institutions" was immediately taken advantage of by certain elements of Chilean society that were enthusiastic admirers of Italian fascism and German National Socialism.[37] One of these was Jorge González von Marées, an emotional and ascetic character, whose admiration for Germany was instilled and nourished by his Prussian mother. While there is no doubt that there were quite a few common points of ideology between the Chilean national socialism and its European congenerics, the principles of the former exhibited a stronger sense of realism in assessing the local socioeconomic situation. The oligarchy was caustically attacked because of its egoism, social insensitivity, and oppression of the peasants. Communism was criticized with no less acridity for trying to turn individuals into slaves of the Party and the state. As an alternative between these two extremes, national socialism in Chile proposed a corporate state, based on the participation of workers and peasants in a movement of national renovation and led by nationalist intellectuals whose role in society would be to emphasize and keep alive the "vernacular values of the Chilean race."[38] This blend of idealism, racial bias, and exacerbated nationalism, and the fact that the movement offered itself as a "third road" in Chilean politics, attracted many students, but did not find an echo among the workers. After six frustrating years of trying to become a respectable and accepted political force, national socialism opted for political conspiracy. In September of 1938, in a desperate attempt to attract attention to his movement and to rebel against the government of Arturo Alessandri, González von Marées sacrificed the lives of sixty-one of his comrades who were gunned down inside a government building.[39] This massacre marked the end of Chilean National Socialism as a political party. Thereafter, National Socialists were generally adventurous underground elements who made ill-fated attempts to topple the solidly established republican democracy. By the 1950s, the young people who had idealistically backed the Chilean National Socialism of the 1930s, had settled down to a bourgeois lifestyle. However, yielding to their juvenile inclinations, they would from time to time rally in political groups that demanded a nationalistic and strong government.

Politicians

For the sake of systematizing the political regimes of Latin America, scholars appear tempted to make generalizations that unfortunately mask the uniqueness of the politicians and the political parties of Chile. In a paper that is otherwise quite faithful to reality, Robert E. Scotts commits just such an error when he states that none of the Latin American countries have full-time professional politicians capable of basic political decision making.[40] As will be seen, this does not apply to Chile, where the complexity of political life and the hectic pace at which it has always been conducted did not allow for dilettantes.

To pursue a political career, a public figure was forced, first of all, to take up residence in Santiago and to keep an attentive eye on his party's internal happenings. At the same time, it was vital for his political survival that he maintain a high profile in the Congress by participating in as many debates as possible and to join in political rallies to keep himself before the media. These requirements were the necessary minimum for a continued and successful political career. There was also a set of unwritten precepts and social norms with which he had to comply in order to progress within the Chilean political establishment.

The first of these was, and continues to be, the political resonance of a person's family name. Although affiliation with one of the oligarchic families was a valuable asset for a political career in any party during a great part of Chile's political history, it later became much easier for descendants of bourgeois or middle-class public figures to consider a career in politics, if they could take advantage of a name with political respectability. One example of this is Luis Maira, a young progressive politician during the Frei and Allende administrations. Even though the Maira family is not of aristocratic lineage, the fact that some of its patriarchs were deputies or ministers during the first quarter of the twentieth century made it easier for descendants of the family to retain a political clientele and to assure the continuity of their name on the Chilean political scene. The example cited here should not be taken to mean that capable and ambitious individuals without the asset of "a name" were discriminated against by the political establishment, just that their political career would be more difficult than that of individuals whose families were already entrenched in political circles.

Another important element affecting a career in politics was the relationship established between members of certain socioeconomic groups in the early years of high school and later on at university. Politicians who were born and raised in the city of Santiago went to fashionable and exclusive establishments generally located in the *Barrio Alto* of the capital city.[41] Among the most conspicuous high schools are those administered by the French Order of the Sacred Heart and by the Jesuits, which have until now preferred to accept children of aristocratic families. More liberal upper-class families send their children to the *Instituto Nacional* and to high schools run by foreign communities or by foreign religious orders such as the Congregation of the Holy Cross and the Order of the Holy Word. High-class families who dare to send their children to a middle-class *liceo* run the risk of losing social acceptability. Social contacts established in these high schools are usually continued at the University of Chile or the Catholic University of Chile, where future politicians generally enroll in the School of Law.

In the preface to his book on American intervention in Chile, Armando Uribe, a typical "career politician," offers a short account of his life in which the reader can recognize several of the elements mentioned above as necessary for a successful political career in Chile, regardless of one's ideological orientation. Uribe's father had been a cabinet minister under the Radicals. First he attended the school of the Congregation of the Holy Cross and after graduation pursued law studies at the University of Chile. He joined the Christian Democracy, but abandoned that party to go with the leftists of the MAPU and unite with the Popular Unity. His loyalty to the "cause of the people" was rewarded by an appointment as ambassador to the People's Republic of China.[42]

Involvement in youth movements at the high school level (e.g., the *Federación de Estudiantes Secundarios*—Federation of High School Students) and at the university level (the FECH—Students Federation of Chile) was very important for the future career of a politician. Elections for offices in student bodies were crucial for established political parties as they were considered training grounds for the combativity and political effectiveness of their youth cadres.[43] These contests tested and exercised the rhetorical ability (more than the political articulation) of a future party leader. Beginning in the 1950s Socialists, Communists, and Christian Democrats concentrated much of their organizational effort on having their young supporters elected to the executive council of the FECH. The young and aggressive students who succeeded would have the best chance of being nominated as candidates for deputy seats in the Congress in the near future. The career of Luis Maira exemplifies this process.

Yet another interesting common denominator among politicians has been their *provinciano* origin. In contrast with their *Santiaguino* counterparts, many of those who go to the capital city to study do so under very stringent financial conditions, interrupting, at least momentarily, the contact with their family nucleus. In the absence of this very important liaison,[44] the *provinciano* student reverts to affinitive groups: young people from the same province, religious or ideological backgrounds. The time previously dedicated to family life is used now to participate in social gatherings within these groups. Political activism or intellectual parties replace family reunions so that the *provinciano* student soon becomes the most militant among his peers and advances to the spearhead of a political party in student bodies. A *provinciano* of prominent name is readily accepted within political and social circles of the capital city, so it is the middle-class student who channels his activities through middle-class or popular parties,[45] at least until he has gained a foothold in Santiago's political establishment.

Once this beachhead has been secured, the next step in achieving social recognition and higher political acceptance occurs through marriage into one of *the* families (see chapter 3) or by joining a fraternity. The Freemasonry has been the most influential fraternity in the political development of the country and has contributed greatly to the formation and continuity of the Chilean political establishment. Student activists from nonoligarchic parties were strongly attracted to its ranks, and students whose parents were affiliated with the fraternity and active in politics were also readily patronized by the organization.[46] During its halcyon years, the Radical party established advantageous political alliances, especially with the Liberal, Democratic, and Socialist parties, that are suspected to have been concocted inside the lodge. In fact, personalities of the Freemasonry were conspicuous members of the Radical or Socialist party and acted frequently as "silver bridges" when political contingencies threatened to shatter center-left alliances. Finally, the significance of the Freemasonry in a successful political career in Chile is obvious from the fact that six of the eight presidents of the Republic between 1932 and 1973 were members of the fraternity.

One last touch in the making of a typical Chilean politician was his "anointment" by the vested economic interest groups of the country. This occurred very early in his career, commonly when he married into affluent circles or when he was elected into the lower Chamber. It was usual that a newly elected deputy would be approached by a corporation and asked to join its board of directors as a councillor (see chapter 3). No ambitious politician would reject such an offer, and initially this offer had no strings attached. In fact, instead of being looked upon with suspicion, his status as councillor added the necessary condiment to sociopolitical and economic recognition within Chilean society. It is also true that few politicians would try to cultivate an image of themselves as *honrado pero tonto* ("honest but stupid"). However, this is not to say that active participation in Chilean politics was considered a highway to riches or that all politicians patronized certain economic interests in order to share in the profits. The point is simply that by being nominated councillor of a company a politician was given public acknowledgment of his ascent, and the company in its turn benefited from the aura of social prestige that surrounded the politician.

The intricate set of relationships outlined here points to the existence of a political elite, an anointed few whose behavioral patterns were specifically geared to what Scott refers to as "the internal control devices" that permit them to operate successfully according to the rules of the political game established by the political system.[47] In a relatively open system such as Chile's there was always a possibility for "lone rangers" and also for mavericks to shatter the basis of the political establishment, but their tempestuous advances were usually short-lived. In contrast, to become a veteran politician one had to play according to the rules at the same time as trying to please the voting public. Experience, oratorical power, passion, and a sense of opportunity produced a good politician, assured him permanence in Congress, and occasionally even made him one of the remarkable statesmen in Latin America. It is therefore difficult to agree with views that deny the existence of capable and efficient politicians in the public administrative cadres of Chile.

Additional proof that Chilean politicians have been individuals generally well prepared to carry out their responsibilities as statesmen is found not only in their early exposure to politics, but also in their occupational background. By and large, deputies, senators, ministers, and presidents of the Republic have a university education and a high percentage have attended law school. In the 1960s, approximately 40 percent of all the congressmen and nearly half of the senators (twenty-one individuals) were lawyers.[48] The party with the highest number of lawyers among its representatives was the Radical party with 55 percent, followed by the Conservative party with 50 percent, and the Christian Democracy with 42 percent. Jurisprudence has always been considered as a most prestigious career in Chilean society. During the nineteenth century the ruling aristocracy, having already established its economic strength by the possession of land, secured the control of Chile's administration by placing in the government its best-trained members, if possible those with a degree in law. George McBride sketched a typical landowner of the 1930s as an individual who "after education was completed, had begun a desultory practice of law that very soon brought him into political life."[49] This casual blend of agriculturalist, lawyer, and politician angered Francisco A. Encina, who, at the beginning of this century, wrote, against the proclivity of Chilean society toward liberal careers: "If one asks one hundred Chilean parents about the career they want for their children, nearly eighty will respond that they prefer law, medicine, or engineering. It is not with syllogisms nor with pompous reasonings that wheat is grown and steel is manufactured...."[50] But his diatribes did not shake the deeply entrenched attitudes of Chilean society. The fact that even in centrist parties like the Radical party and the Christian Democracy more than two-fifths of the prominent politicians had studied law proves that the attitudes of the old aristocracy were copied by the emerging middle class. The so-called popular parties are not excluded from this tendency. In the Socialist party 33 percent were lawyers and only 26 percent blue-collar workers; in the Communist party 35 percent were lawyers and 22 percent blue-collar.[51]

Independent professions such as physicians, dentists, or engineers follow among congressmen with about 20 percent in all the major parties, except in the Christian Democracy where they reach a high of 28 percent. These percentages are indicative of a tendency in the Chilean electorate to give political mandate to professionals who enjoy credibility in social as well as in economic circles. Particularly during the administrations of Jorge Alessandri, Eduardo Frei, and Salvador Allende, responsible ministerial posts were given to experienced professionals—not only lawyers—and being a technician became an asset when contending for a seat in Congress. This tendency appears to be a reaction of the Chilean electorate against the traditional lawyer-politician and intellectual-politician groups that were so conspicuous in the past in both the executive and legislative bodies. Scott identifies as intellectuals those members of society who, through teaching and publishing, gain a reputation as public figures. Although the intellectuals in Congress at the beginning of the twentieth century were chiefly from aristocratic families who had influence in the historical parties, after the "voters' revolt" of the 1920s they came increasingly from the middle class and became the spokesmen of center and left parties. Weston Agor remarks that between 1965 and 1969 there were two professors, one newspaperman, and one writer in the Senate,[52] making up nearly 10 percent of the upper Chamber. If one considers that some of the lawyers in the Senate were also professors—in fact there were three—the percentage increases to more than 15, a figure that is by no means negligible.

Historically, the political power of the oligarchic parties in Chile was based on the ownership of land and the control of the primary sources of the Chilean economy. Correspondingly, the proportion of landowners and entrepreneurs in the two highest powers of the nation was extremely high. Agor reports that between 1933 and 1937 these two groups accounted for 13 and 9 percent, respectively, while in the late 1960s the figures had dropped to 4.5 and 6.8 percent. These figures reveal a dramatic withdrawal of economic groups from the political scene in Chile and their replacement by middle-class politicians. A glance at the distribution of agriculturalists and businessmen, party by party, gives interesting clues to the general characteristics of the Chilean political establishment and the influence exerted upon it by the social values of the ruling classes. Two-thirds of the conservative and one quarter of the liberal congressmen were basically landowners with some profession as their urban activity. Landownership also appears to have been common among representatives from middle-class parties: 18 percent of the Christian Democratic deputies and 11 percent of the radical deputies were landowners.[53] The aforementioned facts confirm the contention that the norm of possessing land as a positive step in political and social acceptance was widespread in the Chilean political establishment. Only congressmen from the Socialist and Communist parties did not conform to that norm, at least not to the same extent; some of them had acquired little farms (*fundos*) or villas (*quintas*) in the Basin of Santiago or in other agrarian provinces close to the nation's capital.

The parties that recruited their main political figures from the middle and lower classes, particularly the Socialist and Communist parties, had a large percentage of salaried workers among their congressmen. The Socialist party seems to have been the more genuine working-class party of the two, since 26 percent of its deputies were blue-collar workers in comparison with only 22 percent in the Communist party; in the latter, 39 percent of the deputies were white-collar workers as compared with 23 percent in the former.

In accordance with its character of being a party for the bureaucratic segment of the country, the Radical party had 37 percent of its congressmen employed as state officials, far more than any other party. Only the Socialist party came close with 23 percent. These figures, which describe the situation in the mid-1960s, may well have changed by the end of the decade as more Christian Democrats and Communists moved into governmental jobs when their parties came into control of the executive.

By no means all who held public office between 1932 and 1973 took the long-winding path described on the preceding pages. The Chilean political system also had room for those individuals who were catapulted onto the political stage by some of the rare tours de force that disturbed the institutional course of the country. A residue of the early 1930s agitation was the participation of the military as elected members in the executive or the Congress. Their eagerness to participate in national politics resulted in their sudden change on September 5, 1924, from a "deliberating passive force" into an "active political force." For the next eight years, until September 1932, the atmosphere of social and political stir catalyzed by the armed forces' "Honorable Mission" created the circumstances in which militaries-turned-politicians had an opportunity to demonstrate their capabilities as statesmen. Colonel Bartolomé Blanche, Admiral Francisco Neff, General Ambrosio Viaux, Captain Carlos Frödden, General Carlos Ibañez del Campo, and Major Marmaduke Grove are just a few of the numerous military figures who replaced professional politicians during the eventful years of the Honorable Mission. As soon as civil rule was restored, most of the military went back to their barracks, with the exception of Carlos Ibañez del Campo and Marmaduke Grove.[54] They returned to politics later as civilians and used the avenues of established parties.

The withdrawal of the military from active politics in 1932 was not complete. Well-known generals and admirals in service were summoned to fill posts in the cabinets of radical administrations and of the presidents Ibañez del Campo and Allende. Other more restless elements attempted to seize political control of the country in ill-fated coups, but found the Chilean democracy too deeply rooted in the souls of the people to be shaken by these adventures. One such attempt was made in 1939 under the leadership of General Ariosto Herrera (the *Ariostazo*), but it failed because of poor organization.[55] In the tense political atmosphere of October 1948, General Ibañez del Campo and a Colonel Vergara were accused of a military-backed conspiracy. When General Ibañez del Campo assumed the executive power in 1952—this time by winning the presidential election—there were rumors of military meddling. And in 1953 it was rumored that some high-ranking military officers were members of a secret organization called the *Línea Recta,* whose objectives were more political than professional.[56] The itch of the military did not disappear during the 1960s. On the contrary, it increased during the populist government of the Christian Democracy. In October of 1969, General Roberto Viaux engineered a mutiny in one of Santiago's garrisons, allegedly protesting salary conditions of the troops. However, the purpose of his protest seems to have been politically oriented.[57] Four years later, Colonel Roberto Souper aimed an abortive coup at Salvador Allende only to be thwarted by officers and troops loyal to the president. In April of 1973, when Chile's history seemed to have made a complete revolution back to the year 1924, President Allende summoned into his cabinet General Pedro Palacios, and in November of the same year, the Generals Carlos Prats and Claudio Sepúlveda and Admiral Ismael Huerta.[58] For a second time in less than fifty years, the military establishment had been taken out of the barracks with a tempting offer to participate in the government of the nation—an offer it was not likely to reject.

Mavericks and adventurers made even more sporadic appearances in Chilean politics than the military. It was in the turbulent early 1930s that figures like Ibañez del Campo, Marmaduke Grove, and González von Marées burst upon the political scene. However, they were front-page news for only a short period of time before they had to retreat under the pressure of personalities from the political establishment. The wave of *Ibañismo* that swept through the country after the election of Carlos Ibañez del Campo as president in 1952 sparked an upsurge of mavericks and adventurers that lasted throughout the decade. Deserving of special mention are the controversial figures of Rafael Tarud, the salesman from Talca; María de la Cruz, without doubt the most histrionic and superficial female politician of the mid-century; Baltazar Castro, the everchanging socialist caudillo; and Antonio Zamorano, the parish priest from the little town of Catapilco. After being suspended by the Catholic church for repeatedly breaking his vows of celibacy, Zamorano turned politician and became deputy in 1957. In 1958, animated by the unconditional support from his followers, he even made an attempt at the presidency. In the 1960s, perhaps the only comparable figure was Jaime Barros Pérez-Cotapos, the aristocratic doctor from Valparaíso. He was elected Communist party senator in 1961, but later was purged from the party because of his *Pekinista* leanings. He then suffered ridicule in the Congress by his peers and former comrades each time he stood up to participate in debate.

It should be emphasized that all these public figures, although initially lodged inside conventionally organized political groups, chose unorthodox methods when dealing with the political establishment and were therefore progressively isolated and sidelined from active politics. Personalism in Chile, unlike in many other Latin American countries, has short legs and does not fit into the country's rigidly structured party system. No matter how strong the charismatic appeal of a leader may be, if he wants to relate to the masses he has to do it via a political party. The caudillo, both at the local and national level, has his chance of political success drastically limited by the widespread influence of party politics and by the establishment of lines of brokerage extending from the highest national offices of a party in Santiago down to the scene of local politics.[59]

3
The Social Texture

In a country with the social variety of Chile, the development of distinct political tendencies reflects very closely the social relations that exist between dominating groups (aristocratic, economic, or political elites) and the urban or rural masses (the middle class, peasantry, and urban proletariat). The political awareness and electoral responses of the latter have been greatly influenced by the perception of their place in Chile's society and by the contracts established with peers and masters. Nevertheless, the relations between individuals and groups were set in a varied geographical environment that has also contributed to political differentiations. In the following pages the social groups will be considered not in dissociation from their geographical contexts but as integral parts of cultural landscapes. Further, the political leanings of these social groups will be assumed to emanate from specific personal and environmental circumstances.

Aristocracy

Political power in Chile was seized by the landowner oligarchy early in the history of the Republic. The economic strength of this class and its use of the peasantry brought independence from Spain and decided in its favor any challenges from competing political groups: liberals, federalists, and even royalists. Apart from the few liberal ordinances of the new rulers, such as the abolition of noble titles and slavery and the suspension of entailed ownership privileges (*mayorazgo*), nothing significant was altered in the colonial system of class relations. Hence a social order that had been instituted during the centuries of Spanish rule and that relied on the possession of land as the main pillar of economic achievement and social prestige continued to prevail in the new regime.[1]

With the triumph in the 1830s of the Portalesian idea of state (*un estado respetado y respetable*), the dominant class began to promote the image of the powerful and incorruptible statesman who wanted only to serve the best interests of the nation. The victories in war of the previous century and the commercial expansion of the country based on an agricultural economy greatly strengthened the conviction of the ruling class that Chile's successes were due to the ability of the landowning aristocracy not only to run efficiently the internal and external affairs of the country, but also to build an economic base for a powerful nation. Detractors and apologists of the Chilean aristocratic oligarchy agree that this social class possessed in addition to wealth certain intellectual attributes that allowed it to seize and hold the political power until the turbulent 1920s. Unlike in other Latin American countries, the aristocracy in Chile was able to keep the nation together during the last century and to turn the state into an institution rather than an instrument of personal enrichment. It had inherited from its ancestors, many of whom were colonial officers, a stubborn adherence to legal procedures, which has always been a remarkable trait of the Spanish spirit. It is not surprising then that Chile's initial republican years were spotted with attempts to create a "state in form" by experimenting with all possible variants of political constitutions. In harmony with this inclination for legal formalities was the idea that the best politician is the one who has been trained as a lawyer; consequently each aristocratic family needed a lawyer to maintain its social and political prestige.

Additional clues to the aristocracy's code of social and political behavior are found in its agricultural background. Holding quite a Hesiodian philosophy, the Basque, Navarran, and Castilian newcomers praised life in the countryside as one of the most sober and virtuous ways of spending one's life and abhorred the decadence of city life. This view surfaces repeatedly in the writings of one of the last apologists of the aristocracy, the landowner and historian Francisco A. Encina. From colonial times on, the landowner class had developed an *encomendero* attitude of patronizing the peasants on their estates and deciding every aspect of their lives. Thus the peculiar myth of the historical role reserved by destiny for the landowner aristocracy—even though it was viewed more as a providential mandate—developed quite early among the members of this social elite and led to the first conflicts with statesmen who tried to run the country without the aristocracy's backing or advice.[2] Their deeply entrenched belief in their own indispensability has been traced masterfully by Alberto Edwards in *La fronda aristocrática*, where he points out the aristocracy's repeated political interventions whenever it felt its influence being threatened by competing sociopolitical groups. Any serious and realistic analysis of Chilean politics in the last decades should by no means omit this important aspect of the oligarchy's attitude as an explanatory element of its political behavior. In this context, the cultivation of history as a favorite literary genre among writers from aristocratic families is keeping alive the memory of that glorious and virtuous past when the traditional aristocracy governed the country.

Nearly two centuries of domination over the rural serfs, an inflated belief in its own importance, and the awareness of its socioeconomic prominence have formed an aristocratic elite whose haughtiness and aloofness may seem ridiculous and puzzling to the foreign observer. A cult of names, which by the turn of the century seemed to have reached a paroxysmal high, incited poor members of the aristocratic families to adopt snob postures unwarranted by their actual social and economic place in society. Many of these individuals, in order to hide their social inferiority, joined the Conservative party, where they could indulge in the comfort of being respected at least for their family name, or they advertised their daughters' debuts in society or marriage in the pages of *El Diario Illustrado*, the former newspaper of the conservative aristocracy.

Apart from the attributes mentioned by Jaime Eyzaguirre,[3] the Basque-Castilian aristocracy also inherited a lack of imagination and a mental inflexibility that made it tremendously intolerant in religious and political matters and deprived it of the slickness necessary to operate successfully in a sophisticated political system. Perhaps in these traits resides the reason for its declining political success in the present century and for its replacement by the more malleable and compliant elements of the bourgeoisie and the middle class. Because of their traditionalism and slow adaptation to social change the aristocratic elite of the country was progressively stripped of their political powers. First, in the 1950s, the introduction of the single ballot took away their electoral control over the peasantry; then, in the 1960s, they were attacked at the main source of their power—possession of the land.

Landowners

The aristocracy had traditionally based its economic, social, and political power mainly on the control of the land. The large estate, the hacienda, was the training ground for the oligarchy. George McBride, an acute observer of the Chilean countryside during the 1930s, described the landed *patrón* ("the master") with the following words:

> *Don Fulano* ('Mister So-and-So') began his career by learning to command. Almost before he could walk or talk he had learned that he could impose his will on most of the circle around him. Servants attended him from dawn until night. His parents he learned to respect and love and among his large family of brothers and sisters he found that he met his peers. Outside of this group his wish was usually law.[4]

Of course, not all contemporary aristocrats originated from the countryside. As early as 1850 the economic life and the political action were shifting into the urban centers. Nevertheless, the landlords who did not actually live on their ancestral estates returned there periodically or sent their children during vacation periods so that they would not forget the "arts" of commanding and inspiring respect. In addition, during election times it was politically profitable for the hacienda owner to be on the estate, as he was usually personally engaged in patronizing campaigns on behalf of the party and candidates he favored. It was also a common custom for the higher rural servants, *mayordomos* ("administrators") and *capataces* ("foremen"), to ask their masters to be godparents to their children, thereby enhancing the paternal image of the landowner. With this, the loyalty of the most important subordinates on the hacienda was assured, and from there the patronizing schemes were expanded into the lower peasant ranks.

The most coveted croplands for the landowner aristocracy that emerged in the eighteenth century were the well-irrigated and fertile alluvial plains of the Chilean Central Vale and its neighboring river valleys. A sample of the estates held by aristocratic families during the last century and the greater part of this century reveals their high concentration in the prime land between the Petorca Valley and the Teno Valley (Table 3). A great number of these families appear also in Table 4 (p. 87), which illustrates the persistent presence of aristocratic clans in the Congress and executive of Chile. It could not have been otherwise since the estates were used by their illustrious patriarchs as recruiting centers for electoral clientele. One notices that competition for the possession of land was more intense in the fertile Aconcagua Valley and in the Basin of Santiago than in the two extreme valleys considered in Table 3. The Cerdas were dominant in what today corresponds to the province of Aconcagua, and the Errázuriz and Valdés in the provinces of O'Higgins and Colchagua. A huge landed estate in this tract of Chile, *La Compañía* near Rancagua, had been purchased cheaply by Mateo Toro y Zambrano from the Jesuit order when it was expelled from the country in 1776; he later sold it to one of the patriarchs of the Correa dynasty.[5] Thereafter it was kept by that family until well into the middle of the present century. Incidentally, the father of the author was born within the boundaries of this almost legendary estate.

In the middle and lower Aconcagua Valley close to Valparaíso, the center of Chile's bourgeoisie, large estates were owned by more families from the capitalistic bourgeoisie (e.g., Eastman, Edwards, Morandé, and Subercaseaux) than anywhere else in central Chile. They initiated the grab for agricultural land near the commercial city of Valparaíso with the purpose of gaining access to the aristocratic circles of Santiago. Abundant water and a good communication with this bustling city ensured the success of agriculture in the picturesque Aconcagua Valley.[6]

North and south of the area discussed here, the absence of an effective expeditious communications system posed difficulties for the development of striving latifundia. Arnold J. Bauer writes pertinently: "Deeper in the provinces conditions were more primitive. In Curicó, Talca, and below the Maule even a huge estate was insufficient to support anything beyond a modestly respectable style to say nothing of a Santiago town house."[7] In the semiarid area of the *Norte Chico* latifundia developed only in the better irrigated valleys. Members of the banker-mining Edwards family have owned large estates in the Huasco and Choapa valleys. Near Illapel in the latter, the Edwards have been competing with the aristocratic Irarrázabals for the control of the land and the politi-

Table 3
Geographical Location of Landed Estates and Political Representation of the Landowner Class

Geographical Unit	Landowner Families	Electoral District
La Ligua Valley	Cerda, Irarrázabal, Ovalle	Petorca, La Ligua
Upper Aconcagua Valley	García-Huidobro, Hurtado, Ovalle, Vicuña	San Felipe, Los Andes
Middle and Lower Aconcagua Valley	Bulnes, Eastman, Edwards, Echeverría, Errázuriz, Larraín, Morandé, Ovalle, Subercaseaux, Undurraga	Quillota, Limache
Puangue Creek	Barros, Correa, Cousiño, Larraín, Montt, Prieto, Riesco	Santiago Second District
Basin of Santiago	Barros, Concha, Correa, Cousiño, García-Huidobro, Irarrázabal, Larraín, Ruiz-Tagle, Toro, Subercaseaux, Undurraga	Santiago Third and Fourth Districts
Lower Maipo Valley	Larraín, Toro	Santiago Fourth District
Basin of Rancagua	Correa, Errázuriz, Gandarillas, Larraín, Ossa	Rancagua, Cachapoal
Rapel Valley	Subercaseaux, Valdés	Cachapoal
Tinguirírica Valley	Correa, Errázuriz, Larraín, Lira, Valdés	San Fernando
Teno Valley	Donoso, Echenique, Vergara	Curicó

cal representation of the valley.

Once the central Chilean railway (Ferrocarril Longitudinal) was built in 1863, latifundia in the style of those in the Santiago Basin flourished close to the rails, south of the Maule Valley. This development led also to the fragmentation of several large haciendas and to the purchasing of land by a new class of entrepreneurs of nonaristocratic background. Along with these newcomers in the landowner class the "anonymous corporations" also arrived. By the middle of the twentieth century, latifundia were no longer an exclusive specialty of the Castilian-Basque aristocracy or of the banking bourgeoisie. Levantines and Italians were also purchasing land in the provinces of Curicó and Talca and became serious competitors of the aristocratic wine growers in the Basin of Santiago.

This trend makes it evident that the landowner class, just like other economic elites of the Chilean society, was becoming variegated and that its base was broadening with the incorporation of bourgeois and upper middle-class elements. The remarkable point, however, is that the new elements did not have a modernizing effect on the sociopolitical attitudes of the traditional landowner group. It worked the other way around: the majority of the new landowners adopted the views of the older class and gave political support to the aristocracy, who represented the interests of all the landowners in the Congress. Therefore, it would be a mistake to think that the increasing number of new proprietors in the countryside created political openings in the traditional strongholds of the aristocracy; on the contrary, it strengthened the control they had exercised for such a long time. In this perspective it is understandable that a great part of the resistance against the agrarian reform of the Frei and Allende administrations came from the new agricultural entrepreneurs who had made the social values and economic interests of the traditional aristocracy their own.

Kinship and Political Continuance

The kinship ties between the Basque and Navarre families that were established in Chile during the last century of Spanish rule surfaced and became quite important in terms of ideological direction during the independence period (1810-1814).[8] Already one can trace back to those years the family alliances that determined the course of the new Republic and the cleavages that were to develop among the members of the aristocracy. For instance, the kinship cluster of the Larrains, or "family of the eight hundred," which rested on two main branches, conservative landowners and aggressive liberal merchants, is well known in Chile's history. Both branches were involved with other no less important families like the Rosales, Pérez, Vicuña, and Infantes, from among whom not only landowner politicians but also clergymen, writers, and military figures were to appear. Another family, originally allied with the Larraíns, was the Errázuriz, who because of their liberal ideas— for which they were labelled *los litres* (shrubs that cause allergic skin eruptions)—kept away from the more conservative Larrains. Another well-known family was the Carrera family. It was related to the Pintos and, in the early years of the Republic, had openly challenged the political power of the Larraíns.

Soon the family alliances that had started in colonial times developed into more politically and economically oriented clans. To the prestige of the family name and landownership was added political influence exerted through public offices. Through convenience marriages certain family groups gained control over particular areas of central Chile, where, consequently, their electoral bases were secured. For families that became isolated in kinship as well as in geographical terms, rise and success in politics were far more difficult than for those who acted together.

Table 4, compiled from Luis Valencias *Anales de la República* and the *Monografía de la Cámara de Diputados: 1811-1945*,[9] illustrates the continuance of patrician family names in Chile's political institutions. The tabulated information offers an insight into which families dominated the political scene during which periods. For a male of lower lineage the incorporation into a family clan occurred mainly through marriage. The offspring bore the family name of the mother after the paternal name and was counted as an integral member of some of the big families listed. In one of the best studies on the Chilean aristocratic elite, Emilio Willems asserts that access to the nation's upper class by a lower-class individual of native or foreign origin was gained most often by marriage. In fact, 42 percent of the sample he studied had risen to the "golden class" by this method. Inversely, males of aristocratic lineage who entered marital unions with plebeian women became socially stigmatized and lost acceptability in their class.[10]

A first glance at the table shows that from the families repre-

Table 4
Representation of Aristocratic Families in the Executive Power and in the Congress of Chile (1810-1953)*

*LEGEND President of the republic - (★)   Senators - (●)
         Minister of state - (■)   Deputies - (○)

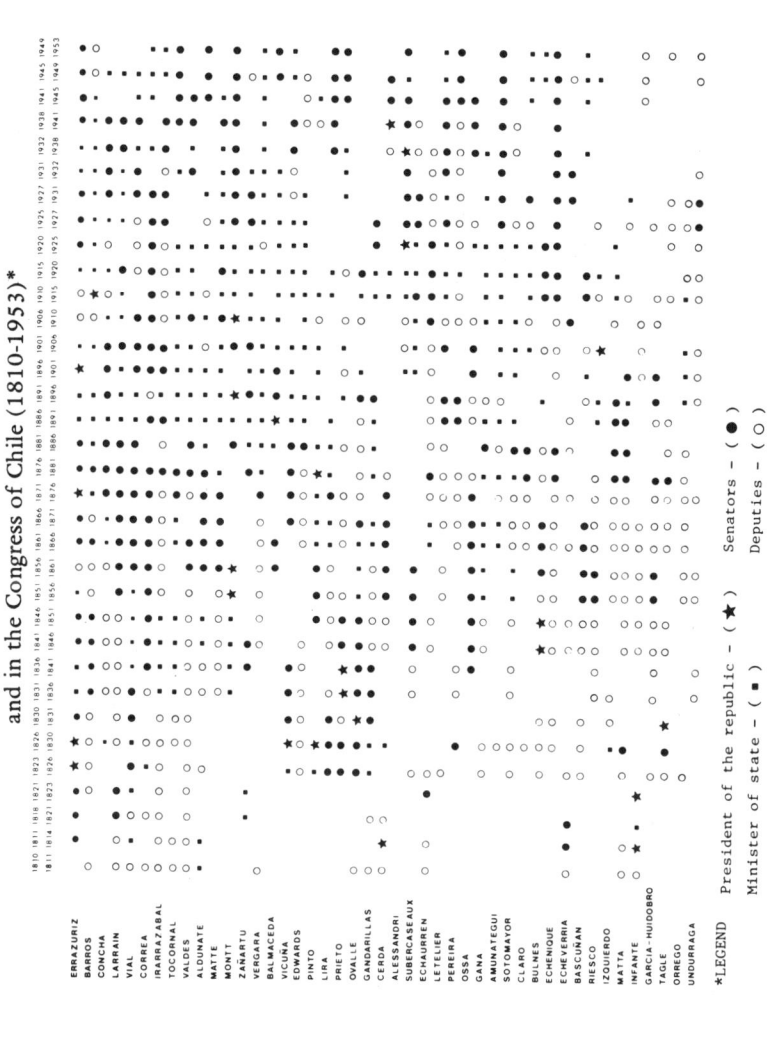

sented, the Errázuriz, Barros, Concha, Larraín, and Vial are the dominating ones. Among these, the Errázuriz stands out clearly as the clan that has produced not only the largest number of members of the executive (presidents or ministers of the state), but also the largest number of representatives in both Chambers of the Congress. A closer look at the mother names of those Errázuriz reveals their connections with other well-known families on the table. In the period of time considered on the table there were five Errázuriz Echaurren, four Errázuriz Sotomayor, four Errázuriz Aldunate, and three Errázuriz Larraín involved in politics. Other prominent Errázuriz personalities bore mother names as aristocratic as Echenique, Pereira, and Valdivieso. The Barros, the second most important family, had about as many representatives in the two highest Chilean powers, but did not establish as many ties with other aristocratic families as did the Errázuriz. There were a few Barros Errázuriz and Barros Valdés, but the rest were descendants from lesser known high families. The Conchas, whose name appears so often as a result of familial alliances like Concha y Cerda, Concha y Toro, or Concha Vergara, occupied seats in the Congress mostly.

The large Larraín representation is due to the existence of the two lines previously mentioned, which resulted in both outspoken conservative family alliances like the Larraín Gandarillas, Larraín Prieto, or Larraín Vial and in alliances of more liberal character like Larraín Zañartu or Larraín Rojas. Unlike the Errázuriz and the Barros who had a family member in the executive most of the time, the Larraíns appear to have been prevented from taking higher offices, perhaps because of their infamous political meddling practices at the beginning of Chile's independence. They nevertheless acquired political relevance by constantly having one or more of their family in one of the Chambers of Congress. The Vials, however, although they had less congressional representation, are found more frequently in the executive, probably due to their connections with other families who were not as aristocratic as themselves but who were well into the country's politics.

Families like the Vergara, the Tocornal, the Gana, the Aldunate, the Montt, and the Matte had a relatively high representation in the executive, although their strength in the Congress was never as overwhelming as that of the Larraín or the Correa. The trend suggests that some aristocratic families were able to evoke sociopolitical respect and to create an image of public service, while others were not. This is particularly true for the Pinto, Balmaceda, and Vicuña families who developed a tradition of supplying ministers of the state from their ranks, although they were never abundant in Congress. The Correa family and to a lesser extent the Irarrázabal, both with numerous connections to other aristocratic landowners like the Toros, Errázuriz, or Larraíns, did not hold many offices in the executive and had to content themselves with seats in one of the Chambers of the Congress.

The table also depicts the emergence and continuity of families who had made their way through economic success and were, in the course of the decades, incorporated into the exclusive circles of the local aristocracy. The Edwards and Subercaseaux deserve special attention. They appeared on the political stage at about the same time, but through somewhat different avenues. The Edwards made an aggressive thrust into the highest political and social spheres from their successfully executed financial operations. By the end of the nineteenth century they were important figures in the executive or integral parts of the local aristocracy, as some of their daughters had married into families like the Irarrázabal, Correa, Gandarillas, or Errázuriz Vergara.[11] As to the Subercaseaux, their record of holding public office is no less impressive. After a period of representation in the Congress, members of this family were integrated into numerous cabinets at the end of the last century and married into aristocratic families like the Vicuña and the Errázuriz.

The Alessandri family's political involvement falls into another category. Again, as in the case of the Edwards, their eruption in politics is due to the activities of the patriarch Arturo Alessandri and his brother José Pedro. From among Arturo's numerous progeny, his sons Jorge, Eduardo, Fernando, and Arturo also ventured into politics and married daughters of aristocratic families like the Izquierdo, Morandé, Valdés, Aldunate, and Besa. Thus, although the founders of the dynasty were common foreigners, their descendants acquired through economic success or political fame the social prestige that made them eligible for incorporation into the highest circles of the Chilean society.

As to the permanence of aristocratic landowner families in politics, Table 4 shows the long trajectory of families like the Irarrázabal, the Barros, the Errázuriz, and the Concha, and the relatively short political life of families like the Ruiz Tagle, Arteaga, and Matta, who are still enjoying, however, the fame of high society.

The Ovalle, a family of great social and political prestige in the early decades of the Republic, has practically vanished from politics in the course of this century. The same applies to the Sotomayor family that was so important in the second half of the nineteenth century. When looking at the representation of aristocratic families in each of the Chambers of Congress, interesting trends emerge. For instance, families like the Errázuriz, the Correa, and the Concha held office as senators for longer periods of time than as deputies, the reason being that the most important public office in the Chilean political system is that of senator because of the length of the term in office and because of the decision-making power of the Senate. Most of the senators spent first terms in the Chamber of Deputies, which for them was only a waiting room for their entrance into the Senate. Furthermore, from 1919 onwards, at the same time as the aristocrats were withdrawing from the lower Chamber, illustrious names like Correa, Errázuriz, Undurraga, Tocornal, Prieto, and Lira became entrenched in the Senate.

The thinning of aristocratic names among deputies, that is in the Chamber that has less decisional power and more conflicting ideologies, becomes visible from 1930 onwards. From the fifty families analyzed here only six were represented in the Chamber of Deputies between 1930 and 1932, and thirteen in the legislative period of 1941-1945. This is a dramatic reduction from the halcyon years of the aristocracy, the 1860s and 1870s, when members of forty-three of the same fifty families occupied benches in the lower Chamber. A more spectacular indication of the eruption of a new social force in Chilean politics, the middle class, cannot be produced. However, is this trend really the result of a democratization of Chile's most popular Chamber? Does it indicate the beginning of the aristocracy's withdrawal from the world of active politics? Certainly not. Although the familiar aristocratic names no longer appear in the foreground, they are still around as the maternal names of many of the "new princes" who enter the Chamber of Deputies as alleged representatives of the middle and working classes: Alamos Barros, Altamirano Orrego, Cañas Letelier, Dávila Larraín, Garcés Gana, González Errázuriz, Marín Balmaceda, Tapia Valdés, and Videla Lira. They keep alive the traditional antics and the arrogance the aristocracy introduced into the Congress a century and a half ago.

Entrepreneurial Bourgeoisie

At the time of the declaration of independence, Chile's economy was based almost exclusively on agrarian commodities that constituted the main source of wealth of the rural landowners. With trade being monopolized by the Spanish Crown through the *consulado* ("consulate"), the development of city-based trading companies was almost negligible; only a few French and English merchants were allowed to establish small trading offices in Valparaíso. But when independence from Spanish rule was achieved in 1818, the United States, Great Britain, France, and Prussia all rushed in to set up commercial relations with the new Republic, and to reap the benefits of free trade. By 1822, there were thirty-one trading establishments in Valparaíso, and that small town of no more than 20,000 inhabitants lodged 3,000 foreigners dedicated to international commerce. In the 1830s, Valparaíso developed into the most important trading port on the South American Pacific coast, shipping grain, hides, tallow, and dried meat. At the same time it became the port of call for vessels sailing around Cape Horn to and from the Atlantic coasts. The city quickly grew into the trading and commercial capital of the country. It was the site of a new socioeconomic class in the making—the entrepreneurial bourgeoisie.[12]

In an enlightening paper, Fernando H. Cardoso underlines the important roles played by exporters of agricultural commodities and by British trading agents in the development of entrepreneurial elites in Latin America.[13] Although he does not refer specifically to Chile, the development of import-export business activities in Valparaíso and the large number of British merchants living in that city typify his statements. Along with other West Europeans, they constituted a social stratum that initially based its power on the trading economy, but later gained control of the national finances and the ownership of mineral resources. When this was achieved, the financial elite was not far from acquiring a predominant place in society and politics.

During the nineteenth century and the beginning of the twentieth century, the migration of nationals into the expanding urban centers was accompanied by a moderate flow of foreign immigrants, whose destination was also the cities. With the exception of the southern provinces from Bío-Bío to Chiloé, which were settled by German agrarian colonists, the mainstreams of European immigrants headed for Santiago and Valparaíso, the principal urban provinces. In this environment, the foreign minorities, made up of British, French, Germans, Italians, Spaniards, Levantines, and Jews, very quickly became economically successful and were then tempted to vie for political power, which had previously been the unchallenged domain of the Castilian-Basque aristocracy of the country. The reception accorded the newcomers varied depending on the perception of the different Chilean social strata. Impoverished high-class families saw with acquiescence a union by marriage of their children with economically successful immigrants.[14] The northern Europeans and French stood in high esteem, followed by the Italians and Spaniards; but Syrians, Jews, and Orientals were accepted reluctantly. The native middle class, and especially intellectuals from this sector of society, looked with misgiving upon the privileges that were granted to foreigners and on their eagerness to obtain land and good-paying jobs for which few or no Chileans could apply.[15] Also contributing to the dislike of immigrants was the fact that they displaced members of the Chilean middle class not only from the free professions but also from their positions as challengers for the political power held by the oligarchic groups in the country. The strong feelings of the Chilean middle class against the participation of even the descendants of immigrants in Chilean politics is exemplified by the vitriolic attack of Nicolás Palacios on the Italians, which seems to have been prompted by the rise of a political star like Arturo Alessandri, a third-generation Italian.[16] The feeling that the immigrants were threatening the social and economic interests of the local middle strata has been mentioned by Solberg who wrote that in 1914, Chilean nationalists, chiefly intellectual figures, were convinced that economic liberalism had permitted foreigners to take control of commerce, industry, and mining and had brought about the economic impoverishment of the nation. The suspension of immigration and a greater involvement of the state in the economy of the country were demanded as a radical solution.[17] But the incorporation of the offspring of these foreigners into the social texture of the nation had already taken place. Children from hardworking immigrant families had entered the universities, had become lawyers, engineers, physicians, or had climbed to key positions in business. In search of self-expression and social recognition, they had become affiliated with political groups and had developed (emulating the aristocracy) a public-figure image. A graphic way of demonstrating the gradual seepage of descendants from foreign families into Chilean politics is by tracing the appearance of non-Spanish names in the records of the Chambers of Deputies and the Senate from 1850 until the present.[18]

The first ethnic group to gain access to Chilean politics was the British, and their names began to crop up in Congress as early as 1860. Family names like Armstrong, Blest, Cox, Eastman, Edwards, Lyon, MacClure, MacIver, Mackenna, Phillips, Ross, Waddington appeared conspicuously in the ranks of the political elite of the nineteenth and the beginning of the twentieth centuries. In recent decades, however, names that had by then become aristocratic have been replaced by others of British, but not necessarily aristocratic, provenance, such as Aylwin, Cash, Chadwick, Hamilton, Leighton, and Thayer.

The French immigrants met a lesser degree of acceptance from the traditional aristocratic elite. Among those who were able to win a place in the Chilean higher classes, because of economic success or political involvement, were the Armanet, Beauchef, Court, Labbé, Letelier (L'Atelier), Morandé (Moran d'Aix), Subercaseaux, and Zegers.

The Germans made a rather late appearance on the Chilean political scene at the beginning of the twentieth century, but their number was greater than that of French and even British immigrants. Among the first German families to be found in politics were the Haverbeck, Koch, Koenig, Monckeberg, Moller, and Philippi.[19] The largest influx of Germans took place between the 1930s and the 1960s, when names like Becker, Brahm, Gardeweg, Holzapfel, Mashke, Piwonka, Rettig, Saelzer, Von Mühlenbrock, and Wiegand were frequently heard in political circles. Lately, however, the German input into Chilean politics has also markedly declined.

Italians who emigrated to Chile during the nineteenth century came predominantly from Liguria and Tuscany. Their physical appearance—tall, fair-skinned, blond-haired, and sometimes blue-eyed—did not differentiate them very much from the rest of the *gringos* (foreigners of Nordic appearance). As a result, Italians in Chile, unlike Italian immigrants in Anglo-Saxon countries, made rapid social and political progress. The most successful has been the Alessandri family, followed by the Bianchis, both of Tuscan origin. With the triumph of the Christian Democracy in 1964 and of the Popular Unity in 1970, there was a remarkable boom in Italian names, especially of descendants of more recent immigrants. They attained offices in Congress as well as in the executive of different political parties: Arnello, Barberis, Cademartori, Gianini, Lorenzini, Pareto, Palestro, Penna, Sivori, Trivelli, Vitale are just a few names of Chilean Italians who were well-known political figures.

Yugoslavians also came to Chile (especially after the collapse of the Austro-Hungarian Empire) and settled mainly in the urban centers of Magallanes and the province of Antofagasta.[20] In the 1940s, the first descendants of these immigrants were already participating in politics, though as "late entries." Among the most prominent Chilean-Yugoslavians were Radomiro Tomic, the unsuccessful presidential candidate of the Christian Democracy in 1970, and Pedro Vuscovic, minister of finance during the Allende administration.

Jews who immigrated to Chile also came relatively recently, and they were not as numerous as those who went to Argentina and Brazil.[21] Jewish immigrants to Chile originated chiefly in Russia and the Baltic states. Although their participation in politics does not show up very much in representative positions (senators, deputies, or ministers), they have been very prominent in the organization cadres of such parties as the Radical, the Socialist, and the Communist. Because of their relatively late arrival after 1912 and again after 1930, the main thrust of Jewish participation in politics has been felt only since 1950. Important Jewish figures in Chilean politics include V. Teitelboim, R. Bernstein, J. Chonchol, A. Faivovich, J. Schaulsohn, O. Waisz, and D. Baytelman.

Another important group of immigrants that became quite active in politics after 1950, when British and French descendants were already fading into the political background, was the Levantines, commonly referred to as *turcos* (because of their Turkish documents of immigration), which include the Lebanese, the Palestinians, and the Syrians. They made a dramatic invasion into Chilean politics during the administration of Ibañez del Campo, who recruited their organizational talents and financial resources for his campaign against his old enemy, the political Right.[22] The outstanding Levantine figure in Chilean politics since 1953 has been Rafael Tarud, who, along with Alejandro Hales, made his entry into politics as a minister of President Ibañez del Campo. Previously only isolated members of this ethnic group had come to Congress, e.g., Carlos Melej, Alfredo Nazar, and Marco A. Salum. After 1964, during the Frei administration, Arab names once again became prominent in the executive and legislative Chambers: Alejandro Chelén, Mario Hamuy, José Musalem, Alejandro Noemi, and José Tohá were conspicuous members of the Christian Democratic and the Socialist parties during the past two decades.

This general survey of the input of descendants of foreign families into Chilean politics illustrates the emergence, rise to power, and assimilation of some of them into the ruling class of Chile through acquired political prestige. The first foreign families to be accepted, not only into politics but also into the exclusive circles of the Castilian-Basque aristocracy of the country, were the children of British families. The Blests, the Mackennas, the Edwards, and the Lyons mixed very early with oligarchic families like the Vicuña, Santa María, Ossandón, Gana, or Matte, thus gaining a coveted place in the economy and in politics as well as among the social elite of Chile.[23] The same thing happened to the French Letelier, Morandés, and Subercaseaux, and to a lesser extent to the German Monckebergs and Mollers. Italians found a more reluctant acceptance by the higher classes; in fact, only the Alessandri family can be considered to have made it into the higher social as well as political spheres. The involvement of the other ethnic groups in politics has not yet brought them access to the oligarchic circles of the country. However, it is significant that some political personalities from less important ethnic groups and members of a middle-class party established linkages with aristocratic families, e.g., Eduardo Frei and Radomiro Tomic, who married María Ruíz-Tagle and Olaya Errázuriz, respectively. This probably lends support to the assertion made by several writers (Pike, Stavenhagen, and Zeitlin) that the middle-class opportunism is characterized by its leanings towards the higher classes and its disdain for the lower. This is particularly true with some sectors of the upper middle class, but it does not apply to all the members of that social group.

The Edwards and the Cousiños exemplify the remarkable rise of some of the bourgeois families. The Edwards empire grew around the descendants of a Welsh surgeon who, in 1807, deserted a British corsair to marry a girl from the quiet provincial town of La Serena. His third child, Agustín Edwards Ossandón, initiated banking activities in the mining city of Copiapó, speculated in copper on the British stock market, founded the first insurance company of Chile, and developed railroad enterprises. Between 1861 and 1879, he was elected a deputy but could not assume a political office because of his many business ventures. His son Agustín Edwards Ross, offspring of his marriage to a member of another bourgeois family of English origin, continued and expanded the enterprises of his father, adding to them the ownership of *El Mercurio,* one of the most influential newspapers of the country.[24] Like his father, Agustín "bought" a seat for himself in the Congress from 1876 until 1895. At the beginning of the twentieth century, the original genealogic trunk of the Edwards tree had branched out to include other bourgeois families (the MacClure and the Matte) and enjoyed a privileged position in the world of finance, society, and politics. Table 4 (p. 87) illustrates the long years of participation in politics that were enjoyed by this family. Not less spectacular was the rise of the Cousiño family. Matías Cousiño, born in Santiago in 1802, set out on the road to financial success, like the Edwards, Subercaseaux, Gallos, and Mattes, in the mining city of Copiapó. From there he expanded his operations to the coal fields of Lota. Since political influence had an important bearing on his financial position, Cousiño also engaged in politics and "bought" a seat for himself in the Congress between 1849 and 1864.[25]

In similar fashion other bourgeois families became wealthy first through mining and then in banking or trading outside Santiago. The move into the capital city was made as soon as a secure economic and political position was reached. The next step on the social and political ladder was the purchase of large estates to round out their prestigious image. In fact, if families like the Cousiño, the Urmeneta, the Eastman, and the Cox are still surrounded by an aura of aristocratic distinction, this is not only due to their financial superiority, but also because their names are associated with famous estates in the agricultural heartland of Chile.[26]

The political ambitions of this rising class did not necessarily coincide with those of the ruling landowner aristocracy and were channeled into less conservative and traditionalist political groups. The bourgeois ideals of economic development, financial laissez-faire, and ideological-religious tolerance found better expression in the Liberal party or National Montt-Varista party than in the Conservative party. Consequently, during a greater part of the nineteenth and at the beginning of the twentieth centuries, each of the two political currents, though both representing the higher classes of Chile, held very distinct and different views on social questions, the welfare of the workers, and the democratization of the masses.

After the 1927-1932 interregnum and the halcyon years of the Popular Front, the ideological currents of the higher classes, the Liberal party and the Conservative party came together and ensured their political survival by merging into the National party of the 1960s. From its origin as an entrepreneurial elite with intertwined interests in banking, trading institutions, and mining consortia, the bourgeoisie moved into manufacturing at the turn of the century as the country began to develop its industrial potential. By the "golden era of industrialization" (the 1930s) the state not only provided great assistance to existing industrial establishments, but it also encouraged fiscal ventures in newly created enterprises.[27] As a result of the combined action of state and private enterprise, a new shade of the bourgeoisie emerged: the managerial elite, which, as characterized by Cardoso, consisted of "state entrepreneurs and professional administrators of foreign concerns." This elite was recruited not only from the traditional higher classes and the growing foreign immigrant minorities, but also from among successful professionals of the native middle class.[28] The infusion of fresh blood into the vessels of an aging plutocracy added a social dynamism to the higher classes and the upper strata of the middle sectors. Accommodation of socioeconomic interests common to the landowner aristocracy, the bourgeoisie, and the professional entrepreneurial elites produced a more apparent than real image of social and economic modernization in the country. Middle-class politicians seized the opportunity to escalate their positions among the economic elites, and the bourgeoisie received in return the support and even the protection of the political establishment. The rearrangement of the bourgeoisie during the twentieth century added variegation to each of the social levels. It amalgamated the traditional landowner oligarchy, the mining entrepreneurial plutocracy, and the newly created industrial managerial elite.

To differentiate the bourgeoisie from the rest of the ruling class is an endeavor by no means easy, because, as Zeitlin and Ratcliff point out, "A conceptualization of large landowners and capitalists in Chile as distinctive class segments may tend to distort [the] perception of their inner connections and to reify them as if they were, in fact, coexisting rather than inseparable elements of a single class."[29] The terms industrial bourgeoisie and entrepreneurial elite apply to a small group of individuals whose amalgamation usually was based not on family lineage, but on mercantile ability. Included in these two categories are bankers, industrialists, landowner capitalists, and managers right down to the small entrepreneurs.

Setting aside the landowner-capitalist sector, let us consider here those members of the bourgeoisie who find themselves still in the rising process towards the socioeconomic levels of the aristocratic plutocracy. They are primarily first-generation immigrants or their descendants. James Petras reports that nearly two-fifths of the entrepreneurs that he surveyed were non-Chileans, predominantly West Europeans. Very interesting is the fact that third-generation Chileans, or the descendants of families that were already accepted by the higher classes of the country, accounted for over 41 percent; the rest came from other ethnic groups. Spaniards, whose dilution in the social texture of the country was achieved by the second generation, restricted themselves to small enterprises.[30] The fact that third-generation Chileans control most of the large enterprises reveals also that access to higher economic spheres appears to be reserved for those who have established family ties with the local elites, and not for aspiring newcomers. Wealth alone, especially in the case of a foreigner, does not seem to warrant social acceptance by the Chilean higher classes. But once a place at any level of the local bourgeoisie is attained, upward mobility seems to be assured. Maria Grossi Ackermann mentions that 60 percent of the business owners and executives she surveyed had fathers who belonged to the entrepreneurial elite, whereas the individuals who descended directly from landowner families accounted for only 5 percent.[31] Petras, in his sample, found 22 percent to have had landowner grandparents.

The available information on how the bourgeoisie perceives itself as a social group is rather contradictory. While some entrepreneurs do not think of themselves as bourgeois and disassociate their social status from that of the landowner aristocracy, Pike found evidence of aristocratic attitudes among them.[32] The Chilean bourgeois who has not yet reached the "golden class" views himself as a nonaristocrat and honestly believes in social mobility. Linked with the image of himself as one of the affluent people of the upper middle class, but not as a plutocrat, is his perception of the working class as a cooperator in the task of national development through economic achievement. The industrial bourgeoisie of the country has been convinced it was this sector of the Chilean society that contributed most to the overall development of the country, and that what was good for business was good for Chile. Such a view implies that this group expected the state not only to encourage but even to warrant the smooth running of entrepreneurial activities, instead of being a hindrance to private initiative in business. Obviously, the acknowledgement that the state has an important say in the economic development of the country attributes great decisional powers to politicians, and consequently they are viewed by the entrepreneurs with rather mixed feelings. While some of them welcome the involvement of the state in the economy of the nation as a waiver of their own economic interests, others strongly reject any intervention by the state.[33] Grossi Ackerman, in her typology of the Chilean industrial bourgeoisie, distinguishes one sector that is inclined to establish alliances with the workers after having achieved political power in the country and another that expects to profit from an alliance with the political establishment. This is an expression, on one hand, of a poli-classistic structure of power, and on the other, of a structure that is based on political and economic power.[34]

All these considerations reflect the important reality that the Chilean bourgeoisie has always had a clear idea of the advantages of political power. They have tried to gain access to this power or to attract to their ranks politicians of modest origin who were willing to adopt bourgeois interests. The fourteen years the Radical party was in power and the six years of Christian Democratic government offer multiple examples of the attraction and integration of the political establishment by what Luis Buñuel has so masterfully called the "enticing pleasures of the bourgeoisie."

Economic Power, Politics, and Social Relations

Diverging views characterize the appraisal of the role of the bourgeoisie in the socioeconomic development of Chilean society. The next pages will focus on the form in which the economic power in the country was organized and will explore the mechanisms of political power that this elite had at its disposal.

During the 1960s and early 1970s, manufacturing and mining, the two sectors of the Chilean economy controlled chiefly by the national bourgeoisie, contributed 25 percent and 9 percent to the gross domestic product.[35] The economic elite owned at least one-third of the total flow of goods and services generated in the country. This is to be considered only the initial basis of the economic power held by the bourgeoisie because, as has been suggested, it went on to control a great part of the agricultural, construction, and services sectors, and created the intricate web of interdependent liaisons that Ricardo Lagos was the first to investigate. Lagos identified a dramatic economic concentration. Only 4 percent of the stock companies controlled nearly 60 percent of the circulating capital. The top financial institutions of the country not only controlled Chile's major industrial establishments but were also financially interrelated and interdependent.[36] At the hub of the system were the banking institutions, which had links with manufacturing enterprises and other businesses, secured through interlocking directorates, kinship relationships, or both. Lagos and others after him pointed to financial institutions, insurance companies, and manufacturing establishments, the directorates of which were dominated by patrician names such as Edwards, Matte, Larraín, Alessandri, Correa, Vial, Sanfuentes, Claro, and Valdés.

When investigating the ownership of corporations in Chile, Zeitlin, Ewen, and Ratcliff discovered that the large majority of the firms classified as having "ultimate managerial control" were in fact controlled by minority interests, generally by one or two families and their associates.[37] The only firm that did not fall into this category because it had a vast array of shareholders did, however, list the names of high-class families in its directory, who no doubt had a great influence in running the enterprise. In yet another paper on the economic power of the capitalist elite of Chile, the same writers identified the economic influence of this sector of the bourgeoisie not only on the manufacturing industries of the country—and needless to say, of course, on the banks—but also on the largest and most productive estates in the agricultural heartland of Chile: 11 percent of the top managers of the country's forty-eight largest corporations and 23 percent of the bankers owned large estates in one of the agricultural provinces of the country. They found a core group of "maximum kinship" (a group of highly interrelated families), which represented 40.9 percent of the landowners, 37.7 percent of the bankers, and 31 percent of the top corporation executives.[38] Conspicuous names in this main core were again Larrain, Riesco, Correa, Infante, Valdés, Lira, and Vicuña, showing that there really exists no conflict between the economic interests of the landed aristocracy and the highest ranks of the industrial bourgeoisie.

Our own survey on the involvement of these families in Chilean politics (Table 4, p. 89) reveals a similar liaison of social and economic power. With only a few exceptions, the family names of the Chilean bourgeoisie appear repeatedly among the families who have occupied elected or appointed positions in Chile's executive or legislature, showing that the national elite did not restrict its dominant role to the social or economic spheres, but defended and promoted its interests in the field of active politics as well. It was not necessary for each of the great capitalist families to have a representative in one of the Chambers of the Congress. Because of kinship ties it was sufficient to have a relative oversee the group interests in the legislature or in the government. If this type of representation did not take place, the landowner-bourgeoisie alliance could attract to its ranks young ambitious politicians from the middle strata. This absorption of successful middle-class politicians by the economic elites has been epitomized in the political and financial career of the Alessandri family, which, although it is not one of the traditional families of the country, rose to a prominent economic and political position through the talents of Arturo Alessandri. Generally the integration of a middle-class politician began with his association with one of the industrial establishments through an appointment to the directory. This appointment made the politician loyal to that industry (in which he may have had a few shares) and committed his political actions to the interests of the industrial bourgeoisie. Cases of such connivance between the economic elites and the political establishment, regardless of the party involved, have been numerous since 1925. One of the criticisms of the Radical party, and probably a major reason why it lost credibility among popular voters, was that many of its members who escalated in political positions quickly succumbed to the temptations of capitalism and used their political influence to reap the economic benefits that the bourgeoisie was willing to pay for political favors.

Socioeconomic escalation by middle-class politicians was not restricted to the Radical party. In different degrees other middle-ground and popular parties were also successful. The rise to power of the Christian Democracy strengthened the established economic interests of some of its members who were engaged in business operations. The most publicized case is that of Edmundo Pérez Zujovic, former minister of the interior under Frei, who had strong commitments in the construction industry and in fish meal factories in the northern part of the country. Also connected with industrial operations in that part of Chile was Radomiro Tomic, who with one of his brothers, owned salt mines in the province of Antofagasta. Sergio Ossa Pretot, another prominent member of the Frei administration, was involved in the construction industry and became one of the directors of the Chilean Chamber of Construction. These and others of the Christian Democracy were associated with the economic interests of the local bourgeoisie, although not to the same degree as members of the Radical party. As Ricardo Lagos suggests, the less intense involvement of the Christian Democracy with the bourgeoisie in 1960 could be attributed to the youth of the party and to the relatively short period of time in which it had been enjoying power both in government and Congress.[39]

Members of leftist parties also involved themselves in bourgeois affairs, although to a lesser extent. Rafael Tarud, former minister of Ibañez del Campo, who hovered over the Left in Chile well into the 1970s, was, along with his brothers Manuel, Arturo, and Raúl, a successful merchant, landowner, and industrialist. Of great importance also for the promotion of the leftist ideology was the fact that two influential publishers, Darío Saint Marie of the tabloid *Clarín* and José Tohá of the evening newspaper *Las Noticias de Ultima Hora*, were doing well in the printing business. Not even the late President Salvador Allende could escape the spell of the bourgeoisie; the 1967 edition of the *Diccionario Biográfico de Chile* lists him as director of the enterprises Casas Prefabricadas, Pascal y Cia S.A.C., Vivocret, and Olivarera del Pacífico.

The dependence of the political establishment on the economic power of the bourgeoisie and vice-versa is shown by the fact that courting of the industrial establishment was carried on by all parties without exception. Donald Bray quotes Chile's textile magnate, Carlos Yarur, as saying:

> It is true that I supported Matte. . . . But it is also true that I supported General Ibañez with money for his campaign when Guillermo del Pedregal came to solicit, and similarly, I contributed to the campaign of Alfonso when Luis Alamos Barros came to see me. The same thing happened with Dr. Salvador Allende. And it could not be otherwise, since capitalists are obliged to be on good terms with everyone.[40]

This is perhaps the most explicit summary of the attitude of the capitalist bourgeoisie toward the political establishment. It is therefore not surprising that, in view of the formidable political influence of the industrial elite, the Socialist coalition that brought Salvador Allende to the presidency in 1970 saw it as a priority to cut the ties between the capitalistic castes and the financial and political circles. Such a task is by no means an easy one, for it implies a frontal attack on the intermingled interests of the plutocracy. It cannot be achieved by stripping this class of its control of banks and enterprises through nationalization, intervention, or other legal mechanisms, without establishing a completely new political and economic system.

The Appeal of the Right

In his study on the Chilean upper class, Emilio Willems reports that members of that class had expressed to him that their involvement in local politics or their occasional work with the diplomatic staff of the country was carried out with "great pecuniary sacrifices" and that they did it only because the image of Chile abroad should be that of a "people with good manners."[41] Along with the image of the master and the solid entrepreneur, the assumption that an upper-class individual is also a farsighted statesman developed as another myth in Chilean politics. Because the landowner or the entrepreneur is rich, he does not need to make a living as a politician; he participates in politics to show his love for the nation.

If that is the arrogance with which the higher classes view their role in politics, it is no wonder that they look down on the middle-class individuals who dispossessed them of political power in the country. With patriarchial scorn they refer to the middle-class political elite by the deprecative term of *politiquero* ("politicaster") and blame all the social and economic ailments of the country on the inefficiency of these newcomers in politics. The upper class has been the initiator of the drive to lower the prestige of all those involved in public administration and to invoke the intervention of the military to prevent extreme politicization of the country. The arrogance of the members of the aristocracy and the air of superiority with which they have surrounded themselves impressed their subordinates, who saw in the affluence and overall success of the master a well-deserved reward for his moral integrity. Voting for such a successful person was common not only among the higher circles, but it also spread into the middle and lower classes whose mental image of a superior man materialized at times in the figure of a prominent politician from the aristocracy.

Conservatism is regarded by the rightist voter not as the negation of social change and progress, but as the expression of an ideology based on the paternalistic order that ruled Chile during a great part of the nineteenth century and that supposedly brought the most convincing economic and military successes to the country. Rightist politicians and their supporters often resort to examples from the past to prove that those times were better and that there existed no social unrest, but only harmony and cooperation among the classes. The main bulk of the rightists is drawn from the landowner stratum, the industrial entrepreneurs, the managerial elites, the successful professionals, the impoverished aristocrats, and the nouveau riche, particularly offspring of European or Levantine immigrants. This conglomerate, often referred to as *pitucos* or *futres* ("fops") by the popular stratum, loves opulence, displays affected manners, and has even a particular fashion of speech, which is frequently ridiculed by cartoonists. In search of self-esteem and identity this class has moved to exclusive city quarters such as the *Barrio Alto* in Santiago or the *Plan* of Viña del Mar, microcosms reminiscent of Europe or the United States but not of Chile. They trail the *siúticos* ("the snobs") and the *medio-pelos*.

The *siútico* in Chile has been sociologically defined by E. Blanco Amor as an individual who believes that his polite manners and superficial education will open for him the gates to the successes that seem to be reserved for members of aristocratic families.[42] In a desperate search for some connecting link with the higher classes he inspects his genealogical background in the hope of finding ancestors who at one time belonged to the "upper ten thousand." He may try to marry the daughter of a family of lineage, for he has realized that many doors still open to an old aristocratic name. The *siútico* despises his middle-class roots and expresses his contempt for the lower classes by adopting not only the customs of the upper classes but also their political ideals. His vote for an aristocratic candidate is proof of that. The behavior of the *medio-pelo* individual whose rank lies somewhat lower than that of the *siútico* because of his lack of dynamism is quite similar. *Medio-pelo* denotes the status of a family that is somehow related to a family of lineage, but has lost social acceptance because of financial misfortune or marriage into a lower class. However, the remembrance that they once belonged to the upper class prompts them to adopt political and social attitudes that are not consistent with their present social status. A *medio-pelo* individual also rejects the values and customs of the lower classes but at the same time nourishes bitter resentment toward the aristocrats and therefore favors ideologies or political groups that aim at their destruction.

Because of the typical rightist's peculiar concept of a glorious past, his political views have strong nationalistic overtones. Significantly, in the 1965 amalgamation of two traditional and conservative forces of the past, the Liberal and Conservative parties, the name of National party was chosen. This name was intended to emphasize that the social postulates of the new party were less significant than interest for the nation as perceived by the higher classes. The propaganda of the Right emphasizes that the common good of the nation, and not international class solidarity, is the main concern of a Chilean statesman. This is why it appealed strongly to the higher officers of the armed forces. The interpretation that the military establishment in Chile supports the political Right because of similar class perceptions, family ties, or even economic interests, should be carefully assessed. The Right and the military go along together because they have the same glorious perception of the past, and both are reluctant to accept political doctrines that stress abrupt social change and political avant-gardism.

Accordingly, the fanatical nationalism found among rightists has led on numerous occasions to the development of ideological groups with fascist tendencies at the far extreme of the Right. The *Línea Recta* military faction of the 1950s and the ill-famed *Patria y Libertad* group of the Allende years were both formed by those ultrarightists. Their basic ideology was that only under capable leadership, a strong hand and rigid discipline, could the Chilean people accomplish as much as they did in the past. The measure in which these ideas penetrated into the lower strata of the population and fulfilled the electorate's longing for a proven statesman determined the share of votes the rightist candidate could expect from the urban proletariat and the peasantry.

Another interesting trait of the rightist political behavior in Chile, observed by Tomás Moulian, is that although the aristocratic segments of the society are strongly committed to traditionalism and the maintenance of social order, they do not completely reject the possibility of rebellion. A strong reaction from the oligarchy is to be expected whenever it sees its social privileges, political power, and economic interests jeopardized by attacks of its political opponents.[43] As will be seen later, the Right can absorb political defeat or electoral wearing, but it will not take institutional or constitutional abuse. Its stubborn opposition to forcibly imposed political measures stems from its profound loyalty to the law. If a political group shows disregard for the rules of the game, the Right will abandon its apparently apathetic attitude and will vehemently call and even fight for a return to the traditional norms of life in the state. Alberto Edwards has dedicated his classic book *La fronda aristocrática* to the strength of this historical constant, the spirit of rebellion that emanates from the Chilean oligarchy, and President Allende, who may have thought that the political muscle of the Right had grown weak, was to have severe problems with the new strength it had gained in the struggle.

Often, and not always with justification, the rightist voter in

The Social Texture

Chile has been assumed to be a clericalist. Though it is true that in the past the Catholic church and the Conservative party supported each other in political as well as in theological matters, the advanced social doctrines developed by a great majority of the Chilean clergy during the second part of the twentieth century have estranged many Catholics from the political and social postulates of the rightist parties. A progressive Catholic would not want to support an obstinate and ultraclerical candidate, and a traditional Conservative would consider it almost a heresy to vote for a progressive Catholic (frequently from the Christian Democracy) whom he perceives as a revolutionary and a "Black Communist."[44] There have been times when serious confrontations developed between Catholic political activists of clerical and secular tendencies. In the 1960s, ultraconservative Catholic and aristocratic elements rallied in a political-religious group, *Fiducia,* whose chief aim was the defense of the traditional social order against the reformist ideas of the Catholic Christian Democracy. Consequently, to identify the religious aspect with a particular group of voters, particularly the Right, is a fallacy that underrates the high degree of political consciousness and ideological independence that characterizes the Chilean voter.

There is another group whose allegiance with the Right has been based neither on class consciousness nor on the nationalistic feelings emphasized by the Right. This group consists of the small entrepreneurs and the retail merchants. In a comprehensive study of the political ideas of that segment of the petty bourgeoisie, Oliveira de Muñoz found that two-thirds of them preferred to see higher-class elements in the government of the nation, and that 83 percent considered the higher class to be more actively involved than any other in the development of the country. Merchants and small entrepreneurs profoundly believe that the economic development of Chile depends on the efforts of the landowners and industrial bourgeoisie, and they know that they too will benefit from economic expansion. Their mercantilistic views outweigh class considerations and they find in their economic interests a common bond with the higher classes.[45]

The Middle Class

Although the landowner class, throughout the nineteenth century, had uncontested control of the agricultural economy and the peasantry and was not threatened by the concentration of power in the cities, the revolt of the voters in the 1920s indicated clearly that a growing number of middle-class and lower-class citizens in urban provinces was emerging to contest the political hegemony. This new and important mass of uncommitted voters was to become the most coveted clientele of political groups from 1925 onwards. In Chile, as also in Argentina and Uruguay, the development of urban centers—an eminently geographical phenomenon—led to the emergence of two social groups, the middle class and the proletariat, whose role in national politics became very important in the period of time encompassed by this book.

Although many of the generalizations uttered about social, cultural, and political conditions in Latin America apply to the Chilean situation only with limitations, a model based on the interdependence of culture, society, politics, and urbanization has been developed by Aníbal Quijano that works adequately in Chile.[46] This author argues that urbanization is a state in which changes in the economic structure, the social texture, the demographic constitution, the cultural attitudes, and the political inclinations are continually taking place. Economically, the urban centers monopolize investment and manpower and develop into poles of attraction for basic, secondary, and tertiary activities to the consequent detriment of the economic value of the countryside. The urbanization of the economy influences also the ecological-demographic development of the society, because it not only draws more people into the urban sectors, but also widens the areas of influence of the cities to comprise smaller towns and villages. The progressive establishment of an urban system incorporates them into major centers and isolates them from the country and from other rural areas. Their dependence on the big centers is thereby established. If the primary expression of the countryside dependence is economic in character, the secondary is cultural. Customs, symbols, and consumer goods introduced first in the big cities invade towns and rural villages, so that the vernacular rural culture becomes infiltrated by values and attitudes alien to its original character, and it sets out on the road to decay. As Quijano asserts, "By the time migration to the town takes place, a different urban culture has grown up, and the culture brought in by the migrants is rural only by comparison with the urban culture of the day."[47]

The urbanization of the social structure is to be considered as an expansion of the urban patterns of social organization, when more population is incorporated into the stratification of urban society. This causes an alteration in the relationships among the various social classes. The traditional ruling class becomes mainly an industrial bourgeoisie; the middle class expands demographically and functionally as its members seek accommodation in the fabric of urban society or seize political power; and a growing working class, the industrial-service proletariat, emerges as a socially and economically marginal sector. It follows that this new social fabric increases the urge for incorporation into national politics of growing sectors of the population, chiefly in the cities where the principal political institutions are located. Thus, if the original power of the oligarchy was based on the dominance of the countryside, the final battle for the control of national politics now takes place in the cities.

Since the author was confronted with the problem of delimiting and defining the middle class, a great deal of time was spent discussing with Chileans, both in Chile and abroad, their notions of "middle class." Early in the enquiry it became obvious that the middle class and bourgeoisie are distinctly separated by wealth and political influence, two attributes of the bourgeoisie. At the lower limit of the scale, the boundary with the working class is established by the level of education, and not by income. Contrary to the assumptions of non-Chilean scholars, the country's middle class—whose attributes are by no means similar to those of other countries of Latin America—is not so much the result of an industrial development as of the "tertiarization" of a society that has grown increasingly urban. State employees, teachers, employees of private firms, and small retailers form a sector of society that can be associated neither with the exploitative groups, as biased scholars have contended, nor with the lower class as is often held by outsiders.[48]

Oscar Alvarez A., "a man of leftist leanings" in the words of Frederick B. Pike and a person with long experience as researcher of Chilean society, distinguishes three levels in the middle class: 1) the upper middle class, which comprises high-rank functionaries, members of the judicial system, doctors, military officers, engineers and commercial entrepreneurs; 2) the common middle class, made up of the large majority of public and private employees, salesmen, bank employees, teachers, and retailers; and 3) the lower middle class, which includes small retailers, farmers, specialized industrial workers, independent landlords, and tradesmen. These three categories established by Alvarez have also been acknowledged by the Chileans who were questioned about this topic, thereby showing that the perception of the middle class is a widespread one and not an arbitrary classification of a few individuals.[49]

The upper sector of the middle class accounts for only 10 percent of the 500,000 families that Alvarez considered middle-class. Access to higher positions in the state's administrative organization had been secured through contacts established in general during years at college, when many men from this sector of society were attracted to politics (regardless of their ideological inclinations) as a means of climbing the socioeconomic ladder. Decisive in obtaining access to university faculties such as law, public administration, medical sciences, or engineering is the high school a student attended before he entered university. Private high schools, especially those that ensured success in the admission examinations to coveted faculties, were preferred because, in addition to the quality of the education they provided, there was about them an aura of social prestige. One might even go so far as to say that there exists a kind of predestination in the educational practices in Chile: as soon as the child of a middle-class family has been accepted into one of the elitist high schools, the parents can be confident that he will continue to the university and into the higher spheres of public administration, the political establishment, or the local business circles. Further, attendance at an elitist school offered more ambitious middle-class members the opportunity of mingling with the progeny of aristocratic and bourgeois families and this was likely to assist them later in becoming accepted by the ruling elites. Nonacceptance by or personality clashes with other members of the upper middle class, or with individuals of higher classes, resulted frequently in abnegation of their class of origin and the adoption of radical ideologies. The complete higher rank of the Movement of the Revolutionary Left was filled in this manner. Also, the most pronounced enemy of the higher classes within the Socialist party was Carlos Altamirano Orrego, a man of by no means humble origins.

An important segment of the upper middle class was formed by foreign immigrants and their descendants. First their economic success and then the entry of their children into college ensured them a place within this social stratum that could be considered as the anteroom to the bourgeoisie. It is remarkable that the foreign elements of the upper middle class as well as its domestic members supplied the directive cadres of almost all the political parties, the exceptions being those that represented strictly the landowner aristocracy and the capitalist bourgeoisie, the Conservative and the Liberal parties. The affluence of a professional career or a well-paid job in the public administration allowed certain upper middle-class individuals to come closer to the aristocracy and the bourgeoisie by living in the same areas of the major cities, by acquiring a cottage in one of the fashionable seaside resorts, and by affiliating with a social club frequented by high-class people. All these practices gave the impression that the middle class as a whole was siding with and imitating the aristocratic-economic elites of the country.

But the same could not be said about the other two majority segments of the middle class, composed mainly of employees, salesmen, small farmers, and craftsmen who had to manage on fixed salaries or modest incomes from independent activities. These sectors of Chilean society that, in the estimation of Alvarez, consist of about 450,000 families (one-third of all Chilean households) can hardly be considered exploiters and enemies of the proletariat. In fact, during the most critical periods of economic stagnation and rampant inflation, they, together with the lower classes, suffered most and paradoxically received most of the criticism. The caricatured image of the middle class depicted by Rodolfo Stavenhagen may well apply to the situation in his native country,[50] but it has nothing to do with the development of the lower sectors of the Chilean middle class. Some of the findings reported by Robert C. Williamson dismiss any ill-based contentions that the Chilean middle sectors are similar to those of other Latin American countries. Among middle-class individuals he detected ardent pleas for social change and a serious commitment to modernization. Questions about the democratization of education and the economic hardships created by inflation were answered quite similarly by middle-class and lower-class individuals. His survey revealed a greater degree of social realism, higher politicization, and more proneness to social change through education in the people of Chile than in the people of Colombia, Costa Rica, and El Salvador, countries investigated previously by the same writer.[51]

Perhaps more than in any other Latin American country, the middle class in Chile has been nationalistic and committed to social and cultural change. Teachers, intellectuals, and political leaders who emerged from the lower strata of the middle class—Pablo Neruda, Gabriela Mistral, Pedro Aguirre Cerda—were seriously concerned with the promotion of an authentic national culture and the establishment of a more equitable social structure in the country. By teaching in poor elementary schools or in dilapidated high schools in humble neighborhoods and by enduring the same deprivations as the poor, they were enticed into political action to bring about structural changes that would alleviate their sufferings. By contrast, speeches about revolutionary change so frequently made by the "progressive thinkers" of the bourgeoisie and the affluent middle class contributed very little to the socioeconomic improvement of the deprived classes, and if these talks had any effect, it was only that of increasing the frustration of the marginated sectors of the people.

A great part of the lower middle class is made up of the numerous rural families who, during the last decades of the nineteenth century, were lured to the growing cities by prospects of work in commerce, industry, or the administrative ranks of the expanding welfare state. The educational requirements of the cityward migrants were supplied by an increasing number of public schools and high schools. These were designed according to French or German standards because Spanish models were considered to be colonial and backward. The *liceo,* an imitation of the Napoleonic lycée, was destined to produce a contingent of liberal individuals who would later enlarge the bureaucracy or make their way to college. Not without a certain degree of justification, the *liceo* institution has been attacked for emphasizing the liberal arts and neglecting the applied sciences and the crafts. However, the blame lies not with the schools themselves, but with those educators of the nineteenth century who planned an institution aimed solely at the production of civil servants. With respect to the criticism that the *liceo* furthered the deprecation of the laboring class and encouraged the emulation of high-class customs,[52] the ideological orientation of the teachers—socialist or Christian democratic—led generally to the contrary. *Liceos* became places of great social awareness, where students were motivated to participation in politics. A great many of the practices are of the Chilean democracy that made Chile exemplary for all Latin America were taught at the *liceos* and not in party assemblies.

Despite its obsolescence and other shortcomings, the *liceo*, more than the private schools of the bourgeoisie and upper middle class, fashioned citizens with democratic and progressive views, though they were badly prepared to join immediately the productive sectors of the country. Thus, for graduates who could not gain admission to college, there was the alternative of joining the ranks of state employees. *Papá Fisco* ("Father State") has provided many middle-class individuals with steady jobs, secure pensions, and the possibilities of social benefits that could not always be guaranteed by a private employer. The civil servant and the industrial worker both being in a position of dependency and economic disadvantage, instead of being antagonistic, as some writers have stated, share common interests and political-economic vindications that lead to concerted political action. A thorough investigation into class consciousness and ideological leanings of public employees conducted by Oliveira de Muñoz left no doubt about the social affinities of this occupational group of the middle class and the lower strata. Both reject any community of interest with the higher classes, accept the intervention of the state in the economic affairs of the nation, and prefer political alliance with blue-collar workers to one with any better-paid or socially higher occupational group.[53] However, this identification with the working class is not so intense as to include a full ideological adhesion to the so-called popular parties or to revolutionary processes of social change. Reform, not revolution, is the means by which public employees want social and economic change to proceed; this does not mean, however, that they are in any way proponents of the status quo.

The middle strata, as defined by Alvarez, are dominant in the urban provinces of Chile, Santiago, Valparaíso, Concepción, Antofagasta, and Magallanes. These provinces also have the highest percentage of population engaged in social, community, and personal services, as well as in manufacturing activities. In the agrarian provinces, where the urban middle strata have been outnumbered by the agrarian working class, and where the political predilections have been more oriented toward the Right, the progressive elements of the middle class preferred to move into the larger cities to improve the prospect of achieving their occupational, social, and political expectations. No wonder, then, that those *provincianos* are so often among the most active individuals in the political groups that flourish in larger cities. Nor is it surprising to find that three-quarters of the active politicians of the twentieth century were not born in metropolitan Santiago, but had come to the capital either to start a career in politics or begin studies at the university, which later led them to the national political scene. In general, these individuals came from an educated middle-class stratum, whose likings, interests, values, and social attitudes were more in accordance with those of the middle strata of the larger cities than with those of rural societies. The migration of this provincial middle class to the city was the early stage of the urbanization of society as proposed by Quijano.

The Middle Ground in Politics

Probably because of the far-reaching effects of its political decisions, the ideological inclinations of the Chilean middle class became the favorite target of both the Left and the Right. Expressions of affection changed quickly to hateful accusations when the middle class leaned to one or another of the extremes of the Chilean political spectrum. For the Left, whose memory is proverbially short, any endorsement by members of the middle class of democratic and reformist doctrines of a non-Marxist character is considered a betrayal of their class, regardless of the fact that their own most enlightened leaders have come from the middle class. For the Right, the progressive social views of the middle class are considered dangerously revolutionary and socially disturbing. The fact is that both the Chilean Left and Right are driven by such strong emotions when judging the middle class that they are unable to realize that this part of the Chilean population has been most cooperative in keeping the texture of the national character alive and in minimizing the shocking social distances that prevail in so many Latin American countries. Contradictory as it may be, the countries in Latin America with the highest sociocultural development and, at the same time, the greatest economic hardships are Chile and Argentina, the two countries with a sizeable middle class.[54] This contradiction arises from the fact that in those countries the middle class constitutes a large sector of the population that is not easily kept satisfied in its economic and cultural demands.

The urban expansion of Chile, at the end of the nineteenth century, required a bureaucratic and educational infrastructure that quickly placed teachers, clerks, and salesmen within the political forces of the country. This salaried section of the populace was initially caught in the dogmatic skirmishes between the traditional oligarchy and the aggressive bourgeoisie, so that its political interests were subordinate to those of the contending parties. With the severe voting restrictions that existed before 1874, only the most fortunate elements of the middle class were given the possibility of casting votes for one of the three major streams of Chilean politics—the Conservatives, the Liberals, or the *Montt-Varista Nacionales*—which represented exclusively the political interests of the higher classes. When in 1888 the Radical party appeared as a faction of the Liberal party, the laicized views of the new group and its separation from the previously existing parties attracted a great many educated people who could not identify themselves with Catholic conservatism or with the bourgeois materialism of the Liberals. Thus, for the first time in Chile's history, a party especially "tailored" for the social aspirations of a growing middle class had appeared on the Chilean scene.

The Democratic party, which stressed the state's involvement in the welfare of urban workers and independent artisans, competed with the Radical party in attracting the growing urban masses. Ideologically, both parties espoused the libertarian ideals of French Jacobinism and the creation of a democratic nonconfessional state. Although the Radical party had been promoted either by rich and ungovernable mine owners from the *Norte Chico* (the Gallo and the Matta brothers), and hence represented the economically successful neobourgeoisie in Chile, or by the gallicized intelligentsia (Enrique MacIver, Valentín Letelier), the Democratic party catered more to the city worker and the independent artisan than to the public employee educated in a *liceo*. To the professionals and the salaried middle class, the propositions of the Radical and the Democratic parties contained ready possibilities for socioeconomic vindications. Accordingly, they enthusiastically endorsed the candidates of both parties. At the time of the voters' revolt in the early 1920s, these two parties received over 40 percent of the votes cast, thereby constituting the main block of opposition to the already fading oligarchic parties.[55] From the stormy 1930s until the end of democracy in 1973, the centrist parties and candidates drew their support mainly from the middle class, which held the balance of power in Chilean politics either by controlling the executive or the legislative power, or by participating in political combinations.

It must be emphasized again that the assumption that the Chilean middle class is unitarian in composition and possesses values and ethics applicable to all members is naive, simplistic, and erroneous. From the varied ethnic backgrounds and occupational diversity as well as the wide differences in income of the middle class, this social stratum spreads itself among all sectors of Chile's political spectrum.[56] Some *siútico* and *medio-pelo* families endorse the oligarchic parties, whereas the socialist-minded and progressives support Marxist parties. Those middle-class individuals whose political decisions are based on a critical scrutiny of the ideologies will reject both the reactionary principles of the oligarchic parties and the totalitarianism of the Marxist parties. Left with the choice between two reformist currents, some lean toward the nonconfessional alternative, whereas others prefer the Christian humanism. As one finds all these possibilities of choice among the middle class, an attempt at ecological explanation reveals itself as futile. Langton and Rapoport have stressed repeatedly that support based on social classification is not to be taken for granted, but that personal job experiences, educational and neighborhood situations determine the direction of the political choice to a much greater extent than class allegiance.[57]

The pluralistic background and wide array of political motivations found among the middle class make it ambivalent in terms of social change and political modernization. Although it is often sincerely committed to sociopolitical progress, it is also cautious and, at times, even supportive of the status quo.[58] Therefore, it is a hazardous assumption for a centrist party to take the support of the middle class for granted. As with certain sectors of the working class, the middle class cannot be relied upon to back unconditionally the progressive centrist parties. Radomiro Tomic, for example, was too radical for some sectors of the middle class, and so he lost his chance of becoming president in 1970.

Contrary to biased opinions, the major contingent of the

Chilean middle class strongly believes that social change is necessary in the country and that an improvement in the internal socioeconomic conditions should be brought about in progressive steps and not by armed revolution.[59] In general terms, its views are reformist rather than revolutionary; it subscribes to a social upgrading of the lower classes and opposes political philosophies that advocate downward social leveling. These views are deeply anchored in the conviction gained especially from North American and West European examples that upward social mobility is possible in a developed and egalitarian society. Along with these general principles goes the unconditional trust of the Chilean middle class in civil guarantees such as freedom, respect for the individual, adequate protection from the government, and limitation of the state's intervention into private matters such as religious, moral, and political beliefs. If these ideals have not been incorporated entirely into the Chilean sociopolitical system, it is not the fault of the middle class but of the political establishment. The blame must rest with the oligarchic interests that have been controlling the economy and the decision-making institutions, which were the generators of a healthy social mobility in the country.

The feeling of frustration that can be caused by the imperfect mechanism of social mobility operating in Chile leaves a middle-class individual very insecure, critical, and dissatisfied with the whole social order and accounts for the great variability of the Chilean parties that has been so characistic during the twentieth century. No ecological or ideological reasons have to be raised to explain why in the last four presidential elections the favor of the Chilean middle-class voters, drifted from nationalist populism (Ibañez del Campo) to rightism (Jorge Alessandri) to Christian developmentism (Frei), finally coming to rest in Marxism (Allende). These shifts in favor are the product of the constant search of the middle class for an adequate and democratic solution to the vast array of social and economic alternatives that nourish its political instability.

Contrary to the negative opinion of some critics, the dissatisfaction and searching of the intermediate strata of the Chilean society prove these people also possess the most critical attitude of all Chileans. With the democratization of education, which developed quickly and comprehensively in the course of the twentieth century, it was the children of the middle class who profited most. The fact that in the public high schools and universities the younger generations came into contact with the doctrines of modern social thinkers such as Rousseau, Proudhon, Stuart Mill, and more recently Marx, Engels, Lenin, and Maritain speaks against the contention of certain writers that the Chilean *liceo,* far from preparing socially dynamic and progressive generations of Chileans, instead contributed to the production of unconditional supporters of the status quo, mere "sycophants of the aristocracy."[60] Contentions of this sort cannot withstand confrontation by the sociopolitical reality of Chile. Indeed, the most caustic critics of the existing order came from the middle class itself, and it was elements from the middle class who assumed the leadership of the political groups most committed to faster social and political change in Chile. If the idea of rebellion against the present order and the incitation of the lower classes to political action are to be attached to a certain social group, this group is the enlightened and most socially critical within the middle class.

The frustration and dissatisfaction of the middle class arise when it perceives that, although a few can reach a certain degree of affluence and gain some political power, the class as a whole, because of the steady deterioration of the Chilean economy, has been incapable of keeping up with the economic demands of a modern style of life. Escalating prices and diminishing buying power in the recent past resulted in the members of the middle class being affected most and paying the highest tolls in the Chilean drive for modernization. The wealth of the oligarchy allowed this sector of the society to cope with, and even benefit from inflation, but members of the middle class experienced only the declining buying power of their salaries and an increase in the gap between their material expectations (to own homes, electric appliances and, most of all, cars) and their economic capabilities. Confronted with this, the reaction of the middle class was rejection of the political alternatives that did not pursue the abolition of the present system and endorsement of parties that promised a fair share of wealth for all citizens. As rightist regimes were discarded because they meant more economic benefits for the rich, by the same token the political views that excluded the possibility of socioeconomic growth for the individual were rejected.

The Social Texture

Anyone who is familiar with the expectations of the middle-class workers will recognize that although they were sincerely committed to social change, they were also sympathetic to parties that offered social justice and economic development within a framework of freedom and respect for the views of the individual, which can often be in conflict with those of the state. As Moulian has indicated, longings of the middle class for changes in the economic and social structures of the country produced an "encounter" first with the liberal-democratic, and later with the social-democratic postulates of the Radical party, at a moment when the clerical autocratism of the nineteenth century was becoming obsolete and when liberalism was proving beneficial only for the bourgeoisie.[61] The original rationalism and anticlericalism of the Radicals—adopted obviously from Voltaire—appeared very appealing to new generations of urbanites who were not attached to the past and felt liberated through better education. During the first five decades of the century, the ranks of the Radical party swelled with young people who sought upward social mobility by securing positions in the public service[62] and by affiliating with Freemasonry, the main spiritual supporter of the Radical party. Enlightened teachers and intellectuals found in these two institutions much of the spiritual freedom they sought from religious beliefs as well as the humanist principles of class redemption. In the small cities and towns of the countryside, where the political influence of the conservative landowners was not so strong, lawyers, doctors, and teachers who had come into touch with the philosophical-political principles of radicalism while at university became the leaders of the community. For the greater part of this century the main attribute of small-town public figures was their affiliation with the Radical party, with Freemasonry, and with the local firemen's association as honorary members. Tomás Moulian contends that the political vacuum left in the provincial towns by the Conservative and Liberal parties was favorable for the endorsement by the middle class of the reformist doctrines of the Radical party, while in the larger cities, where the oligarchic parties dominated in traditional upper-class circles and the bourgeoisie, this party's support came from nonaristocratic professionals, alumni from the universities, and the bureaucratic masses. Among them a well-developed network of reciprocated favors and loyalties was established, so that in the flourishing years of the Radical party

(1938-1952) it was common knowledge that affiliation with that party meant occupational and social escalation and probably the absence of political scruples.[63] Proving the aphorism that "power corrupts," the Radical party, which was the dominant political force for more than three decades, started in the 1950s its irrecoverable fall. It had been prepared by the loss of faith among the middle and lower classes when they saw the party's upper ranks become rich and enjoy their power, showing blatant disregard for the social demands of the party.

By 1952 the abandoned clientele were searching for new political currents that would be more in keeping with their aspirations. After a short-lived honeymoon with Ibañez populism, they drifted into the emerging legions of the Christian Democracy and the Marxist Popular Unity. Confronted with the egocentricity of the rightist parties and the prospect of a society rigidly ruled by the single and omnipresent party advocated by Marxism, the moderate voter in Chile, regardless of his class, fell under the spell of the Christian humanism and the communitarian society propagated by a party of young people who, until 1958, had not had the opportunity to partake of the executive as a major political force.

From 1957 to 1963, the Christian Democracy increased its national vote by 13 percent. The party's electoral growth took place mainly in the industrialized and metropolitan provinces of Valparaíso and Santiago, where it attracted non-Marxist but progressive professionals, teachers, and intellectuals. But the total identification of the Christian Democracy with broader sectors of the middle class had not yet occurred. Anticlerical individuals of the middle class who had supported the Radical party in the past preferred to join the less radical parties of the Left or the Socialist party, some of whose members still respected bourgeois institutions, instead of a party that was perceived as a prolongation of the Catholic church. The opportunist elements of the upper middle class, especially the *siúticos* and the *medio-pelo,* abhorred the corporate ideology and the redemptionist social efforts of the Christian Democracy and the progressive clergy, because they saw in these endeavors only the perturbing social stirring of a group of naive revolutionaries. Consequently, the definite "encounter" of the Christian Democracy with the middle and lower classes occurred when the politicians and partisans of this party were able to promote the image of a socially pluralist group that was interested in the political integration of the urban settlers as well as the peasants, who had so far been sidelined from national politics.

Detractors of the middle class, who overlook the social diversity and economic cleavages of this stratum of society, are prone to identify its political, economic, and social interests with those of the higher class. Included in this erroneous generalization is the contention that in politics, middle-class individuals tend to reject the so-called popular parties and prefer to support the oligarchic parties. Indeed, these schemes do not hold true in Chile's trends of political behavior, as has been documented in several studies on the ideological leanings of the middle class. When surveying the political loyalties of retailers and public employees, Oliveira de Muñoz[64] underlined the blatant differences and the astonishing discrepancies that exist within the middle class. Salesmen and merchants openly recognize that their economic and social interests are more closely linked to the interests of the higher classes than to those of other groups in Chilean society. Public employees, on the other hand, find their interest incompatible with those of the higher classes, but at the same time they do not identify themselves with the blue-collar workers either. Economic and political linkages between the bourgeoisie and the merchants stand out clearly (p. 107); they encourage consumer habits, since both groups will profit from them. For this reason they reject intervention by the state in the national economy and are actively antileftist. Civil servants, however, have a different attitude because of their dependence on the state. As salaried employees they feel closer to other workers (miners, industrial workers, private employees) and join them in their plea for economic vindication. However, from an ideological point of view, they do not fully subscribe to the leftist tendencies of some organized worker groups. Reformism rather than revolutionary change is more meaningful to them and consequently they tend to endorse the political options offered by the centrist parties.

Oliveira de Muñoz's well-chosen sampling offers valuable insight into the political ambivalence of the middle class. It shows that the upper sector sides with the socially and economically dominant higher classes, whereas the lower sector rejects the higher classes and finds more identification with its own peers or, in cases of conflict, with the lower class. Consequently, the middle class cannot be expected to react uniformly to political stimuli, and, therefore, its political decisions are more heterogeneous than those of the lower class.[65] It is fallacious, then, to state that the economic and social aspirations of the middle class proved in the past to be detrimental to the vindications of the lower class. In fact, the drive towards structural change initiated by progressive elements of the middle class worked not only for their own benefit but for that of the lower class as well. In the quest for better living conditions and a more egalitarian society, the middle-class individual, the teacher, the civil servant, the small retailer, and the artisan have always been closer to the salariat of the lower class than to the plutocrats.

From these considerations it becomes more understandable that the identification of the middle with the lower class is not so much a question of occupational (or class) consciousness as of economics. At the upper extreme of the middle class, small entrepreneurs, lawyers, doctors, engineers, and the military appear to adjust their aspirations for social and economic rise to the status enjoyed by the plutocracy. Politically, they dislike reformism, endorse liberalism, and support status-quo parties. Since the great majority of the political elite of Chile for the last fifty years came from the upper middle class,[66] regardless of the ideology they represented, the misconception has developed that the whole middle class had the opportunist antics of this upper layer and that they were more interested in gaining social and economic advantages for themselves than in promoting the overall development of Chilean society. Sincere commitment to social change prompted the revolutionary activism typical of upper middle-class individuals, such as Andrés Pascal Allende, Miguel and Edgardo Enríquez, Luciano Rodríguez, Rodrigo Ambrosio and others of the MIR, MAPU, and the Christian Left. Likewise, the directive cadres of the Radical party and the Christian Democracy came from the upper middle class, giving the impression that Chilean politics of the last forty years were the exclusive affair of a political elite of nonpopular and quasi-aristocratic background. In a way identical to what happened to the aristocracy, internal feuds for political dominance tore apart and ideologically dismembered the upper middle class and engendered the passionate hate that divided and dispersed them over the whole political spectrum of Chile.

The Urban Working Class

The development of the urban proletariat in Chile is linked with the early urbanization of the country and the emergence of mining and manufacturing industries. Even before the formation of an industrial proletariat, there rose a mining working class that moved from mining-agrarian provinces, such as Coquimbo and Aconcagua, into the nitrate fields of Tarapacá and Antofagasta. Aníbal Pinto links the early awakening of class consciousness to the migration of workers from central Chile to the northern mines and holds that this migration produced a certain improvement in employment opportunities for the agrarian workers that stayed in the demographic core of the country.[67] The emergence of the mining proletariat in the northern provinces of Chile certainly prepared the ground in which the seeds of socialist ideologies were to germinate earlier than anywhere else in the country.

At the time when the mining working class was growing stronger in the provinces of the North, the major cities of the country (Santiago, Valparaíso, and Concepción) were transformed from trading centers for agricultural commodities into manufacturing centers. Initially, the labor force was recruited from specialized craftsmen who had come from industrialized European nations.[68] Soon these immigrants were on the road to economic success and set up their own small businesses and enterprises. This vacuum was then filled with labor recruited from within the country. The first cityward migrants were mainly agricultural workers, often ill-prepared for jobs in manufacturing establishments. The wages paid to these new industrial laborers were far below what a specialized journeyman would have received, and this started the custom of industrialists to underpay newcomers because there were always sufficient rural migrants to fill positions left vacant by those who were dissatisfied with a low salary. The fact that many rural migrants found work in the new industrial establishments that had been opened in the cities by their former *patrones* (bosses) from the countryside is also very important for the understanding of employer-worker relations in Chile. This frequently overlooked aspect of employment practices of entrepreneurs in Chile, which persisted well into the 1960s, explains the paternalistic relationship that has surprised some foreign observers.[69] Until very recently a factory owner or businessman would prefer as his foreman a recent rural migrant of middle age to an urbanite, because the former would show more loyalty to his boss and to the firm.

The group behavior of the mining workers, who when confronted by large foreign-owned corporations and disdainful *gringo* administrators learned to defend their rights by means of strikes and open confrontations, has been much different.[70] United by hard fighting and tough bargaining they very early developed a sense of comradeship and class solidarity.

Adjustment of rural families to the requirements of modern industrialization came in the second generation, as the children of migrants attended better elementary schools and had the opportunity of learning a trade in some of the vocational or art schools that sprang up everywhere during the first quarter of the nineteenth century. Those children of urban workers who did not obtain positions in the public services had, because of their education, a better chance of becoming specialized industrial workers, which placed them one step ahead of rural migrants employed in tertiary activities. A sample of industrial workers, analyzed by Víctor Nazar, revealed that a scant 12 percent were former agricultural workers and that most of the contemporary industrial labor came from an urban background. His survey showed that rural migrants involved in manufacturing were more literate and appeared to have fewer difficulties finding jobs and adapting to new working environments than less educated workers.[71]

The Internal Structure of the Working Class

Differentiation within the urban labor force occurred chiefly on two bases: early arrivals received better employment opportunities, particularly in the manufacturing sector, and those with a higher degree of industrial specialization received better wages. Less skilled and later arriving rural migrants were left with the unstable and usually poorly remunerated jobs of the tertiary sector. These general rules of employment, based obviously on the social division of labor, were responsible for the formation of a distinct structure within the urban working masses.

If salary is considered the main criterion of differentiation, three major sectors of industrial workers can be observed.[72] At the top there is a well-paid group in resource exploitation or secondary industries that maintains exports and dominates the economic life of the country. Workers in this group have the most powerful and influential unions and these are very adept at getting the political establishment to fulfill their vindicative claims. Next come the workers in manufacturing industries, usually located in urban districts, whose unions are less powerful. Nevertheless, through coordinated activity, they are able to improve their salaries more effectively than the workers located at the bottom end of the scale, those in textile and food processing. The latter are the poorest paid industrial workers, probably because of the large proportion of female workers in that industrial category and the fragmented labor organization. In fact, it is common for each food processing plant and each textile factory to have its own union that, in times of conflict, finds that it has little bargaining power with the entrepreneurs.

The wage differences are also reflected in the workers' views about their role in society and participation in the political life of the nation. In a study on the social consciousness of the working class, Lalive d'Epinay and Zylberberg[73] developed an interesting typology of Chilean workers, the application of which to the social analysis of national politics is very relevant (Table 5). From the formulation of the types it is evident that the working class, far from having the monolithic consistency assumed by some authors, was historically quite variegated in ideology. Because of differences in sociopolitical consciousness, the workers were spread across the whole political spectrum, making any prediction of their political behavior extremely untrustworthy.

To the political, cultural, and economic characteristics pointed out by Lalive D'Epinay and Zylberberg should be added the different degrees of self-esteem that each worker entertained about himself and about the group to which he belonged. The modernizing developmentalists, e.g., the longshoremen, and the Marxist reformists, e.g., the copper miners, were well rewarded in their vindicative demands and shared the consumer habits of the higher classes. Well aware of their importance in the national economy, they knew that wage demands would be promptly satisfied, because the country could not afford long strikes. This group of workers preferred a gradual change in the economic-industrial structure over a radical one to ensure the maintenance of their favorable position among the salaried workers. The violent strikes

Table 5

Typology of Chilean Workers Based on Their Sociopolitical Awareness

Type	Infrastructural Base	Cultural Influences	Political Identification	Degree of Representation
Modernizing Developmentalist	Consumer-workers Early integration	Legalism Modern Catholics Ideology of modernism	Christian Democracy Centrist parties	Highly represented
Reformist	Consumer-workers Proletarians Early integration	Cultural paradigm is predominant Orthodox Marxism	Traditional Left: Communists and Socialists	Highly represented
Global Revolutionary	Proletarian workers	Ideology of conflict Heterodox Marxism	Diverse groups of the Ultraleft	Poorly represented
Populist	Proletarian workers	Cultural paradigm is dominant Mixed or confused ideologies	Erratic identification Prefers the Socialist party and the Ultraleft	Highly represented
Conformist	Proletarian workers	Cultural paradigm is dominant	Erratic political preferences: from abstention to identification with diverse groups	Highly represented

Source: Christian Lalive d'Epinay and Jacques Zylberberg, Dichotomie sociale et pluralisme culturel: la dispersion politique de la classe ouvrière chilienne, p. 270.

of the workers of the copper mines nationalized during the last years of the Allende administration are a case in point.

Very different perceptions regarding their sociopolitical power prevailed among proletarian workers, especially those from the industrial sectors with traditionally low wages. The nonessential character of their products, poor union organization, and sudden and continuous layoffs led to the development of a sharp conflict between the working-class interests and the managerial-bourgeois elite's profit making. Further, suppression by the police and military forces in cases of labor disputes and prolonged strikes convinced the workers of the manufacturing industries that acceptable structural changes could be achieved only by radical methods. During the last ten years of Chilean democratic life it was in coal-mining areas, in large textile establishments, and in small food and appliance factories of the urban centers that the extreme Left, especially the Movement of the Revolutionary Left, made its most obvious advances and eventually created the Front of Revolutionary Workers.[74] A high degree of political mobilization and aggressiveness—at times beyond the expectations of the Popular Unity government—characterized this sector of the urban working class that until the 1960s had been neglected by the government and was considered by labor leaders as the "poor relations" of the Chilean labor force.

The workers termed "populist protestors" include the large number of urban industrial workers and employees in the area of personal services who have in common low wages, occupational instability, and a poor unionization. The construction workers, whose jobs are subject to drastic seasonal and yearly variations, should also be included in this group. In total they comprised 53 percent of the labor force of Greater Santiago in 1971.[75] Their sense of occupational insecurity and economic frustration resulted in a very erratic sociopolitical response, and a lack of organization led to uncoordinated action in pressing their demands. The political inclinations of this group have been inconsistent, and they have usually yielded to political factions that based their actions on populist redemption and not on ideological postulates. Because of political inconsistency and lack of discipline, it became very difficult, even during the halcyon days of the Popular Unity, to capitalize on the political dissatisfaction of this large mass of urban workers. Thus, their participation in active politics was limited to short-lived periods of revolutionary outbursts.[76]

Regarding the workers whose attitude to sociopolitical changes was marked by conformism rather than by commitment to political action, Lalive d'Epinay and Zylberberg hypothesized that such an attitude was strongly influenced by their religious background. Their rejection of ideologies based on violent change led them to support the status quo or the progressive change advocated by developmentalist ideologies. Nevertheless, the low level of wages of these generally independent journeymen and small factory workers placed them within the proletariat and below the consumer sectors of the working class.[77] From 1932 to 1973, these workers had been drifting from one part to another of the Center-Left, attracted alternately by the radical or Christian Democratic reformism, the populism of Ibañez del Campo, or even Allende's socialist reformism. Some of them rallied in times of presidential elections in political factions of clear religious overtones such as the Christian Allendista Movement, the Christian Left, the populist masses of Antonio Zamorano, the Evangelic *Ibañismo,* and the picturesque group headed by Pastor Umaña.

Surveys on the influence of religious beliefs on social consciousness and political leanings, conducted by Lucy Behrman,[78] revealed both similarities and differences when compared to the findings of Lalive d'Epinay and Zylberberg. Behrman found that practicants could be involved in community organizations and elections, showing that an intense religious life need not exclude an interest in such secular matters as politics. Only in the case of Pentecostals did she observe political apathy. Furthermore, better educated and occupationally more successful workers exhibited greater interest in participating in religious services and community activities. Those workers of Behrman's sample who were actively engaged in unions and were militant in leftist parties obviously found religious practices inconsistent with their ideological views, so that they refrained from participating in religious activities; some socialist workers, however, considered attending church service as part of their community obligation.

In general, Behrman came to the conclusion, in keeping with other observations on the sociopolitical consciousness of the Chilean urban working class, that where hopelessness, frustration, and a failure to find meaning in life exist, there is also an understandable apathy toward possible religious or political solutions.

On the other hand, among proletarian individuals who through religious or ideological beliefs had been provided with an incentive in life, participation in communal, political, or religious activities became keen.

The Organization of the Labor Force

The great role in the incorporation of the urban proletariat into the political life of the country was played by the unions. These organizations, which appeared early as a by-product of industrialization and urbanization, were first of a vindicative character, but later developed into groups of political pressure. Indeed, the trade unions became for most workers the only institutions through which they could channel their desires of participation in politics as well as their social and economic demands. The unions represented for many, especially for the rural migrants, a substitute for the close relationships with their peers they were used to from the countryside, which they missed greatly in the environment of the cities. In addition to connecting them with their urban peers, the unions provided also information and propositions on how they could use their potential political power and instilled in them the feeling of being "subjects" and not mere "objects" in national politics.

Organized labor groups appeared early in Chile's social history. As early as 1834 the aristocratic philanthropist José Gandarillas had proposed the formation of craftsmen associations to provide social and economic assistance for disadvantaged urban artisans. But his social concern accomplished little more than the establishment of small welfare and charitable institutions. More successful were the mutualist institutions prompted by a desire for social security and mutual assistance among particular groups of workers, such as the typesetters of Santiago and Valparaíso, who started mutualist societies in 1853 and 1854 respectively.[79] In 1858 mutualist associations called *Sociedad de Artesanos* were also created in those major cities. The artisans' associations soon spread into other urban centers of the country and included not only craftsmen but also industrial workers. Unionism was not specifically one of their concerns, but they offered the training and education programs that would be required later for the formation of unions. When, in the 1910s and 1920s, the Chilean state assumed a great part of the social-security responsibilities for the working class, especially through the creation of the *Caja del Seguro Social Obligatorio* ("Corporation of Obligatory Social Services") and the *Juntas de Beneficencia* ("Boards of Social Welfare"), the mutualist associations withered into little more than charitable institutions that by the 1950s were barely kept alive by aging clerks and specialized workers.

More of a union character and political activism appeared in the *mancomunales* that were established at the turn of the century in the nitrate exporting ports of northern Chile. These associations of workers from various trades emphasized economic vindications, improvement of social conditions, and educational opportunities for the workers and their dependants.[80] It was not the political but the social aspirations of their members in the deteriorating situation of an urban environment that kept the *mancomunales* alive, at least until the first unions were strong enough to survive.

A more militant posture in politics was adopted by "resistance societies" organized by active groups of workers within a certain occupational sector. The stirring of the otherwise passive workers of central Chile into protest movements began about the time when European urban workers appeared on the country's labor scene. These immigrants were imbued with the principles of anarcho-syndicalism, very much in fashion in Europe in the 1890s.[81]

The seeds that these three early forms of workers' organizations had sown in the Chilean labor class germinated into the first trade unions in the country. In 1902 a Federation of Print Workers was formed in Santiago, and in 1907, with allegedly anarchist backing, the Federation of Carpenters and Similar Trades was founded. In 1909 the mounting wave of unionization resulted in the formation of the Grand Workers Federation of Chile (FOCH). Other similar organizations, such as the Regional Federation of Nitrate Workers and the Federation of Maritime Workers, were to follow later on the example of FOCH, which had developed under the auspices of the railway workers. Between 1917 and 1919 FOCH offered membership in its federation to organized *mancomunales* and semiorganized worker groups of the country. This move gave political activists, Luis E. Recabarren among them, the opportunity of gaining access to FOCH and of steering it into a politically more active role either by seeking association with the Democratic party or by becoming the platform for the *Partido Obrero Socialista*, later the Communist Party of Chile.[82]

The Social Texture 131

The association of FOCH with political parties turned out to have negative consequences for the working class because from 1920 to 1925 it was torn apart by the dissensions and rivalries of different Marxist groups. A blow was dealt to the organization by the dictator Carlos Ibañez del Campo who disbanded workers' organizations and imprisoned political activists who opposed him. The revival of the Chilean democratic system after 1932 brought also the instauration of FOCH under the dominance of the Communist party. This caused ideological disputes with the newly formed Socialist party, which patronized the National Confederation of Unions of Chile. Meanwhile, another setback was experienced by the Chilean labor movement when the anarcho-syndicalists separated from FOCH and created the General Confederation of Workers.[83]

By 1936 all the loose ends of the working class came together and the *Confederación de Trabajadores de Chile* (CTCH) emerged. This organization, yielding to the political interests of the Communist, Socialist, Democratic, and Radical parties, played an important role in the emergence of the Popular Front and represented the highly politicized working class during the period from 1938 to 1946, when the Radical party held the executive. In 1946 the bitter fight between Communists and Socialists for the control of the CTCH ended with a split in the organization and an ensuing negative effect on the social demands of the working class and on the prestige of the politicized labor leaders of the country. In the years to follow the organization was wracked by internal disputes and intrigues that further damaged the interests of organized workers in Chile.[84]

In 1950, with the Communist party underground, Socialists of all factions as well as syndicalists, Radicals, and a few Falangists joined efforts to launch a new major workers' organization. This time they avoided dependence on a specific political party, chose union leaders who were more flexible in political terms, and opened the organization to all members of the working class regardless of their ideological leanings. Thus the *Central Unica de Trabajadores de Chile* (CUT or CUTCH) came into existence on February 16, 1953, under the direction of the prestigious Clotario Blest. From then until the final takeover of the organization by the military in 1973, this highest body of the working class grew until it had a membership of over 700,000 and played an active role in the political life of the country during the next two decades.

The importance of the unions in Chilean politics and the eagerness of popular parties to dominate the directorships of trade unions has been regarded by Tomás Moulian as an outcome of the absence of any other intermediate organizations between the atomized populace and the state. Thus, as soon as the first signs of workers' organizations appear, their potential electoral support is canvassed by a political party. Once the annexations occur, the unions become dependent on the party for whatever actions they expect from entrepreneurs or from the state. Under these circumstances "the union movement becomes a parasite and a satellite of the political organism whose influence is needed to achieve any kind of political benefit for its members."[85]

Alan Angell has summarized the effects of politicization on the major organism of the Chilean labor movement. In reference to the situation before 1970 he cites as one of the positive aspects of politicization the greater opportunities for political participation that were granted to the unions and the training in bargaining tactics that CUTCH provided for the executive cadres of its affiliated unions. On the negative side there were sectarian cleavages that the parties inserted into a movement that needed badly to remain united to achieve its sociopolitical goals. Further, the stern bargaining tactics that were introduced into the labor movement by partisanship prevented a fast and favorable solution of many labor conflicts, acted to the detriment of the union members, and increased the public's apprehension regarding what the unions really wanted in periods of labor unrest.[86]

An impressive number of organized laborers backed with enthusiasm the movements of economic vindications that erupted repeatedly as a consequence of the country's ailing economy and chronic inflation. A survey of the objectives of labor leaders, carried out by Samuel Valenzuela, makes it clear that economic vindications were one of the main purposes of a union. Other goals, such as raising the educational level, the morale of the workers, or a promoting of the unity of the Chilean labor movement were considered less important. The role of the union as a promoter of political consciousness among the working class was minimal.[87] Similar results were reported in a pioneer work of Landsberger, Barrera, and Toro. They wrote: "The main goal of the Chilean union leader is that of trying to satisfy the members' rising expectations through straight wage increases, modern style. He is not devoting much energy to the obtaining of paternalistic benefits nor to the use of the union to prepare the worker for a coming revolution."[88] However, these surveys were conducted in the 1960s, when the political militancy of the trade unions had not yet reached the intensity of the Allende years. Until then social protest movements by the organized working class were usually not internally generated, but were induced by the political establishment, especially in critical periods when there was widespread dissatisfaction, galloping inflation, sagging industrial production, and rising unemployment. Investigations on the political allegiance of industrial workers with the Left coincide in assigning an important role to the trade unions and union leadership in the ideological orientation of the industrial proletariat. Atilio Borón suggests that after 1962 organized labor was an activator that promoted participation in elections among the new voters who were incorporated into the stream of the Chilean electorate.[89]

In spite of the importance of the union as a recruiting ground for the Left, its influence upon the popular voter is not to be considered as absolute. The worker perceived in his trade organization the main vehicle for expressing his social and political views, but there were also other factors that could balance his identification with his fellow workers and let him vote for a party or a candidate not promoted by his union leaders. The first researchers who applied ecological approaches to electoral results made a rather startling discovery. It was found that the working class in Chile did not react as a coherent unit to progressive ideologies. Whatever reason was chosen to explain the split in the electoral behavior of the Chilean working class, the fact remained that "popular" vote could not be identified as "votes for the Left." By using data of 1969, before the polarization years of Allende, Alejandro Portes found that the generalized statement that the lower class correlates with a radical political preference did not hold true in Chile. In fact, less than one-third of those interviewed advocated at that time radical political solutions for the problems of the country. As he correctly stated, these results revealed that "lower-class support for extreme leftist and radical parties was anything but secure."[90]

Part of the explanation for the far-from-unanimous political reaction of the working class to an ideological current that appeared to reflect its aspirations is to be found in the heterogeneous nature of the Chilean lower classes, not to mention the dichotomy of the "consuming working class" and the "proletarian working class" that Lalive d'Epinay and Zylberberg detected among the urban workers.[91] The overgeneralized statement that from 1958 to 1970, the industrial workers of Greater Santiago were solidly backing the Left has also been critically reviewed by Smith and Rodríguez. Using public opinion surveys from that time, they found that the support for the Left from manual workers amounted to, at the most, two-fifths of the electorate, whereas the rest constituted significant electoral support for moderate and even rightist parties. These findings (whose general validity can be argued since they proceed from survey polls) are in keeping with the electoral results obtained by the Left during that period and are evidence, once again, that there has not been much class-cohesive political behavior among the urban industrial workers in the recent political history of the country.[92]

In a geographical view, the high degree of activism that characterizes the mining and manufacturing unions undoubtedly had a strong influence on the political development in the areas where these activities are concentrated. For example, in the provinces of Atacama and Antofagasta, miners and industrial workers make up 40 and 30 percent respectively of the total labor force and their political influence is very decisive for the leftist parties. In Santiago and Valparaíso, where nearly one-third of the workers are employed in the poorly organized sector of services and where the industrial workers represent only one-fifth of the total labor force, united action by the working class based on the unions was less effective than in the mining provinces. In a stronger position was Concepción, a province where the political commitment of the coal miners, the textile workers, and the steel workers to the cause of the Left has kept the Socialist and Communist parties continually in the foreground of the political scene. When correlating the levels of labor organization with the geographical concentration of economic activities and with political preferences, the case of the province of Magallanes, which has traditional leanings to the Left associated not with industrial or mining development, but with the existence of a large sector of public employees of progressive views and with the development of a strong Federation of Oil Workers, is also significant.

The case of the provinces that are predominantly agricultural, where the poor unionization before 1967 was not able to entice the rural workers into united participation in national politics is very different. It was only during the government of the Christian Democracy and the Popular Unity that these large portions of the Chilean working class assumed a significant role in the political scene.

The Peasantry

In a comparison of Chile's urban society with its rural counterpart, the main difference is that the former has been socially diversified and modernized, while rural society, structured according to the norms of fifteenth century rural Europe, remained essentially the same well into the 1960s. A sociopolitical elite, whose power was based on wealth and the possession of land, controlled the country, while a large mass of peasants stood at its service without sharing the economic and sociopolitical advantages of their masters.

Large in number, the peasantry proved to be a social compound that was always readily available to be used by its masters of the moment. Peasants from Chiloé and Colchagua fought against each other in the battles of independence; peasants from Curicó and Colchagua were engaged by local entrepreneurs to work in the placers of California or in the nitrate fields of Antofagasta, or to fight in the wars against Peru and Bolivia. They had been utilized for the electoral purposes of the oligarchy and had shot at each other when the feuds within the ruling class unleashed the Civil War of 1891. Further, when the country embarked on the process of industrialization the capitalist bourgeoisie recruited its first laborers from the masses in the countryside. Thus, by force of a custom it never understood, the peasantry developed into the social class that nurtured the political-economic ventures on which the ruling class chose to embark.

In 1970 more than half a million individuals (20 percent of the country's active labor force) were engaged in agricultural activities. In the sixteen provinces of intensive agriculture in Middle Chile, 40 to 50 percent of the working population were so employed; in nine provinces rural workers made up more than half of the labor force and in Chiloé they reached 64 percent. Even in the industrialized and urban provinces of Concepción, Valparaíso, and Santiago, farmers and agrarian workers accounted for 16, 12, and 8 percent, respectively, of the provincial active labor force. Furthermore, in Coquimbo, a province where agricultural activities had been severely hampered by recurring droughts and by loss of manpower to mining, the agricultural labor force still reached one-third of the active population.

Until the beginning of the land reform process, agricultural labor in Chile fell into two distinct categories: dependent workers and independent small farmers. The first group comprised the personnel that performed functions on large estates, e.g., *inquilinos*—permanent workers on farms who were remunerated in part by cash, in part by payments in kind, housing, and the usufruct of a plot of land—and *voluntarios,* known also as *peones* or *gañanes* in the Chilean terminology—rural workers who were paid in cash on a daily basis.[93] The second group was composed of individual owners such as *pequeños propietarios* or *parceleros* ("owner cultivators" or "parcel owners") as well as sharecroppers.

The dependence of the permanent rural workers on the landowners has conventionally been regarded as the perpetuation of the personal relation between master and servant, dating back to the time when granted land and entrusted workers formed the bases for the first *estancias* (estates dedicated to the raising of cattle) and later for the *haciendas* (landed estates that combine intensive agriculture with stock raising). As George McBride wrote in the 1930s, "The system of rural labor established in colonial times has survived to the present day, little changed by a century and a quarter of nominal democracy."[94] And if one examines the observations on the human condition of the rural workers made by Gene Martin in the 1950s or by Emilio Klein in the 1960s, one finds that in three or four decades very little, if anything, happened that altered class relations within the country's rural society.[95]

Paternalism has been cited by many analysts of the rural society as one of the main reasons for the dependence of the servant on the master. This explanation first surfaced in the early works of Nicolás Palacios and Francisco A. Encina and is still cited in recent studies on Chile's peasantry.[96] There exists, however, the danger of overemphasizing the fatherly solicitude of the landowner and the reciprocal obedience of the rural tenant in these noncontractual associations. The ties between the two were more complex than the personal and affectionate relationships that go with paternalism and there was also included an economic aspect. For instance, there existed no legal bindings (contracts, obligations, or bondage to the land) of the agrarian worker to a particular landed estate, so that his permanence on a hacienda and his submission to the authority of a landowner needed to be assured through another type of rapport, one more material in nature. The adoption of sharecropping practices was an enticement for the rural worker to remain on the estate or in its vicinity. In addition to this, the landowner's "monopoly of the resources," as defined by Klein,[97] resulted in a dependence of the *inquilino* on the perquisites associated with his services to the estate. Payments in kind—groceries from the estate's store, water for irrigation of the family plot, use of agricultural implements from the hacienda pool—were not comparable to an industrial worker's salary and, in addition, greatly increased the *inquilino*'s attachment to the landowner. His dependence was much more than a paternalistic relationship: it was a situation of economic, and even political, dependence since it also included support of the electoral decisions of the master "for the good of the whole rural community." So it was this economic dependence of the rural workers that posed one of the serious problems for the implementation of the agrarian reform;[98] the traditional attachment to former masters had already been removed through political mobilization by the Christian Democracy and the Popular Unity.

If the dependent rural workers were a disadvantaged social group in the countryside, the small independent farmers, the *minifundistas,* were even more so. In 1965, almost 50 percent of the landowners in Chile possessed holdings of only five hectares or less, which in total comprised an incredibly low 1 percent of the entire privately owned rural land.[99] In the provinces of O'Higgins and Santiago alone, 69 and 62 percent of the rural holdings were two hectares or less. Even when cultivating only the most productive crops, owners could barely reach subsistence level. Thus, this sector of the rural society was plagued by the social and economic effects of a concentration of oversized landholdings on the one side and an overfragmentation of small holdings on the other. Demonstrating misjudgement of reality and an absurd academism, some authors refer to this group of small farmers as "petty bourgeoisie" or worse, "rural middle class," designations that do not reflect the desolate social and economic condition of these far from successful farmers. Even a superficial survey of the abundant literature produced on minifundia and small farmers in Chile reveals the severe economic limitations of these rural dwellers and their economic as well as their political dependence on local bosses and urban brokers.[100]

Clearly laid out minifundia pockets are spread all over the mediterranean agricultural heartland of the country from Coquimbo to Bío-Bío. In the river oases of the North, small and highly productive properties form the majority of the landholdings: 64 percent of Tarapacá's and 77 percent of Antofagasta's estates are under five hectares in size. Also widespread, but in many cases not so small, are the minifundia on the island of Chiloé and in the provinces of Cautín and Maule. But it is not so much the size of the properties that determined the poor life-styles among rural dwellers; rather it was the backward agricultural techniques by which they exploited their holdings and the lack of financial support from governmental or private agencies. Physically and economically cornered as they were, they could never hope for political independence. In local as well as in national politics, both characterized by a high degree of centralism and tight interdependence between local, regional, and national politicians,[101] the numerical potential of the small farmers was completely lost, and they had to remain loyal to political brokers and oligarchic landowners for favors received. For these reasons traditional minifundia areas seldom departed from the pattern of political behavior observed in districts with large landholdings. Since the agrarian reform was carried out for the purpose of depriving the landowner class of the political subservience of the peasantry, the small independent proprietor received no benefits from it and continued to be excluded from a significant role in the nation's political life.

Changes in Chile's Rural Society

During the 1960s and 1970s, a most ambitious sociopolitical project was undertaken by farsighted individuals and progressive political groups to implement changes in the agrarian structures and the rural society, two sectors that had remained almost untouched by the country's modernization and social development.

As long as the ruling oligarchy had been able to incorporate into its ranks the newly emerged bourgeoisie and to impose on them the axiom of landownership as a source of social prestige and as long as politicians from the middle class were imbued with the same attitudes, there was no possibility of successfully proposing land-tenure changes against the interests of the landowners entrenched as they were in Congress and the executive. It was only in the 1920s, when the foundations of the oligarchic state were shattered by the rebellion of the middle class and when the aristocracy withdrew partially from Congress and the executive, that the first serious attempts to curtail the power of the landowner class were undertaken by the "new adventurers" in Chilean politics. In 1928, under the Ibañez del Campo dictatorship, the *Caja de Colonización Agrícola* was established for the purpose of promoting agrarian settlements on state property and of buying poorly administered estates to be subdivided and sold to small cultivator-proprietors.

The efficiency of the *Caja* as the country's only legal institution dealing with land redistribution hit its peak at the end of the 1930s when the Popular Front attained control of the executive and tried to implement the reforms in the agricultural sector that had been included in Aguirre Cerda's presidential campaign. They consisted mainly of vague promises of land reform, financial aid to small and medium proprietors, and further incentives for the colonization of state-owned land. Moreover, in the social part of the program new legislation on behalf of agricultural laborers and small proprietors was announced.[102] The changes foreseen for the rural workers were minimal in comparison with the rest of the economic and social program of the Popular Front and did not arouse the enthusiasm of the rural proletariat. The landowner aristocracy was opposed to the program, since it hoped for government help to recuperate from the financial slump of the Great Depression, and observed with apprehension the growing socialization of the country.

In the early 1960s, under the government of the rightist Jorge Alessandri, improved legislation made the *Caja de Colonización Agrícola* operative again, and a number of *huertos* ("vegetable gardens") and *parcelas* were distributed to former service tenants from estates purchased by the government. In the framework of this program, 420 family parcels and 527 vegetable gardens were allocated[103] —too few and too late! Mounting pressures for drastic changes in land-tenure patterns and social justice in the countryside required more radical and far-reaching measures. In November 1962, President Jorge Alessandri signed Law No. 15020, which was to become the legal instrument during the early stages of the agrarian reform. An important feature of the new law was the creation of the *Corporación de la Reforma Agraria* (CORA) and the *Instituto de Desarrollo Agropecuario* (INDAP). The state was given the right to expropriate poorly managed or underexploited estates as well as landholdings owned by judicial persons who did not exploit them directly.[104]

As soon as the Christian Democracy was in government in 1964, it began to carry out changes in the countryside within the framework of Law No. 15020. With Rafael Moreno as head of the Corporation of the Agrarian Reform and Jacques Chonchol (with credentials as FAO advisor in Socialist Cuba) director of INDAP, swift moves were made toward expropriating holdings of staunch rightist landowners and organizing rural workers for the political benefit of the party in power.[105] The mobilization of the peasants was actively pursued by Christian Democrats through the Christian Peasant Union and the Union of Chilean Peasants, while the Marxist parties backed the Federation of Peasants and Indigenous People, later called *Ranquil*.[106] Thus, regardless of which party dominated throughout the country, the exposure of the peasants to unionization and their manipulation as elements of political pressure had the effect of encroaching on the last strongholds of landowner resistance in Congress and the National Society of Agriculture (SNA). As impending expropriations began to threaten traditional landowners, they moved swiftly to subdivide their estates into as many parcels of less than twenty economic units[107] as they could and to distribute them among members of their families. However, these moves did not weaken the determination of Moreno and Chonchol. In his final address to Congress in May 1970, President Frei summarized the achievements of the agrarian reform after his six years in office in the following words:

> In these years and until today 1,224 estates with a surface of 3,200,000 hectares have been expropriated. This surface is made up of 265,000 hectares of irrigated and 2,935,000 hectares of not-irrigated land. Until now more than 900 *asentamientos*[108] have been established,

benefiting 28,000 families, which means a total of 150,000 rural individuals. . . . According to the law and after having met the prerequisites determined by the long term plans for the agrarian reform, titles of individual properties are being issued to families where this is technically and rationally feasible, since this has been our aim and our ultimate goal. . . . I am convinced that the agrarian reform is one of the most transcendental events of this period and one of the most important achievements of this government. It was impossible to elude this problem. In the countryside, access to ownership had to be granted to the peasants as well as the opportunity to exert their citizens' rights and the possibility to change the patterns of land tenure. If this task had not been undertaken now, it would have become unavoidable later on, and under much more difficult circumstances.[109]

Five months later President Frei handed over the executive power to Salvador Allende, leader of the Popular Unity and winner of the September 1970 presidential election. The views on the land reform of Allende's political coalition were in general outline similar to those of the Christian Democracy. In fact, the new government had only to adjust its agrarian policies to the legal clauses of Law No. 16640 (passed by Congress in July 1967), which had been drafted by members of the Christian Democratic party who later defected and joined the Popular Unity under the name of MAPU; as the reason for their defection they adduced the slow pace in structural changes, particularly in the agrarian reform, adopted by the government of Frei.[110]

As promised before the election of 1970, the government of the Popular Unity, with Jacques Chonchol as minister of agriculture, proceeded to accelerate the pace of expropriation, announcing at the same time that the measures would also affect estates of less than eighty basic hectares whenever, in the judgment of the peasants, an estate's land of reserve was obstructing the development of a rural community.[111] This clause opened the doors to a practice of expropriation that became typical for the years of the Popular Unity: the land seizure (*toma*), the fastest method of forcing a proprietor to relinquish his rights to the land of reserve and CORA officials to recognize the accomplished fact before legal procedures had even been initiated.[112]

Between November 1970 and August 1972, 3,440 landowners were eased out of nearly 5.5 million hectares of land, which were turned over to CORA for administration or subdivision. The surface involved was 61 percent of all the irrigated land of the country and 43 percent of the total cultivated land. In the first five months of 1972 alone, 1,525 estates were expropriated, 250 were intervened by the government, and 150 were in the process of being expropriated after being intervened. Most affected by the redistribution of irrigated land were the provinces with extensive agriculture in the Central Valley: Linares (82 percent), Colchagua (73 percent), Concepción (73 percent), Talca (68 percent).[113] In all these provinces and others adjacent to them, the main thrust of the agrarian reform occurred during Allende's administration, which suggests that under Frei the pace of the reform in these highly productive provinces had been comparatively slow. In fact, during the Christian Democracy's government, expropriation had been directed more toward land in the *Norte Chico* (51 and 50 percent of the irrigated land in the provinces of Coquimbo and Aconcagua) and the province of Valparaíso (43 percent), so that there was not much land left there for expropriation by the Popular Unity government. However, in the recently colonized provinces, which had remained practically untouched under Frei, the government redistributed 37 percent of the cultivated land in the province of Osorno, 30 percent in Llanquihue, and 29 percent in Valdivia. In Valdivia and Cautín alone, 79 and 67 percent of the redistributions were effectuated during the Allende government, as compared with 36 percent in Santiago, 41 percent in Colchagua, 29 percent in O'Higgins, 30 percent in Ñuble, and 31 percent in Coquimbo during the same period of time. These figures are clear indications that the agrarian reform was applied differently by the two governments as each responded to its political commitments to different rural groups and to its own social priorities. The total of the beneficiaries from the land turnovers is difficult to assess; 53,576 or 61,739 families that had previously resided and worked on the estates are cited figures.[114] In correspondence with the intensity of the land exploitation and the sociopolitical pressures, the provinces with the largest number of beneficiaries were Santiago (7,937 families), Coquimbo (4,869), Colchagua (4,517), O'Higgins (4,301), Talca (3,746), and Linares (3,431), all, with the exception of Coquimbo, located in the Central Valley.

There was a drastic change not only in the land-tenure patterns but also in the concepts of exploitation of the agricultural resources and of the social organization of the rural workers. On one side, the *Centros de Reforma Agraria* (CERA) were envisaged as collective farms on which specialized work, such as livestock raising or crop production, would be taken care of by a management committee. Profits from the farm operation would be used for "socialized consumption" and not shared on an individual basis. Individual property would gradually evolve into communal ownership and provisions were made to incorporate into the CERA nuclei the migrant workers and *minifundistas* who had not found a place in the previously established *asentamientos*. The other form of socialist organization in the countryside consisted of the *comités campesinos* ("peasant committees"), which were provisionally in charge of expropriated estates under the control of CORA until the *inquilinos* living there should decide to turn them into a CERA nucleus or an *asentamiento*.[115]

The institutionalized change of the land-tenure patterns conducted by the government of the Popular Unity was accompanied by an escalation of peasant mobilization. The membership of the communist-controlled *Ranquil* rose from 43,867 in 1970 to 105,990 in 1972, thus surpassing the Christian Democratic-controlled federations of *Triunfo Campesino* and *Libertad*, which counted only 54,767 and 23,203 members, a decrease of 14 and 20 percent respectively from their 1970 memberships. These figures illustrate how intensive the patronage of the government of the Popular Unity was over the rural workers. Such patronage previously had been a matter of reproach of the Christian Democracy by more than one author but was passed over in silence in the case of the Popular Unity.[116] Alain Labrousse holds that the peasant unionization was pursued by the official organizations of the Popular Unity (the INDAP among the small independent farmers and agricultural cooperatives and the CORA in the *asentamientos* and Centers of Agrarian Reform) for the purpose of politicization in the same way as unionization of the urban proletariat was pursued by the CUT.[117]

In addition to the government's increased patronage of the rural workers, the peasants were mobilized by nongovernmental bodies, e.g., the MIR. That organization was pushing much harder than the Communist or Socialist parties for the rapid achievement of a global revolution, and the methods employed differed very much from those of the Communist party, a fact that led to bitter confrontation.[118] The MIR promoted the *Movimiento Campesino Revolucionario,* which, unlike *Ranquil,* focused its attention on the deprived peasants and *minifundistas* in the southern provinces of Cautín and Malleco. All this clearly indicates that the accelerated pace of structural change in the countryside was prompted by political motivation.

As Brian Loveman succinctly put it, "The Allende regime made a prime commitment to the final destruction of the hacienda system. . . . Allende symbolized the end of the existing system of property and the political regime which served as its foundation."[119] For a progressive Chilean, whether Communist, Socialist, Radical, or Christian Democrat, this social aim of the agrarian reform was not an exclusive concern of the Popular Unity, but one common to all parties. It was simply a concern of rendering social justice to a segment of Chilean society that had been marginated, exploited, and oppressed for centuries. However, the disagreement between the different progressive groups arose over the ideological direction in which they wanted to lead the "liberated" peasant class. For the Christian Democracy, the sociopolitical changes in the countryside were understood within the framework of a "communitarian" ideology that directs its social actions to the individual and to the common good. Consistent with these postulates were President Frei's efforts to establish individual holdings as well as cooperative enterprises, as he emphasized in his last presidential message.

For the government of the Popular Unity, the sociopolitical aims of the agrarian reform were different. The words of President Allende speak for themselves.

> In the modern world, when the fundamental conflict has reached the stage of socialist transformations, it is accepted that a far-reaching Land Reform, corresponding to the interests of the agricultural laborers and the various categories of medium-sized and small peasants, can only be carried out through an alliance of all the oppressed classes, headed by the working class. In our case, Land Reform is not accompanied by the maintenance of capitalism, but by the destruction of its fundamental nucleus: national and foreign monopolistic capitalism. It is not, therefore, a case of developing capitalism in the countryside, but a process of guiding tenurial structures towards Socialism by the means which are best suited to the character of our historical and social development.

It is understood that in some cases the new structure will be of the most advanced type—communal ownership; elsewhere various forms of cooperative systems, and finally, the survival of sectors of small private ownership will have to be considered.[120]

The Appeal of the Left

Nowhere in Latin America have socialist tendencies developed for as long and as continuously as in Chile, where accessibility to information made the lower classes more susceptible to the principles of social justice. In addition to the growing number of eligible voters, there has been the steadily rising number of people who, after 1952, voted for a party that advocated social change, class struggle, and the abolition of the old system. It is no coincidence, therefore, that the last two freely elected governments in Chile subscribed to some, if not to all of those postulates, and that the Christian Democracy in 1964 and a Socialist-Communist coalition in 1970 won the executive in free elections.

Chile's proclivity toward ideologies based on socialism is not a recent development. Earlier than in other Latin American republics social thinkers sparked an awakening of class consciousness by calling attention to the social and economic limitations that affected the deprived classes. A literary figure of the early twentieth century, Baldomero Lillo, in his short stories *Sub Sole* and *Sub Terra* described the steadfastness with which the peasants and miners endured their grim sufferings, and Nicomedes Guzmán in his contemporary novel *La Sangre y la Esperanza* dramatized the hardships of the fast growing urban proletariat in the 1930s. The perception of social injustice and the search for a political solution had to come from environments where the proletariat was little protected against exploitation by entrepreneurs: in the mines of the North and the rapidly growing manufacturing cities of central Chile. The first leftist voting trends developed in conjunction with mining and manufacturing unions that proliferated in the northern provinces and in the three largest cities of Chile (Santiago, Valparaíso, and Concepción) after the War of the Pacific.[121] Initially it was the Democratic party, which had been founded in Santiago by Malaquías Concha in 1887, that won the votes of the urban laborers and the coal and nitrate workers.

But before this, the notion of the working class was perceived and understood only by the mining and the manufacturing workers who had attained an advanced degree of group identification and organization. Class solidarity became more real during the first worker strikes in Chile—the ship liners' strike in Valparaíso (1903); the meat packers' strike in Santiago (1905); and the nitrate miners' strikes in Antofagasta (1906) and Iquique (1907).[122] The popular ferment generated by those union-led movements was channeled into a political struggle by dedicated activists such as Luis E. Recabarren, Manuel Hidalgo, and Carlos A. Martínez, who, in July of 1912, laid the foundations of the Socialist Labor Party (*Partido Obrero Socialista*). In urban centers, the public employees of the welfare state that Chile had become after the War of the Pacific chose also to establish a union in 1918 that, under the name of the Employees Union of Chile (*Unión de Empleados de Chile*), maintained political independence and did not permit patronizing by any political group.[123]

In the 1921 congressional elections, which marked the beginning of the so-called voters' revolt, socialist voters accounted for only 1.5 percent, while the Democratic party, which at that time represented socially progressive views, rose to the third political force in the country with 12.4 percent of the total returns. These figures indicate that very early in the development of the socialist electorate, and in spite of vote bribery and rampant electoral intervention by the parties of the Right, the Left was able to win 14 percent of the popular vote. Further increases occurred in the parliamentary elections of 1925 and during the days of the Popular Front in the late 1930s, indicating how appealing the Left had become, especially among unionized workers and state employees. But its popularity declined after the Second World War as a result of the economic bonanza created by Chile's copper and nitrate exports and the rivalries between the Communist and Socialist parties for control of workers and state employees.

In the 1950s, the Left changed from its purely unionist character into a movement based on an ideology and attracted not only workers but also professionals, civil servants, teachers, and students. At the University of Chile in Santiago and at the University of Concepción, socialist and communist professors adopted a militant attitude seldom seen before and used their positions to proselytize and entice into political activism the mass of students that had remained indifferent to politics since the effervescent years of the Popular Front.[124] So it is not surprising that in the 1960s, as alumni from politicized universities were incorporated into professional life, Marxism was no longer a doctrine for the working class, but a fashionable ideology in intellectual and professional circles.

Progressively, sympathizers of the Left attained governing positions in the artists' guilds and journalists' union. This obviously meant better possibilities for electoral mobilization than in previous years when the thrust of the Left rested only on the militancy of the trade unions. A desire for social change was shared by the two groups of such different sociocultural background as the university-educated elite and the proletariat. Though their socialist views were the same, their motivations were definitely different. For the worker, the aspiration for structural social change stemmed from his daily experiences of life in a capitalist society, whereas in the case of the educated leftist it was based on intellectual sophistication. Langton and Rapoport have drawn an interesting parallel between the political motivations of the leftist intelligentsia in Chile and the increasing appeal of the Left for upper and middle classes in Western Europe.[125] The individuals from these classes who, through university education, have reached a comfortable living standard tend to give priority to postbourgeois symbols, such as civil liberties and political participation as they are promoted by the leftist parties. It becomes obvious that with more individuals from higher classes endorsing the political principles of the Left, the movement became more heterogeneous and ideological in content.[126]

In Chile the perception of belonging to the lowest class stems fundamentally from an awareness of the comparative degree of deprivation. *"Nosotros los pobres, y los demás"* ("We the poor, and the others") is a phrase that expresses the socioeconomic distance between unemployed or underemployed individuals and the rest of the population. The postulates of Marx and Durkheim that economic deprivation leads to social alienation are well exemplified in Chile by many exasperating experiences of daily life that increase the sense of frustration among the poor. Underemployed and temporary workers are usually not protected by social security schemes, and they have suffered most from the escalating prices of food, clothing, and medication that were unleashed by the rampaging inflation in the country during the last fifty years. Thus, the sad reality of deprivation in a national economy eroded by inflation created a multiple picture of misery with not only individuals becoming demoralized, but whole family groups falling apart in a scenario of poor neighborhoods and insanitary dwellings.

All these elements contributed to the creation of an image of hopelessness that appeared to be inherent both in individuals and in the groups among whom they lived. Consequently, as soon as any of them succeeded in getting steady jobs with the benefits of unionization, they would consider themselves above their former peers, who, in their turn, would place them in the group of the *demás*. The frustration that arises from a situation of this sort is what social researchers have found to motivate many members of the urban proletariat to endorse the Marxist solution. Several authors have indicated that it was frustration that made the urban populace adopt aggressive attitudes not only against classes that were perceived as socially and economically favored, but also against sectors of the urban proletariat that seemed to be reaping more benefits from the current economic structure, obtaining a better chance of achieving a higher level of comfort. A class concept based solely on the grounds of appurtenance to the proletariat or working class was by no means consciously recognized by the lowest strata of the urban societies. Active leftism was adopted because its ultimate aim was the liquidation of the present social and economic orders and their replacement by a political system that would benefit people who had nothing to lose. The benefits mentioned were of material nature, since the most deprived classes are more concerned with their economic shortcomings than with their social positions.

The urban proletariat's rejection of ethical values and behavioral norms as imposed by the existing social order has been mentioned as another motive for endorsing the Left. Coincident observations by Soares and Hamblin as well as by Isuani and Cervini reveal that divorced individuals and unmarried couples from the lower strata favored the Left more than individuals of the same civil status from higher classes. In addition, this sector of the Chilean populace was unruly in character; it even rejected religious conformity and endorsed radical ways of change.[127] Such a blend of libertarianism and anarchic leftism got into difficulties with the disciplined and ideologically strict Communist party, so that this sector of the population felt more at ease with the political directions of the Socialist party or the Movement of the Revolutionary Left (MIR).

The frustration and the rejection of established social norms previously mentioned go along with the state of social rebellion and normlessness that Emile Durkheim referred to as *anomie*.[128] From Durkheim's viewpoint it can be inferred that the leftist vote is also the consequence of a deeply anchored feeling of alienation, which in this context means exclusion from political power. Thus understood, alienation is not only a feeling common to the lower strata of the Chilean society; it is also an operative political motivation in higher strata. Carl Stone argues that political alienation as a reason for voting for the Left should not be considered as a motivation only among the deprived classes, because this reasoning would not explain why large sectors of the proletariat supported the Christian Democracy.[129] Furthermore, Smith and Rodríguez expressed doubts about the validity of the argument that all leftist votes originated from the lower class. They held that many of those votes came from alienated individuals of higher classes.

As to the influence of class consciousness as a motivation for leftist voters, the extensive research on this topic carried out by Alejandro Portes[130] shows, first, that preference for leftist ideologies is to be found more among individuals who are frustrated with their family or social situation and blame society for their condition than among those who, though also frustrated, do not. Second, interaction between feelings of frustration and personal-structural conditions lead to a higher degree of class consciousness and so will be reflected in more individuals endorsing leftist politics. The second situation appeared to be absent in Chile, at least until the 1960s. Indeed, as Portes suggested, without class awareness the protests of the working class remain restricted to economic issues and do not become a political struggle, just as was pointed out in the preceding pages. But the question still remains whether the consciousness of belonging to the lower class had an important bearing on the vote for the Left and whether there was any real class awareness among the members of the proletariat. Alan Angell has bluntly stated that the Chilean lower class exhibits a lack of cohesion and awareness, two requirements that Marx considered indispensable for the development of a politically active class. Apart from short periods of electoral enthusiasm, no common political strategy has effectively united organized labor, the peasantry, and the "marginals."[131]

In revealing terms, Torcuato Di Tella and his coresearchers

established that the development of a proletarian class consciousness among the coal miners of Lota was based more on the experiences of labor struggles between workers and entrepreneurs than on a perception of the social distances that separated them from other elements of the Chilean society.[132] The important implication of this notion of lower-class consciousness is that large sectors of the proletariat, e.g., independent craftsmen, journeymen, maids, and street peddlars, developed hardly any class awareness and that their voting for the Left was based on feelings of anomie and frustration. Only the organized workers who became aware, through their active union leaders, of the conflicting dualism of the exploiter-exploitee relationship, were able to develop a class consciousness that expressed itself in leftist militancy and political rebellion.[133]

Commitment to social change as an element of decision making among the Chilean electorate is to be considered as more complex than other political motivations, because it contains personal overtones that are not subject to ecological norms. In the development of change-oriented political views, an awareness of the country's social conditions was necessary. The degree of this awareness depended to a great extent on the ideological exposure of the individual to media and partisan indoctrination. The latter occurred mainly in union gatherings and university classrooms, where it made an enormous impact on individuals from the middle class; they in fact became the ones who prompted their lower-class counterparts to political action. As both Robert C. Williamson and Sandra Powell have pertinently stated, up to the Allende years there existed more predisposition to social change in the middle class than in the lower class. The latter, due to their disadvantaged social conditions, were not in a position to conceive of any kind of social mobility.[134] It is not surprising that there were elements from the middle class that assumed leadership positions in political groups with postulates of social justice and structural change. So now, instead of having class-based political currents, the country aligned itself according to group-based ideologies, and the parties became more aggregative. As one author has put it, the desire for institutional change resulted in brokerage politics instead of in politics of contending classes.[135]

The quest for social change had indeed become common among progressive social forces in Chile and was no longer an exclusive goal of the Marxist Left. This desire revealed not so much a class consciousness as an awareness of the shortcomings of the existing social structures and the willingness to alter the situation through personal commitment to action. Political mobilization and integration were expressed through interest in electoral participation, protest movements, revolutionary outbursts, active partisanship, and even outbreaks of political-religious mysticism.[136]

Urbanization and Progressive Vote. Urbanization in developing countries has been regarded as a process that affects the individual both positively and negatively. The move into cities increases literacy, education, access to health care, and exposure to information sources. Politically, this meant in Chile that the peasant was weaned from his political dependence on his former employer, the landowner. These positive sides of urbanization, that are partially covered by the generic term "modernization" as it has been proposed by Daniel Lerner,[137] have to be confronted, however, with the negative aspects of urban immigration: alienation from the traditional roots of a rural society increases anomie and political instability. Furthermore, the move into an urban environment, instead of bringing the expected rise in living standards, often results in a greater economic deprivation than that experienced in the original rural environment and in a social downgrading that leads not only to political but also to emotional instability, with accompanying high rates of crime.

Ecological analysts of Chilean elections resorted early to the urbanization process as an explanatory variable of the leftist, or perhaps better, progressive vote. In his precursory work on the geography of Chilean politics, Ricardo Cruz Coke argued that the increasing urbanization was leading toward the strengthening of leftist and reformist parties because of the combined political participation of lower and middle classes.[138] However, more recent research on the psychology of voters and the political leanings of the urban proletariat in Chile has suggested that a high degree of urbanization per se does not condition leftist radicalism, but that it contributes to it by augmenting occupational dissatisfaction and by unleashing anomic reactions. Using sound analytic techniques, Portes and Ross were able to measure and quantify the weight of occupational insecurity and the individual's blaming of this on the structure as more conducive for leftist inclinations than frustration, rootlessness, low socioeconomic status, and mobility together.[139]

It is perhaps because of this situation that Ricardo Cinta[140] found the same negative correlations in the different provinces of Chile between the degree of urbanization and industrialization and the preference for the Left that Kornhauser had established.[141] Thus, urbanization seems to be a political indicator from a double viewpoint. On one side, it inhibits leftist proclivity, as the migrant individual is able to fulfill the socioeconomic expectations he envisaged upon leaving the countryside; on the other, it promotes leftism among those who cannot obtain better jobs, convincing them that the social system and government have denied them satisfying work opportunities.

In sociopolitical terms these twofold reactions are coupled with two different types of socialization that are associated with urbanization. There is the incorporative urbanism that not only integrates the individual into the working force of the city, but also provides him with material facilities and social mobility. It is among this type of urbanites that a higher degree of satisfaction with their present status exists and that the leftist ideology is not enthusiastically endorsed. Guillermo Briones found to his surprise that in some provinces of Chile (Antofagasta, Malleco, and Cautín), leftist votes were fewer than the degree of urbanization would have led one to expect. This situation prompted him to calculate indexes of political discrepancy that showed that urban provinces, such as Valparaíso, Santiago, Antofagasta, and Concepción, yielded (at least during the 1969 congressional elections) fewer leftist votes than one would have anticipated from their number of urban dwellers. Only in the province of Mallaganes did the votes for the Left match the percentage of urban population, a fact that can be attributed to its degree of information and to the activities of the organized unions in an urban environment.[142]

This trend, established by statistical analysis of aggregate data, rejects again the common assumption that the urban proletariat has been solidly behind the leftist parties. Reformist parties such as the Christian Democracy and the Radical party have gained more popular support from the urban proletariat than some political analysts had expected. Especially during the Frei administration, the Christian Democracy greatly increased its appeal among the urban proletariat through its programs of Popular Development (*Promoción Popular* and *Operación Sitio*), which were designed not only to improve the living conditions of the deprived urbanites, but to arouse their political consciousness and to mobilize them to the party's electoral advantage.[143] Since these programs were initiated by Frei in 1964, it is not surprising to find, as several scholars have done, that the *pobladores* ("urban settlers") patronized by the Christian Democracy found their occupational, housing, educational, and health needs satisfied by the early 1970s and were prepared to endorse a political philosophy that promised gradual reform instead of violent revolution.

Those *pobladores*, however, who had not benefited from these assistance programs were still dissatisfied and, as Daniel Goldrich states so pertinently, fell easy prey to the leftist opposition.[144] Portes and Ross have emphasized that an important operating motivation of leftist radicalism is a high degree of political socialization, activated by personal contact within families and in poor neighborhoods where social interaction is more intense than in single-family-housing neighborhoods.[145] And this is where "excluding urbanism" is found: in the proliferation of shanty towns (*poblaciones callampas, campamentos*) in the peripheries of the cities, where physical marginality is accompanied by social segregation from the rest of the city and in the urban slums (*conventillos* and degraded block buildings), which host a growing number of unemployed or underemployed males and overworked females. The women, many of whom live in common-law unions, raise numerous children and, in addition, support the whole family by working as part-time maids or by doing laundry for middle-class households. These marginated masses are not necessarily to be associated, as several authors have asserted, with the increasing flow of rural migrants, but rather with urbanites who are lacking an upward drive and whose children enter marital unions before they can earn a living.

By the end of the 1960s the peripheral settlements and the socially marginal masses had fallen under the spell of the Socialist and Communist parties. These parties supplied them with activist leaders (generally outsiders) and the infrastructure (use of propaganda material, access to leftist radios and newspapers) necessary to exert more pressure on the government.[146] The mounting mobilization promoted by the two parties increased the political momentum in the poorer neighborhoods to such an extent that when Salvador Allende was elected president, both the Socialist and Communist parties began to lose control over the *pobladores* and they fell into the grip of the more radical groups of the Left— the Movement of the Revolutionary Left, the People's Organized Vanguard (VOP), and the Movement of Revolutionary Pobladores. Leaders as well as members of the *pobladores* groups, Víctor Toro and Alejandro Villalobos for example, received indoctrination and manpower support from the MIR and during the Allende years they frequently challenged the authority and political direction of the Popular Unity, thereby becoming the most active endorsers of the Chilean road to revolution. To maximize the political weight of the mobilized *pobladores*, the ultraleft organizations strengthened them by consolidating several neighborhood committees into so-called *comandos comunales* ("community commands"), which also included local groups for the distribution of food (JAP) and cells of activist workers organized in the *cordones industriales* ("industrial belts"). They were so called because they comprised clusters of industrial establishments in different sectors of a city. There is no doubt that the takeover of the mobilized worker-*poblador* masses by the Ultraleft caused justifiable concern among the established Left, especially the Communist and Socialist parties.[147] Evidently the hypermobilization of the urban proletariat, which the parties of the Popular Unity had initiated during the Frei years, was reaching uncontrollable proportions by 1973 and was leading to the rejection of the established authority. The unruliness of the *pobladores* would finally threaten from within the institutional stability of the government of the Popular Unity. Since the mobilization of the *pobladores* had been intended to lend ideological content to the demands of the settlers and to prepare them through political indoctrination for the inevitable class struggle,[148] the political intentions of this action spread a feeling of uneasiness and alienation among other social classes, especially the middle class, and turned them increasingly anti-Allende. There has been widespread consensus among objective writers that the mobilization of the lower class in Chile, and especially of the *poblador*, was undertaken not for the purpose of achieving structural change, since marginal settlements continued to spread under the same miserable conditions, but for the purpose of capitalizing on the electoral weight of this mass of voters. In the latter the Left had undeniable success, but in the long run it brought about some of the "unanticipated" consequences that have been mentioned above.

The lesson Chile learned from the extreme mobilization of the urban poor is that even though in itself it may be a positive undertaking on behalf of the popular parties, it has proven to be more of an obstacle for social change than a help for a progressive government.[149] Furthermore, the mobilization of the lower class in urban centers came under the control of the Ultraleft, which was more interested in ultimate revolution than in the creation of a socialist-democratic society. Thus, the support Allende received from the masses was overridden by the ultraleftist revolutionary urgency and created more trouble for the socialist government of the Popular Unity, which was already under fire from the non-Marxist opposition.[150]

4
Forty Years of Democratic Life

The period between October 1932 and March 1973 comprised a chapter in Chile's history in which political freedom was never seriously endangered and in which elections proceeded without a party or a pressure group forcibly taking control of the executive or the legislative power. Even if it is debatable whether civil liberties were respected at all times during that period and whether there were attempts by certain parties to seize power illegally or to abolish the constitutionally established institutions, elections were held without interference and the verdicts of the polls were accepted. Also during these forty years, the efforts of the political establishment to encourage political participation by enfranchising new groups of voters—women, illiterates, and young people—were successful, and the electoral vices that had plagued the country in previous decades were gradually eradicated. These developments made it possible for the democratic system to thrive and for the parties and populist movements to share power in proportion to the popular support received. Nowhere in Latin America did there exist such ideological variety, such pluralism, such respect for the constitution, and such political participation as in Chile during this period.[1]

Prelude: 1924-1932

The "night of the rattling sabres" and the military *pronunciamiento* of September 5, 1924, unleashed a crisis that the political establishment was not prepared to cope with. After being forced by the military to admit into his cabinet three senior officers, President Arturo Alessandri was asked to resign on September 12.

On the same day, Congress was dissolved without resistance, and the government was taken over by a military junta that ruled the country until January 23, 1925, when it was overthrown in turn. The leaders of the conspiracy, a group of young army officers and the eldest sons of Alessandri, requested the return of President Alessandri to finish his term in office, which was due to expire in December of the same year.[2] Although this was a setback for the military, their retreat from the political scene was by no means complete. With Colonel Carlos Ibañez del Campo as minister of defense during the last months of the Alessandri administration and as minister of the interior under Emiliano Figueroa, who succeeded Alessandri in the presidency, the military continued to hover over the troubled politics of the country. Unable to resist the pressures exerted by Ibañez del Campo, the weak President Figueroa relinquished his office in May 1927 and left the scene to the ambitious military.[3]

Ibañez del Campo, by now a general, easily engineered his election as president of the Republic and immediately embarked on a "legal" dictatorship that lasted until May 1931, when he was forced to resign under pressure of the political establishment and the economic crisis.[4] The political suppression that all parties had suffered during the dictatorship had aroused them to such an extent that they were only too eager to jump into the political arena to prove the quality of their doctrines. Overenthusiasm led to yet another period of political instability, which lasted from August 1931 to September 1932.

During that time, the executive power shifted from the vice-president of the Republic to the chairman of the Senate, and from there to a radical president, Juan E. Montero. In June 1932, it came under the control of a junta headed by Carlos Dávila, a progressive Radical; Eugenio Matte, an outspoken Socialist; and Colonel Marmaduke Grove, a Socialist commander of the air force. The junta, which had come to power through a coup d'état, leaned heavily toward socialism, and its rule is known in Chilean history as the "Socialist Republic." Like other socialist experiments, the Socialist Republic devoured its children one after the other. First Dávila was ousted from the junta for allegedly conservative views.[5] In revenge he mounted a conspiracy against his former comrades and, with the assistance of members from the Santiago garrison, deposed them. With the complete power now in his hands alone, he began the so-called One-Hundred-Days-Dictatorship. On September 14, 1932, worn down by the burden of power, he relinquished his office to General Bartolomé Blanche, who held the presidency for less than one month and then handed it over to the president of the Supreme Court, Judge Abraham Oyanedel. This man, sensing the country's weariness of political intrigues and military plots, promptly called presidential and congressional elections for the end of October 1932. This put an end to the political turbulence that had lasted for seven long years.

The Emergence of Socialism: 1932-1941

The election date of October 30, 1932, announced by Judge Oyanedel, gave the political parties less than four weeks to campaign. Nevertheless, five presidential candidates were ready for the contest. Arturo Alessandri, supported by Liberals, Radicals, and Democrats; Marmaduke Grove, backed by Socialist groups; Héctor Rodríguez de la Sotta, a Conservative; Enrique Zañartu Prieto, an aristocrat supported by Liberal-Democrats and pro–Ibañez del Campo forces; and Elías Lafferte, the candidate of the Communist party.[6] This slate represented all the political currents that had developed in the country during the unsettled 1920s and early 1930s.

On election day the national returns recorded a triumph for Arturo Alessandri with 54 percent of the votes. He had been able to gain pluralities of over 65 percent in the northern provinces and in the provinces of *La Frontera;* in Malleco alone he received 90 percent of the votes. Not less impressive was his sweep in the agricultural provinces with over 50 percent against a low 20 percent for the second candidate, the Conservative Rodríguez de la Sotta. In the urban provinces Alessandri was not quite so strong. In Aconcagua he obtained 46 percent against 35 percent for Marmaduke Grove, while in the province of Valparaíso he scored 48 percent against 32 for Grove. In the province of Santiago, Alessandri won over Grove with 42 percent against 33. However, these provincial figures mask the remarkable differences at municipal levels. In the urban municipalities of Greater Santiago, Alessandri secured an advantage of 43 percent over Grove's 35, whereas in the rural municipalities of the same province he scored 41 percent over 32 for Grove.[7]

The returns of the presidential election established that the Chilean electorate had decisively turned its back on an executive dominated by conservative and dictatorial forces (Rodríguez de la Sotta and Zañartu Prieto together obtained only 26 percent of the vote) and that it preferred a more liberal and progressive government. And Grove's second finish came as no surprise. With 18 percent of the returns in his favor, it was clear how popular his Socialist personality had become. Amazingly, it was not in the northern provinces and in Concepción, which later became strongholds of the Left, but in the urban provinces of central Chile that Grove received his greatest support, thereby making it evident that the seeds of socialism had found a more fertile ground among the urban masses than among the miners. The Communist candidate's highest total was 2.5 percent of the votes in the provinces of Tarapacá, Curicó, and Concepción, whereas his national percentage was a low 1.2 percent.

If the presidential election seemed to have been decided by personal appeal and ideological background, this was not so much the case in the congressional elections that were held on the same day. The Alessandri parties were supported by only 42 percent of the electorate, 12 percent less than Alessandri in his presidential victory. The Socialist candidates received only 6.5 percent of the total returns, a figure that reflected also the substantial gains of Grove himself, whose 18 percent of the national vote was not shared by his party. More successful were the Conservatives who managed to exceed by 3 percent the 14 percent of their presidential candidate Rodríguez de la Sotta.[8] The big winners in the 1932 congressional elections were the Radicals who claimed thirty-four deputy and nine senatorial seats and 18 percent of the popular vote. Their greatest gains came in the southern agricultural provinces, from Ñuble to Chiloé, where they were backed by the rich agriculturists, a different breed from the landowners in the agricultural heartland of the country.[9] In Santiago and Valparaíso the gains of the Radical party were less impressive because of the overwhelming support given by these provinces to rightist candidates. Santiago alone elected twelve deputies from the Conservative party (two-thirds of the seats allocated to the capital province) against three from the Radical party. In the province of Valparaíso Conservatives and Radicals elected three deputies each. As expected, the Conservatives were strong in the traditional agricultural provinces from Colchagua to Maule, with ten out of the nineteen deputy seats. The parties of the Left obtained their highest returns in the northern provinces of Tarapacá and Antofagasta, where they won four of the five senatorial and six of the eleven deputy seats. In the rest of the country the electorate's response to the parties of the Left was poor.

In general, the returns of the 1932 elections indicated that in a major contest the personal attraction, so characteristic of the turbulent 1920s, still persisted and that in congressional elections the electorate was moving slightly toward the Center and the Left. The shift was causing a compensatory polarization of rightist forces in benefit of the Conservative party, with its gain in support in the core of the country. Thus, the political forces that were to do battle at the end of the 1930s were moving into clear positions of antagonism and combat by 1932.[10]

Very soon after the elections the realignment of the political parties was in process, with the Left under the leadership of Eugenio Matte and Marmaduke Grove swiftly moving into belligerent opposition to the Alessandri government. The president did not hesitate to counterattack. To parry any sedition from the military or the Left, he tacitly agreed with the development of the Republican Militia, a paramilitary organization pledged to defend the constitutional order in the country. The Left observed with alarm the president's acquiescence in the growth of this organization and the rise of the National Socialist party in the country. It became even more alarmed when President Alessandri asked Congress to impeach Senator Eugenio Matte and jailed Marmaduke Grove for alleged conspiratory activities with the support of *Ibañistas*.[11] In both instances the president of the Republic had made use of the extraordinary powers with which he had been vested by the Constitution of 1925.

The hard line adopted by Alessandri not only led to a breach with the Left, but also contributed to the estrangement of the Radicals, his allies in the presidential election of 1932. In April of 1934, the Radical party, the most powerful political group at that time, withdrew from the government, as did a large part of the Democratic party. Left only with the Liberal party (his party of origin), Alessandri had to turn to the Conservatives for political support of his government. By so doing he prompted the rallying of the rightist parties and the grouping of the Left with the centrist Radicals in the opposition. Although the Left had not shown great strength in the 1932 congressional elections, the popularity of Grove with the proletarian electorate was undeniable, and it became the strategy of the Left to take advantage of that attraction. On January 6, 1933, left-wing Radicals, Democrats, and Social Republicans (a group of social-democratic intellectuals formed in 1931) joined forces in a Block of the Left. This combination held nineteen seats in the Chamber of Deputies and nine in the Senate. Since Radicals and Communists were not included, the Block was no match for the forces backing President Alessandri. However, when the Radicals left the government, fed up with the abuses from the aristocratic Minister of Finance Gustavo Ross, the strength of the Block increased with their entry. When in April of 1935 municipal elections in the country proved favorable to the Liberals and Conservatives, the two parties in power, it became clear to the opposition that the only effective way to topple the rightist government of Alessandri would be by means of a union of Center and Left parties.[12]

In March 1936, after long internal disputes in the Radical party, the alliance of that party with Socialists, Democrats, Communists, and the Workers Federation of Chile gave birth to the Popular Front. The aims of this political federation were to fight against the oppression of the oligarchy and to strive for a socioeconomic system that would benefit the middle and lower classes.[13] In the years that followed, the slogan *pan, techo y abrigo* ("bread, shelter, and overcoat") synthesized the vindicatory postulates of the coalition.

The congressional elections of March 1937 provided the first opportunity for the realigned forces to test their strength, and the results of the elections clearly demonstrated the polarization that had occurred within the Chilean electorate. The rightist coalition that backed President Alessandri obtained a solid 49 percent of the popular vote (Conservatives—21 percent; Liberals—21 percent; Democrats—5 percent; Agrarians—2.3 percent), giving them a total of eighty deputies (a majority in the lower Chamber) and twelve senators and adding strength to the majority the Right already held in the upper Chamber. This Congress, so outspokenly rightist, was to become a formidable challenger of the next president, Aguirre Cerda, the victorious candidate of the Popular Front in 1938. The forces of the opposition were led by the Radical party with 18.7 percent of the popular vote, but only twenty-nine elected deputies. This is an example of the incongruities that could be caused by the D'Hont dividing number: in the 1932 elections the Radicals, with fewer votes (18 percent), had won thirty-five deputy seats. Second place in the opposition went to the Socialist party with 11.2 percent of the popular vote, nineteen deputies, and three seats in the Senate. The Communist party also made gains, electing six deputies and one senator. A party that made its debut in these elections with a relatively poor showing was the National Socialist party, with 3.5 percent of the votes and three deputies. The left-wing faction of the former Democratic party emerged the big loser, holding only five of its former fourteen seats in Congress. The salaried workers had clearly transferred their loyalties to the Socialist and Communist parties.

In a regional review of the results (Figure 2), the Socialists made imposing gains in the provinces of the North and in Magallanes, where their social message had gained the approval of the miners. In the provinces of Santiago and Valparaíso the Socialist party won eight of the forty-five deputy seats, an impressive figure because it equalled the number of deputies elected in those provinces by the powerful Radical party. Concepción also demonstrated its growing leftist proclivity by electing three deputies from the Marxist parties against four from the rightist forces.[14] The Radical party continued to show its strength in Greater Santiago, where it appealed to the urban middle class, and in the southernmost agricultural provinces, where it enjoyed the support of the agriculturists.

Among the forces of the Right, the Conservative party showed greatest strength, especially in the province of Santiago, where it secured nine deputies of the possible eighteen, and three senators of the possible five to be elected. As expected, the party also did well in the agricultural provinces from O'Higgins to Ñuble. The Liberals had to share the gains of the Conservatives in those provinces; only in Aconcagua did they obtain a plurality. In the province of Cautín the largest vote went to the Agrarian party, which represented the interests of agricultural entrepreneurs. Ricardo Donoso argues that the electoral success of the Right and especially the election of liberal candidates were the result of a grand-scale bribery campaign run by the hated Minister Ross, an action that convinced even more disgusted young Conserva-

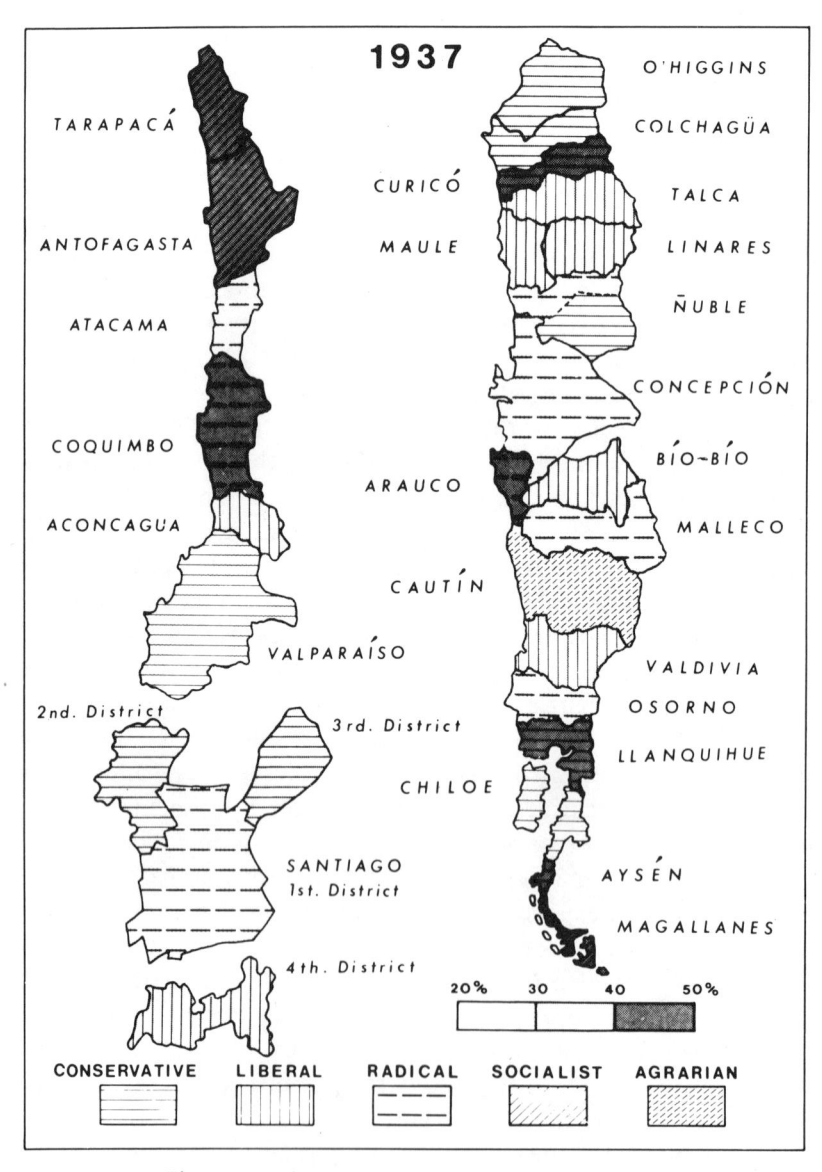

Figure 2.—The congressional elections of 1937.

tives that they should create a political party dissociated from the corrupt practices of the traditional rightist parties; thus, the National Falange came into existence.[15]

The electoral victory of the Right, instead of reducing the revolutionary fervor of the Popular Front, inflamed its combative spirit and promoted greater solidarity among the parties of the coalition. The Radical party, whose right wing had continued to cooperate with the government of Alessandri in spite of the repeated attacks of Gustavo Ross on the leftist leanings and the middle-class provenance of its members, embarked on a more enthusiastic participation within the Popular Front alliance. It has been mentioned that one of the peculiar traits of the rightists in Chile is their scorn for the participation of middle- and lower-class individuals in politics, since they consider themselves as the best prepared and most capable. This attitude is exemplified in the disdainful manner and ruthlessness by which Ross, against the wishes of President Alessandri, alienated the Radicals.

As early as April of 1937, the members of the Popular Front began preparations for the presidential contest to be held in 1938. The Socialist party nominated Marmaduke Grove as candidate for the Popular Front, whereas the Radicals—the majority party in the coalition—nominated Pedro Aguirre Cerda, a moderate member of the party's right wing. In a dramatic convention in April of 1938, the Socialists yielded to the demands of the majority party and endorsed the candidacy of Aguirre Cerda.[16] In the ranks of the Right the candidacy of Gustavo Ross was imposed by hardliners from the Liberal and Conservative parties on the more moderate majority in both parties. The presidential slate for 1938 was almost complete when in June a picturesque group called the Popular Liberating Alliance—composed of National Socialists, *Ibañista* forces, and sparsed Socialists—nominated Carlos Ibañez del Campo.

This latest entry appeared to lessen the chances of the candidate of the Popular Front since a significant sector of the uncommitted middle-class voters seemed inclined, fearing the radical socio-economic changes of a Socialist government, to forgive Ibañez del Campo his past sins. But then, several events occurred to ensure victory for Aguirre Cerda in the upcoming election. His opponent Gustavo Ross had a very unpleasant character and his economic measures had made him most unpopular. Further, the

Alessandri administration suffered a loss of prestige when, in September of 1938, police forces massacred a group of Nazi youths, and Ibañez del Campo withdrew his candidacy as a result of that tragic event.[17] It also turned the forces that had rallied under the Liberating Popular Alliance toward the Popular Front and enlarged the support of Aguirre Cerda.

After a bitter presidential campaign on October 25, 1938, the candidate of the Popular Front emerged as the winner, with a slim advantage of 4,111 votes. The triumph of Aguirre Cerda changed the electoral picture that had resulted from the congressional contest of 1937. The strongholds of the Left and the Right acquired clear contours (Figure 3). The candidate of the Popular Front was successful in the provinces of the North with percentages close to or even over 60, while his rightist contender swept the agricultural provinces with percentages oscillating between 59 and 79. In the traditional agricultural province of Colchagua, Gustavo Ross peaked with 79 percent, showing the enormous influence of the landowner aristocracy. To counterbalance the Right's high returns in the agricultural provinces Aguirre Cerda obtained a large number of votes in the urban industrial provinces of Santiago, Valparaíso, and Concepción, where a definite swing of the urban middle and lower classes away from the traditional Right was taking place. The greatest plurality for the Popular Front was achieved in Magallanes, where Aguirre Cerda won over Ross with 4,215 votes against 526. Even in the two provinces of recent colonization, Cautín and Valdivia, the candidate of the Popular Front managed a slim edge over his opponent, and that was decisive for his victory.[18]

If the strong vote for the Right in the agricultural provinces of the country was to be explained to a great extent by vote-buying practices, the good showing of the Popular Front in the industrial and mining provinces was a response to the deteriorating economic situation of the labor class, created by inflation, low wages, and unemployment. No less conducive to the defeat of the Right were the repressive measures taken by Alessandri against union organizations that had voiced the proletariat's protests and the unpopularity of Gustavo Ross himself among the workers. The strong support of Magallanes for Aguirre Cerda is to be attributed to scandalous land grants made in that province by the *Caja de Colonización Agrícola* for the benefit of some affluent Santiago

167

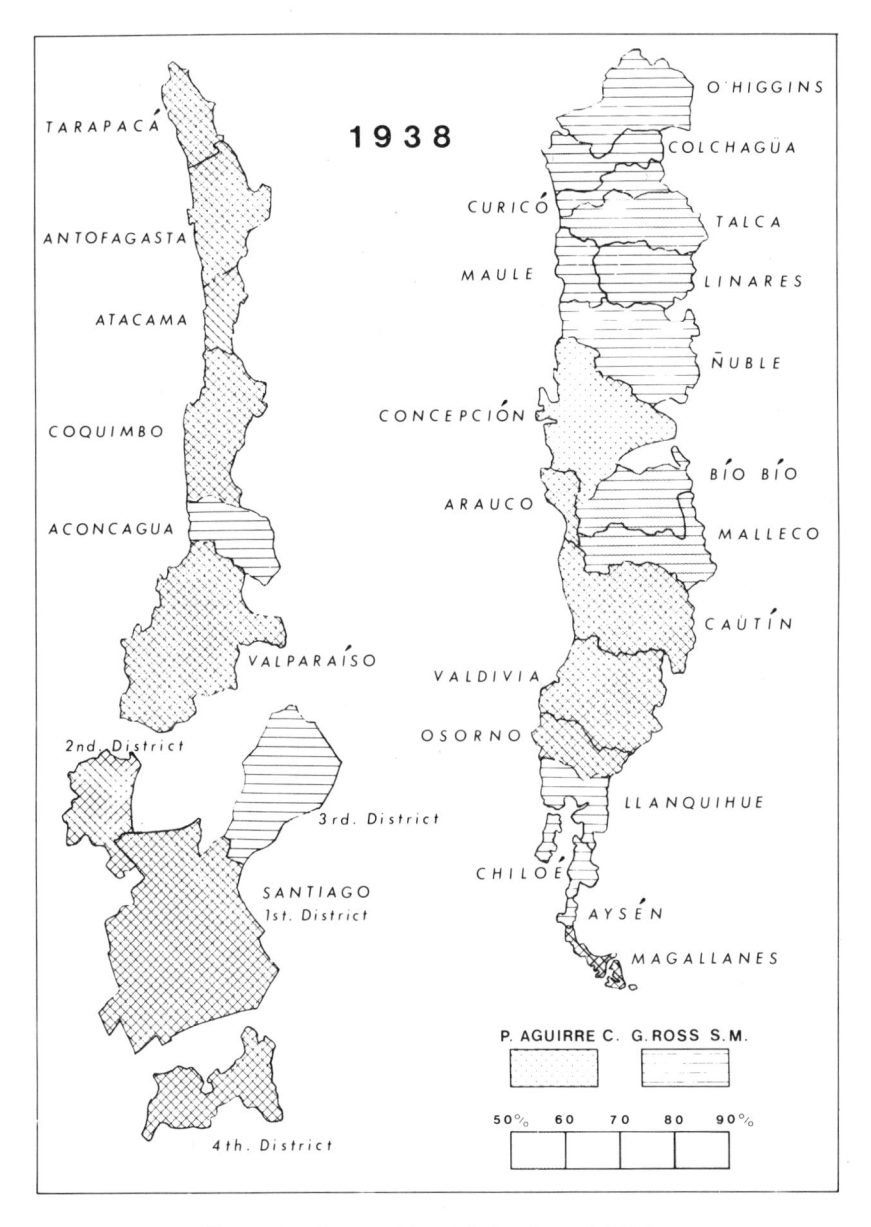

Figure 3.—The presidential election of 1938.

residents and large companies.[19]

The election of the Popular Front to the executive marked the beginning of a new regime in Chile. Aristocrats and bourgeois were removed from all appointed administrative positions in the country and abroad and replaced from the ranks of the Radical party.[20] Thus the characteristic "bureaucratic" clientele of the radical years began its development. To overcome economic prostration and unemployment a series of measures destined to give the government a more important role in the national economy and in the control of the natural resources of the country were implemented. The creation of new government agencies opened jobs to more members of the party and alleviated the unemployment situation. Furthermore, although several provinces of agricultural Chile were devastated by an earthquake in 1939, the outbreak of World War II stimulated the country's nitrate and copper exports and gave an overall boost to the economy.[21]

The major difficulties for the Popular Front during their early years in power arose from the rightist opposition still firmly entrenched in Congress. Favorite obstructionist tactics included impeachment of ministers, stalling the passage of legislation, and abstaining from attending congressional sessions to prevent the necessary quorum. The National Falange and the National Socialists came to the assistance of the hard-pressed Popular Front in those bitter skirmishes with the Right.

But the most serious threats to the Popular Front coalition and the reason for its ultimate collapse came from within the alliance itself. On one side, the Socialists disliked the government's growing bureaucracy and criticized the slow pace with which structural changes were carried out, while on the other side, the Communists began to cater to the labor unions and censured the Socialists for collaboration with a government that was not revolutionary enough.[22] Within the Socialist party itself things were not running smoothly. The ambitious César Godoy started to rock the boat, challenging the authority of Marmaduke Grove and causing the party's first scission in 1941 by pushing the formation of a Socialist Workers party.[23] The Radical party was no more successful in keeping its ideological purity and unity while in the Popular Front. Slowly the party began to develop a "conservative" faction that moved silently into a centrist position and isolated the "progressive" faction. Such a development was sure to be resented by the

Marxist members of the coalition. Against all the efforts of President Aguirre Cerda, who still believed in the union of the middle and lower classes within the Popular Front and wanted to keep the union alive, at least until the congressional elections of 1941, the Front collapsed on January 16, 1941. As John R. Stevenson accurately remarked, even though the coalition had been in control of the executive power for only twenty-three months, it had survived longer than the French and the Spanish popular fronts.[24] The split forces of the former alliance were now heading independently for the congressional elections, in which they would find out that it was their union that had really found favor with the electorate of the country and that the Right had succeeded only in discrediting itself by its obstructionist tactics.

The March 1941 elections were an astounding success for the forces of the Left especially for the Communist party, which received 12 percent of the popular vote and increased its representation in the Chamber of Deputies from seven to sixteen and in the Senate from two to four. The years of active proselytism among organized workers, and under the umbrella of the Popular Front, had been well rewarded. The Communists made an impressive show in the provinces of the North (Figure 4) with 32 percent of the votes in Tarapacá and 41 percent in Antofagasta, marking the beginning of a trend that was to persist for three decades. The party also obtained nearly one-fifth of the popular vote in the provinces of Coquimbo and Concepción, both with strong mining developments. Nationwide the Communists emerged second behind the Radicals.

The Socialists received 17 percent of the popular vote and increased their representation in the lower Chamber by five and in the upper by one. The party obtained pluralities in the province of Valparaíso and in the First District of Santiago—the urban area of the capital province. Demonstrating that the appeal of prestigious local figures of the Left could successfully challenge the political power of the oligarchy, the Socialists won by a slim margin in the traditionally agricultural province of Colchagua. A shift toward Socialist candidates could be observed also in the provinces of Valdivia and Llanquihue (former strongholds of Radicals and Conservatives) where the party obtained nearly 30 percent of the votes. The splinter Socialist Workers party elected only one deputy—in the province of Concepción. The Democratic party

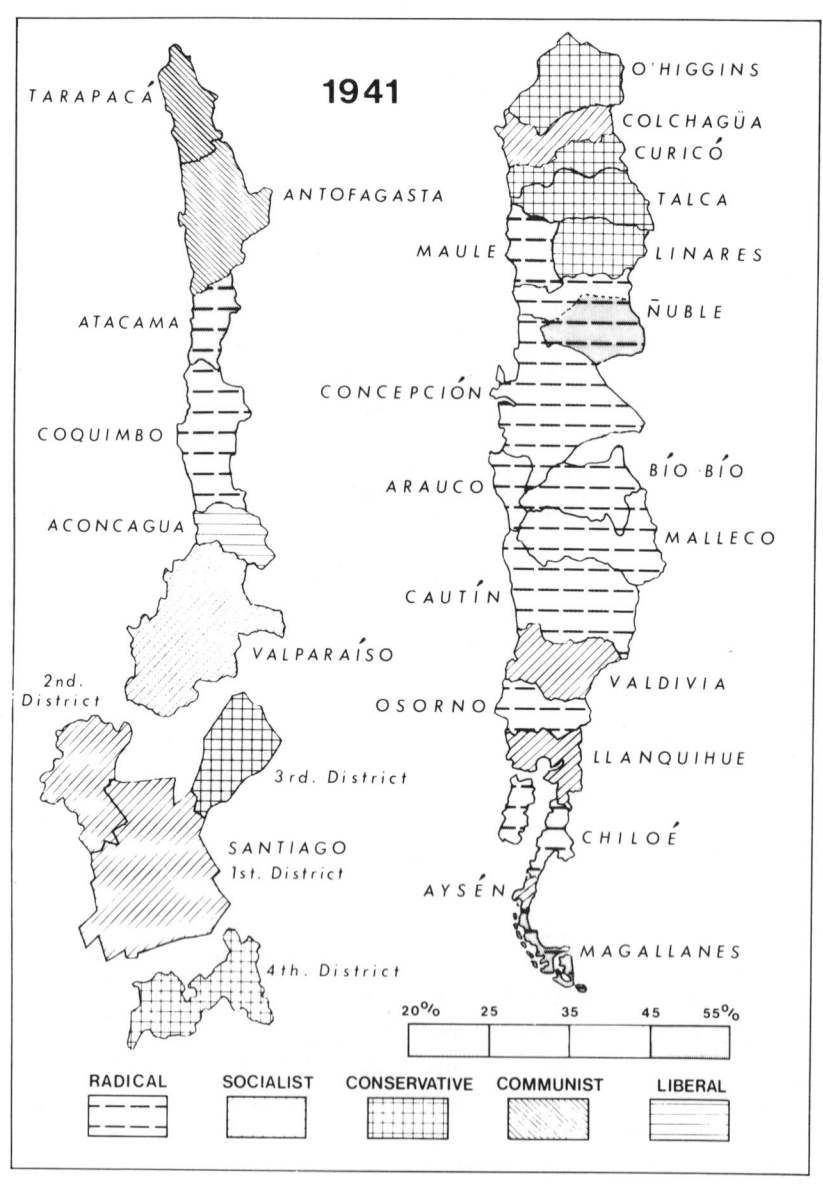

Figure 4.—The congressional elections of 1941.

continued to decline and obtained only 4.2 percent of the national vote; nevertheless, through convenient local alliances (joined lists), it elected six deputies to Congress. Its highest returns came from the provinces with a large urban proletariat, Concepción and Santiago.

Great upsets in the 1941 congressional elections were experienced by the National Socialist party, by then in complete disrepute because of the conspiratory activities of González von Marées and the National Falange. The latter, although it mustered 3.5 percent of the national vote, elected only three of its forty-three candidates because it presented candidates in places where the party had little or no support.

The Radical party came out of the elections again as the leading political force in the country with 22 percent of the popular vote (a gain of 3 percent over the results of 1937) and a significant gain of thirteen deputies and one senator. The party obtained pluralities in most of the mining-agricultural provinces of the *Norte Chico* and in all the agricultural provinces south of Linares. The rest of the South was claimed by the Socialists. Thus it appeared that the Radicals had made inroads among small mining entrepreneurs, wheat producers, and also among the bureaucracy in the southern part of the country.

Conservatives and Liberals, the main pillars of the Right, felt the siege by the popular and middle-class parties. While the Conservative party managed to retain its twenty-nine seats in Congress, the Liberal party saw its representation fall from thirty-five to twenty-two deputies. In the Senate these parties lost one and three seats respectively. The Conservatives dropped from 21 percent of the national vote in 1937 to 17 in 1941, and the Liberals from 21 percent to 14. The Conservatives managed to maintain their traditional strength in the agrarian districts of the province of Santiago and in a few of the traditional agricultural provinces of Middle Chile (O'Higgins, Curicó, Talca, Maule, and Linares). The Liberals could keep a firm grip only on the province of Aconcagua, probably because of the personal appeal of Abelardo Pizarro H., a local caudillo of San Felipe. The Democrats, the rightist faction of the Democratic party, emerged from the election with a heavy loss, retaining only two of seven seats, and were ready to be absorbed by one of the giants of the Right. The Agrarians were more fortunate, keeping three seats in the Congress with the support of rightist voters of the provinces of Cautín, Concepción, and Linares.

The congressional elections of 1941 marked the culmination in the development of the progressive forces that started in 1932. During those ten years, a definite shift of the middle and lower-class electorate toward political positions postulated by the Popular Front had taken place, and the Right had seen its political power eroded by a new wave of socialist aspirations. The alliance of parties that emphasized socioeconomic changes had certainly had the positive effect of mobilizing the popular forces and of eliciting an electoral response from them. Consequently, it is not an exaggeration to state that this period in the political history of Chile saw the first attempt by organized forces of the middle and lower classes to seize control of the highest powers in the country through concerted electoral action. The endorsement of socialist postulates by the urban masses and the working class, especially the miners, was particularly important for the future of the popular parties. However, the directive cadres of the Marxist parties misused the salaried classes' mandate and confidence. Instead of closing ranks in their struggle against the oligarchy, the popular parties engaged in competition with each other for the same clientele—the organized unions—and became entangled in internal disputes that led only to estrangement among the Marxist groups and the atomization of ideologically weaker parties.

Chile's electorate in the late 1930s and early 1940s appeared to be ready to support progressive parties in their pursuit of structural changes, but the directive cadres were too busy "playing politics" in the old tradition and were wasting their opportunity to use the mandate of the electorate to effect a real change in the socioeconomic situation of the country. The gradual shift of the Radical party in the direction of more moderate views on socioeconomic change and the tendency of the bourgeois circles of the party to control the radicalism, particularly toward the end of this period, was also significant. Gradually the party abandoned its leftist grass roots to the Socialist and Communist parties and concentrated on the white-collar workers and the bureaucracy that were to become its future clientele. In the years to come, the party was to enter alliances with rightist groups, and this was to lead to the eventual alienation of its supporters in the 1950s.

The Golden Years of the Bourgeoisie: 1942-1952

The world-war economy of the early 1940s had very positive effects on the country. By maintaining a neutral position Chile had managed to avoid severing its relations with the Axis at the same time as it entertained active trade relations with the United States. In this way, it had accumulated a considerable surplus of foreign currency by the end of World War II. However, these favorable conditions of the economy that peaked in 1944-1946 benefited only the upper strata and the growing bureaucracy, whereas the urban proletariat and the rural workers gained little from the flourishing economy. It is not surprising, then, that the Radical party, as the major political force of the country and the indisputable holder of power in both the executive and the legislative, now catered to the bourgeoisie and bureaucracy and gradually moved away from its commitment to the deprived classes that Aguirre Cerda had proclaimed in 1938. The 1940s were no longer the years of popular optimism that the late 1930s had been—they became the halcyon decade for the bourgeoisie of the country.

At the end of 1941 President Aguirre Cerda suddenly fell ill and died within a few weeks. A presidential election was called for February 2, 1942. The first groups to announce their candidate were the former *Ibañistas,* gathered under the banner of the Liberating Popular Alliance, and some Agrarians; they nominated Carlos Ibañez del Campo. This candidacy immediately polarized the Right and the Left. While some Liberals, headed by former President Alessandri, stubbornly opposed Ibañez del Campo, other Liberals and Conservatives endorsed him as the only figure capable of stemming the advances of the Left. The Socialists nominated a patriarch of the party, Oscar Schnake, who could not, however, count on the support of the Communists because of verbal attacks he had leveled at them a few years earlier regarding their subservience to the dictates of Moscow.[25] The Left was severely divided. Within the Radical party two geographically well-defined groups were competing for the nomination of their candidates. On one side the congressmen of the *Norte Chico* pressed for the nomination of the mercurial Gabriel González Videla, a candidate palatable to the Communists, on the other the wealthy farmers of the southern agricultural provinces put forward the name of the moderate Juan A. Ríos.[26] When the latter won the nomination for the Radicals, the Socialists quickly dropped the candidacy of

Schnake and joined them, as did the National Falange, the Agrarians, the Democrats, and the *Alessandrista* faction of the Liberal party. The presidential election coalition of the Democratic Alliance thus came into existence. The Conservative party and the National Socialists had now no choice but to support Ibañez del Campo.

In the quiet election of February 1942, Juan A. Ríos won a comfortable victory with 55.7 percent of the electorate (260,034 votes) against 44 percent (204,635 votes) for Carlos Ibañez del Campo. In the northern provinces the triumph of Ríos was overwhelming with more than 70 percent of the vote. The *Norte Chico* also supported him solidly, as the Radical party strengthened its grip on these agricultural mining provinces (Figure 5). In the four districts of the province of Santiago, Juan A. Ríos secured only a very slight margin, in no case more than 52 percent of the total vote. The neighboring province of O'Higgins also gave the Radical candidate a narrow victory, mainly because of the votes of the El Teniente copper miners. In the agricultural province of Ñuble, where a strong nucleus of radical support had been growing since the presidency of Aguirre Cerda, the official candidate also won with a percentage of 54. In the mining districts of the provinces of Concepción and Arauco, Ríos also made impressive gains: 70 and 94 percent respectively of the total returns. The Radical party had found solid acceptance among the owners of medium-sized landholdings in the southern agricultural provinces, as evidenced by the fact that Ríos won all the recently colonized provinces with the exception of Llanquihue, and the rest of the South as well.

Carlos Ibañez del Campo obtained the highest number of votes in the traditional agricultural provinces of central Chile, with the exception of O'Higgins, but his overall plurality was not impressive since he polled just 50 percent; his best showing was in the province of Colchagua where he reached 61 percent. Because of the strong Socialist vote in 1941, his victory in the urban province of Valparaiso, where he obtained 52 percent of the returns, possibly because of a recovery of the conservative forces of that province, was somewhat unexpected.

An interesting aspect of this presidential contest is the series of mixed feelings that the heterogeneous alliances must have provoked among their participants.[27] For the Communist party it was a matter of sheer convenience to support a candidate like

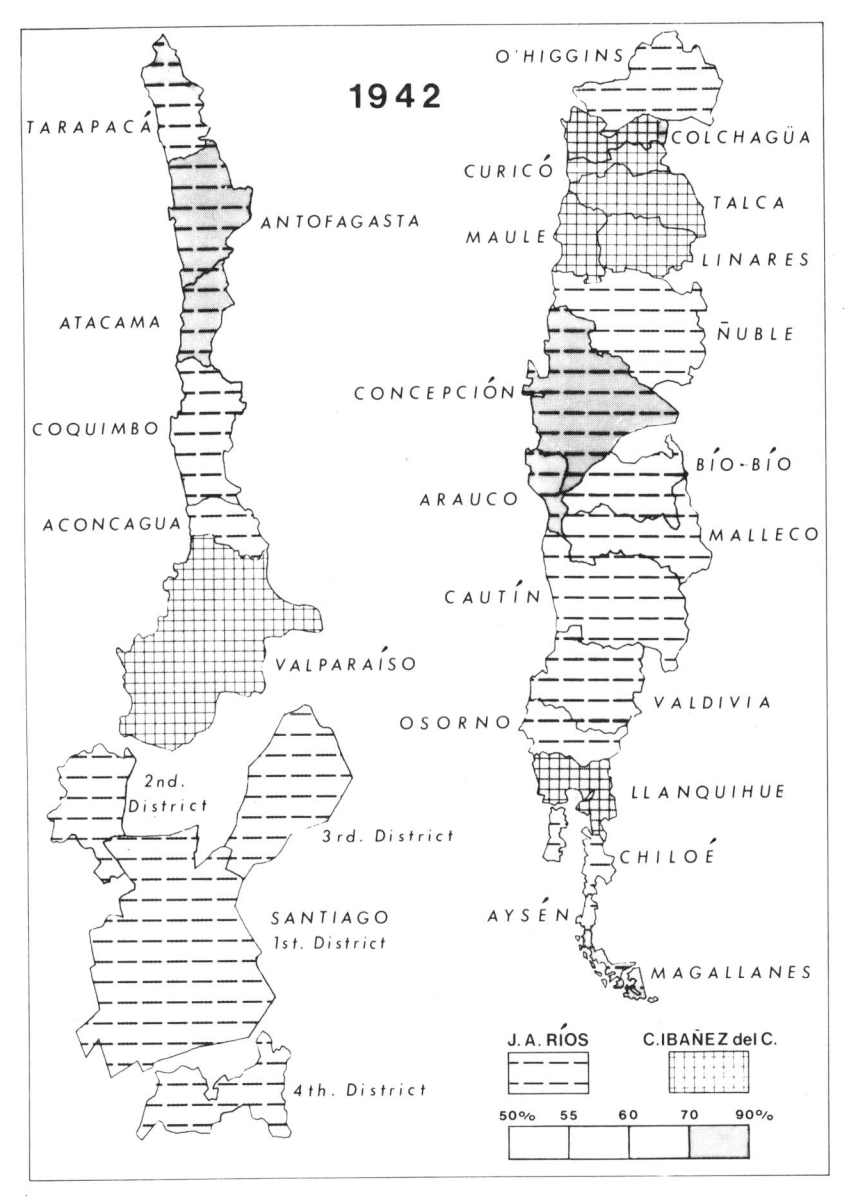

Figure 5.—The presidential election of 1942.

Ríos who had publicly expressed his anti-communist position. It was also with reluctance that they entered an electoral alliance with the *Alessandristas* and with the "reactionary" landowners of the Agrarian party. Ríos's ties with the latter are understandable, since he himself came from an agriculturalist family. Moreover, Ríos had not been popular with the former President Alessandri because of the attack he had launched, while a deputy minister, against Gustavo Ross. Thus, in supporting Ríos, Alessandri chose the lesser of two evils, because he saw in Carlos Ibañez del Campo the man who had provoked his fall from the presidency in 1925. As Federico Gil correctly states, the party alliance that elected Ríos, although made up from the same parties that had triumphed with Aguirre Cerda, was by no means a resurrection of the Popular Front, but only a kind of "marriage of convenience."[28] In the coalition that supported Ibañez del Campo, the Conservatives really did not have great enthusiasm for the man who had tried between 1925 and 1931 in his position as strong man in the executive to humiliate the oligarchy.[29] It was only the presidential election that produced these strange bedfellows.

So it is not surprising that after the election of Juan A. Ríos the centrifugal forces affected not only this circumstantial political marriage, but also each of the participating parties. The years between 1942 and 1945 witnessed indeed the most destructive split that had occurred within the parties in the country since the early 1930s.

The Radical party, now under the firm control of the conservative wing, initially governed with the support of the Socialists; but when the latter withdrew because of internal conflicts, the former began to cut its ties with the popular parties and to look to nonpartisans and even to politicians of centrist-rightist leanings to keep the government operating. This move was to bring about the final breach between rightists and leftists, which led to the secession of the rightists and the formation of the Democratic Radical party in 1946.[30] The Liberals continued the separation that had occurred on the eve of the 1942 elections, and while the majority agreed to cooperate with the government of President Ríos, a faction called the Progressive Liberals decided to remain aloof from the mainstream of the party. Nor was there complete harmony within the Conservative party. As in the 1930s, a group with progressive social ideas had started to gather and finally moved away from the party in 1948 under Eduardo Cruz Coke.[31]

But it was within the Socialist party that the wave of dissension was to produce the greatest damage. Marmaduke Grove's acquiescence to collaboration with the Radical government was particularly criticized by Salvador Allende and Raúl Ampuero, two young and ambitious leaders of the Socialist party who in January of 1943 had started to challenge the leadership of the legendary figure. In the following year the old leader, besieged by the young Socialists, left the party with some of his more faithful followers and formed the Authentic Socialist party, a party that did not, however, survive the congressional elections of 1949.[32] This withdrawal did not render the remaining segment of the Socialist party immune to schism, and in 1948 it was to suffer perhaps its most devastating split.

Only the Communists, by capitalizing on their inroads among organized labor and constantly keeping the Radical government in check, maintained their unity intact and entered a period of rapid expansion. This was accomplished at the expense of the debilitated Socialist party, which, because of internal disputes, was not able to keep a firm grip on the labor movement, its clientele since the late 1930s.

In the municipal elections of 1944 the Radical party emerged as a solid winner gathering 24 percent of the national vote, an improvement of 2 percent over 1941. Second came the Conservatives who, taking advantage of the division among the Liberals, garnered 22 percent of the vote and swept not only rural but also some urban municipalities. The Socialist party, which obtained only 8 percent of the total vote, experienced the major setback in the elections, which was as expected because of the crisis it was going through. But the worst was yet to come.

The issues in the congressional elections of 1945 were threefold: first, the Radical party tried to convince the voters that its government had brought institutional and economic stability to the country; second, a momentarily unified Right denounced the Radical government for being too lenient with the spread of Communism among workers unions and opposing the patronage of the Radicals over the civil servants; and third, the Communist party, now the most powerful party of the Left, embarked on a campaign of expansion based on its criticism of the bourgeois leanings of the Radical government and on the split among the Socialists. The political forces in between these three main currents had no ideological influence in the election, and this the returns confirmed.

Winners, in terms of both the popular vote and representatives elected, were the Conservative and Liberal parties with 23.6 and 18 percent of the total vote respectively. The gains of the Conservatives were impressive as they increased their representation from twenty-nine to thirty-six deputies, although they lost one seat in the Senate. The Liberals increased their representation in the Congress from twenty-two to thirty-one; and in the Senate from eight to ten. Unlike the 1941 election, the Conservatives won all the traditional agricultural provinces of central Chile, from Aconcagua to Ñuble, including the urban provinces of Valparaíso and Santiago (Figure 6). The Liberals were victorious in the province of Coquimbo, where the appeal of two emerging figures, Hugo Zepeda and Raúl Marín Balmaceda, counteracted the Radical hegemony over the province that was based on the prestige of Gabriel González Videla. Also to the Liberals fell the province of Malleco. Thus the Right made its comeback as had been anticipated by the returns of the 1944 municipal elections.

The Radical party came second in the elections, dropping from 22 percent in 1941 to 20 percent in 1945. Five of its forty-four representatives in Congress lost their seats and one in the Senate. The southern agricultural provinces, with the exception of Malleco, remained loyal to the Radical party, proving that the economic measures taken by Juan A. Ríos had found a good reception among his peers, the southern agriculturists.[33] In the North, only the mining province of Atacama—the cradle of radicalism— endorsed the Radical candidates.

All the mining provinces in the extreme North and Concepción returned majorities for the Communist party, which, however, saw its national percentage of 12 in 1941 drop to 10. While the Communists lost one deputy, they gained one senator. Their strength in the northern provinces is attested by the fact that they won two of the five senatorial seats in the provincial grouping of Tarapacá and Antofagasta. One of the seats was won by the patriarch of Communism, Elías Lafferte, the other by the poet Pablo Neruda.

Decimating losses hit both factions of the Socialists. The

179

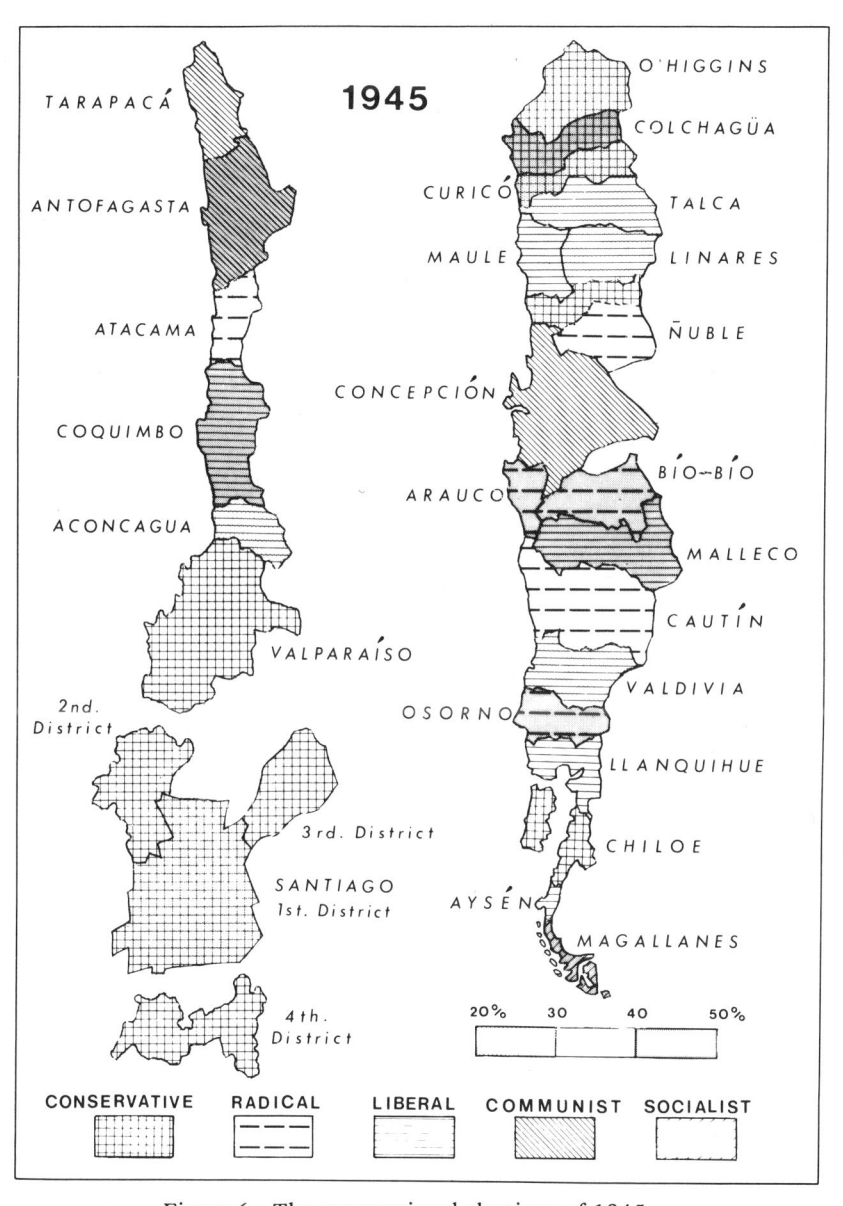

Figure 6.—The congressional elections of 1945.

Authentic Socialist party, which had presented sixty-one candidates, elected only three of them as the party polled only 5.5 percent of the popular vote. Marmaduke Grove, still holding his senatorial seat, became the leader of a "ghost" party.[34] The mainstream of the Socialists fared little better. Out of twenty-nine candidates they elected only six, and their national percentage was a pale 7 percent as compared with the 17 percent obtained in 1941. In the Senate the Socialist factions retained two seats each. Their most serious losses occurred in the urban provinces of Santiago and Valparaíso, where their former supporters seemed to have deserted them for the rightist parties. The Conservatives lost the province of Colchagua, whereas the provinces of Valdivia and Llanquihue shifted from the Socialists to the Radicals. The only province to provide some consolation for the battered Socialists was Magallanes with its only deputy. The Left had suffered a dramatic setback due to the contraction of the Socialists, although the Communists were able to conserve their popular support.

Of the other parties, only epigones of the three main currents on the political scene, the Democratic party and the Agrarian party, came out of the elections with their forces intact, each of them with three deputies and two senators. The Democratic party recovered in Santiago's First District and in the province of Concepción with the influence of some local labor leaders who were party members while the Agrarians continued to be strong among the landowners of the province of Cautín. The National Falange retained its three deputies, although its percentage dropped from 3.4 in 1941 to 2.6 in 1945.

Thus, in a fashion that has occurred repeatedly in the political history of the country during the twentieth century, the electoral gains attained by parties were senselessly wasted through internal disputes and did not result in positive parliamentary action on behalf of the social groups that had supported them. Parties like the Socialist of the early 1940s, which were not properly prepared for the highest powers of the nation, were doomed to lose quickly their electoral advantages as they became entangled in the treacherous and futile skirmishes that were so common in Congress and in the executive. Further, the congressional elections of 1945 made it clear to those who believed in the decline of the Right that Conservatives and Liberals could recuperate lost ground and capitalize on any dissensions among their rivals. This was to reoccur in the next decades against the predictions of all those who thought that the political Right was extinct.

The opportunity for the Right to test the strength of its clientele's support came in 1946 when President Juan A. Ríos succumbed to a short but fatal illness. In July of that year, Conservatives, Liberals, and Agrarians gathered in a convention to decide on a candidate from a slate of three nominees: the old Arturo Alessandri for the Liberals, the Social Christian Eduardo Cruz Coke for the Conservatives, and the aristocratic landowner Jaime Larraín for the Agrarians. The Liberals and Conservatives each tried to impose on the others their own candidate based on the argument that each of them had been received well by the voters in the 1945 election. The convention was thus doomed, and by misusing its newly regained support from the electorate the divided Right embarked on a fruitless campaign to seize control of the executive in the coming presidential election.[35]

By the end of July the left wing of the Radicals proclaimed the candidacy of Gabriel González Videla and immediately obtained the support of the Communist party. The Conservatives and the Falange reacted by officially nominating Eduardo Cruz Coke. Liberals, rightist Radicals, Agrarians, Democrats, and Authentic Socialists endorsed the candidacy of Fernando Alessandri, a son of Arturo, who had withdrawn his nomination in favor of his son. Totally isolated on the Left the Socialist party nominated Bernardo Ibañez, a labor leader, as its candidate for the presidential contest.

With a divided Right, the triumph of Gabriel González Videla became assured, and the only question to be answered by the election was the number of votes that he would obtain, because that would determine whether the *congreso pleno,* in the control of his opponents, would confirm his election or appoint the second majority candidate. On September 4, 1946, Gabriel González Videla obtained 40 percent of the votes cast, and in second place (rather unexpectedly) came the candidate of the Catholics, Cruz Coke, with 29 percent. His second finish was a surprise, because according to the returns of the Conservatives and Falange in the 1945 congressional elections, he was not expected to pass the 24 percent mark. The great loser was clearly Eduardo Alessandri, whose political alliance had been expected to reach 37 percent;

instead he obtained a poor 26 percent. The Socialists under Bernardo Ibañez received another proof of their advanced stage of decline in that they attracted only 2.5 percent of the electorate, a significant drop of 4.7 percent compared with the returns in the congressional elections of the previous year.

The Radical and Communist alliance swept all the provinces of the mining North and of the *Norte Chico,* and carried the urban districts in the province of Santiago as well (Figure 7). In the province of Antofagasta, Gabriel González Videla obtained 70 percent of the votes, which was an impressive shift of the electorate toward Democratic Socialism and Communism. The agricultural province of Curicó also gave a slight margin to the Radicals showing that it was relatively independent from the grip of the Right. Concepción and Arauco were won by the Radical-Communist candidate without difficulty. But the agricultural provinces of recent colonization, where the moderate faction of the Radicals had been so dominant during the Juan A. Ríos administration, supported Eduardo Alessandri. Only the province of Valdivia went to the left wing of the Radicals as did the provinces of the extreme South.

As expected, the candidate of the Conservatives did well in the traditional agricultural provinces from O'Higgins to Ñuble. Only Curicó, which went to the Radicals, and Maule, won by Eduardo Alessandri, disrupted the Conservative hegemony over that part of central Chile. The province of Valparaíso, again displaying its preference for the Conservatives, gave the first majority to Cruz Coke. His triumph in that province had been anticipated since the Conservatives and the National Falange had received 36 percent of the provincial vote in the 1945 electoral returns. Continuing their trend as Conservative strongholds the provinces of Llanquihue and Chiloé gave Cruz Coke the plurality.

The coalition that supported Fernando Alessandri and that appeared the strongest came first only in the agrarian provinces where the bases of the moderate Radicals and the Agrarians were solid. The province of Coquimbo, which had shown liberal preference in the 1945 election, succumbed this time to the appeal of González Videla, a native of that province.

For the Socialists the results throughout the nation were catastrophic. In Magallanes, the province that gave them the highest percentage (17), Bernardo Ibañez received only 948 from the

183

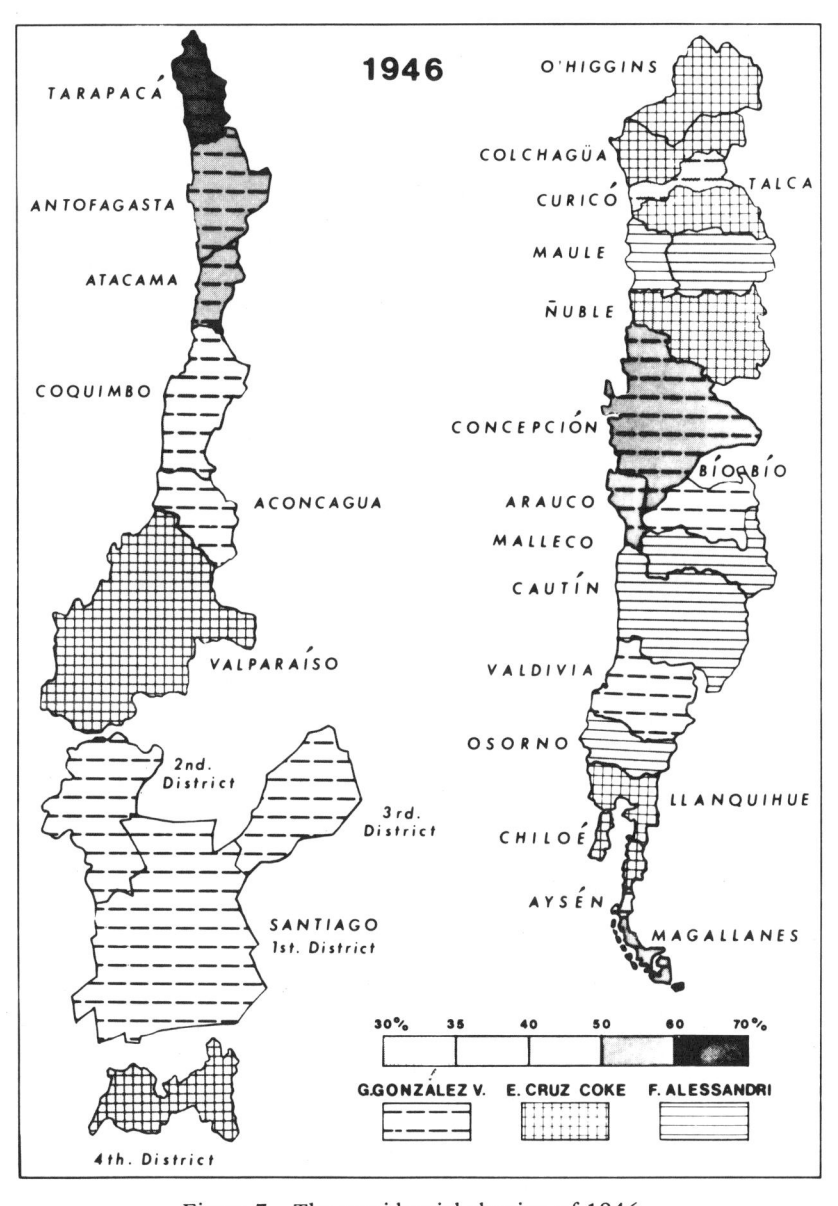

Figure 7.—The presidential election of 1946.

total of 5,530 votes cast. In the mining provinces of the North, the highest mark they could reach was in Atacama with 6.2 percent of the provincial vote. In none of the four districts of the province of Santiago did Ibañez surpass the 4.5 percent mark.

As soon as it became evident that it was the election of Gabriel González Videla that was to be confirmed by Congress, the right-wing Radicals rushed to support the winner to share the ride on his bandwagon. The Liberals followed suit thus tipping the balance of power and ensuring González Videla's proclamation by the *congreso pleno*. This concentration of political forces had the double effect of dividing the Left even more than before the election and of isolating the Conservatives on the Right.

Alone on the Left, the Socialist party continued to lose popular support and to be torn by internal disputes. The Communists, now in the government, used all their influence to cater to organized labor, estranging this electoral clientele further from the Socialists. In December of 1946 the unbearable situation the Socialist party faced regarding the increasing control of the Communists over organized labor precipitated the total rupture of relations between the two and led to a split within the Confederation of Workers (CTCH).[36]

In the next electoral contest, the municipal elections of 1947, the indisputable winners were the Communists who doubled their 1944 returns and amassed 16 percent of the national vote. Liberals and Conservatives reached their 1944 totals but polled a smaller vote than in the congressional elections of 1945. The Radicals maintained their 1945 level: 20 percent of the national vote. It was not without apprehension, however, that they had been observing the steady growth of the Communist clientele, especially among organized labor, so that González Videla finally decided to break with the Communists and to govern with the support of the Radicals alone. On April 16, 1947, he asked for the resignation of his three Liberal and three Communist ministers. This move relegated the Communists to the opposition where they immediately started to mobilize the unions (coal miners, nitrate miners, port workers, and construction workers) in an open challenge to the government.[37] The confrontation between the Radical president and the Communist party reached its peak during a strike of the coal miners of Lota in the province of Concepción. In August of 1947, using extraordinary powers approved by the acquiescent

Radicals, Conservatives, and Liberals, President González Videla set out to settle the unrest of the unions. The Socialists, sensing the opportunity to deprive the Communists of their control of the unions, volunteered their help.[38]

It was now the Communists' turn to become beleaguered. By March of 1948, when the government of Chile had broken relations with the Soviet Union, Yugoslavia, and Czechoslovakia for their alleged intervention in the nation's internal affairs, González Videla was determined to eliminate the Communist party as a political organization. Thus in July 1948, with the backing of the Radicals, Liberals, Conservatives, Agrarians, and Authentic Socialists, and opposed only by the Communists and a small group of Socialists, the "Law for the Permanent Defense of Democracy" was passed by Congress. In September 1948 the Communist party was outlawed, its major directives were relegated to remote corners of the Republic, Communist labor leaders were demoted, and the newspaper *El Siglo* was closed down.[39] Except for a protest by some Socialists, the proscription of the Communist party was received by the public with a certain indifference, as the party had gained a reputation of troublemaker, and from its endorsement of Moscow's Communism, people assumed that the party did not disapprove of the state takeovers that had occurred in many prewar democracies of Eastern Europe. Among those who reacted against the prohibition of the Communist party was the Socialist group headed by Salvador Allende and Raúl Ampuero, who, with their supporters, moved away from the mainstream of socialism and adopted the name of the Popular Socialist party. The remainder, mainly old-guard leaders headed by Bernardo Ibañez and Juan B. Rossetti, continued with the traditional line of the party under the name of the Socialist Party of Chile. Resentful of their loss of popular support because of the offensive of the Communists since the early 1940s, this group welcomed the banning of the Communists.[40] After this move against the Communists, the president turned to the Conservatives and Liberals to run the country in a coalition called the "Government of National Concentration." The thrust of the opposition now fell to the Falange, the Agrarians, the Socialists, and some Doctrinarian Radicals, who formed an alliance referred to as the Social Action Front (FRAS).[41]

By the end of 1948 after all the internal stir caused by the banning of the Communist party, the country embarked once again on an electoral campaign that was to culminate in the congressional elections of March 1949. Eighteen different political groups registered candidates for the contest. That high number reflects the numerous splits that had affected all major parties during the administration of González Videla. One branch torn away from Radicalism had formed a small group called the Doctrinarian Radicals; the Social Christian faction of the Conservatives had finally separated but kept the original name of that party, while the aristocratic sector of the party, willing to collaborate with the government of González Videla, had adopted the name of Traditionalist Conservative party. The Socialists went into the elections as two separate groups plus the Authentic Socialist party of Marmaduke Grove. The Democratic party had also suffered a schism when a minority faction in Santiago formed the People's Democratic party. The Liberal party was still separated from the Liberal Progressive party, the branch that had split in 1942. Fragmentation was the name of the political situation at the end of the 1940s.

Notwithstanding the unsteady course of the Radicals in the previous three years, they won the 1949 elections with 22 percent of the total vote, thirty-four deputies, and thirteen senators. Their best returns came from the northern provinces and the *Norte Chico*. In the province of Santiago the Radicals obtained a plurality in the populous Third District, and they also led in the provinces of Ñuble and Concepción, probably because of the Communists' absence. In the southern part of Middle Chile the Radicals regained the province of Llanquihue (Figure 8).

The Traditionalist Conservatives obtained 21 percent of the popular vote, which elected twenty-one deputies, and retained their six seats in the upper Chamber. The party achieved its best results in the traditional agricultural provinces from O'Higgins to Talca and in the rural province of Chiloé.[42] The Conservatives of Social-Christian orientation had good returns in the urban provinces of Valparaíso and Santiago, where their reformist views held more appeal than among the easily bribed peasants in the agricultural provinces. The Liberals won in the provinces of recent colonization, apparently because the Agrarians and Radicals were losing ground after nearly ten years of dominance. They did well in the provinces of Tarapacá and Coquimbo, where they came

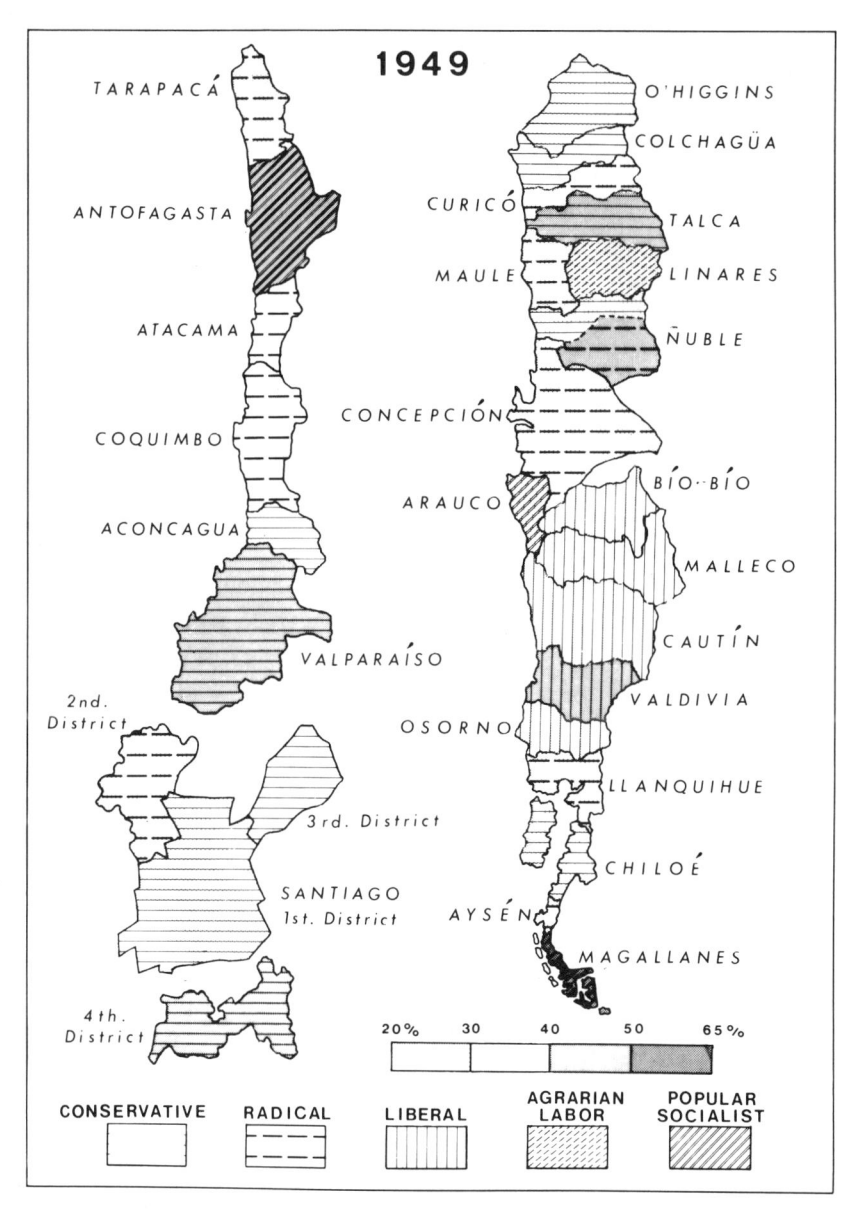

Figure 8.—The congressional elections of 1949.

second after the Radicals, and also obtained high returns in the traditional agricultural provinces of central Chile. The former Agrarians entered the elections merged with a group of Ibañez del Campo supporters under the name of Agrarian Laborites and gained a plurality in the agricultural province of Linares; they also made a showing in Santiago's Second and Third districts, as well as in the provinces of Ñuble and Bío-Bío. The upsurge of this group, backed by influential agricultural entrepreneurs, appeared to be in response to a growing dissatisfaction among landowners who, disenchanted with the traditional parties, were preparing to launch Carlos Ibañez del Campo as candidate for the presidential election of 1952.

The Popular Socialist party elected only six deputies and one senator. Its highest returns came from the provinces of Antofagasta and Arauco, where it received the support of an electoral clientele that had favored the Communist party in previous elections. In the provinces of Magallanes, the Popular Socialists retained the province's only seat. The other faction of the Socialists gathered only 3.4 percent of the vote and they elected five deputies. If one adds the six deputies obtained by the Popular Socialists, the representation reached by all the Socialist branches had improved by two deputies over the congressional elections of 1945. However, it must be remembered that many of the votes that went to the Popular Socialists came from the orphan clientele of the Communists, so that their showing continued to be very poor.

Among the minority parties the best results were obtained by the Democratic party, which elected three deputies in the First District of Santiago. The National Falange raised its percentage from 2.6 in 1945 to 3.9 in 1949, retaining its three deputy seats and electing Eduardo Frei as its only senator.

The results of this last election of the 1940s revealed the extent of the political changes that had occurred during the decade. Throughout the 1940s the Radical party had proven to be the first political force in the country, but its ideological foundations had changed remarkably. At the beginning of the decade the party exhibited a definitely popular flavor that had won many supporters from the proletariat and the lower middle class and had given strength to the Popular Front. In 1941 Radicals, Socialists, and Communists, together representing 57 percent of the electorate, had managed to corner the Right and had the popular support that augured structural changes in the country. However, the chance to carry out the socioeconomic reforms the voters expected from the parties of the Popular Front was missed, as Socialists and Communists quarreled and as the Radical party had moved toward the moderate and even conservative position that characterized its last ten years in the executive.

By the end of the 1940s the Radical party had clearly become a bourgeois party. Its alliance with Liberals and Conservatives had tilted the balance of power to the other extreme of the political spectrum. After the congressional elections of 1949 it was the Right and the Radicals who, with 61 percent of the total vote, isolated the other parties in a defensive opposition. Further, the enjoyment of power contributed to the ideological metamorphosis of the Radicals from a popular party into a political group controlled by individuals deeply involved in financial activities and sharing interests in common with the landowner class. The socioeconomic transformation of the directive cadres of the party is exemplified by the career of President González Videla himself, who, having been a socialist Radical in the 1930s, turned into a bourgeois while heading the government.

The contention that the late 1940s are to be regarded as the halcyon years of the bourgeoisie is substantiated not only by the notorious economic profits made by the plutocratic strata of the country,[43] but also by the extent of political influence regained by the oligarchic parties. In fact in the municipal elections of 1950 the Conservatives received 26 percent of the vote, the Radicals 23 percent, and the Liberals 16 percent. Only 36 percent were shared by the other parties. Of this, 10 percent went to the various Socialist groups and 4 percent to the National Falange. The Right was having a windfall.

Political Messianism: 1952-1964

The period that stretches from the early 1950s into the mid-1960s is characterized by a weakening of the monopoly of the political parties and a turning of the electorate toward nonpartisan public figures who were perceived as alternatives to discredited political parties. The election of Carlos Ibañez del Campo and Jorge Alessandri was an expression of the disenchantment of the voters. Nevertheless, as these "saviors" also failed to solve the chronic economic and social problems of the country, the political establishment had another opportunity to respond to the demands of the electorate. This time, however, the renaissance of the political parties was based on ideological arguments and not on short-term prescriptions for economic and social well-being.

During the last years of González Videla's administration, the dissensions and alliances of convenience, designed with the sole purpose of sharing the executive power, involved almost all organized political groups. The Radical party, controlled by a central executive committee completely in the hands of the bourgeoisie (bankers, entrepreneurs, and landowners) became increasingly detached from the popular basis and isolated itself in the top ranks of the party. Liberals and Conservatives withdrew from the government and were replaced by Social Christian Conservatives, Falangists, and Democrats in a cabinet that was referred to as the "Cabinet of Social Sensibility."[44] This political combination in the executive exposed the Radical party as frivolous and opportunist, prepared to recruit support from any quarter in order to stay in power. Such alliances discredited all the participants to just the same extent as the economy continued to deteriorate.

Within the Socialist and Communist parties the situation was not less bleak. The Socialists were as divided as ever. Their party continued to cooperate with the administration of Gabriel González Videla, while the Socialist Popular party remained in a position of rather unsustained opposition to the government. Within the Communist party, now underground, there had also developed two diverging currents. One, led by Luis Reinoso and Daniel Palma, advocated an active clandestinity, which involved terrorism and armed insurrection, while the hierarchy of the party, with Galo Gonzalez at its head, preferred to keep a low profile and hoped for an early reestablishment of the party to legality. As usual, the struggle between the two factions was resolved by the central committee purging the violent elements in 1950.[45]

Under these circumstances of political disarray it was not difficult for the supporters of Carlos Ibañez del Campo to launch his presidential campaign on an electoral platform that promised political purification and the rule of a populist government. The main organization behind his candidacy was the Agrarian Laborite party, whose ideological postulates blended elements of nationalism, puritanism, and populism with subtle touches of fascism. As expressed by the leaders of the movement, their political commitment was the fight against internationalist doctrines such as Freemasonry, Marxism, and Christian socialism, which had penetrated the country to exploit the Chilean people after the withdrawal of the Castilian-Basque aristocracy from public functions.[46] But ideological postulates were not even necessary, now that the populace was tired of promises and longing for a strong leader who would remove incapable politicians and finally undertake some positive action on behalf of the deprived masses. Such motivation explains why authoritarian figures, who had never been accepted by the political establishment and had been distrusted by the electorate, saw opening before them a political avenue that had not been tried before: authoritarian populism.[47] In the atmosphere of general political disrepute there was little the traditional parties could do against the mounting *Ibañista* wave. However, encouraged by the returns of the 1950 municipal election and committing again the inexcusable mistake of taking that electoral support for granted, the Right nominated Arturo Matte and the Radicals Pedro E. Alfonso as their presidential candidates. On the Left, the Socialist Party of Chile and the outlawed Communists presented, for the first time, Salvador Allende. This prominent leader of the Popular Socialist party had returned to the Socialist party (which had now relinquished its avowed anticommunist stand) when Raúl Ampuero's Popular Socialists endorsed with enthusiasm the candidacy of Ibañez del Campo.[48] Once again the Socialists exhibited their political versatility in establishing political alliances just as if such alliances had not already caused enough trouble within the party and had not estranged so many of its electoral clientele during the 1940s.

The results of the September 1952 presidential election saw Ibañez del Campo an easy winner (46.8 percent of the popular vote) over the rightist Arturo Matte (27.8 percent). Alfonso of the Radicals received 20 percent, and Salvador Allende came in last with 5.5 percent of the national vote.

Ibañez del Campo's victory was spread over the whole North, in the urban provinces of Middle Chile, and in the agricultural provinces of recent colonization (Figure 9). In none of the northern provinces were his returns lower than 40 percent, and in urban Santiago and Valparaíso he received more than half of the total vote. The province of Magallanes gave Ibañez del Campo his

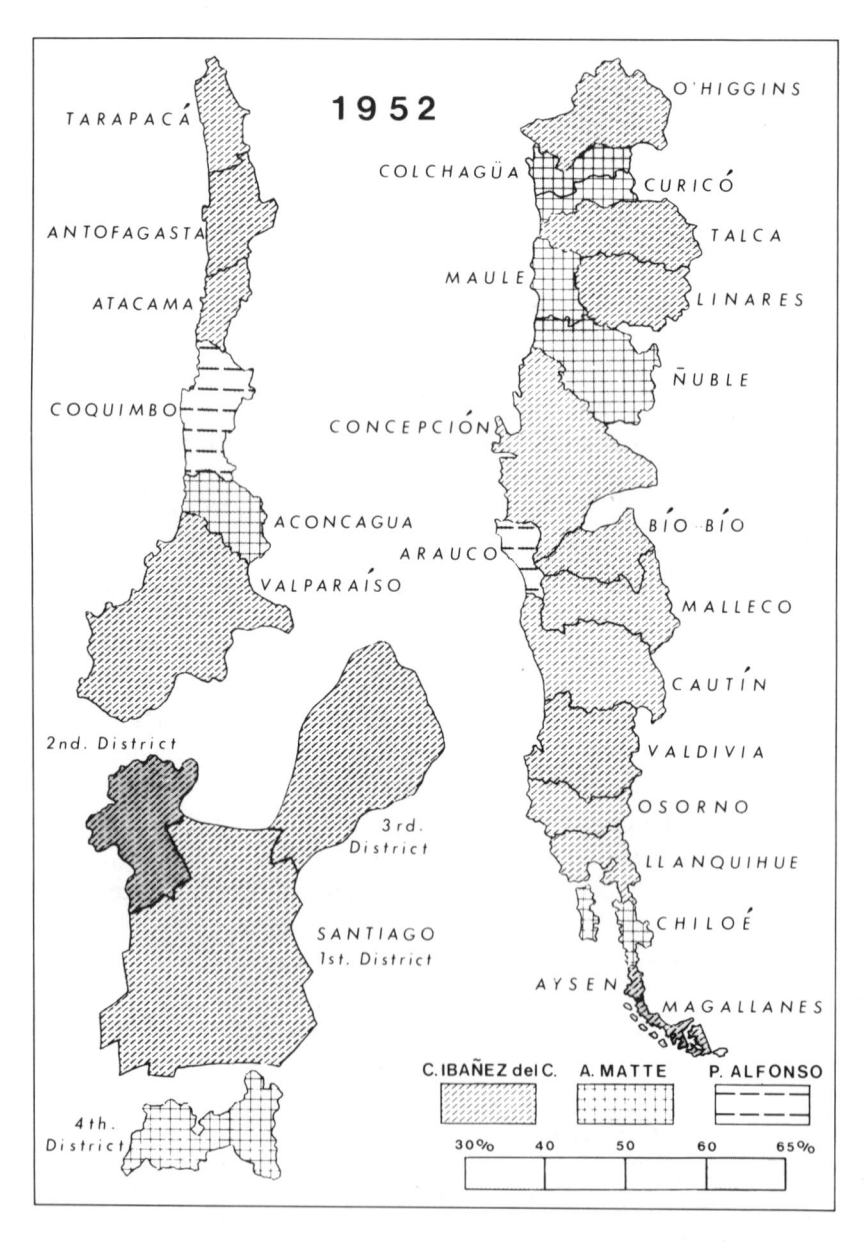

Figure 9.—The presidential election of 1952.

strongest support, 65 percent of the total provincial vote. From these results it is clear that the former dictator received heterogeneous backing, including the workers of the northern provinces, the urban-industrial masses of the country's center, the agricultural entrepreneurs of the South, and the rural proletariat of some of the traditional agricultural provinces (O'Higgins, Talca, and Linares). What the *Ibañista* landslide proved to the country was that, notwithstanding the existence of a well-developed party system and party politics, none of the parties could count on the electorate's unconditional acceptance of options offered by the political establishment and that charismatic leaders could magnetize a large mass of noncommitted voters.[49] To substantiate this last contention, the actual results can be compared with those forecast for each of the four contestants in the 1952 presidential election as computed from the results of the 1949 congressional and 1950 municipal elections. On this basis Arturo Matte was expected to get 42 percent of the vote, Pedro E. Alfonso 38 percent, Ibañez del Campo 14 percent, and Salvador Allende 4 percent.[50] The inaccuracy of the forecast stemmed from the fact that one-third of the electorate was not bound to any particular political party and thus could decide the outcome of an election. This was a fact of political life that the parties had to take into account if they wanted to recover their lost strength.

The Right obtained pluralities in the agricultural provinces of Aconcagua, Colchagua, Curicó, Maule, and Ñuble and also retained the province of Chiloé. With the exception of Colchagua (52.8 percent for Matte), in none of the agricultural provinces did the rightist candidate get more than 42 percent. These figures showed that the political Right no longer enjoyed unchallenged control over agricultural Chile. Matte came second in the province of Coquimbo, close behind the Radicals, owing to the strong appeal of the Liberals. In the urban provinces, the Right maintained second place, but far behind Ibañez del Campo.

For the Radicals, the presidential contest was the first blow in a series that they were to suffer in the future. Pedro E. Alfonso came first in the province of Coquimbo where the Radical vote had increased dramatically during the administration of Gabriel González Videla. The province of Arauco, where public employees and the lower middle class had remained loyal to the Radicals, also gave plurality to Alfonso. But these were the only two provinces the Radicals could salvage from the eight they had held in the congressional elections of 1949. In the provinces of the North, Alfonso ran second, again far behind Ibañez del Campo. In general, the outlook for the Radicals was grim, and these results were to indicate only the beginning of the decay of the party as a dominant political force in the country.

Despite the discouragingly low returns for Salvador Allende, there were some positive signs in the results for the Socialists of Chile and the Communists. Although the winner, Ibañez del Campo, exerted a great attraction over the working class in the northern provinces as well as in Concepción and Arauco, there was still close to 10 percent of the electorate in these provinces who resisted the *Ibañista* wave and voted for the Marxist candidate. The appeal of the Left was apparently lost, however, in the urban provinces of Valparaíso and Santiago, where Allende obtained no more than 7 percent of the provincial vote. The highest return for Allende came from the province of Arauco, still a poor 15 percent.

After his landslide victory, Ibañez del Campo conducted as president a widely advertised, though not greatly effective, campaign against inflation and speculation on food commodities. Measures to implement this increased the political momentum of *Ibañismo* so much that the windfall in its favor was expressed by the motto "A Parliament for Ibañez" during the electoral campaign that precluded the congressional elections of March 1953.

The social forces that rallied behind the former dictator consisted of an amorphous conglomerate of populist groups, each led by momentary caudillos who drew their electoral clientele from the established parties and ran under a banner of administrative correction and austerity. The political demands of each group were quite different and at times conflicted with one another.[51] There were fascists, feminist revindicationists, militarists, nationalists, and even fanatic leaders of religious groups. All these elements made *Ibañismo* very colorful indeed, but politically ineffective as each group strove for the fulfillment of its specific aspirations or depended on its respective caudillo to obtain favors from the government.

Twelve traditional parties and sixteen different *Ibañista* groups entered the congressional contest that proved to be as expected a resounding triumph for the supporters of the aging president. The Agrarian Laborite party, the main pillar of the new government, emerged from the election with twenty-five deputies, five senators, and 15 percent of the national vote. These results made this party the major organized political force of the moment. The diverse *Ibañista* factions obtained more votes than the Agrarian Laborites, 21 percent, but because of the complications of the dividing-number system, they elected only twenty-five deputies. After years of trying to secure an electoral elientele, the association of the Popular Socialist party with the victorious *Ibañismo* yielded gratifying political rewards to these Socialists, as they seized 8.3 percent of the popular vote, elected six deputies, and obtained one seat in the Senate. On the whole, the government candidates were supported by 40 percent of the national electorate (included in this figure are the votes of other small groups that supported Ibañez del Campo's government) and obtained a majority in the lower Chamber with seventy-five deputies. With catastrophic consequences for the government, the Senate as usual stayed in control of the opposition made up by Radicals, Conservatives, Liberals and the National Falange.

The electoral returns indicated that the wave of *Ibañismo* was very strong in the urban industrialized provinces of Middle Chile (Valparaíso, Santiago, and Concepción) as well as in the agricultural provinces of recent colonization (Figure 10). The province of Magallanes, a stronghold of the Popular Socialist party, also yielded to the government forces. It is significant that the urban-mining provinces of the North as well as certain provinces in the agricultural core of the country withdrew their support of Ibañez del Campo. The important implication of this trend is that in all the provinces where the support for him had been a spontaneous response from masses of dissatisfied urban and nonorganized workers, the populist movement, fostered by the former dictator, continued its momentum; whereas in the provinces with militant and organized workers (the North) and in the provinces dominated by traditional landowners (the agricultural core of the country), the caudillos if *Ibañismo* were unable to capitalize on the charismatic attraction of their leader.

Among the ranks of the opposition the Radical party suffered the greatest losses as it collected only 14 percent of the national vote and saw its deputy representation drop from thirty-four to nineteen. In the Senate they retained ten seats. Their pluralities of past elections were lost almost everywhere, and only the

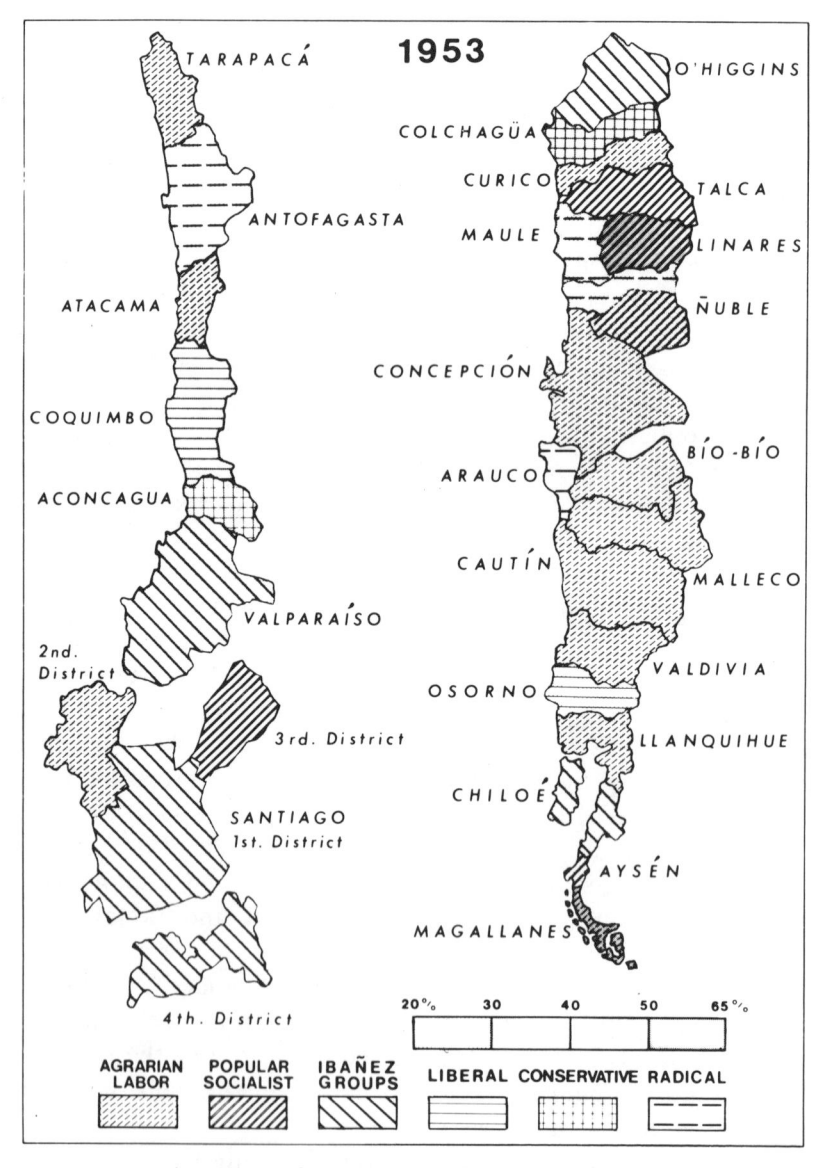

Figure 10.—The congressional elections of 1953.

province of Maule and one district in Ñuble provided some comfort to this beleaguered party.

The results of the 1953 elections were less catastrophic for the Liberal party, which, with 10.5 percent of the vote, was still able to elect twenty-three deputies (ten fewer than in 1949) and eleven senators. The party showed particular strength in the province of Coquimbo, where it took over the leadership from the Radicals. In the northern provinces, as well as in the provinces of recent colonization, the party came second. It proved to have no appeal at all in the urban industrialized provinces. The Conservatives, divided into Traditionalists and Social Christians, obtained 14.5 percent of the national vote, but elected only eighteen deputies and six senators. The drop from the 1949 returns was 7.7 percent with a loss of fifteen deputies. Of the provinces commonly under the control of the Conservatives, only Colchagua remained in the fold. They had just one first-time victory in the agricultural-mining province of Aconcagua. As in the case of the Liberals, support for the Conservatives from urban voters weakened considerably.

The Socialist Party of Chile, which had done so poorly with Allende as presidential candidate in 1952, emerged from the 1953 elections with increased vigor. The party improved its deputy representation from five to nine and was able to match the appeal of the Popular Socialist party in the northern province of Tarapacá as well as in the First District of Santiago. The total vote for the two factions of the Socialists reached 12.5 percent, an optimistic sign of recovery for the Socialists, notwithstanding the wave of populism that the *Ibañismo* had introduced into the country.

Smaller groups like the Democratic party and the National Falange met the *Ibañista* thrust with difficulty and were fortunate to keep their deputies and senators in the Congress. These two parties seemed to have a faithful clientele that roughly equalled the number of registered members. The Democrats had chief support in the provinces of Concepción, Arauco, and Ñuble, while the Falange continued to draw its strength from among urban minorities in Antofagasta, Santiago, and Valdivia.

Even though Ibañez del Campo was supported by the populace and enjoyed a majority in the Chamber of Deputies, he still had to cope with a strong opposition in the Senate. Throughout his term in office he, or his ministers, constantly came under fire from the upper House, which tried by all means to subdue the stubborn personality of Ibañez and to demonstrate to him the power of the political establishment over mavericks. On the other hand, Ibañez del Campo offered Congress, right from the start, many targets. Among the first issues for the Senate to attack was the badly concealed help the *Ibañista* electoral coffers had received from Argentina's "justicialist" movement and the too obvious ideological concurrences between Juan Perón and Ibañez del Campo. Feelings of uneasiness had grown strong in Chile as Peronism was developing in Argentina not only as a social doctrine, but also as a military and expansionist regime.[52] These ill feelings and suspicions provided considerable ammunition for attacks by Radical senators, particularly Isauro Torres and Exequiel González Madariaga, who became vocal denouncers of the Argentinean infiltration into the ranks of Ibañez del Campo. As a consequence of this linkage, María de la Cruz, the histrionic leader of the Feminist Party of Chile, was ousted from the upper House by the senators in the opposition.[53]

Another target of the opposition's attacks was the much too obvious contact the ex-dictator had entertained and still retained as president of the Republic with certain "deliberative" military characters. It was an open secret that Ibañez del Campo had never abandoned his intention of subduing the political establishment with military support. The *Ariostazo* in 1939 and the "plot of Colliguay" during the administration of González Videla had radiated a touch of his conspiratory spirit,[54] and this made him vulnerable. During his term in office, leading figures of the military again adopted a very "deliberative" attitude and appeared willing to use their power to support the president in his struggle against the political establishment. Within the military influential officers had founded a lodge, known as *Linea Recta* ("the Straight Line"), which, once its existence leaked out, prompted an alacritous denouncement from the politicians and a congressional investigation.[55] The president's proclivity to use military commanders on active service to solve the frequent ministerial crises that were created either by dissensions among the *Ibañista* forces or by attacks of the Congress complicated his stand further before the Senate.

Although, after the congressional elections of 1953, President Ibañez del Campo had obtained control over the lower Chamber with three deputies more than the opposition, the flight to Venezuela of the *Ibañista* deputy "Pincho" Ojeda under charges of fraud and the withdrawal from the government of the Popular Socialist party in October of 1953 had left the president without support from either of the two Chambers and at the mercy of Congress as a whole. It was not long before the political establishment started to dismantle his government. Not only were his pro-Argentinean leanings and his militarist inclinations grounds for attack, but also his continuous threats to use a *mano firme* ("strong hand") to subdue any sedition from the political establishment and from the restive unions. The latter had begun to be used by politicians in their siege of the executive, and this had aroused the wrath of the president. As the confrontations of the executive with the political establishment and the unions became more frequent, criticism by the media also mounted. Reports in the newspapers or on the radio that harshly criticized the actions of the president or his ministers were frequently confiscated or silenced to demonstrate the seriousness of the president's *mano firme* stand, and by mid-1954 such action had put him on a collision course with Congress and the Office of the Comptroller General.

Two basic issues of the Ibañez del Campo presidential campaign had been governmental integrity and the defeat of inflation, but in practice neither was achieved under his administration. The "Pincho" Ojeda case, and the venality incurred by the *Comisión de Hombres Buenos*, a group of retired military officers who had been appointed by the president himself to investigate financial and administrative wrongdoings in the free port of Arica, revealed that many *Ibañistas* were no less corrupt than the Radicals whom they had replaced in the government.

But it was in his fight against inflation that the president lost popular support even more rapidly. For 1954 Chile set the world record with a 70 percent inflation, and those most affected were the salaried classes. In an effort to curtail inflation, Ibañez del Campo tried to implement an economic plan developed by Frei in 1954 and another by Jorge Prat in 1954-1955. When neither plan resulted in a significant reduction of the inflation rate, the Klein and Saks financial consultants from Washington were contracted to develop a program. Because the program of stabilization they recommended was implemented only partially (tax increases for economically privileged groups and shared financial sacrifices were flatly rejected as "politically unpleasant measures"), and since the Left would not cooperate with those "Yankee-made" plans that might have saved the political prestige of the president, the Klein and Saks mission proved just another costly failure of the Ibañez del Campo administration.[56] The soaring prices, the shortage of food items, and the devaluation of the currency added fuel to the fire that had been ignited by the political confrontation between the unions, controlled by the political establishment, and the government. The president, in the belief that every vindicatory strike of the workers was incited by leftist agitators, moved with extreme harshness against the trade unions and their leaders. Between 1954 and 1957 union leaders were repeatedly incarcerated, which served only to increase the animosity and militancy of organized laborers against the government. *Ibañismo* was clearly slackening among the very workers that had supported Ibañez del Campo in 1952, and the political parties were ready to retaliate for all they had suffered at his hands in 1952 and 1953.

The first concrete sign of the return of the electorate to the old political parties was the municipal elections of 1956, in which the Radicals collected 23 percent, the Conservatives 18 percent, and the Liberals 12 percent of the national vote. In a clear indication that the electoral clientele had deserted Ibañez del Campo and was moving toward centrist parties, not only did the Radical party receive increased support, but the Christian Democracy, by winning 8 percent of the total vote, also gained markedly. The Socialist party, however, dropped to 10 percent, 2.5 percent less than it had obtained in the congressional elections of 1953.

The people's disenchantment with Ibañez del Campo's unsuccessful political venture became even more evident in the congressional elections of March 1957 when his main pillar of support, the Agrarian Laborite party, lost sixteen of its deputies and retained only four of its senators. The splinter *Ibañista* groups salvaged only six deputies of the twenty-two they had elected in 1953. Such was the collapse of *Ibañismo* after four years in power! In only two provinces, Llanquihue and Maule, did the government parties obtain pluralities; everywhere else the victory of the opposition was overwhelming (Figure 11).

As leader at the polls, with thirty-five deputies elected, the Radical party won all the provinces of the North, from Tarapacá

201

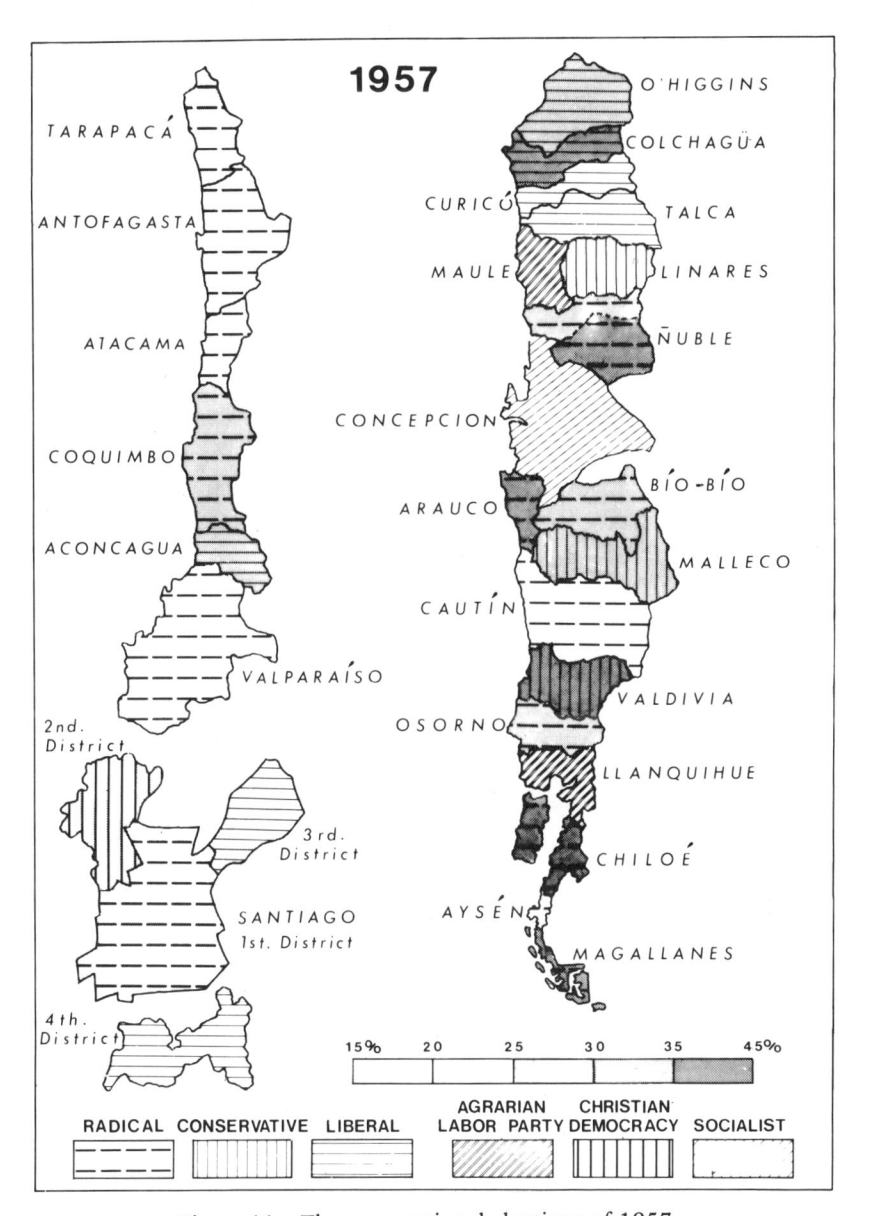

Figure 11.—The congressional elections of 1957.

to Coquimbo, where the miners and the urban population had little confidence in the effectiveness of the Popular Socialist party in opposition to Ibañez del Campo. The Radicals also scored well in the province of Valparaíso and in all the urban districts of Santiago. They regained the agricultural provinces of Ñuble, Arauco, Bío-Bío, and Osorno, which had been lost to Ibañez del Campo in 1953. The strongest showing in the rightist opposition was that of the Liberal party, with twenty-five deputies and ten senators elected. The party also obtained good returns in the province of Linares (the home province of Ibañez del Campo), where the Agrarian Laborites were upset, as well as in the provinces of Malleco and Valdivia. Strong second place showings were realized in the mining-agrarian provinces of the *Norte Chico*. The Conservatives emerged from the contest as the third strongest political group in the country, with twenty-three deputies and six senators. They won in the traditional agricultural provinces, from O'Higgins to Talca, as well as in the mining-agricultural province of Aconcagua. In the province of Santiago, the rural Fourth District also went to the Conservative party.

The successes of the three major parties of the opposition, Radicals, Liberals, and Conservatives, appeared to suggest that the old order in Chilean politics had been restored after the Ibañist parenthesis; the Radicals had recovered their former clientele in the North and in the urban provinces, and the Conservatives in the agricultural provinces. Nevertheless, there were changes in the nation's electoral mosaic that were to be factors in future elections. The Popular Socialist party no longer controlled the northern provinces or the industrial province of Concepción (lost to the Socialist Party of Chile) and was left with only eight deputies out of its nineteen of 1953. The Socialist Party of Chile had done little better losing two of its nine deputies. In the Senate, the two Socialist factions held eight seats. Thus the electoral results had been far from happy for the divided forces of Socialism. The Communist party, which had entered the 1957 congressional contest under the cover name of *Partido del Trabajo* (Workers Party) elected four deputies, but no senators, and received a bare 2 percent of the total vote. In short, the elections had not proven auspicious for the popular parties, which polled only 12.6 percent of the national vote, but there were signs of recovery.

The most impressive gains in these elections were made by the

National Falange, which jumped to 9.4 percent in 1957 from 2.8 percent in 1953. It increased its three deputies to seventeen and in the Senate it won two seats. The highest returns for this growing party came from the Third District of Santiago, where it gained plurality, and the provinces of Tarapacá and Linares, where it ran second to the Radicals and Liberals. The Falange increased its strength in the urban provinces of central Chile, but became weaker in the traditional agricultural provinces. Among the senators elected in the province of Santiago were Jorge Alessandri, who ran as an independent, and the Falangist Eduardo Frei. They were to be two of the contendors in the next presidential election.

By 1957 Ibañez del Campo was a disillusioned, embittered old man. Under attack from the political establishment, abandoned by all parties, and with the *Ibañismo* completely dismantled, he surrounded himself with a group of personal friends to keep the government running until the end of his term in office. Donald W. Bray reported that he summoned to his cabinet personalities from the Arab community, men like Alejandro Hales and Rafael Tarud, who were accepted reluctantly by the political establishment. In order to express his contempt for the political establishment Ibañez del Campo apparently decided to give the Arabs an opportunity to demonstrate their administrative skills.[57] Other friends included old authoritarians like Tobías Barros, Sótero del Río, Abdón Parra, Santiago Wilson, and Osvaldo Koch, who had always been close to him. Also conspicuous in government during these years were the Sainte Marie brothers, Osvaldo and Darío. The former acted as minister of foreign relations from 1956 on and finished his political career under impeachment for alleged involvement in the escape of a Peronist delinquent from the Santiago penitentiary. Darío Sainte Marie, "a typical opportunist and a master of intrigue,"[58] ran the government newspaper *La Nación*, in which he lost no opportunity to praise the president. The total lack of scruples of this wealthy man is evident from his political vagaries. During the presidential campaign of 1952 he had beaten the propaganda drums for the rightist Arturo Matte against Ibañez del Campo. In 1964 he changed his loyalty to Eduardo Frei, an opponent of Ibañez del Campo, and five years later he turned his back on Frei and chose Salvador Allende as the new god to praise in the pages of his personally owned tabloid, *El Clarín*.

Ibañez del Campo did not, however, let his term in office go by without hitting back at his political opponents, especially the rightist parties and the Radical party. In 1958 he initiated legislation to reestablish the legality of the Communist party (despite the many problems it had given him during its semiclandestine status) by abolishing the "Law for the Permanent Defense of Democracy." Furthermore, with the support of *Ibañistas*, Christian Democrats, Socialists, and Communists (*Bloque de Saneamiento Democrático*), he dealt a second blow to the Right by passing the electoral law that introduced the single official ballot as a measure for eradicating the vote-buying practices from which the rightist parties had been the main beneficiaries.[59] With these two maneuvers Ibañez del Campo ensured that his political enemies would not forget him after his retirement from politics.

The reinstallment of the Communists could not have come at a more opportune moment. Since 1956, all the splinter groups of the Left had begun to push for the formation of the Popular Action Front (FRAP). This new alliance of leftist forces had been proposed within the Socialist Popular party during the Fifteenth National Congress of 1955 with the purpose of uniting the "workers parties" and the Central Workers Union (CUT) and of excluding all "bourgeois" parties. The Communists still preferred a broader alliance of progressive democratic forces within the growing coalition by including the Christian Democrats and the leftist Radicals as well, but the views of the Popular Socialists prevailed, and on February 29, 1956, the FRAP was born. It comprised the two branches of Chilean Socialism, the Communist party, the Popular Democratic party, and the *Frente Nacional del Pueblo* (a group of Socialists under the direction of Baltazar Castro, who had remained faithful to Ibañez del Campo).[60] In the congressional elections of 1957 the leftist coalition made its timid political debut by agreeing to respect another ally's right to nominate candidates in electoral units where that party was strong without competing for the same seat. This gentlemen's agreement, however, did not work to the satisfaction of the subscribers of the alliance, probably because there were still feelings of distrust and uneasiness that stemmed from their dissensions of the past fifteen years. A positive circumstance in the buildup of leftist forces in the country occurred in July of 1957, when the two main branches of Socialism, on the occasion of the

Seventeenth National Congress of the Socialist Popular party, merged again under the name of Socialist party.[61]

With the reunion of the Left and the concentration of Conservatives, Liberals, and Agrarian Laborites in the Right, the forces that were to contest the presidential election of 1958 were already taking up their positions. The refusal of the FRAP to establish electoral alliances with "bourgeois" parties prevented a Radical–Christian Democratic–FRAP coalition and isolated the first two parties in the political middle ground. The Radicals, encouraged by their electoral gains in the 1957 congressional elections, nominated Luis Bossay, one of their moderate senators. Also relying on the good showing of 1957, the Christian Democrats nominated Eduardo Frei, a man with great personal appeal. The Radicals expected support from the rightist parties and had therefore nominated a candidate who appeared attractive to the reformist grass roots of the party and also to the conservative taste of the Right. The Christian Democracy, since it was not seeking alliances with any of the other three major political forces (the Radicals, the Left, or the Right), relied very heavily on Frei's personality and ran its candidate to test its electoral appeal as a young political force. By insisting on their own candidates both Radicals and Christian Democrats had created an unwise split of the centrist forces that, in theory, gave electoral advantages to the Left and the Right.

The Right, counting on the support of 33 percent of the national vote (as in the 1957 congressional elections) and capitalizing on the economic disaster created by the Ibañez del Campo administration, nominated Jorge Alessandri, the eldest son of Arturo. His position as an independent politician and his fame as a successful manager were stressed by the propaganda machine as requisites necessary for the efficient operation of a country that had been mismanaged by the political establishment and by incapable caudillos.

The Left stood united behind the Socialist Salvador Allende, a man with experience in presidential campaigns, of solid oratorical skills, and without an equal within the FRAP. Although on paper Allende was supported by only 13 percent of the national vote, the FRAP expected to attract the dispersed supporters of the *Ibañismo* and dissatisfied leftist Radicals. If the possibility of a centrist victory had been lessened by the Radicals and Christian

Democrats running their own candidates, so was that of a leftist triumph, when the picturesque figure of the priest of Catapilco, Antonio Zamorano, entered the presidential contest with the support of independent populist forces. Zamorano's candidacy was hopeless from the very beginning and, although there was talk about his withdrawing and joining the forces of FRAP, he stayed in the race to the end and thus spoiled the chances of Salvador Allende.

On September 4, 1958, victory went to Jorge Alessandri; he polled 389,948 votes (31.5 percent) against Allende's 356,499 (28.8 percent). Eduardo Frei was far back with 255,777 votes (20.7 percent), and Bossay fourth with 192,110 votes (15.5 percent). The figures indicated that the 41,305 votes (3.3 percent) that went to Antonio Zamorano, which would have gone to Allende if Zamorano had relinquished his candidacy, would have been more than sufficient for Allende to overtake Alessandri.

Alessandri gained a plurality in all the agricultural provinces of the country, including those of recent colonization, and in the province of Chiloé (Figure 12). The urban metropolitan provinces of Valparaíso and Santiago, with the exception of Santiago's Second District, also supported Jorge Alessandri with percentages between 30 and 40. Alessandri reached his highest mark (48 percent) in Colchagua. Thus, a trend that had been characteristic in the past, namely the agricultural provinces, Valparaíso, and some of Santiago's districts voting for the Right, was repeated in 1958, and this time without vote-buying practices, at least in theory, because of the use of the single voting ballot in the election.

Salvador Allende won pluralities in all the provinces of Chile's North from Tarapacá to Coquimbo. The latter province, which had previously been held by the Radicals and Liberals, shifted to the Left, a trend that was to continue in future elections. In the province of Santiago, the popular Second District also gave pluralities to Allende, showing how efficient the FRAP organization had been among the poor urbanites of the capital. Initiating a new trend, the industrial urban province of Concepción supported Allende with a solid 41 percent, as did the neighboring province of Arauco with 47 percent. In both, just as in the provinces of the North, the support Salvador Allende obtained from organized labor and from a united Left was obvious. The southernmost provinces of Aysén and Magallanes also showed their pre-

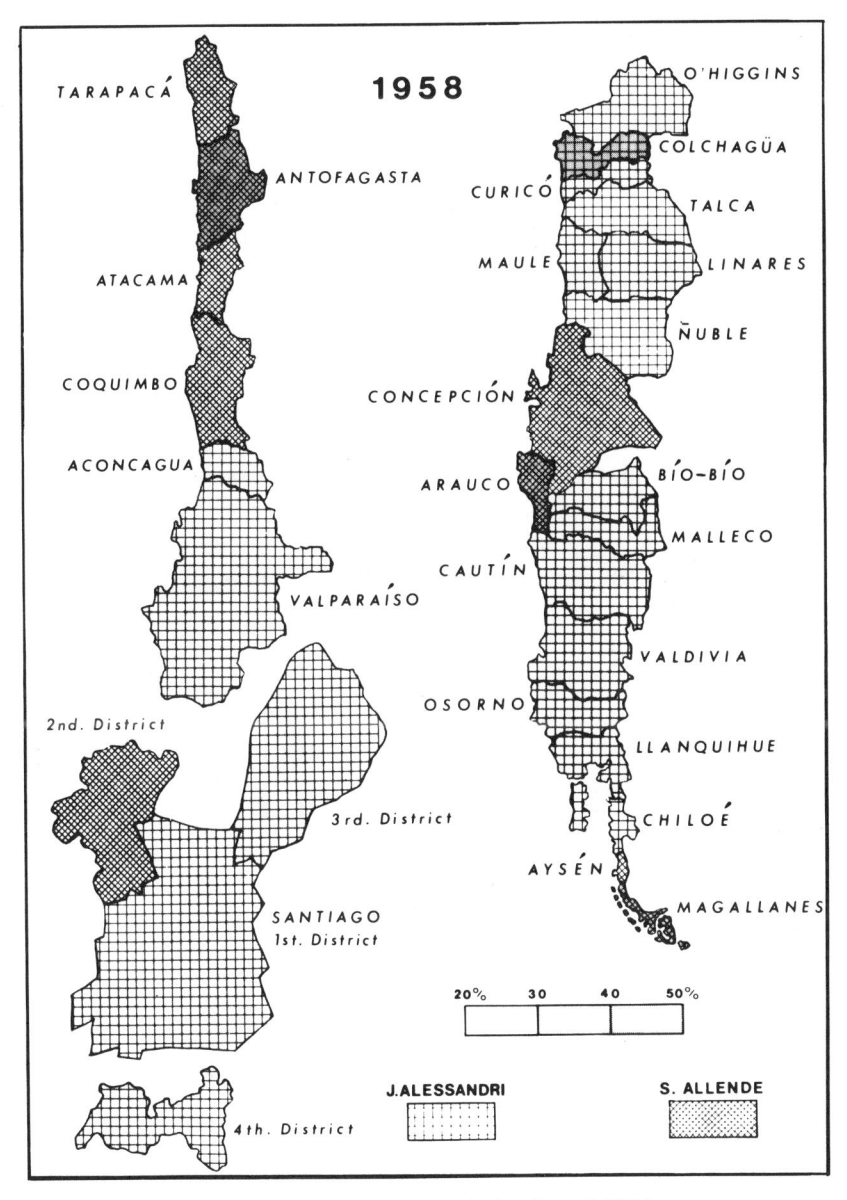

Figure 12.—The presidential election of 1958.

ference for the candidate of FRAP, especially the province of Magallanes, where 48 percent voted in favor of the popular candidate.

Eduardo Frei, even though he came third with 20.7 percent, made a very satisfactory showing in view of the fact that the highest percentage of votes the Christian Democracy had ever reached in twenty years of existence had been 9.4 in the congressional elections of 1957. The most encouraging results for the Christian Democratic candidate came from several urban provinces in Middle Chile. In Valparaíso, for instance, Frei ran second to Alessandri with 26 percent of the provincial vote, and in Concepción, with 21 percent, he came second to Allende. Frei also obtained good returns from the northern mining provinces as well as from Magallanes, where he held second place, though far behind Salvador Allende.

The Radical party with Luis Bossay suffered another discouraging defeat. Its 15.5 percent of the vote was much lower than the good results of the 1957 congressional elections, and it left the Radicals in fourth place behind the united Right, the FRAP, and the Christian Democracy. In none of the provinces where they had scored so well in 1957 (Tarapacá, Coquimbo, Santiago's Second District, Arauco, or Bío-Bío) did their candidate place higher than third. Prior to the 1958 election rumors had circulated that the rightist Radicals, who controlled the central committee of the party, were less than happy about the candidacy of Bossay and that they had secretly agreed to push their electoral clientele to support Jorge Alessandri. Even if this was only a rumor, it fitted well, as later became evident, with the intention of the right-wing Radicals to collaborate with the Alessandri administration.

The fifth candidate in the contest, Antonio Zamorano, obtained an unexpected high of 20 percent of the total provincial vote in Talca and 13 percent in Linares, two of the former strongholds of *Ibañismo*, a fact that suggests a certain propensity of populist voters toward being swayed by picturesque characters rather than by abstract ideologies. After his presidential venture the "priest of Catapilco" held an office of deputy until 1961, then moved to Valparaíso and settled down with his several children to a bourgeois life.

The 1958 presidential election, although it was not a victorious one for the FRAP or the Christian Democracy, marked a significant turning point in the recent political history of the country as it revealed the emergence of the united Left as a formidable alliance and the inception of the Christian Democracy as the major centrist political force. For the Radicals, displaced from the Center-Left by these two future political giants, there would be a short recovery in 1961 before their final collapse in the 1970s.

The momentous success of the Right with Jorge Alessandri stemmed not so much from the ideological appeal of conservatism or liberalism as from the personal appeal of Alessandri as a capable manager and a frugal bachelor, two qualities that were skillfully exploited by his campaign managers. From the time when Alessandri accepted the candidacy offered to him by the Liberal and Conservative parties he insisted on running his government without concessions to either of them and on following a policy of economic reconstruction for the country, so shattered by the mismanagement of the previous administration. In this Alessandri, just as Ibañez del Campo in 1952, underlined his image as a noncareer politician whose only interest was the improvement of the country's economic situation. To the same degree as Ibañez del Campo was perceived by the independent voter as the national savior after the frustrating Radical government, Jorge Alessandri scored on his image as an economic healer of the country. This may well provide sound grounds for the statement that in 1952, as well as in 1958, a major factor in the electoral decision of the uncommitted voter was not his belief in the ideology of the Right so much as his conviction that an upright man was needed to regenerate the stagnant economic situation of the country.

Despite the fact that it is unlikely that Ibañez del Campo and Jorge Alessandri will be remembered as having similar traits of character, both did in fact emphasize their independence from the established parties and postulated a solid presidential authoritarianism,[62] and for their views both came under constant attack from the political establishment. Furthermore, to underline the seriousness of his dedication to the economic melioration of the country, Alessandri did not select ministers for his cabinet from the established parties but surrounded himself with technocrats and entrepreneurs. Not only did this manager approach to the administration of the country prove beneficial for the economy, but it also greatly increased Alessandri's credibility. In the municipal elections of 1960 the Liberal party, from which most of Alessandri's political advisors came, made substantial electoral gains. However, the Conservatives, who also backed the president, did not profit to the same extent. The Radicals, by evincing an attentive and friendly attitude toward Alessandri and by exercising restraint in their opposition in Congress, also benefited from his electoral success, however transitory.

In the opposition there were the Christian Democracy and the FRAP, which, in the early 1960s, mounted a strong political offensive against the Alessandri government. Since in the municipal elections of 1960 a reduction in the leftist vote to 21 percent strengthened the conviction that only through popular agitation could the Left make gains in the congressional elections scheduled for March 1961, the Socialists and Communists stirred up organized labor by using their control over the CUT. The Christian Democrats, on the other hand, limited their assault on the government to congressional debates since they wished to avoid alienating the middle-of-the-road voters who still believed in, and sympathised with, the austere economic measures proposed by the president. Moreover, the Christian Democracy, which, by obtaining 15 percent of the vote in the municipal elections of 1960, had done much better than anticipated, was also looking toward political gains for the next congressional elections. And they considered that a good way of achieving this was by scoring on the government in Congress. Once again, after a hiatus of twenty years, ideologies were to be the basis of the congressional contest of 1961 between the Right in the government and the Center-Left in the opposition.

The Radical party, in one last resurgence before its final collapse, secured 20 percent of the national vote and elected twenty-three deputies and seven senators. The whole North from Tarapacá to Coquimbo gave pluralities to radical candidates (Figure 13). In the urban province of Valparaíso the Radical party won narrowly over the Christian Democrats. The First and Second districts of Santiago also gave pluralities to the Radicals. In the agricultural provinces the Radicals made the most remarkable comeback since the time of Gabriel González Videla, as they gained a solid victory in Ñuble II (Chillán, Bulnes, Yungay) with 36 percent of the vote and in Linares with 25 percent. In another unexpected show of electoral strength, the party defeated the Communists to win the

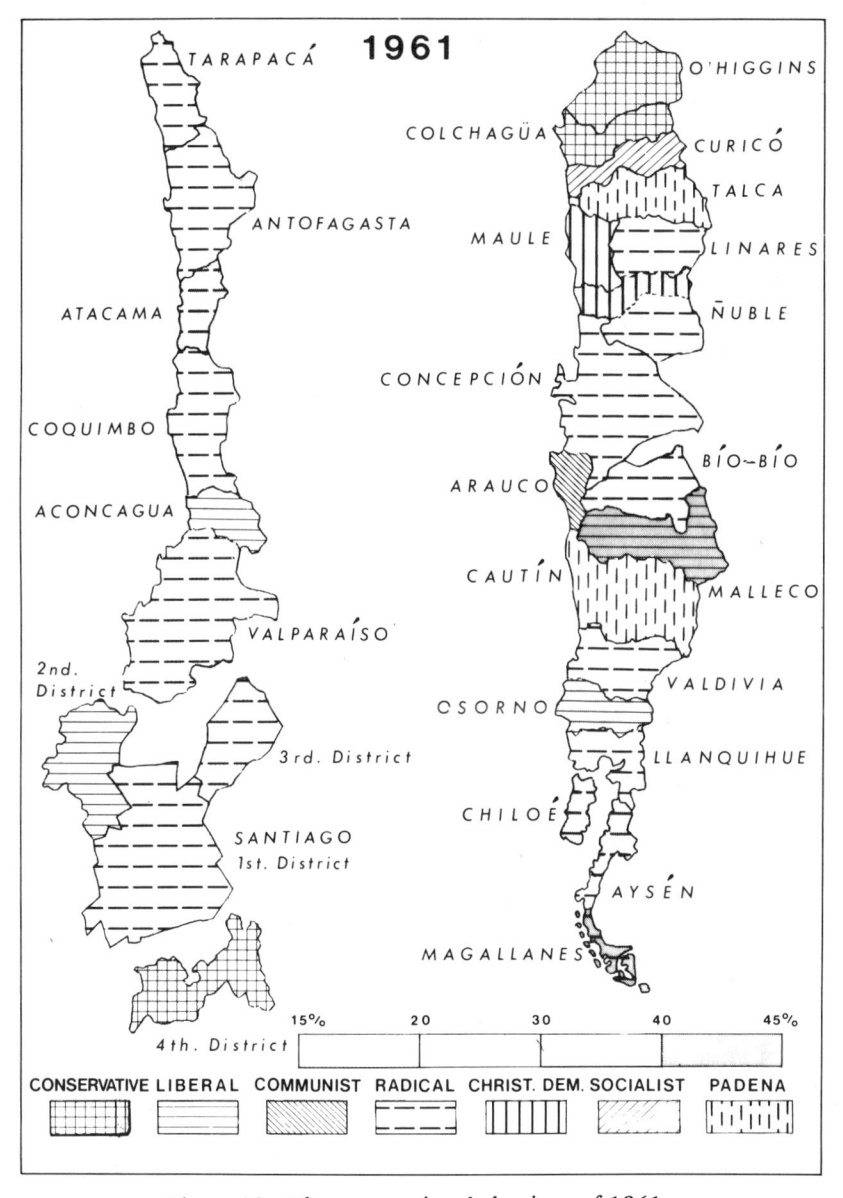

Figure 13.—The congressional elections of 1961.

province of Concepción with 25 percent of the total vote and three deputies. The regained vigor of the Radicals also became evident in the agricultural provinces of recent colonization, Bío-Bío, Valdivia, and Llanquihue, where they won five of the twelve deputy seats. They also led the polls in the provinces of Chiloé (33 percent of the provincial vote) and Magallanes (45 percent).

To find a general explanation for the success of the Radical party in provinces that differ so markedly in character is difficult, if not impossible. Although in the North the electoral clientele that had previously supported *Ibañismo* may have turned to the Radicals, in other parts of the country their success may simply have been because they had not let their fingers get burned in the executive during the previous nine years, so that the image of their candidates had improved in comparison with that of the candidates of the Right, the Left, or the Christian Democrats. Further, many nonreligious and liberal-minded individuals preferred to vote for a liberal-laicist party rather than a clerical party or either of the two extremes of the political spectrum. The victory of the Radicals in Concepción and Magallanes, where traditionally the Left had been strong, was probably because of a wise choice of candidates. For instance, in Magallanes, always a stronghold of the Socialists, the appeal of a prestigious local figure, Jorge Cvitanic, turned the tide in favor of the Radicals.

The Liberal party again in 1961 emerged as the second strongest political force of the country, electing twenty-eight deputies, three more than in 1957, and five senators, totaling nine in all. The Liberals obtained pluralities in the provinces of Malleco (40 percent) and Osorno (31 percent), and in most of the provinces of the country they were able to elect at least one or two deputies. In the province of Coquimbo the Liberals lost to the Radicals, but they themselves received twice as many votes as the Communists who placed third. The fact that they could elect deputies in the northern provinces where the Left had traditionally been strong suggests that the Liberal party still catered to an electoral clientele of bourgeois leaning that would not, however, support the more traditional Conservative party. The parties of the Right retained a certain degree of attraction for those who considered the economic measures of President Alessandri appropriate for the economic ailments of the country.

With 16 percent of the national vote in 1961, the Christian

Democratic party (ex-National Falange) became the third political force in the country. The party increased its 1957 congressional representation by more than 40 percent, electing twenty-three deputies and two senators. As in previous elections, the highest returns for the Christian Democracy came from the urban provinces of Chile. In the province of Valparaíso the party collected 18 percent of the vote and came second to the Radicals, whereas in the Third District of Santiago it lost to the Liberals with 16 percent. For the first time in the history of the party the Christian Democracy elected deputies in traditional agricultural provinces such as Colchagua, Curicó, and Maule, as well as in some of the provinces of *La Frontera,* Bío-Bío and Malleco. The party was clearly gaining a foothold in areas where it had previously not met with the slightest response.

The parties of the Left also made significant advances in the 1961 congressional contest. As a result of a careful study of the party's electoral possibilities the Communist party, with only 12 percent of the national vote, elected sixteen deputies and four senators. In fact, with roughly the same number of votes in the senatorial contest as the Christian Democrats, they elected four senators, whereas the Christian Democrats elected only two. This is attributable to the unwise use of the Christian Democratic electoral forces. In the two northernmost provinces, Tarapacá and Antofagasta, the Communists trailed the Radicals but outdistanced the other parties. In the agricultural-mining province of O'Higgins, the Communist party was second to the Conservative party. As in the 1940s, the Communists had become an important electoral force in the industrial mining provinces of Concepción and Arauco, where, for only a short interval, they had been overtaken by the Radicals.

The Socialist party, even though it emerged with 10.7 percent of the national returns and only 14,500 votes fewer than the Communist party, had used its popular support less carefully than the Communists and elected only twelve deputies and four senators. In fact, in the northern provinces of the country the Communists elected three times as many deputies as the Socialists, even though they polled only twice as many votes. In the provinces of O'Higgins and Concepción, where mining is an important economic activity, the Socialists again gave up votes to their allies. The advantages of the Communists over the Socialists were more conspicuous in the province of Santiago, where the former, with only 40 percent more votes than the Socialists, elected six deputies against only one for the Socialists. In electoral units where both parties had presented candidates, the North and the urban provinces of Middle Chile, in most cases it was the Communist candidate who won. Only in provinces where the Communists had no candidates (Aconcagua, Curicó, Linares, and Osorno) did the Socialist party win seats in the lower Chamber. Very early in the development of the FRAP, the alliance of the two Marxist parties was obviously proving more favorable for the Communists than for the Socialists just as in the early 1940s, the difference being that the Socialists accepted the situation with greater calmness for the sake of unity between the two popular parties.

The Conservatives scored considerably below the 1957 mark. Their 15 percent of the national vote and the seventeen deputies they elected put them in fourth place, two places lower than in 1957. Their major losses occurred in the urban provinces of Valparaíso and Santiago, where Conservative candidates polled fewer votes than the rising Radicals and Christian Democrats, and in several of the traditional agricultural provinces that had now turned to the Christian Democrats or the FRAP. The only agricultural provinces that remained loyal to the Conservatives were O'Higgins and Colchagua. Valparaíso and the first three districts of Santiago had switched their support to the Radicals or the Liberal party. Only the rural Fourth District voted conservative. In the rural province of Chiloé, where the strength of the Conservatives had become proverbial, they had to accept second place behind the Radicals. They also gave up two traditional agricultural provinces, Talca and Maule, which went to the PADENA, a conglomerate of the remnants from the *Ibañismo* including the National People's party, the Democratic party, and the People's Democratic party.[63] This heterogeneous party gained a plurality in the province of Talca (owing to the appeal of a local figure, Rafael Tarud) and in the province of Cautín, where the former *Ibañistas* were still strong. The PADENA also obtained good returns in the province of Valparaíso (13 percent of the provincial vote) and won twelve seats in the lower Chamber.

Since the PADENA was an ally of the FRAP, this whole block was now represented in Congress by forty deputies and twelve senators against forty-five deputies and thirteen senators of the two rightist parties. This basic alignment of forces in Congress left the two centrist parties, the Radicals and the Christian Democrats, in a position of holding the balance of power and even of forming a centrist opposition front in both Chambers of Congress. But this alternative, which might have been of great value for the next presidential election, was not in keeping with the Radicals' typical sense of timing and of political opportunism. In August of 1961 Jorge Alessandri, in view of the increasing difficulties his independent government and his cabinet of experts were facing with the political establishment and the labor unrest provoked by the Left, accepted the collaboration of Radical, Liberal, and Conservative ministers.[64] The Christian Democrats were now isolated in the middle, but this did not upset them unduly. The past three elections had convinced them of the greater benefits to be gained from ideological and political independence when compared with their years of cooperation with the Radicals of González Videla.

From then on the FRAP adopted an aggressive opposition stand toward Jorge Alessandri's government, knowing that it could bring only political advantage and that, if need arose, they could depend on the support of the Christian Democracy in Congress whenever an opportunity for a checkmate on the government forces might occur.

The alignment of forces after the congressional elections of 1961 shows that an important turning point in Chilean politics had been reached, the prelude to the strong polarization that would sweep the country from the mid-1960s until 1973. It became evident that the centrist parties held the winning edge for any political combination that might develop. However, the refusal of the Christian Democrats to compromise their ideological purity and to enter into political alliances (which had been so deleterious for the Radicals) isolated them from prospective allies and created difficult political situations for them. The swing of the Radicals to the Right in 1961 had not only moved the political center of gravity toward the Right, but it had also brought about the polarization of the Left as a compensatory movement, and this was to become very decisive in the late 1960s.

In October of 1962, after widespread union unrest and sustained attacks from the Left in Congress, right-wing and moderate Radicals called for the formation of the Democratic Front in an alliance with Liberals and Conservatives.[65] This alliance, which appeared powerful on paper, got the first opportunity to test its strength in the municipal elections of 1963. But the returns from these contests, instead of revealing gains for the pro-Alessandri coalition, showed the political benefit of opposition to the government. In fact, while the opposition made substantial electoral gains, in the Democratic Front only the Radicals managed to keep the same percentage of the national vote as they had held in 1960 and 1961. The Conservatives and Liberals suffered serious setbacks, losing 6 of the 14 and 17 percent they had received in the two earlier years. The highest losses sustained by the Conservatives took place in the provinces of Aconcagua, Santiago, and in all the agricultural provinces of Middle Chile with the exception of Maule. Liberal municipal candidates suffered defeat in the northern provinces and in the urban provinces of central Chile, whereas in the traditional agricultural provinces they made some gains, probably at the expense of the Conservatives, supporting a trend suggested earlier.

The results attained by the FRAP parties showed little improvement on their overall electoral achievements of 1960 and 1961. Their most significant gains occurred in the agricultural province of Maule, where the Left appeared to be building up strength, and in the province of Atacama, which they won from the Radicals. The extreme North and the extreme South produced favorable returns for the Left, whereas in the provinces of recent colonization, in Valparaíso, Aconcagua, and Curicó the FRAP received little support as many electors shifted their preference to the rising Christian Democracy.

The winners in the municipal elections of 1963 were the Christian Democrats, who not only obtained their first plurality (narrowly surpassing the vote for the Radical party) but also made significant electoral advances in several provinces (Concepción, Linares, Aconcagua, and Tarapacá) that previously had given them little or no support. Furthermore, the Christian Democrats were developing strength in the provinces of Antofagasta, Ñuble, and Santiago. Only in Cautín, Malleco, Colchagua, and Arauco did they fail to match their successes in the other provinces. Just as important as the numerical total of these good electoral results of the Christian Democracy in 1963 was where they were achieved. For it was clear that the Christian Democrats were no longer attracting only the urban electorate but were making considerable inroads into agricultural and mining provinces that had previously denied them any support.[66]

In a national perspective, the high electoral returns obtained by the two centrist parties clearly indicated that the Chilean electorate was weary of political extremes, rejected radical alternatives, and was now more in favor of reformist democratic parties. The gains of the Christian Democracy in the mining provinces of the North and in the agricultural provinces of central Chile revealed that its reformist message was reaching the progressive elements of the middle class as well as the proletariat in those provinces.

In 1963 and 1964, the last two years of Jorge Alessandri's government, the economy of the nation, which had been auspicious and healthy at the beginning of his term in office, began to stagnate again and even to regress. An inflationary relapse, increases in the national debt, currency devaluation, and a halt in the growth of the GDP led as in the past to the disenchantment of the masses, to mounting labor unrest, and to harsh attacks on the government by the parties in opposition.[67] Under such discouraging social and economic circumstances, there was no doubt that the opposition was capitalizing on the deteriorating situation and that the government was losing popular support. To allow Alessandri full freedom in coping with the national economy and to dissociate themselves from the government in view of the impending presidential election of 1964, the parties of the Democratic Front withdrew from the government in 1963 and started to prepare for the coming electoral contest.

Julio Durán, an affluent member of the Radical party's right wing, had been nominated by the Democratic Front and appeared to be the candidate with the best chance in the 1964 election. The leftist coalition, FRAP, after an initial wavering between Rafael Tarud, Pablo Neruda, and Salvador Allende, decided to nominate Allende. This would be his third candidacy for the office of president of the Republic. The combined strength of the Communists, Socialists, the PADENA, and the National People's Vanguard—the group led by the Socialist Baltazar Castro—was estimated as approaching 29 percent of the national total (based on the returns of the 1961 elections), which would give them second place. The third place in the 1964 contest was expected to go to the Christian Democracy with Eduardo Frei who had proven his appeal as a presidential candidate in 1958.

A by-election to fill a vacant seat in Congress shortly before a presidential election has always been considered in Chile as a preview of the election or at least a gauging of public opinion. The presidential election of September 1964 was preceded by a by-election on March 15, 1964. A deceased deputy was to be replaced in the agricultural province of Curicó. Confident of the traditional strength of the Right in that province and ignoring the fact that the deceased deputy had been a member of the Socialist party, the campaign managers of the Democratic Front rushed to call this by-election a muster case, even a plebiscite of how Chileans as a whole were likely to vote in the upcoming presidential election, even though Curicó constituted only 1.2 percent of the national electorate.[68] The victory went to Dr. Oscar Naranjo, the candidate of the FRAP, with over 12 percent more votes than his rightist opponent, and 17 percent more than the candidate of the Christian Democracy. The *"Naranjazo"* ("Naranjo's smashing blow"), as this defeat of the Right was called, spread havoc on the Democratic Front: the Radical Julio Durán withdrew his candidacy for the rightist alliance, allowing the Liberals and Conservatives to endorse a presidential candidate with a better chance— Eduardo Frei.[69] The Radical party, still the second political force in the country, had the choice either of supporting the candidacy of Salvador Allende, since the anticlerical radical grass roots would never vote for a Roman Catholic like Frei, or for keeping Durán in the running solely as a Radical candidate in the hope of attracting a few uncommited voters between March and September. During these months, Allende courted the Radicals, but he was not successful in accomplishing the withdrawal of Julio Durán. Nevertheless, it appeared that the leftist Radicals, knowing that Durán had little chance, preferred Allende and intended to withdraw their support from the party's official candidate. Thus, just the opposite of what had happened within the Radical party during the 1958 presidential campaign took place; this time it was the leftist faction that turned its back on the official candidate of the party.

Not only the schism within the Radical party, but also the onslaught of the Liberals and Conservatives on the Frei candidacy, forecast the oncoming presidential contest as one drawn between only two political forces: the Marxist Left and its opponents. This development was the consequence of the *Naranjazo,* the by-election in Curicó that, under normal circumstances, would have passed almost unnoticed. Now, however, it had become the turning point that marked the end of personalism in Chilean politics and the beginning of an era in which ideology was to decide electoral contests. To render it even more evident that the period between 1952 and 1964 had been one dominated by messianic figures, Jorge Alessandri continued to enjoy the respect, if not the appreciation, of a great part of the public as an honest and dedicated person right to the end of his presidency. In fact, ignoring the attacks of the political establishment, it is fair to assert that the public considered that the limitations and failures of his government should not be blamed so much on Alessandri as on his collaborators and on the obstructionism of the opposition.[70] It does not come then as a surprise that there were suggestions from independents for his nomination as presidential candidate for a second term, if constitutional ammendments to that effect could be introduced. Alessandri himself declined these propositions.

Ideology and Polarization: 1964-1973

The nine years between September 4, 1964, and September 11, 1973, witnessed the culmination of a steady process of democratization and social progress that had begun in 1925. Never before the administrations of Frei and Allende had the country seen such a political mobilization of urban and rural masses. At the same time as militancy increased, the bases for political participation were broadened through a lessening of the restrictions of the electoral laws. Heightened politicization brought the ferment of change to the university, the church, the barracks, and the consumer; in short, it raised the political consciousness of social groups that had been in the past relatively unresponsive to political stimuli. This rising politicization of Chilean society was further strengthened by positive structural changes that occurred during this period. The agrarian reform not only altered land-tenure patterns, but it also deprived the landowner class of its traditional source of political power—the peasantry. Rural tenants emerged as a social force with an important input into the political life of the country. In a different field, "Chileanization" (Frei) or "nationalization" (Allende) of copper brought the most important export commodity of the country under Chilean control and established the principle that the nationals, including the workers, should own the primary resources of the nation. Later, when the government of the Popular Unity moved against the interests of the bourgeoisie by nationalizing banks and the means of production, it became evident that a profound transformation was taking place in the social and political texture of the country as well as in its economic structure.

While many Chileans thought that structural changes were possible within the existing constitututional order, for others no pace of change was rapid enough except global revolution and the substitution of the "bourgeois state" by the "dictatorship of the proletariat." In a country with the democratic tradition of Chile, the latter encountered the fiercest opposition from the democratic forces. Intransigence and steady confrontation replaced the customary composure in political dealings. The extreme Left and the extreme Right were soon on the road to antiregime attitudes and physical violence, and the danger of terminating forty years of democratic life was imminent.[71] More than a frontal encounter of reactionary and Marxist forces, these years of polarization witnessed antagonism between reformism and revolutionary change. By the mid-1960s it had become evident that political conservatism had no echoes and no future with the ever increasing electorate. Thus if a political party expected to entice the Chilean voters, it had to advance a platform of structural change. Since other political alternatives had failed in the past, two positions with strong ideological content confronted the electorate—the Christian Democratic communitarianism and the Popular Unity's Socialism.[72]

The Christian Democracy offered a government based on the participation of the people, social justice, and humanist respect for the individual. In the words of Radomiro Tomic:

> The Christian Democratic ideology holds forth to Chile a social order that can replace the individualist and Marxist collectivist schemes. It is the communitarian society [which], in our view, should be grounded in the following values and able to give them institutional being: On the philosophical and moral plane the Christian Democracy adheres to the principle that the human person as such, and not the state, or class, or race is the supreme value in the community social order. On the social plane the Christian Democratic ideology accords full support to the principle that to fulfill his destiny, the human person must simultaneously integrate organisms and social groups such as the family, the labor

union, and profession, the cooperative, the neighborhood, the municipality, the region, the political party and the like. On the political plane the communitarian society has to be based on the dominant participation of the majorities in the effective centres of power—social, economic and political power—the control of which determines the national destiny. This has to be achieved within the spirit and practice of democracy.[73]

The Socialists and Communists, the major forces of the Left, pursued a global transformation of society, economy, and culture according to the Marxist postulates. President Allende himself expressed the aims of the Popular Unity government: "Indeed the people of Chile chose the road of revolution and we have not forgotten a fundamental principle of Marxism: the class struggle. During the electoral campaign we said that the purpose of our struggle was to change the regime, the system. That we sought to form a government in order to obtain the power to carry out the revolutionary transformation which Chile needs, to break the nation's economic, political, cultural and trade union dependency."[74] To clarify the intentions of his government vis-à-vis the state apparatus of Chile, President Allende added a little later: "Through this government the majority of the people will replace the minority which has been in power until now.... As for the bourgeois state, at the present moment we are seeking to overcome it. To overthrow it!" These are clear statements of the purposes of the two major contending forces on the political scene of the 1960s. And because of the vehemence with which each proponent pursued its aims, dogmatism, intransigence, and polarization reached the intensity that led to the collapse of the Chilean democracy in 1973. For the Left the corporative reformism of the Christian Democracy became a deceiving term for what they considered a sellout to international imperialism and to the local bourgeoisie.[75] For the non-Marxist parties the intentions of the Left were geared toward creating in Chile the dictatorship of a single party, the submission to international communism, and the destruction of the national soul.[76] With such disparate views there was no room for common sense, dialogue, or compromise.

The Government of the Christian Democracy

After the election of Oscar Naranjo as deputy for Curicó, it became clear to Liberals and Conservatives alike that the force to be stopped in the presidential contest was not the Christian Democracy but the fast-growing FRAP. Accordingly, in April of 1964, they officially rescinded their pact with the Radicals and announced their unconditional backing of the candidate of the Christian Democracy. From the point of view of electoral strength, this endorsement appeared favorable for Eduardo Frei, but by the same token, it made him vulnerable to attacks from the Left. It went so far, in fact, that as a consequence of the support from the Right, the media and the politicians of the FRAP began to refer to Frei's candidacy as "the other face of reaction."[77]

That denotation backfired at the candidate of the Left, Salvador Allende. His open sympathy for Marxist regimes that had come into power by violent means and his pronouncements that he was a convinced democrat and a constitutionalist created an image of ambivalence that was far from attractive to the uncommitted voter. Allende's close contact with Fidel Castro and the installment of a Communist regime in Cuba gave his political opponents grounds for propagandizing that Chile would become another Cuba and a Soviet satellite if Salvador Allende was elected president.[78] Thus the campaign developed in an atmosphere charged with mutual recrimination and defamation that served only to increase polarization and animosity. With Julio Durán as the sole candidate of the Radicals, the rest of Chile's political forces rallied around Allende and Frei. The mainstay of Allende was the FRAP, a coalition in which the Socialist and Communist parties played the main role. Secondary forces behind Allende were the PADENA, the Socialist People's National Vanguard, a significant group of anticlerical Radicals (the Radical Movement of Doctrinary Recuperation), and a handful of Liberals under the leadership of the aristocrat Gregorio Amunátegui, who refused to support a Catholic candidate. Unabashed by the Marxist views on religion, Rafael Tarud headed a group called the Allendista Catholic Movement, which worked effectively for Allende.

The Christian Democracy counted on the appeal of Eduardo Frei and the enthusiastic support of the young party. Liberals and Conservatives had joined the Christian Democrats without commitment and, although they conducted a lukewarm campaign in support of Frei, they used the funds at their disposal primarily for their so-called "campaign of terror" to convince the uncommitted middle-ground electorate of the impending catastrophy for the country if the Marxist Allende was elected.[79] Other sectors that rallied under Frei were splinter parties, remnants from the deceased *Ibañismo,* such as the Agrarian Laborite party, and elements from the PADENA led by Carlos Montero, who had defected because of the hegemonic dominion of Socialists and Communists within the FRAP coalition.

Once a definite alignment of the various political factions had taken place, the main task of the two major contending forces (Durán had become little more than an onlooker) was the intensification of the electoral propaganda in the populous provinces of the country where, because of the incorporation of new voters, it was thought that the election would be decided. The FRAP was conceded the support of those provinces in which organized workers and laicist middle-class individuals (normally supporters of the Radical party) had rarely shown any significant support of Catholic parties—the mining provinces of the North, the coal mining provinces of Concepción and Arauco, and Magallanes. Rallies and speeches conveyed the impression that there was no doubt about the FRAP candidate's victory by a wide margin; as a result, little effort was spent on publicity. Frei's organization, on the other hand, did not depend on its previous electoral gains and adopted an active campaign policy, especially in the agricultural provinces. The Curicó by-election and Tarud's success in the agrarian province of Talca had taught the lesson that traditionally conservative provinces could be won over to the Left if the personal appeal of the candidate was strong enough to attract the ideologically uncommited part of the electorate.

The main battleground of the election promised to be the provinces of Valparaíso and Santiago, which contained 51 percent of the nation's electorate and which had the greatest number of newly registered voters. The primary targets of Frei's electoral campaign were the feminine voters and the youth. The support of women was sought by promises of socioeconomic changes without violence and by emphasizing "revolution in freedom," while for the young people populist rallies were held that catered to their idealism. An asset of the propaganda machine of the Christian Democracy was the organization of the *Marcha de la Patria Joven,* a 1,000-kilometer hike from Puerto Montt to Santiago conducted by Frei supporters with great media coverage.

September 4, 1964, was a sunny spring day, and the presidential election passed without violent incidents. Eduardo Frei won 56.1 percent of the electorate with 431,110 votes more than Salvador Allende's 38.9 percent. From the feminine electorate Frei won 63 percent! As expected, the polarization of the electorate had stripped the Radical Julio Durán of all chance of making a decorous electoral showing; he attained only 4.9 percent of the national vote.

Just as the campaign managers of the two major contending forces had anticipated, the winner was decided in the two most populous provinces of the country. Valparaíso was won by Frei with 60.3 percent and Santiago with 60.9 percent (Figure 14). In those two provinces alone Frei gained an advantage of more than 320,000 votes over Allende. Contrary to what was expected, Frei won majorities in all four districts of the province of Santiago, including the proletarian Second District, where his 59 percent was his lowest return in that province. It is significant that he carried all the agricultural provinces, traditional and of recent colonization. However, with the exception of Cautín and Llanquihue, where he obtained 63 percent of the provincial vote, in no constituency did he poll more than 58 percent as he did in the urban provinces of Valparaíso and Santiago. He was also the winner in the largest cities of the country (Greater Santiago, Valparaíso, Viña del Mar, Concepción, and Antofagasta) although Allende held first place in the provincial totals of Concepción and Antofagasta.[80]

Whether this means that the urban working class voted for Frei is pure speculation, just as is the argument that the fact that Allende received more votes from among male voters in certain urban centers was proof that he was backed only by the workers. The first places obtained by Frei in the major urban centers cannot be interpreted as a weak response of the working class to the appeal of Allende, as Halperin suggests,[81] the reason being that electoral results cannot be matched with contemporary data on occupation in a given electoral unit, at least not at the level of municipalities. It remains little more than a guess to assert which occupational strata backed which candidates. For the same reason, attempts to prove that the votes Allende received came from the working class contain little of factual value; they are but warranted assumptions. As soon as selective distinctions are introduced the element of partisan bias vitiates the objective analysis. Of course, at times an analyst may be determined to prove that *his* candidate

Forty Years of Democratic Life 225

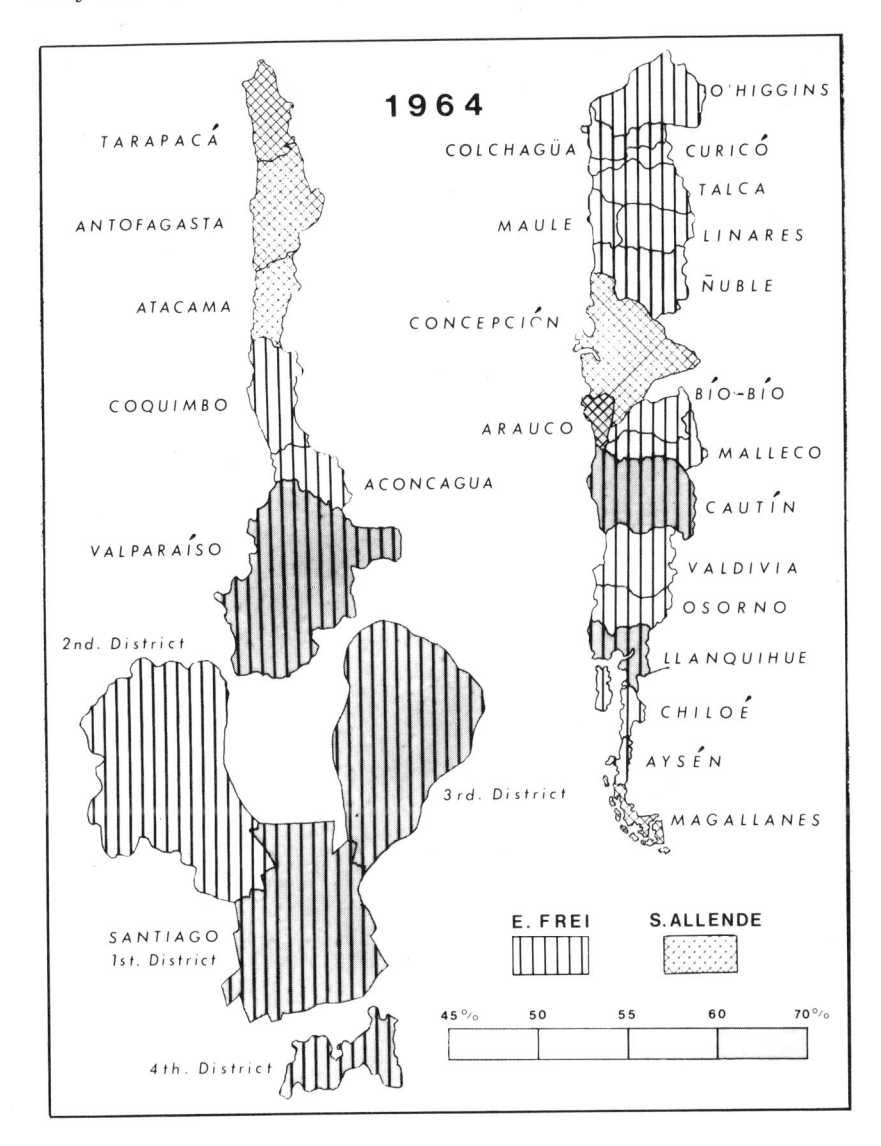

Figure 14.—The presidential election of 1964.

won (as a comfort in distress); electoral returns have always been susceptible to misinterpretation.[82] With the limitations imposed by the absence of reliable contemporary data on occupation, ecological interpretations remain just that—interpretations, viewpoints. The only conclusion that can be drawn from electoral returns is for whom people voted and where; from that trends may be established that, in general, can be parallel with ecological situations.

It has been mentioned above that the vote for Frei in agricultural provinces never surpassed 58 percent. The remarkable aspect here is that Allende scored better than anticipated in those provinces; indeed, in the traditional agricultural provinces he obtained between 34 and 45 percent of the vote, more than he received in the presidential election of 1958, when he never rose above 25 percent in those provinces. These percentages suggest that in the 1964 polarization (in 1958 there were five presidential candidates) the candidate of the Left was able to rally votes from sectors that were not customary clientele of the Marxist parties, thereby refuting once again the interpretation that votes for Allende had to come from the working class or were votes based on ideological commitment.

Salvador Allende carried the northern provinces of Tarapacá, Antofagasta, and Atacama, with percentages fluctuating between 44.6 and 48.3. He won the urban municipalities of Arica, Iquique, Tocopilla, and Copiapó, but his advantage over Frei was never more than 12 percent of the municipal electorate. The two major cities in the province of Antofagasta and Calama, fell to Frei by only a narrow margin. The municipality of Calama, which includes the largest copper mine of the country (Chuquicamata), voted 10,603 for Frei against 9,279 for Allende. These results were interpreted by Halperin as a rejection by the miners of Allende's nationalization program and prompted comments from Zeitlin and Petras that Allende had won over the working class because he scored 5.4 percent more than Frei among male voters.[83] What these foreign observers fail to realize is that it is impossible to prove that all the male votes for Allende came from workers and that few of the workers voted for Frei. It is also a fragile argument to state that Frei's victory in the commune of Calama meant a rejection of Allende's copper policies. How can it be determined from the total votes in Calama which came from miners and which political alternative miners had chosen?

Sandra Powell has made the very pertinent observation that in the 1964 election both Frei and Allende obtained less stratified support (votes from only certain sectors of society) than they had received in the electoral contest of 1958. Thus both candidates, instead of monopolizing the votes of certain occupational groups, e.g., copper miners, urban workers, or peasants, competed against each other for the support from these sectors, and the appeal of the Christian Democracy proved to be as strong as that of the FRAP.[84] Similar remarks on the character of Frei's total electoral support in 1964 have been advanced by Smith and Rodríguez, who contend that it is fallacious to assume that only a vote for the Left is a genuine working-class vote. There were high returns for Frei in some municipalities of indisputably proletarian character to prove their point.[85]

Particularly significant is the fact that in the most popular municipalities of Greater Santiago, e.g., Barrancas, San Miguel, La Cisterna, Quinta Normal, and Renca, Frei won over Allende with advantages of 1, 6, 11, 14, and 11 percent respectively. Zeitlin and Petras argue that these total results do not mean that the Christian Democracy was able to "wrest the workers allegiances from Socialists and Communists, with whom the workers have been identified throughout most of their struggles in this century," because in these municipalities it was Allende and not Frei who captured the majority of the male votes.[86] With all due respect for the ideological leanings of these authors, they are so obsessed with proving the triumph of Allende among the working class that they do not hesitate to assume that only *men* constitute the working class and to separate the Chilean proletarian couple in their political views. Moreover, to ascribe the overwhelming feminine vote for Frei to the influence of the Catholic church on women is overemphasizing the church's influence in Chile as well.

In short, it is only the aggregation, and not the stratification of the vote that explains the relatively high returns for Frei in the proletarian areas of urban centers and the good showing of Allende in the agricultural provinces. This general statement does not exclude cases of extreme polarization during the 1964 election. For example, in the traditionally rightist communes of Providencia and Las Condes in Greater Santiago, Frei overwhelmed Allende in the proportion of five to one and three to one, respectively. Is this an indication that the master voted for Frei and the butler and maid for Allende? Definitely not. Votes for Allende in these well-to-do neighborhoods may also have proceeded from accommodated leftist bourgeois and intellectuals.

Conversely, Salvador Allende obtained solid preferences in the mining centers of the country, with the exception of the mining districts in the provinces of Aconcagua and O'Higgins. In the municipalities of Catemu (Aconcagua) and Machalí (O'Higgins), where there is a high concentration of copper miners, the advantage of Allende over Frei was 14 and 28 percent respectively. This is really not an indication of an overwhelming victory for the FRAP candidate because those areas had always been solid strongholds of the Left.[87] More convincing victories were gained by Allende in smaller mining centers in the northern provinces of the country, e.g., Tocopilla, Toco, Sierra Gorda, and Tierra Amarilla, and in the mining municipalities of Lota, Coronel, and Curanilahue (provinces of Conception and Arauco) as he doubled and at times even tripled the results of Frei. In the municipality of Tomé inces of Concepción and Arauco) as he doubled and at times facturing, the candidate of the FRAP also did well by winning 60 percent of the municipal total. In this case there exists more ground for the interpretation that the working class preferred Allende over Frei. Moreover, in the southernmost province of Magallanes, Allende triumphed not only in the provincial capital, Punta Arenas, but also in the oil-producing municipality of Porvenir and the packing-plant town of Puerto Natales. In this traditionally leftist province Allende had obtained 47 percent of the vote in 1958 when running against four other candidates, so that the 49 percent he obtained in 1964 indicated but a slight growth when compared with the 42 percent for Frei, who in 1958 had only 21 percent of the provincial total. This and other improved results for Frei in places where the Christian Democracy or a Catholic candidate had previously scored rather poorly suggest that the electorate in these provinces had become more receptive to the social message of the Christian Democracy, or, as some observers prefer to say, the appeal of Frei was sufficient to attract progressive individuals whose vote for the Left had been in the past determined by the absence of more appealing candidates from the Center or the Right.

Julio Durán, the Radical candidate, did not meet even the most pessimistic expectations of party officials. His highest mark of 13.5 percent was in the province of Chiloé where Luis Bossay, the candidate of the Radicals in the presidential contest of 1958, had received 28 percent of the provincial vote. This exemplifies the devastating effect that polarization, added to a lack of appeal from the Radical candidate, had produced among the electorate.

Durán's lowest returns came from the province of Santiago where he obtained 3.1 percent, a mark that was 16 percentage points lower than Bossay's total in 1958. The mining province of Atacama, which in that year had given to the radical candidate well over 30 percent of its vote and which in the municipal elections of 1963 had returned 38 percent for the radical candidates, yielded only 12.1 percent for Durán. And this happened in his second best province in the country! In the contest between two solidly founded political parties, the Radicals had nothing to offer and, in addition to losing their credibility as politicians, they also lost their appeal among the middle class and the bureaucratic sectors of the country.

Partisan argumentations aside, the triumph of Frei was the response to his political platform of non-Marxist, but progressive, forces of the country. To attribute Frei's landslide to the "campaign of terror" is an underrating of the political education and common sense of the Chilean electorate, which has been considered the best informed and most difficult to please in all of Latin America. Furthermore, to maintain that the working class stood solidly behind Allende, while the oligarchy, the bourgeoisie, and the middle class were aligned with Frei, is to commit the inexcusable fallacy of ignoring the aggregation within the major ideological currents of the mid-1960s—the Christian Democracy and the Left. The increase of votes for the Christian Democracy in urban industrialized municipalities and the unusual strength of the FRAP in agricultural provinces were signs of ideological rather than ecological polarization.

The euphoria over Frei's triumph made the directive cadres of the Christian Democracy realize they had to move fast if they wanted to capitalize on their candidate's enormous appeal. Frei's overwhelming victory at the polls in September of 1964 had by no means changed the antidemocratic attitudes of the leftist opposition—the Communist and Socialist congressmen boycotted the sessions of the Congress in which Frei was to be proclaimed president of the Republic. However, since he had obtained more than 51 percent of the popular vote there was no need for a congressional vote.

The unfair tactics of the opposition went against the tradition of fair acknowledgment of defeat and served as a warning to the Christian Democracy of what to expect if such an unfriendly opposition were to become entrenched in the Congress. It was therefore vital for Frei to have a majority in the Congress if he expected to carry out the reforms promised during his electoral campaign. In November of 1964 the Right (Liberals, Conservatives, and Radicals) had eighty-four deputies and twenty-seven senators, and the leftist FRAP had forty deputies and thirteen senators. The Christian Democracy with only twenty-three deputies and four senators was in a comparatively weak position. The Right had supported Frei during his campaign, but no actual agreement had been made so that he could not rely on its cooperation in the Congress. The leftist parties resented the defeat of Allende and were not at all friendly toward the Christian Democrats; their boycott of the *congreso pleno* had shown how far they were prepared to go.

But, like ex-President Carlos Ibañez del Campo, Frei had been fortunate to have been elected president only six months before a scheduled congressional election, when the popular support from his election to the presidency had not yet worn off. With the slogan of "a Congress for Frei," the Christian Democratic party initiated an aggressive campaign to rally forces for the congressional elections of March 1965. They also capitalized on the Left's obstructionist tactics in the Congress and their negative effects on the Chilean public and on the government's intended structural reforms. Already in December of 1964, Minister Bernardo Leighton had announced urgent reforms of the public administration and of the taxation system to bring them in line with the proposed social programs.[88] Obviously, such a statement of action assured the low- and middle-class supporters of the Christian Democracy of the government's serious intentions to change the country's socioeconomic conditions. Activation of the agrarian reform was widely advertised in order to win the peasantry, who had shown less than total allegiance to Frei in 1964. For the urban electorate the Christian Democracy had also a message of redemption in the programs of Popular Promotion. Finally, to appease the nationalistic feelings of those who disliked the American ownership of the country's natural resources, especially copper, the party made the first step toward the "Chileanization" of the copper mines (51 percent ownership of the Chilean state), which was to precede a complete nationalization of the mines.[89]

For the congressional elections of 1965 the opposition of the

Christian Democratic government had developed few constructive points with which to attract the electorate. In an attempt to regain the votes that, in September of 1964, had gone to Frei as the alternative to the Marxist Allende, the Right tried to frighten the conservative elements of the Chilean society by telling them that their interests were jeopardized by the reforms announced by the government. The Left showed no intention of compromising with the Christian Democracy and was determined to use the hard line in its dealings with the newly elected government. According to the reputed economist Aníbal Pinto, the feasible alternatives for the Left were: a frontal attack opposition to the Frei government; a possible cooperation; conventional opposition (with the help of the Right in the Congress); or positive opposition, which means a selective support of those government policies that would benefit the supporters of the Left.[90] By March 1965 the FRAP coalition had chosen the frontal attack opposition to the government knowing that the Christian Democrats, in view of the structural reforms they had announced, could not hope to establish a political alliance with the Right.

The polls gave a smashing victory to the party in government. The Christian Democracy obtained 41 percent of the national vote, which made it the most formidable single party in the modern history of Chile. The Radical party, which had been second in the 1965 elections, obtained only 13 percent of the national vote. Although in September 1964 the FRAP had reached 38.9 percent with Salvador Allende, it showed now only 26 percent. In the lower Chamber the Christian Democrats elected eighty-two deputies (55 percent of the seats) and in the Senate they secured twelve out of the twenty-one contested seats. In the province of Santiago the Christian Democracy could have elected an additional senator if it had included a fourth candidate in the list; and in the province of Valparaíso it could have elected one more deputy if, again, the list had contained one additional candidate. The most optimistic forecasts had predicted a maximum of sixty-five deputies and nine senators, and the party surpassed these predictions by seventeen deputies and three senators.[91]

Although the marks for the FRAP did not equal Allende's vote in 1964, the Communist and Socialist parties increased their representation in the Congress. The Communists, the most important force in the FRAP alliance, emerged with 12 percent of the national vote, seventeen deputies, and two senators. The Socialists, as usual, trailed behind with 10 percent of the national vote, fifteen deputies, but three senators. PADENA, the third force in the FRAP, scored a poor 3.1 percent (in 1961 its mark had been 6.8 percent), which gave that party three deputies and one senator.

Although the 13 percent obtained by the Radical party was an improvement over Julio Durán's performance in the 1964 presidential contest, the results of the congressional elections could not be considered as auspicious for the party. In fact, it had elected only twenty-one deputies and three senators, a loss of nineteen deputies and three senators when compared to the 1961 election. Obviously, the Radicals had seen part of their support go over to the Christian Democrats and, to a lesser extent, to the FRAP. But most noticeable was the attraction of the emerging Christian Democracy among the traditional supporters of the Right. Tremendous electoral losses affected the Liberal party: national support fell from 16.5 percent in 1961 to 7.3 percent; only five deputies could be elected against the twenty-eight the party had obtained in 1961; and in the Senate the Liberals could not add a single representative. The Conservatives did no better than their allies; they came out with only 5.3 percent of the national vote, three deputies, and no senators. So devastating was the defeat of the Right that its political survival seemed in jeopardy. From these elections stems the epithet of "mummies."

The global results of the 1965 congressional elections refute the interpretation that the vote for Frei in 1964 had been the product of the fear of communism and that many traditional rightist voters had chosen Frei as the lesser of two evils and not because of his programmatic appeal.[92] The return of the rightist voters to their former positions revealed, however, that this sector of the electorate comprised not more than 15 percent of the nation's voters. Moreover, the diminution of the Radical party, a party of the middle class, was a clear indication that its clientele had shifted to the Christian Democracy, attracted by the programs of social reform and respect for democracy outlined by the young party before the elections.

As to whether the electorate responded to this political platform, one need only look at the results of the congressional elections of 1965. With even more intensity than in 1964, as the competition was now between the Christian Democracy and five other major parties, the party scored its major victories in the urban industrial provinces of the country (Figure 15). All the districts of Santiago voted overwhelmingly (between 46 and 49 percent) for Christian Democratic candidates. There was no question here of separating "bourgeois" districts from "proletarian" ones. In the popular Second District of Santiago the Christian Democracy convincingly defeated the Communist and Socialist parties among both male and female voters. While the Christian Democrats won 43.6 percent of the male vote, the Communists scored 17 and the Socialists 13. The feminine response was even more pronounced: 52 percent for the Christian Democrats against 12 percent for the Communists and 7 for the Socialists.[93] In the province of Valparaíso the winning party attained, with 51.5 percent, its highest provincial mark. The Communist party came second with 13.7 percent of the popular vote. Without precedence in the last forty years, a party with a religious connotation was able to obtain plurality in the province of Concepción, while the Communist party came second with 24 percent. As was customary the coal mining municipalities yielded to leftist candidates. Also for the first time the Christian Democracy won in the province of Antofagasta with 33 percent of the vote against 21 percent for the Communists. Unexpectedly, the mining province of Atacama, which in the past had voted for Radical or Socialist candidates, gave 40 percent to the Christian Democrats against 20 percent to the Radicals.

If in 1964 there were doubts about the preferences of the electorate in the agricultural provinces of central Chile, they were dissipated in March of 1965. The Christian Democrats swept them all with percentages oscillating between 44 and 31. The highest mark was obtained in the two districts of the province of Ñuble, where the Christian Democracy had already started to show some strength in 1961, due to the influence of local personalities. In the province of O'Higgins, where the importance of mining is not to be underrated, the party won with only 39 percent. Whereas the Communists came second in that province, in the rest of the agricultural provinces the Socialists or the PADENA trailed the Christian Democrats, although at great distance. It is remarkable that plurality had been given to a party that had voiced its intentions of accelerating the agrarian reform, and that the second preference had gone to parties that advocated even more radical

234

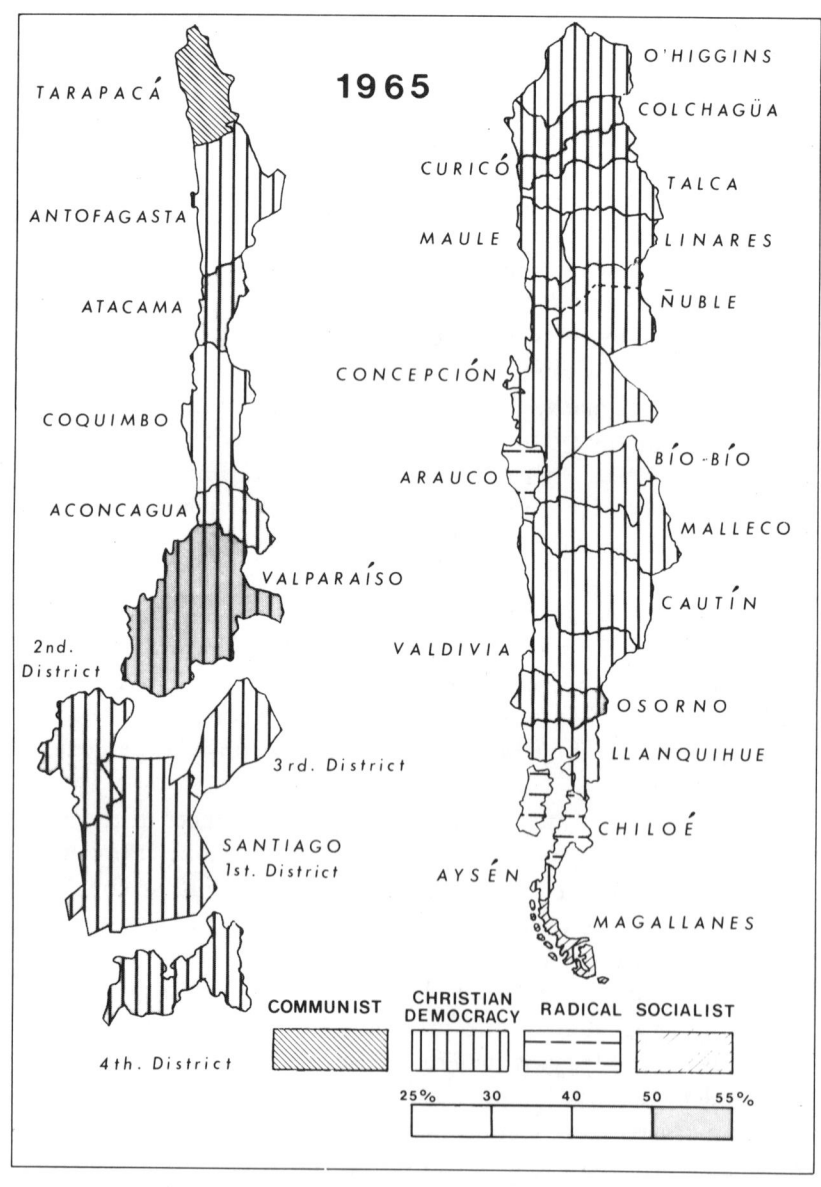

Figure 15.—The congressional elections of 1965.

reforms in land tenure. This reveals that as early as 1965, when the Christian Democracy had not yet established its grip over the peasantry of central Chile, the agrarian workers had already gained their political liberation from the landowners. It is significant that nowhere in the traditional agrarian provinces could any of the rightist parties attract more than 12 percent of the vote and that in general they came fourth behind the Christian Democrats, Communists, Socialists, or even Radicals.

In the agricultural provinces of recent colonization the pluralities for the Christian Democrats were widespread, but the Radicals and not the leftist parties were given second preference, which suggests that the agriculturalists of that part of Chile did not endorse the radical land policies advocated by the FRAP parties. The PADENA scored very well in the province of Cautín, where, owing to the appeal of local figures of moderate social-democratic views, it came second to the Christian Democrats. The Radicals obtained first preference only in the coal mining province of Arauco and in the rural province of Chiloé with percentages below 30. Formerly successful in the provinces of recent colonization, as well as in Ñuble, Bío-Bío, and Atacama, the party still came in second, but in the rest of the country it had to settle for third place behind the Christian Democrats and the Communists or Socialists.

Among the Marxist parties the Communists showed the greatest strength. With 37 percent they were first in the northern province of Tarapacá and second to the Christian Democrats in the provinces of Antofagasta, Valparaíso, O'Higgins, Concepción, and in all four districts of Santiago. The Communist successes in the mining provinces of the North and in all urban industrial provinces are an indication that their strength was due to the existence of nuclei of organized industrial workers and miners.

Since the Communists had not presented candidates in the agricultural provinces of Middle Chile, the Socialist candidates did well there, electing one deputy each in O'Higgins, Colchagua, and Curicó, provinces where they had seldom had electoral gratification. The province of Magallanes' only deputy office went to the Socialists with the support of other parties in the FRAP coalition, whereas the non-Marxist parties rallied around the unsuccessful candidate of the Radical party. Second place in provincial returns was obtained by the Socialists in the provinces of Aconcagua, Curicó, Arauco, Valdivia, and Aysén, all rural provinces, an indication that the support of the party was becoming increasingly aggregative by adding agrarian workers to the established base of industrial workers.

As in the presidential election of 1964, the feminine vote went first to the Christian Democracy (45 percent), second to the Radical party (12.8 percent), and third to the Communists (10 percent) as compared with the 38 percent for the Christian Democrats, the 14 percent for the Communists, and the 13.7 percent for the Radicals among male voters. The Left's obviously poor appeal among the female voters had to be considered seriously by its strategists in the future. Support from the women could mean the winning edge if close returns should occur in the future. In this context it is understandable that the Left increased its number of female politicians: Julieta Campusano, María Elena Carrera, Mireya Baltra, Carmen Lazo, Laura Allende, just to name a few. There were more leftist female politicians than rightist or centrist, but the response from female voters was still negative.

The formidable representation of the Christian Democracy in the Chamber of Deputies, which became known as the *aplanadora* ("steam roller"), augured a smooth running of affairs. Still, the party had not reached the coveted number of ninety-eight deputies (two-thirds of the lower Chamber) that would have allowed Frei to force the Senate to act on matters introduced into Congress by the executive.[94] Also, since five out of six Christian Democratic deputies were men without experience in the legislature they were entrusted to the experienced Deputy Alfredo Lorca, who was appropriately nicknamed "Mother Superior." In the Senate, the Christian Democrats were outnumbered thirteen to thirty-two, so that they could expect the most tenacious opposition.

Encouraged by the mandate from the people and relying on the high representation in the lower Chamber, Frei's government moved swiftly to introduce bills concerning the major programmatic points outlined during the electoral campaigns: nationalization of copper, agrarian reform, tax reform, unionization, and university reform. In the parliamentary debate on these bills, the necessary prelude to legislation, the lines that were to characterize the political strategy of the Christian Democracy in the years to come surfaced. On one side, alliances with the Right would assure the Senate's passing of legislation on the "Chileanization" of the copper mines. On the other side, alliances with the

Left would secure legislation on the agrarian reform. Of course, in the copper question the Left pursued total nationalization without payments to the American companies (in opposition to the plans of the Christian Democracy), whereas in the agrarian reform it favored acceleration of changes in the land-tenure schemes, which aroused opposition from Liberals and Conservatives.[95]

Apart from momentary shifts of alliances in the Congress, the Christian Democracy tried to avoid permanent bonds with either the Left or the Right, and indeed there was no need for them since the 1965 elections had given such enormous support to Frei and his government. But excessive power caused problems for the majority party. Arrogance and a lack of political flexibility in its dealings with the political establishment, *falta de muñequeo político* (i.e., lack of wrist wrestling ability), heightened the animosity of the other parties and inspired their attacks on the government. The Left's continuous stirring of organized labor into rebelling against the government forced the Christian Democracy to apply harsh measures with militant workers, which led to an erosion of its prestige among them.

In addition to the external pressures, in its first year in power the Christian Democracy began to experience factional differences that cracked the apparent solid unity of the party. It should be remembered that the Christian Democratic party had become highly aggregative in the 1960s, quite unlike the National Falange, which, during its first two decades of existence, had been "a small fraternal cadre party embracing young, middle-class Catholic intellectuals."[96] The conquest of the executive power had placed the old cadres of the party in key governmental positions. Mellowed by age and long years of experience, they appeared to be too cautious and even conservative for the young and impatient lower ranks of the party.

The preparation of the Christian Democratic bill on agrarian reform and a new legislation on labor organization revealed the internal cleavages that were developing as early as July of 1965. An "officialist" faction made up of middle-aged party members, mostly professionals, and long since committed to the social-Christian postulates of the party, dominated the state agencies and the executive. In the course of time they had been joined by landowners and industrialists who had formerly militated in center-right parties such as the Agrarian Laborite party, the National party, and the *Partido Demócrata*. The landowner elements were not at all eager to bring forward a swift and radical agrarian reform, but left the initiative to the younger and more dynamic elements headed by Jacques Chonchol and Rafael Moreno.[97]

Basic disagreements on the pace of the "revolution in freedom," the attitude toward the rightist parties, and the party's policies regarding the organization of workers separated the "officialists" from the "nonconformists." One of the nonconformist groups rallied around an old but restive professional politician of the party, Rafael Agustín Gumucio. He was surrounded by younger men like Rodrigo Ambrosio, Alberto Jerez, and Julio Silva Solar, whose social-Christian views emulsified with elements of ill-digested Marxism. This faction, known as the "rebels," stood for a swift and radical implementation of the agrarian reform, total nationalization of the copper mines, cooperation with the Marxist-controlled Central Workers Union, and the establishment of political alliances with the Left in order to accelerate revolutionary developments in Chile.[98]

Realizing that the program of the "rebels" could bring the Christian Democrats into ideological competition with the Marxists in which the former's pluralistic views would put them at a disadvantage, but at the same time rejecting a capitalistic approach to development, a third faction, the *terceristas*, emerged in 1966. Its leaders were progressive, realistic professionals without the ideological confusion of the "rebels" and without the conservative attitudes of the officialists. Among the *terceristas* were Renán Fuentealba, a man with long-standing tradition as a parliamentary fighter, Bosco Parra, and a group of young politicians like Luis Maira and Pedro F. Ramírez, whose affinity with the leftist "rebels" was difficult to hide. Nevertheless, the *terceristas* preferred to keep their criticism of the official politics within the circles of the party in order to present a façade of party unity.

Undoubtedly, the internal strife among Christian Democrats was only a side effect of the trouble the party was facing from outside. The fear that proceeding too fast with the structural changes could cause panic in both national and international financial circles had kept the government from intervening in the economic structure of the country. This drew harsh criticism from the Left and from the trade unions. Correctly assuming that the government would be reluctant to move against labor protest movements, the Left incited the unions to escalate their demands and back the upsurges in the mining provinces. The tragedies that resulted gave the leftist opposition the opportunity to call the government of President Frei "reactionary" and "repressive."[99] At the University of Chile and at the University of Concepción, Marxist students disrupted activities at will to make a show of the impotence of the government. Thus, the effects of external circumstances as well as the conflict within the party and the lack of energy to back the government initiated an irreversible *desgaste* ("popular erosion") of the Christian Democracy.[100] This reverse of fortune became visible early in 1967 when the Senate refused President Frei permission to accept an invitation from President Lyndon Johnson to visit the United States. Without a majority in the Senate, and with less than two-thirds in the Chamber of Deputies, any appeal would have been fruitless. So once again the Christian Democracy asked the people to show their disapproval of the unprecedented behavior of the opposition by voting against them in the upcoming municipal elections of April 1967.[101]

The results of that contest were most disheartening for the Christian Democrats. They won only 36.5 percent of the vote, 7 percent less than in the congressional elections of 1965. All the other parties experienced gains, the Socialist, Radical, Communist, and National (merged Liberals and Conservatives) parties. The major upsets of the Christian Democracy occurred in the urban centers that, only two years before, had been so favorable toward them. Strikingly low support was shown in highly urbanized communes of the provinces of Santiago and Valparaíso, where the lost votes went to the Nationals, who, as a result, doubled their 1965 ballot support in some places. The Socialists increased their returns in the northern provinces and in the populous districts of the province of Santiago. The Communists, as usual, had victories in the northern mining provinces as well as in the coal mining municipalities of Concepción and Arauco. The Radicals showed signs of recovery in Coquimbo, Valparaíso, and in the agricultural provinces of recent colonization.[102]

In the rural municipalities, from where the first reactions to the agrarian reform were expected, the Christian Democracy suffered fewer losses than in urban communes and even had gains in the rural municipalities in which *asentamientos* had been established. Robert R. Kaufman advanced the hypothesis that since the leftist

FRAP and the Christian Democracy exhibited electoral gains or moderate losses in those municipalities in which the rightist National party and the Radicals had heavy losses, it could mean that the FRAP coalition and the Christian Democracy were not competing against each other, but were in fact both contending with the Right for the rural vote. He also states that from the 1967 municipal returns it may be concluded that the support for the Radicals and the Right came from small land proprietors, whereas the vote of *asentamiento* peasants and landless rural workers was divided between the Christian Democracy and the FRAP.[103]

In general, the results of the municipal elections showed the Christian Democracy was being deserted by the two major sectors of the Chilean society that had favored it in the past. On one side, the support from popular sources had slackened and moved to the Left (from whom the Christian Democracy was no longer able to subtract votes), and on the other side the urban middle-class voters had already gotten over their honeymoon with Frei and, worn down by the cost of reforms that were of no benefit to them, had started to shift over to the Nationals and Radicals.

In 1965, the extremely low electoral returns for the Radicals and the rightist parties had been interpreted as a sign of their definite decline, but two years later it was proven otherwise. Thus, the strategists of the Christian Democracy turned their batteries against the Right, who they believed responsible for their loss of popularity. By attacking the Right's antireformist views they hoped to win support from progressive workers and middle-class individuals who had not yet endorsed the Christian Democracy. But this was poor strategy. As it turned out, there was no additional support forthcoming. Therefore, instead of benefiting Frei's government, a leaning to the Left hastened the erosion of the party, as moderate middle-class elements abandoned the Christian Democracy and moved into conservative positions, and leftist individuals who once had favored the party felt more inclined to support the aggressive FRAP.

Already in 1965 Socialist party spokesmen had declared war without truce against the government of Frei,[104] and in the following years a mounting offensive was conducted by making use of the Marxists' control over the labor unions. Attempts to gain control over the Central Workers Union (CUT) were completely unsuccessful, and the proposal of Labor Minister William Thayer to create freedom of unionization to counteract the Communist control of the CUT brought not only an outcry of "nonconformists," but also a most strident reaction from the national and international Left.[105]

The Christian Democrats' attempted opening to the Left and their failure to counteract the Marxist influence within organized labor elicited the most formidable offensive from the Left and from labor since Ibañez del Campo's second term in office. Violent strikes rampaged the country between 1966 and 1968,[106] proving that the government was unable to cope with labor unrest and that by trying to use a firm hand it only damaged its image of a popular regime. At the same time, the democratization of the university and the adaptation of education to the needs of the nation led to violent confrontations and partisan struggles, as the political parties, especially the Communists, seized the opportunity to gain power and influence in teachers' guilds and student unions. To add fuel to the fire, guerrilla activity was reported in remote areas of the South, and the major urban centers of the country were plagued by bomb explosions and armed bank assaults, perpetrated by groups of the Ultraleft (MIR, VOP). Armed subversion and contempt of authority were becoming the order of the day in Chile. Ironically, all these by-products of extreme politization, which under different circumstances would have been welcomed by the Christian Democracy as signs of political mobilization, were working to its disadvantage. Frei's government became increasingly beleaguered by the Left's capitalization on the dissatisfaction of the middle- and lower-class workers.

Developments in the sphere of congressional politics also were most unfavorable for the Christian Democracy. The Radical party, which appeared to be making a comeback in the 1967 municipal elections, sensing the attrition of the Christian Democratic government and the intensity of the leftist tide in the country, decided to break off with the Right and began to approach the Left under the direction of Professor Alberto Baltra. A bourgeois figure, Baltra belonged to the old guard of Radicals who, in the years of the Popular Front, had been on good terms with the Left. In the mid-1960s his relations with the People's Republic of China made him the most appropriate "silver bridge" between his party and the FRAP. At the end of 1967 the new alignment of the Radicals with the Left was put to its first test. In a senatorial by-election, held in the provinces of recent colonization, Baltra, supported by Communists and Socialists, won a narrow margin over the Christian Democrat Jorge Lavanderos, an affluent agriculturalist.[107] In view of this victory of a leftist coalition in an area of rather conservative farmers, the comments of Luis Corvalán, secretary-general of the Communist Party of Chile, to the *New York Times* were quite realistic in the sense that power was within reach for the Left if the strengthened union of Communists and Socialists could be maintained in the elections of 1969 and 1970, and if defectors from the Christian Democracy and the Radical party would join the Left.[108]

The bickering inside the Christian Democratic party took its first victim in November of 1968, when Jacques Chonchol, the main force behind the agrarian reform, resigned as vice-president of the Agrarian Livestock Development Institute (INDAP) to protest alleged budget curtailments from the government on instigation of the "officialist" Minister of the Interior Pérez Zujovic. This incident dramatized the seriousness of the internal conflict that was developing on the eve of such an important parliamentary contest as the one of March 1969 promised to be.

Chonchol's resignation, which meant a stalling of the agrarian reform, offered the "nonconformists" sufficient grounds to plead that the executive had fallen into the hands of conservative and regressive elements and that they were in collusion with the threatened interests of the oligarchy.[109]

The growing radicalization of the Christian Democrats led to similar developments among young laymen and priests who rallied in a militant group known as *Iglesia Jóven* ("Young Church"). They denounced liberal capitalism for its exploitative connotations, acridly criticized the formalism of the upper hierarchy of the Roman Catholic church, and saw an association with Marxism as the only means to abolish socioeconomic inequities and to attain a socialist society.[110] Since *Iglesia Jóven* was made up almost exclusively of ultraprogressive Jesuits and accommodated members of the upper middle class, the movement was too intellectual and sophisticated to find support among the proletariat; it only shattered the Catholic church in Chile and contributed to the internal dissension within the troubled Christian Democracy. It is incomprehensible that nobody in the party seemed to realize the impending catastrophe as the diverse factions drifted, in complete paranoia, into the hands of their avowed enemies. The frontal attacks by "rebels" and *terceristas* on the party leaders had driven them into more conservative and autocratic positions, and the acquiescence to the leftist parties had diminished the external strength of the party. No political or electoral gains could be expected from the sectors of the electorate that had fallen under the control of the FRAP as a result of the government's awkward handling of inflation and labor unrest.

With the very modest hope of winning 35 percent of the national electorate, the Christian Democracy embarked on an electoral campaign that did not so much draw attention to the merits of the party as to the qualities of President Frei as a statesman. At a time in which the structural reforms advocated by the Christian Democracy had caused heightened animosity, alienation, and ingratitude between the losers and the beneficiaries, the campaign was aimed at giving the president the parliamentary support to circumvent congressional obstructionism and to speed up legislation in benefit of the masses. The rightist National party based its campaign on the contention that Christian Democratic government had brought to the country only social unrest, institutional chaos, and economic distress, and that the only winners in this situation had been the Marxist parties. The FRAP had several things with which to reproach the government: none of the much publicized reforms of the Christian Democracy had really progressed at a revolutionary pace, inflation was taking its heaviest toll from the proletariat, and the response of the government to the protests of the working class had been repression. As in the past, the attention of political observers focused on the electoral appeal of Frei and his "revolution in liberty" as opposed to the radical revolution pursued by the FRAP.

This was the situation for the congressional elections of March 2, 1969, from which the Christian Democracy emerged with 31 percent of the national vote and the FRAP 30 percent. The Nationals enjoyed an unexpected high return of 20 percent—the "mummies" had risen from their sarcophagi!

The erosion of the Christian Democrats cost them twenty-seven deputies, as they took only fifty-five seats in the lower Chamber. The highest gain in that Chamber was made by the Nationals who increased their seven seats to thirty-four. Less dramatic were the gains of the Communists and the Radicals each with four seats more than in 1965. The Socialists, even though their national support was 3 percent higher than in 1965, could not raise their fifteen seats in the lower Chamber. Polarization had progressed so much in the last four years that splinter parties like the Popular Socialist Union and the PADENA together could barely get 3 percent of the national vote.

Quite different from the past when the number of elected deputies had been closely proportional to the number of elected senators, the Christian Democrats claimed a great success in the Senate as they obtained thirteen new senators, which raised their representation to twenty-three. Apparently, in the 1969 congressional elections the Christian Democracy offered an attractive slate of "heavyweights" who really appealed to the electorate. Dominating political figures of the past like Luis Bossay and Ramón Silva Ullaa were elected senators, although the party they represented did poorly in the deputies elections. Despite the importance of political parties as channels of political expression, a strong personality could still attract many electors.[111] The Communists, in comparison, elected only four senators and kept the same six seats they had in 1965. Nationals and Radicals elected five senators each, a loss of two and three senators, respectively, from the numbers obtained in 1965. The Socialists also experienced losses in the Senate, winning only three seats as compared with the seven they had obtained in 1965.

In the provincial distribution of electoral strength (Figure 16), the Christian Democracy obtained pluralities in eighteen provinces; it lost Maule to the Nationals, the Second District of Ñuble and Osorno to the Radicals, and Valdivia to the Socialists. In a strange shift considering its former leftist leanings, the province of Arauco was won by the Christian Democrats. But almost everywhere, except in the agricultural province of Malleco and the southern province of Aysén, they lowered their 1965 marks by an average of 13 percent. The lowest results for the party in government came from the urban-industrial provinces where it had made dramatic inroads in the mid-1960s, especially from the Second and Third districts of Santiago, where the lost votes apparently went to the FRAP and the Nationals. In the province of Valparaíso the Christian Democrats lowered their 1965 marks by 17 percent, whereas the Communists made an impressive gain of 23 percent, the Nationals improved by 7, and the Socialists by 2 percent. In

245

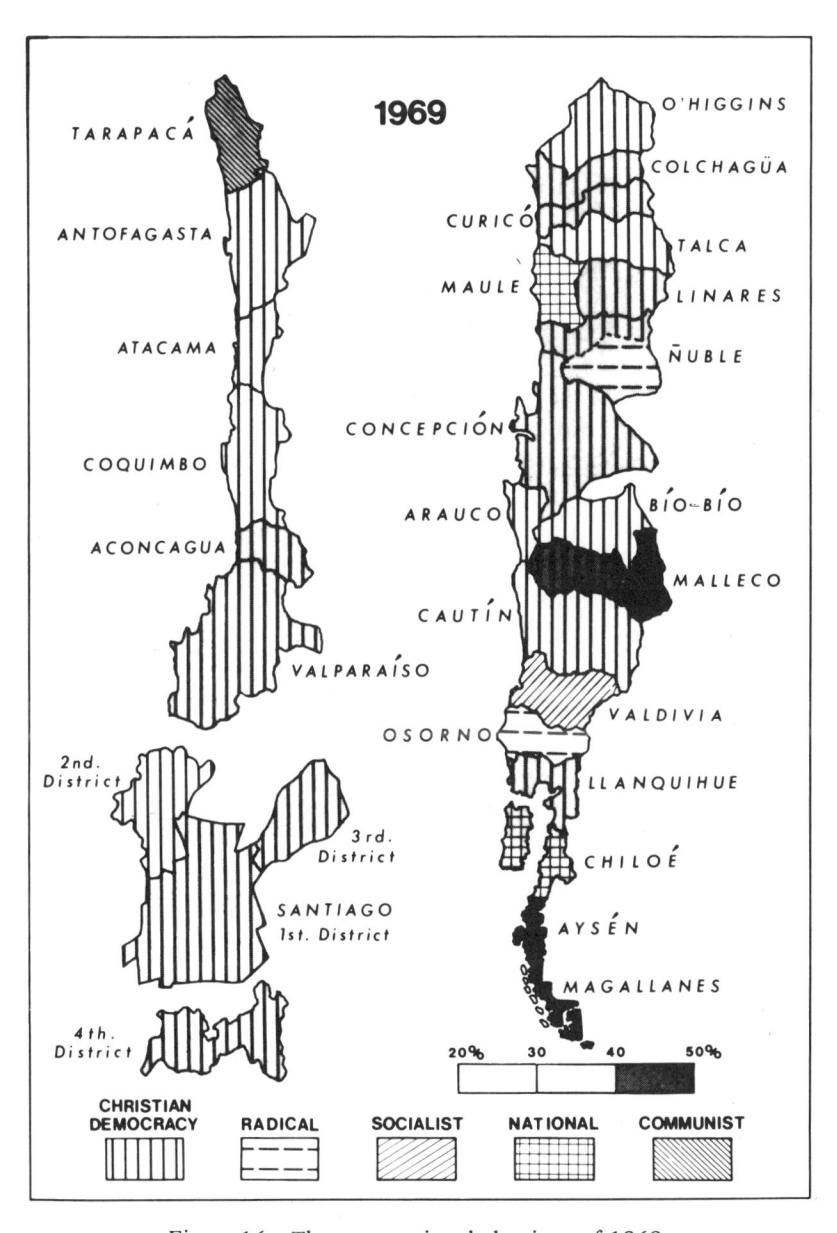

Figure 16.—The congressional elections of 1969.

the province of Concepción the reduction of the Christian Democracy from 39 to 31 percent seemed to be related to the electoral growth of the Communists from 24 to 27 percent. Even the Nationals gained ground in leftist Concepción and raised their poor 5.8 percent in 1965 (no deputy) to 11.5 percent (one deputy) in 1969.

Unexpectedly, in the northern provinces of the country (Tarapacá and Antofagasta) the Christian Democrats' losses were no greater than 5 percent in deputies, indicating a certain competition with the powerful leftist parties that had been dominant in that region. This point was further proved in the election of three Christian Democratic senators in those provinces against only two Communist senators. However, the mining province of Atacama upset the Christian Democrats; although they obtained the plurality there with 26 percent, this figure was 14 percent lower than in 1965.

In the agrarian provinces the Christian Democrats' decline, averaging 11 percent, was less acute.[112] The greatest loss occurred in the province of Ñuble (14 percent below the 1965 mark) and the least occurred in Maule where the party held its ground—32 percent of the provincial vote. Further south, in the provinces of recent colonization, the party had more auspicious results. The province of Malleco gave them 44.5 percent of the vote, a 14 percent increase over 1965. Arauco and Aysén gave the Christian Democrats pluralities, and in Chiloé, although trailing the Nationals, they improved their 1965 mark by 7 percent.

Second place in the total return went to the Nationals who won pluralities in the provinces of Maule and Chiloé. As pointed out before, the major recoveries of the rightists occurred in three of the districts of Santiago, in urban Valparaíso, and in the agrarian provinces. A differentiation must be made, however, between the returns from the traditional agricultural provinces and those from the agricultural provinces of recent colonization. In the traditional agricultural provinces the rise of the Nationals, their former political masters, was on the order of 5 percent (with the exception of the provinces of Colchagua and Talca where the Right continued to decline); in the other agricultural provinces the improvement was more significant—9 percent, and in the case of Cautín even 14 percent over the 1965 results. Quite unexpectedly the Nationals also made a comeback in some of the northern provinces.

They elected one deputy and obtained 18 percent of the vote in the province of Tarapacá, one deputy and 13 percent in Coquimbo, and one deputy and 22 percent in the province of Aconcagua.

The Communist party came in third with 16.7 percent of the country's electorate, twenty-two deputies, and six senators. Their most convincing show occurred in the province of Tarapacá, which gave them the plurality; in Antofagasta they were second to the Christian Democrats with 24 percent of the provincial vote. Other good marks were scored in Valparaíso—23 percent, in Santiago's First District—15 percent, Second District—21 percent, Third District—18 percent, and in Concepción—27 percent. It is noteworthy that all these provinces or districts are either copper or coal mining provinces or urban industrial provinces. The Communists also made inroads into the agricultural provinces of Talca and Bío-Bío, where they elected one deputy each. The Socialists, their companions in the FRAP, could not keep up with them; they collected only 12.8 percent of the national vote and elected fifteen deputies and three senators. Again, as in previous elections, even though the Socialists came close to the Communists' percentage of the total vote (only 3 percent less), they elected 23 percent fewer candidates because of poorly distributed electoral efforts. The Socialists came first in the provinces of Valdivia (two deputies) and Magallanes (one deputy); in Coquimbo and O'Higgins they obtained second place behind the Christian Democrats. A contraction of the Socialists, probably to the advantage of their Communist allies, occurred in the northern provinces as well as in Valparaíso, the First District of Santiago, Concepción, and Arauco. Only in the Second, Third, and Fourth districts of Santiago did they match the votes for the Communists, but they won only two out of the fifteen contested seats in the lower Chamber, while the Communists took three.

The comeback of the battered Radical party was more modest than that of the National party. It managed to obtain 13.5 percent of the national vote, a meager 0.7 percent improvement over its 1965 percentage. By using their support in a more intelligent way than the Socialists and even the Communists, the Radicals elected twenty-four deputies and five senators and appeared to be the most favored, and the smartest, political group of the 1969 congressional elections. Their best showings occurred in the Second District of Ñuble and in the province of Osorno, where they attained pluralities, and in the provinces of Coquimbo, Linares, Arauco and Maule, where they came second to the Christian Democrats or Nationals. Relatively good percentages were obtained in the urban industrial provinces of Valparaíso and Concepción, with provincial returns below only those of the Christian Democrats or Communists. The rural province of Chiloé revived a little of its old faith in the Radicals and gave them 25 percent of the provincial vote and one deputy. The populous Second and Third districts of Santiago, from where the party had drawn a great part of its support in the past, were definitely lost for the Radicals probably to the Christian Democrats and the FRAP.

As to the smaller parties of Chile's political spectrum, there was not much left for them after the five giants had made their electoral grab. Ampuero's Popular Socialist party could not obtain a single seat in the lower Chamber, but it remained a legal party because of the senatorial seat of its leader. It had a useless show of support in the provinces of Antofagasta (9 percent), Colchagua (12 percent), and Llanquihue (10 percent). The PADENA fared no better as it won only 1.5 percent of the national vote and failed to elect deputies in any of the provinces in which it presented candidates: Cautín (5.6 percent), Santiago's Third District (2.7 percent), and Santiago's First District (2 percent).

The Congress elected in 1969 was of great importance, for it would be in office during the first three years of the next president's term, and half of the senators would stay in the upper Chamber until 1977. Now whatever political force, the FRAP, the Right, or the Christian Democracy, was to win the executive power in 1970, it was evident that it would not have a majority in either of the two Chambers. This circumstance would create the same problems for the future government as it did for its predecessors.[113] The only combination that could have reached a comfortable majority in both Chambers would have been a centrist coalition of Christian Democrats and Radicals. However, the latter were reluctant to enter into an alliance with a party in government whose support was obviously declining and saw a greater advantage in remaining in the opposition. The Christian Democrats, on the other hand, persisted in their obtuse policy of "ideological purism" and independence that had caused nothing but trouble in their dealings with the Congress.

The returns from the urban provinces in the 1969 congressional elections showed that the leftist inclinations of some sectors of the Christian Democracy had caused the flight of middle-class voters to the Nationals. The fact that the officialist candidates of the Christian Democracy (most of the thirteen senators) scored clear victories, rather than the "rebels" and *terceristas,* revealed that the moderate line of the Christian Democrats was more appreciated by its electoral supporters than the nonconformist positions. Furthermore, in the urban provinces where the Communists had made substantial gains, the desertion of Christian Democrat voters was a likely consequence of the mounting mobilization among the *pobladores,* who, long neglected by the governmental agencies, had found in the revolutionary message of leftist activities a new road toward structural change and political participation.[114] Guillermo Briones maintains that although the highly urbanized provinces showed a correlation with electoral support for the Left, the results of the 1969 election revealed little correlation between leftist preferences and the labor force in manufacturing industries, a finding that denies the common talk that the industrial-urban proletariat has been solidly behind leftist parties in Chile. Instead he affirms that this sector of the Chilean society supports those parties that postulate development and reform as well as Marxist parties.[115] Perhaps with this consideration in mind one can understand why the Christian Democracy and also the Radical party did not fall far behind the FRAP in the provinces where manufacturing industries are an important sector of the economy: Antofagasta, Valparaíso, Santiago's Third District, and Concepción.

The loss of middle-class support (the swing of voters to the Nationals and the corresponding reduction of Christian Democrat votes in urban provinces) may be interpreted as the result of the middle-class's disenchantment with the Frei government. Inflation added to overtaxation had its maximum impact on the salaried workers of the middle strata, the only ones whose taxes are automatically deducted from their paychecks. Since the affluent classes were always able to cope with rising prices (and even profit from them) and often had the legal knowledge or connections to dodge tax regulations, they were not greatly affected by inflation and taxes. No wonder, therefore, that the salaried voters disliked political platforms such as "Let the rich pay," knowing that it was not the rich but themselves who would pay in the end. George W.

Grayson has suggested that the withdrawal of electoral support by middle-class individuals could also have been caused by the bickering inside the Christian Democratic party as well as by "electoral fatigue" (1963, 1965, 1969 were election years and 1970 was to be the next one). He adds that the unusual high percentage of abstentions (27 percent) is yet another sign of disenchantment, not only with the Christian Democracy but with the extreme politization of the institutional life in Chile in general.[116]

However the erosion of the party in government and the shift of voters to the two extremes of the political spectrum is explained, after the 1969 elections it was evident that the euphoria of *Freismo* had subsided and that the Christian Democracy had been unable to hold the uncommitted voters it had attracted during the mid-1960s. By 1969 the dissatisfied electorate was aligning once again in those extreme ideological positions that announced times of tension and polarization in Chilean politics.

Not long after the March 1969 congressional elections the electoral party machines were being tuned up for the presidential contest of the next year. After the impressive show of the Nationals and the election of two members of the Alessandri family, it was obvious for the Right that its candidate for 1970 would be the aged ex-President Jorge Alessandri. This forced the Christian Democracy to make its own decision very early in 1969 and to choose one of three alternatives: (1) to nominate a candidate acceptable to the Right to thwart the candidacy of Jorge Alessandri and repeat the situation of 1964—a Christian Democratic candidate unconditionally backed by the Right; (2) to seek an alliance with the Left under the umbrella of a Christian Democratic candidate; or (3) to run its own candidate, trusting in his personal appeal and the prestige of the party to ensure electoral victory.

As to the first possibility, the recent electoral recovery of the Right made it unnecessary for it to become again the unacknowledged partner of the Christian Democracy. Also, the proposed successor of Eduardo Frei, Radomiro Tomic, another founder of the party, was completely unpalatable to the Right because of his leftist posture. The second alternative, an electoral alliance with the Left centered around a Christian Democratic candidate, was as unacceptable to the Left as the support of a leftist candidate was to the Christian Democracy. As early as 1968, when the party in the government had voiced its intentions of running one of its men, the Communist party had made it known that it would never support a Christian Democratic presidential candidate, and the Socialists, through their ultraleft spokesman Carlos Altamirano, had rejected in even harsher terms any possibility of electoral collaboration with the Christian Democracy.[117] Thus the only alternative for the Christian Democrats was to run their own candidate alone, fully aware that his chances of winning would be the slimmest of the three major candidates. In May 1969 the official wing of the party approved by a very narrow margin a resolution to reject an alliance with the Left. This move precipitated the defection of a group of "nonconformists" who formed the Movement of United Popular Action (MAPU). On August 15, 1969, the Christian Democratic party officially announced the candidacy of Radomiro Tomic.

The expectations of the parties of the Left were much better than those of the Christian Democrats. Socialists and Communists had been very cautious in the choice of their nominees. They were trying not to spark premature dissension within the ranks of the Popular Unity (UP), the new name of the alliance of the Left. The Radical party, whose independence from the leftist alliance allowed its members to express their views more freely, entered its candidate in the person of Alberto Baltra in June 1969. His nomination reflected the overtly leftist tendency the party had adopted in the last years. Rightist dissidents were subsequently expelled or resigned and rallied in a faction called Radical Democracy, which shortly after announced its endorsement of Jorge Alessandri's nomination. On August 29, the Socialist party finally managed to agree on Salvador Allende as their entry for the nominating contest of the Popular Unity. The other members of the leftist union soon followed suit: on September 7 the Popular Independent Action (API) forwarded the name of Rafael Tarud; on September 27 the Movement of United Popular Action (MAPU) nominated Jacques Chonchol; and at the end of September the Communist party entered Pablo Neruda. The decision of who would be the candidate of the Left was to be made at the end of the year. On November 2, 1969, Jorge Alessandri officially agreed to run for the National party and thus averted an alliance between the Right and the Christian Democracy. The parties of the Left, sensing victory now that the Center and the Right were divided in the presidential contest, smoothed out their differences, and by January 1970 Salvador Allende emerged once again as the candidate of a united Left.[118]

In its basic issues the electoral campaign of 1970 did not vary greatly from the campaign of 1964. Radomiro Tomic had the difficult task of conducting a cautious campaign; he had to play down the shortcomings of the first Christian Democratic administration (inflation, housing shortage, copper policies, and sluggish pace of the agrarian reform) and to stress further structural reforms in the country. This brought acrid attacks from the Right and prompted the flight of the moderates to the National party, increasing the growing political polarization. Special care was taken by Tomic's electoral machine to maintain his support among the peasants favored by the agrarian reform and to recover the electoral clientele of the poor urban neighborhoods. In both these sectors, however, the real challenger of the Christian Democracy was not the Right but the Popular Unity, and Tomic showed an astonishing lack of political realism in mistaking his political adversary.

For the Left this presidential campaign appeared less difficult than previous campaigns. From its advantageous opposition stand, the Popular Unity could easily point out and criticize the failures of its two opponents when they had held the executive power. Contrary to reports that the mass media of the country and the church worked against a possible triumph of the Left in 1970,[119] the Popular Unity experienced a most impressive backing from the media. The journalists' union, the crew of the state's television network, the artists' guild, more than ten newspapers and weekly magazines, and half a dozen radio stations in Greater Santiago were at the disposal of Salvador Allende during his campaign. And the firm grip of Communists and Socialists over the student unions at the University of Chile, the University of Concepción, and the Technical State University assured the party of a large and militant contingent of political campaigners. With such a communication infrastructure and the enthusiastic collaboration of artists and students, the thrust of the campaign for Allende zeroed in on the urban proletariat and the dissatisfied peasants who had not benefited from the Christian Democrats' agrarian reform. Less attention than in previous campaigns was given to the coal and copper miners, whose loyalty to the Left rested on very solid bases.

In Jorge Alessandri the Right had found a prestigious but less than enthusiastic candidate. Knowing that nobody from the ranks of the National party had the political appeal or image of righteousness he had, Alessandri agreed to run as candidate at seventy-three years of age. His campaign was based on the contention that the six years of Christian Democratic administration had brought agitation to the countryside, inflation, hyperpolitization, and contempt of the institutional authority. The Christian Democracy was accused of having permitted the penetration of Marxism into the universities, the media, and ultimately among the peasants.[120] The mounting terrorism by ultraleftists, the violence in the country, and the growing dissatisfaction among the armed forces were blamed on the Christian Democracy's inability to cope with political insurrection and military insubordination. A particularly serious example of the latter had been the mutiny of the Artillery Regiment Tacna in Santiago on October 21, 1969 (the *Tacnazo*), in which General Roberto Viaux unskillfully mixed wage demands with unmistakable putschist intentions.[121]

To a middle-of-the-road electorate, Alessandri's criticism of the Christian Democracy and the Popular Unity was more than welcome, especially among the urban middle classes who had suffered the brunt of Frei's tax reforms and the physical inconvenience of the Left's agitation. With more political sense than the Christian Democrats, the electoral propaganda of Alessandri (financially boosted by U.S. funds)[122] was aimed at the moderate, antipolitical, and independent voters of the provinces of Santiago and Valparaíso, which the strategists of the Right thought would be the decisive provinces. Unlike in previous elections, the Right left the countryside almost completely to its adversaries. It made no efforts in areas where the Christian Democracy and the Popular Unity had already proven their strength. To not even have tried was one of the costly mistakes of Alessandri's electoral strategy.

The Government of the Popular Unity

After an election day without incidents, the official results were announced in the early hours of September 5, 1970. Salvador Allende had won with 1,070,344 votes (36.2 percent of the electors) over Jorge Alessandri with 1,031,151 votes (34.9 percent). In a distant third place came Radomiro Tomic with 821,342 (27.8 percent). The 39,175 votes separating Allende from Alessandri were reminiscent of the slim margin that had made Alessandri president in 1958. This time, however, Allende was the one favored by the slight edge. Salvador Allende had won his victory in the 50,570 votes obtained over Alessandri in the province of Concepción and the 41,965 votes in the four northernmost provinces.[123] As indicated before, the disinterest of Alessandri's campaigners to challenge the Popular Unity in the provinces where it was firmly rooted had allowed Allende to move out of reach. Inversely, the emphasis put on the urban centers of Middle Chile did not bring the necessary gains to the candidate of the Right; in the province of Santiago Alessandri fell 100,000 votes short of what he would have needed to balance Allende's gains in the northern provinces. With percentages of over 43 Allende's victories were solid in the northern provinces (Figure 17). It is interesting that Atacama and not the traditionally leftist Tarapacá gave Allende the highest plurality with 50 percent, an indication that the northern pole of leftism had shifted from the industrialized province of Tarapacá into the less developed mining province of Atacama. In comparison with the 1964 presidential contest, Allende improved his support in Tarapacá and Atacama by 1.7 and 5.6 percent, respectively, but lost support in Antofagasta and Coquimbo (-3.6 and -1.9 percent, respectively). Political analysts disagree in the interpretation of these electoral fluctuations,[124] but they all recognize that political backing should never be taken for granted in any area in Chile. For example, in the mining town of Chuquicamata, Alessandri, and not Allende as was expected, obtained the majority. And in all the provinces of the North the rightist candidate and not the candidate of the Christian Democracy was second to Allende. As has been previously indicated, such a trend means that electoral polarization rather than ideological diversification decided the leanings of the voters in these highly politicized provinces. In northern Chile the Christian Democracy could barely keep up with the Left and furthermore lost voters to the Right. Even in the province of Antofagasta, where the Tomic family holds economic interests and the Yugoslavian community is influential, Radomiro Tomic came in only third, 12 percent behind Jorge Alessandri.

One of Allende's most convincing returns occurred in the coal-mining areas of Concepción and Arauco, where he obtained roughly seven times more votes from the male electors than did Alessandri and six times more than Tomic. In the industrial areas around the city of Concepción Allende's advantage was not quite as conclusive;

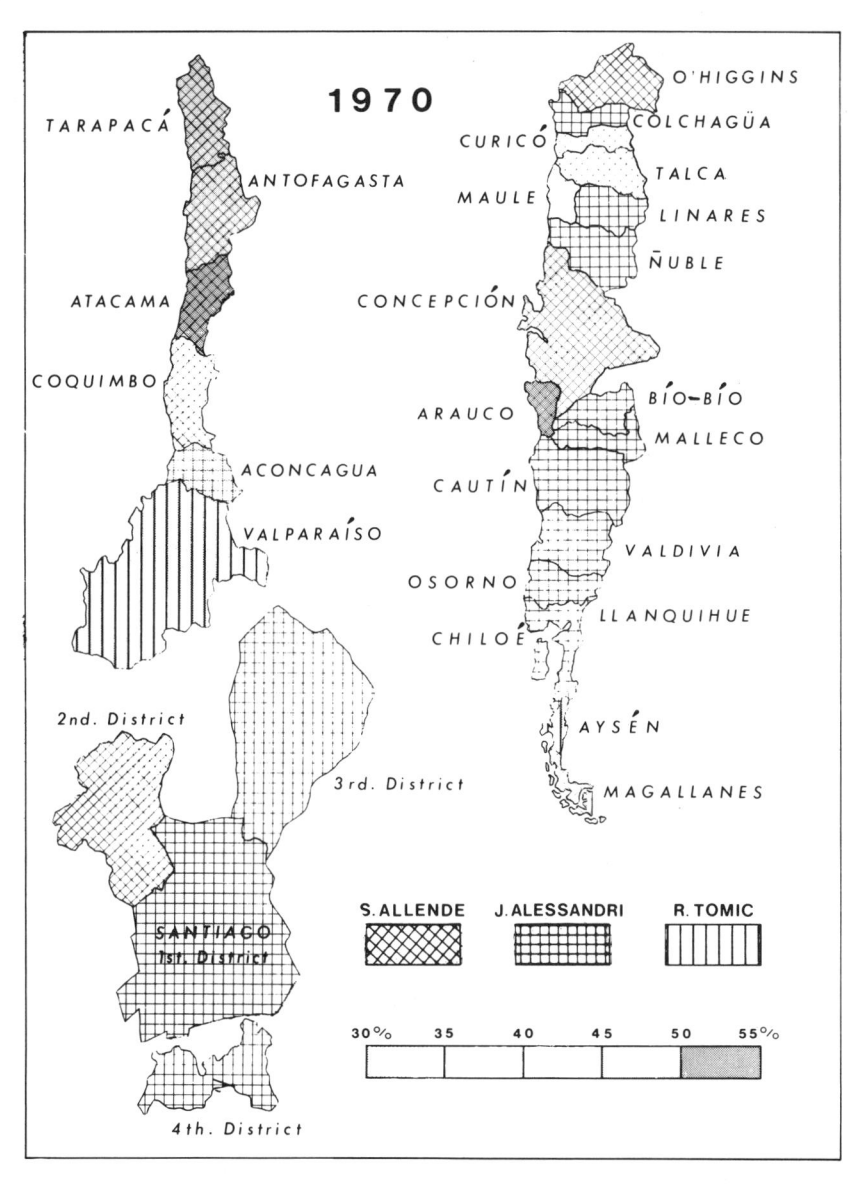

Figure 17.—The presidential election of 1970.

still, it accounted for nearly 50 percent more than the other two contestants together. Compared with 1964, his support in Concepción and Arauco was 0.7 and 4.3 percent lower. Also in the province of Magallanes, which he won with 47 percent of the provincial vote, Allende's 1970 support was 2.6 percent lower than in 1964.[125] For the first time in four tries for the presidency Salvador Allende obtained pluralities in the traditional agricultural provinces of central Chile. In O'Higgins, Curicó, and Talca he obtained first place with percentages of about 40. Unexpectedly again, second place went to Alessandri and not to Tomic in all three provinces. During the years of the Christian Democratic government there had been continuous accusations from the Right and from the Left that the agrarian reform had been conducted in those provinces with the purpose of creating a political following for the Christian Democracy. However, the results of the election revealed the opposite.

In an excellent study of the peasants' reaction to the 1970 presidential election Benno Galjart clarified many questions as to which party the peasants did support.[126] First he established that by no means was their response united. Allende emerged as the winner predominantly in the rural communes of agricultural Middle Chile where minifundia and temporary workers were numerous. Tomic obtained more votes than the other candidates in the municipalities where peasants had been permanently settled in *asentamientos* and where the peasant organizations were dependent on the Christian Democracy. Nevertheless, the rural communes where the peasant organizations had fallen under the control of the Marxist Ranquil Union voted for Allende, even though the subdivision of the land had been initiated by the Christian Democratic government. However, Galjart warns against overemphasizing the peasant unions' influence in the political decision of the individual peasant. Furthermore, the 1970 election proved that the rural workers had attained complete political independence from their former masters, the landowners. If the rightist vote was high in some agricultural communes, it was not due to patronization, as in the past, but to personal conviction. Small farmers, family estate owners, and sharecroppers supported Alessandri and rejected Tomic and Allende in the same order. Also, the competition between Allende and Tomic for the vote of the peasants, favored or not by the agrarian reform, was resolved in favor of Allende. As has been frequently argued here, the electoral campaign conducted by the Christian Democracy against the Right hardly helped to win votes for Tomic; on the contrary, in the end it was Allende who profited from the promotion of political polarization. As Galjart points out, in the rural places where Tomic won over Allende, or vice versa, the votes for Alessandri remained unaltered, revealing that his were the only stable votes in the agrarian provinces.

Also to be underlined is the fact that in the rural provinces of *La Frontera* and the provinces of recent colonization, where, until then, the agrarian structure consisted of large to medium-sized landholdings, the plurality was won by Jorge Alessandri and second place usually went to Tomic. Only in the provinces of Bío-Bío, Valdivia, and Chiloé did Allende have clear advantages over Tomic. Significantly, in none of these provinces had the agrarian reform been actively introduced.

Jorge Alessandri obtained pluralities in three of the four districts of the province of Santiago. In the Fourth District his victory was the slimmest with 35.8 percent; in the other two his percentages were 40 or over. Only in the populous Second District did the plurality go to Allende with 40 percent, 10 percent more than Alessandri could achieve. It has been contended that Allende's winning the Second District of Santiago was due to the backing of the working class, and the proportion of male votes received was the proof.[127] Such an interpretation implies the fallacious ecological assumption that the male vote for Allende came only from working class elements, something that may well apply to areas like Concepción or Arauco that have traditionally voted for the Left, but does not apply to the industrial municipalities of Santiago, where electoral variety has been quite remarkable. Moreover, the vote for Allende in the populous Second District of Santiago was 1.5 percent lower than in 1964, which reveals that his alleged solid backing by the working class was sagging in 1970.

Jorge Alessandri won the agrarian provinces of Aconcagua, Colchagua, Maule, Linares, and Ñuble, as well as all the rural provinces of the South. In the province of Valparaiso he came 0.6 percent below Allende's second place. He was less successful in the provinces of Concepción and Magallanes, where his third place was a sizable distance from Tomic's second. In general, according to Michael Francis, the vote for Jorge Alessandri was much higher than in the presidential contest of 1958, and this applies especially to the northern provinces of the country. Obviously polarization had once again favored first Allende and then Alessandri, as the latter received the votes from alienated middle-ground voters.[128]

Rodomiro Tomic came in third as had been predicted. Only the provinces of Valparaíso and Aysén yielded pluralities to him, and even these were by very narrow margins. The most demoralizing returns for Tomic came from the northern provinces, where the Christian Democracy had been gaining ground in the course of the last decade. A great setback also occurred in the agricultural provinces of Middle Chile and in Santiago's First District. Tomic's 27.8 percent of the national vote was another reduction of the Christian Democratic vote, which in 1969 had already sagged to 29.8 percent after its highest ever (41 percent) in the 1965 congressional elections. Not even among women, traditional supporters of the Christian Democracy, did Tomic receive satisfactory responses. They favored Alessandri with 38 and Allende with 30.5 percent, whereas Tomic came in third again with 29.9 percent. The male electorate showed strong support for Allende (41.6 percent) and gave the second preference to Alessandri (31.5 percent).

The fifty days between the election of Salvador Allende and its ratification by Congress on October 24, 1970, were extremely tense and eventful. Since Allende's first place at the polls did not represent an absolute majority it had to be ratified by Congress, and for this the backing of Christian Democratic congressmen was indispensable. This support was offered by the party still in government under the condition that Allende would subscribe to a package of constitutional amendments aimed at preventing any attempt by the new government to restrict civil rights, to act against the constitution, or to establish a totalitarian regime in Chile. So, a "Statute of Democratic Guarantees" was drawn up by the Christian Democracy and by representatives of the Popular Unity; it included provisions pertaining to the total control of media by any political body, the freedom of speech and education, and the prohibition of private militias.[129] In mid-October the package was approved by the two Chambers of the Congress and on January 9, 1971, was signed into law by President Allende.

By accepting these constitutional guarantees Allende had assured himself of the support of the Christian Democracy at the meeting of the *congreso pleno*, which on October 24, 1970, constitutionally proclaimed Salvador Allende as president of the Republic. On November 3 the new president inaugurated his government and announced his first cabinet, composed of four Socialists, three Communists, three Radicals, and one member each of the MAPU, the API, and the Socialist Democratic party.

The meeting of the *congreso pleno* had been preluded by the fatal shooting of the commander-in-chief of the army, General René Schneider, on October 22. He had publicly stated the army's nonpolitical position and respect of the constitution, a statement that had infuriated extreme rightist conspirators who had hoped to get the military involved in a coup to prevent the inauguration of Allende as president of the Republic.[130] Schneider's slaying was the first eruption of the violence that was to stain Chile's political history of the 1970s.

Once in office, President Allende and his Popular Unity administration moved swiftly on the most pressing issues of their electoral platform. Manufacturing establishments owned by foreign concerns or by local capitalists were nationalized; the Central Workers Union was recognized as a legal body representing the interests of the workers in their dealings with the state; total nationalization of the copper industry and of financial institutions was announced; and provisions were made by the minister of agriculture, the well-known Jacques Chonchol, to accelerate the pace of the agrarian reform. These measures, added to others of a more impressionistic nature, such as distribution of milk among the children of the poor (another campaign promise) and the raising of workers' salaries, elicited great fervor for Allende among the deprived classes. The government of the Popular Unity was enjoying a windfall that became increasingly evident in the municipal elections of April 4, 1971.

In this first test of the strength of the new government the parties of the Popular Unity were able to improve their 1970 mark to 49.7 percent of the total electorate (by then the voting age had been lowered to eighteen), whereas the opposition parties fell back to 48 percent. The most impressive advances were made by Allende's own party, the Socialist, which attracted 22.4 percent of the national vote, 10 percent more than in the congressional elections of 1969. By comparison the Communists' 17 percent meant an increase of only a fraction of 1 percent over their 1969 mark. A slight reduction in electoral support (-1.5 percent) was experienced by the divided Radicals: the leftist faction obtained 8 percent, while the rightist faction collected only 3.8 percent of the vote.

The party hurt most by electoral desertion was the Christian Democracy whose 25.6 percent was a new slump since it started to decline in 1967. That figure lay 2.2 percent below the votes of Tomic in September 1970 and 5.5 percent below the congressional elections of 1969.[131] As to the rightist National party, its vote was also 2 percent lower than in 1969. Considering the local factors that influence municipal elections, the turnout for the Socialists did not mean a shift of independent voters from the Christian Democrats or the Radicals (these two parties did not receive fewer votes than in March 1969); rather it meant a strong endorsement of President Allende by a new contingent of young voters. It should be remembered that the electoral body of April 1971 had increased by about 210,000 new voters (10 percent) over that of September 1970.

Trends that had been showing up in the previous election appeared even stronger now. The Popular Unity conquered larger numbers of votes in the northern provinces, in Concepción, and in Magallanes, and increased the gains obtained by Allende in the agricultural provinces of Middle Chile. The most significant advances in urban provinces were made in Santiago. There, all the popular communes gave pluralities to Socialist or Communist aldermen, and this time not only with a strong male vote but also with increased support from the female electorate.[132] The parties in opposition could not improve their absolute numbers of votes in the province of Valparaíso; the only party that did was the Socialist, mostly due to the support of new voters.

In total, the Popular Unity managed to get 45 percent of the contested seats, and the forces in the opposition came through with the remaining 55 percent. The apparent contradiction in these figures with the 49.7 percent of the total national vote obtained by the Popular Unity stems from the fact that there are rural communes in Chile where aldermen positions can be won through relatively low numbers of votes and that in some of those communes the Left had never been strong. Also on April 4, 1971, the Senate seat left vacant by Salvador Allende was to be filled. It fell to the Socialist Adonis Sepúlveda, who with 51 percent won over the Christian Democrat ex-Minister Andrés Zaldívar. This triumph of the Popular Unity in the southernmost provinces of the country increased the conviction among Allende supporters that the government had indeed received a strong mandate from the people.

The political developments between early 1971 and September 1973 have been covered more extensively than any other period in the history of the country because of their significance as the democratic inception of a Socialist regime. Since that coverage comprises the most varied and contradictory interpretations,[133] the following analysis of these years will focus on the reaction of the Chilean people to the political events and on the polarization as expressed in the results of the electoral contests that took place between April 1971 and March 1973.

President Allende started his administration in the same situation as most of his predecessors—with the opposition in control of the Chamber of Deputies and the Senate. This circumstance, bitterly lamented by the apologists of the Popular Unity government, but very well understood by the president himself, was initially solved by Allende making use of all the legal loopholes at his disposal. He respected Chile's political traditions even though his most "hotheaded" followers, using obstruction from Congress as a pretext, claimed that the "bourgeois state" had to be destroyed to make way for the ultimate triumph of the people's revolution.[134] Such views could only lead to an escalation of polarization and violence. After April 1971 no social or political conflict was considered as an expression of genuine concern—every issue was interpreted as a confrontation between a "reactionary Right" and a "totalitarian Left."

When in July 1971 the death of a Christian Democratic deputy left a vacant seat in the province of Valparaíso, both the government and the opposition took the contest as a referendum on the popularity of the government. It seemed to matter to neither of them that the election had strong local overtones, namely that one of the contenders was a local Christian Democrat, Oscar Marín, a well-known physician and public figure from Viña del Mar, while the other was Hernán del Canto, a Socialist unionist from Santiago. The election of Marín, although narrow (50.1 percent), came as no surprise to the residents of Valparaíso, but it was readily interpreted by the parties in opposition as a rebuff of Allende's government, while the Popular Unity called it "a triumph of the collusion of the Christian Democracy and the Right."[135]

It is not surprising then that, as the months went by, the hostilities between the Popular Unity and the Christian Democracy increased to such an extent that a reconciliation between these two progressive forces became highly problematic. The internal tearing the polarization was causing among political groups in Chile became even more evident as leftist sympathizers of the Christian Democracy defected from the party to found the *Izquierda Cristiana* (Christian Left) under the leadership of Bosco Parra and six deputies.[136] Around mid-1971 the Radical party also split on internal disagreements between pro-Marxist and anti-Marxist factions. Senior members of the party left, alleging that the Radical party was not so much Marxist as Social Democratic in its leanings. Eventually they rallied under the name of the Party of the Radical Left (PIR) maintaining initially an uncommitted collaboration with the Allende government.

Two by-elections in January 1972, one for a vacant senator seat in the agricultural provinces of O'Higgins and Colchagua and one for a deputy seat in agrarian Linares, were considered another test of the government's standing. In O'Higgins and Colchagua the candidate of the Christian Democracy, tacitly supported by the National party, was Rafael Moreno, who had been the vice-president of CORA, the Corporation of the Agrarian Reform, during the Frei government. Since Moreno had been instrumental in an intensive drive for expropriations and land redistributions in both these provinces, he was expected to win the senatorial seat. And this is what happened; he obtained 52.7 percent against 46.4 percent for his Socialist opponent Héctor Olivares. Olivares, however, was able to carry the city of Rancagua including the El Teniente copper mine, where he was a union leader. Setbacks for the government had taken place in two provinces where *asentamientos* were already well established and where the Popular Unity had therefore relatively little by which to mobilize the peasant masses.

In the more center-right province of Linares the National party put forward one of its strongest men, the conservative lawyer-landowner Sergio Diez who had once been deputy for the province of Talca and, as such, was well known among the landowners of the region. His opponent, María Elena Mery from the MAPU, had no less impressive credentials. She was the widow of Hernán Mery, a CORA officer who, in April of 1970, had been fatally wounded by a landowner about to be expropriated in the province of Linares. The contest promised to be a close one. Still, Diez won with an unexpected 57 percent over 41 percent for María Elena Mery. This defeat contained perhaps more warning signs than the by-election in O'Higgins and Colchagua. The province of Linares had 57 percent of its farmland already expropriated and redistributed, and the rest of the cultivable land fell into the category of small property not subject to the agrarian reform. Nevertheless, rural agitators of the MIR had succeeded in inciting peasants to unlawfull seizures of farms. Not only small and medium-sized agriculturalists but also Allende's government harbored ill feelings against the MIR's uncontrolled revolutionary excesses in the countryside.[137] And the electoral results of Linares were a clear indication of the state of affairs in agrarian Chile after more than one year of the Popular Unity's government.

As usual, the results of the by-elections prompted reactions within the political forces of the country. This time it was the Popular Unity coalition that suffered the consequences. President Allende, realizing that a hasty radicalism caused inhibition rather than mobilization, reshuffled his cabinet to accommodate more moderate elements from the Popular Unity. Four members of the two factions of the Radical party were given portfolios, so that that party became the most represented in Allende's cabinet and underlined the government's centrist outlook. President Allende's move obviously inflamed the Ultraleft and caused unwanted strain within the Popular Unity coalition.

In February 1972 at the conclave at Arrayán, a meeting of all the participants in the government's coalition, it was agreed that to minimize vote losses, the coalition should present joined lists for the congressional elections of the next year. Allende was hoping at that moment to conquer eighty-four deputy and twenty-nine senator seats for the coalition.[138] An introduction of joined lists into the electoral contest was agreeable to the Christian Democracy and was approved by Congress in early May 1972. The new rules of the electoral game were in fact a legalization of the political polarization that was in full swing in 1972.

At the same time as the government and the opposition arranged themselves in their irreconcilable positions, the political parties aligned for the congressional contest of March 1973. In April 1972 the Party of the Radical Left (PIR) withdrew its two ministers from the cabinet of Allende and went over to the opposition. This occurred shortly after talks concerning a merge with the Popular Independent Action (API), the party of Senator Rafael Tarud, who had decided to stay with the Popular Unity after all. The realignment of the PIR with the forces of the opposition was tested on July 16, 1972, when another by-election was held in the province of Coquimbo to elect a successor for a deceased deputy. The Communist Amanda Altamirano received 52 percent of the vote against 46 percent for her opponent, the Radical Orlando Poblete. This victory was a relief for the Popular Unity after it had lost three previous by-elections. Still Coquimbo was a province in which the Popular Unity had been building up its forces consistently during the last years and so these returns were not as high as expected. The opposition, in its turn, no longer regarded the province of Coquimbo as the stronghold of radicalism it had been in the past; it was satisfied with the results since it had managed to increase its number of supporters by 9,000 and to reduce the plurality held by the Popular Unity.[139]

From August 1972 until the end of the year Chilean politics followed a turbulent course. Inflation, the most feared scourge of any government, grew in uncontrollable proportions and the unsettled conditions in the countryside as well as in the food industry caused a mounting shortage of food. Strikes, turmoil, and confrontation, the typical sequels of popular dissatisfaction, plagued the government of the Popular Unity. The latter, just like the other governments, reacted with harshness against its critics and gave the opposition grounds to accuse the government of repression, brutality, and antidemocratic attitudes. How many times had this sequence of events repeated itself in Chilean politics!

The 1973 congressional election campaigns were conducted in an unbearable atmosphere of hatred and mutual suspicion of an impending coup d'etat. For the government coalition the electoral contest was to prove that despite the economic and social cost of the "road to socialism," the people of Chile were still backing the irreversible changes that were taking place in the country. The increased mobilization of urban workers and peasants was an element the government wanted to make use of. Notwithstanding the deteriorated economic situation, food was still available to the poor through the JAP organization (Committees for Supplies and Price Control). Disclosures by Jack Anderson of the *Washing-*

ton Post that the ITT multinational corporation, the CIA, and the Nixon administration had conspired to topple the government of Allende since the day of his election were also advantageous to the Allende administration.[140] These allegations, later proven right, inflamed the nationalistic feeling of more than a few uncommitted voters; they saw in those actions just what the Ultraleft in Chile had been declaiming: a collusion between the imperialist United States and the putschist oligarchy of the country.[141]

For the parties in opposition the issue at stake was the continuance of democracy and pluralism. Both the National party and the Christian Democracy emphasized that the elections of March 1973 should be considered a plebiscite on the government of the Popular Unity's intention to transform Chile into a totalitarian state. The Nationals went even further by asking the electorate to secure for the opposition more than two-thirds of the seats in Congress, the proportion necessary to request a president's demise.[142] Apart from their traditional sources of political support, the Right and the Left were addressing the urban middle class, the peasants who had benefited from the agrarian reform, and certain worker groups like the copper miners, whose loyalties to the Left had been shaken after clashes with the government on salary demands. More than in any other congressional election in contemporary Chile, both of the political combinations, the Federation of the Popular Unity (Socialists, Communists, Radicals, MAPU, API, and Christian Left) and the Confederation of Democracy (Christian Democracy, National party, Radical Party of the Left, and Radical Democratic party) knew exactly which sectors of the electorate to cater to and which language to use. With the existence of these two well-defined ideological positions there was, as proven later, no room for small eclectic parties.

The unusually delayed election results were announced in blocks: the Confederation of Democracy (CODE) obtained 2,003,047 votes (54.74 percent) in deputies elections and 1,237,692 (56.2 percent) in the senatorial elections held in five provincial groupings. The Federation of the Popular Unity (UP) obtained 1,589,025 votes in deputies elections (43.39 percent) and 926,302 votes in senatorial elections (42.1 percent). The contested seats were allocated as follows in the Chamber of Deputies: Christian Democracy, fifty; National party, thirty-four; Socialist party, twenty-seven; Communist party, twenty-six; Radical party, five; Radical

Democracy, Popular Independent Action, and Movement of United Popular Action, two each; Radical Party of the Left and Christian Left, one deputy each. To the Senate the Christian Democrats elected ten, the Communists five, the Socialists five, and the Nationals four representatives. CODE now had eighty-seven deputies (58 percent) in the lower Chamber and thirty-two senators (64 percent) in the Senate against nineteen from the Federation. These results, compared with those of the congressional elections of 1969, meant gains for the Nationals (four), Socialists (three), Communists (three), and Christian Democrats (one) in the Senate. Losses in that Chamber were experienced by the leftist faction of the Radical party, which emerged with only two of its former six senators; and several microparties had vanished before or during the elections.

Repeating previous patterns, the main parties in the opposition, the Christian Democracy and the National party, did well among the female electorate as they won 60 percent against 39 percent for the Popular Unity. Among the male voters the opposition also led, but its margin was a scarce 2 percent: 51 percent for the Confederation of the Democracy against 49 percent for the Federation of the Popular Unity.

A regional analysis of the 1973 congressional elections can be carried out in two ways; one, by studying the electoral strength of each of the two contending alliances; the other, by surveying the appeal of each party in the provinces of the country. Considering the electoral results from the first point of view, CODE carried pluralities in more provinces than the Popular Unity, eighteen against seven. However, the entire North gave the Popular Unity pluralities between 50 and 54 percent. The province of Coquimbo yielded the highest percentage to the Popular Unity (54 percent), while in the traditionally leftist province of Tarapacá the governmental coalition won by a fraction of 1 percent. The North as a whole remained with the Left, but the center of this support had shifted to the more depressed transitional *Norte Chico*. It seems that in the socioeconomically better-off provinces of the extreme North the Allende administration could no longer count on the intense support the Left had enjoyed in the past.

Solidly behind the government of the Popular Unity were the industrial-mining province of Concepción and its satellite, the province of Arauco. Here the forces of President Allende scored their major pluralities, 55 and 65 percent of the provincial vote respectively. The agricultural province of Talca also remained faithful to the government, but not so the mining-agricultural province of O'Higgins. After decades of loyalty to the Left, the swing of the southernmost province of Magallanes over to the center-right coalition (51 percent) was also unexpected. It can be assumed that this province, with a relatively high standard of living and in spite of declared leftist leanings in the past, was not fully satisfied with the government of the Popular Unity.

The opposition alliance achieved highest pluralities in the urban provinces of Valparaíso and Santiago with 59 percent of the vote. All the districts of Santiago, including the populous Second District, gave pluralities to the CODE. Except for Talca the agricultural provinces of Middle Chile did the same. The percentages fluctuated between 52 in the province of O'Higgins and 67 in Ñuble II (Chillán, Bulnes, Yungay). Still higher percentages were obtained by the opposition in the *Frontera* provinces and in the provinces of recent colonization: Cautín voted 64.9 percent in favor of CODE candidates against 34.6 percent for the Popular Unity; but the highest marks of this alliance were obtained in the province of Valdivia with 48.6 percent. Finally, the two southern provinces of Chiloé and Aysén also favored the opposition with 58 percent.

Regionally, the electoral patterns in these first congressional elections during the Popular Unity administration appeared the same as in the past. All the northern provinces and the industrial-mining area of Concepción-Arauco favored the Left, and the urban provinces of Middle Chile as well as the rural provinces supported the Center and the Right.

These general results by coalition, however, mask the changes in party support that had occurred since the last congressional elections. In a party-by-party consideration the major winner was without doubt the Socialist party, the president's party, which had raised its former mark of 13 percent to 18 percent. It was followed by the National party, whose increase was 1.6 percent over its 20.9 percent in 1969. The Communist party, for the first time in the last two decades, could not keep up with its traditional partner, the Socialists, and obtained the same 16 percent as in 1969. The most severely damaged party was the Radical party, which slumped down from its 13.3 percent in 1969 to 3.8 percent.

Also comparatively weaker in this contest was the Christian Democracy, whose 30 percent was 2 percent lower than in the 1969 congressional elections.

The striking similarity between the added percentages of the CODE members and the Popular Unity in 1973 and the marks reached by those parties in 1969 (52 percent for Nationals and Christian Democrats against 46.2 percent of the Communists, two factions of the Socialists, the Radical party, and the PADENA) suggests a startling situation. Despite the bitterness, the polarization, and the partisan viciousness of the last four years, and notwithstanding the incorporation of new voters (24 percent of the total), the basic distribution of electoral forces had remained unchanged. Of course there had been shifts of electoral support from ideologically weaker to stronger parties. For instance, the Socialists appeared to have received the support of an electorate that had in the past favored minor parties of the Left, whereas the lost forces of the Christian Democracy and the right wing of the Radical party seemed to have enlarged the National party. These trends lend substance to the contention that, even with the general alignment of the electoral forces unaltered, there were obviously shifts taking place within each of the blocks toward the more militant and aggressive parties, the Socialist and the National.[143] And the internal movements of voters were another sign of polarization behind an external appearance of the electoral status quo.

How great the local variations of party appeal were in the 1973 elections can be seen in a province-by-province analysis of the returns for each party (Figure 18). The Christian Democracy, which continued to be the majority party of the country, had drawn the greatest support from three districts of the province of Santiago and some from the agricultural provinces of Middle Chile (Curicó, Maule, Ñuble). One of the paradoxes of the 1973 elections is that the Christian Democracy seemed to be losing the dominant position it had held until 1969 in the traditional agricultural provinces of Middle Chile, while on the other hand, it won pluralities in provinces like Chiloé and Magallanes where, even in the best years of Frei, it had not been able to make any inroads. Also the provinces of Coquimbo, and Concepción which had never been very fond of the Christian Democracy, gave the winning edge to that party as did all the provinces of Valdivia.

269

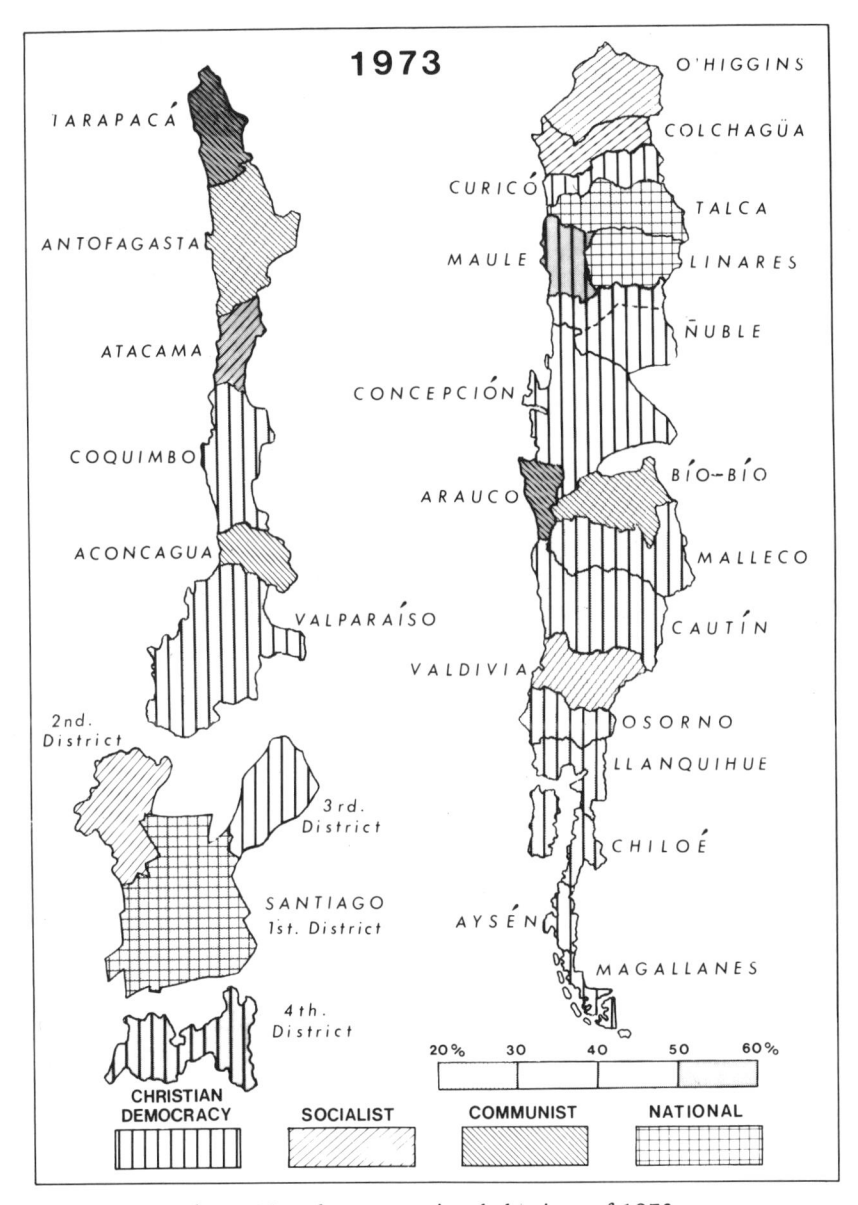

Figure 18.—The congressional elections of 1973.

By the number of votes and congressmen elected the National party emerged as the second major political group in the country. Pluralities were obtained in urban-industrial Valparaíso and in the traditional agricultural provinces of Talca and Linares. But perhaps its most remarkable result was the election of one deputy in each of the northern provinces of Tarapacá and Antofagasta as well as in Concepción. Since the early 1960s the rightist parties had been barely existing in these strongly leftist provinces. The advances of the National party were also impressive in all the agricultural provinces of Chile where, once again, this party had consistently lost support during the 1960s. To appreciate the enormous electoral comeback of the "mummies" it must be mentioned that only in five of Chile's twenty-five provinces did the Nationals fail to elect at least one deputy. By comparison, in 1969 they had not been represented in seven and in 1965 not in sixteen provinces!

As during the years of the Popular Front the Socialist party held a prominent place in the national political spectrum. Pluralities were obtained in mining Atacama, in the populous Second District of Santiago where Mario Palestro, a local figure, reached the highest vote for a deputy in the country,[144] and in the agricultural provinces of O'Higgins and Colchagua. Also following a more recent trend, the Socialist party obtained the plurality in Valdivia. Compared with the 1969 congressional elections, the Socialist party made inroads in almost all the agricultural provinces of the country. Breaking with another trend it was able to successfully compete with the Communists in those provinces in which both parties had run candidates. The Socialists fared particularly well, far better than the Communists, in Greater Santiago. After the impressive majority of Palestro, Laura Allende (a sister of the president) obtained the largest number of votes in the Third District, doubling those of the elected Communist deputy. In the First District as well, the Communists were outdistanced by the Socialists. Definitely, after so many years of struggling in the shadow of the Communists, the hard line of the Socialist party within the Popular Unity and the attraction of President Allende had yielded benefits.

The Communist party, making use of its usual clever electoral strategy, concentrated its efforts on the northern provinces. Tarapacá and Antofagasta gave pluralities to Communist candidates, but they were not as impressive as they had been in the late 1960s.

The results were more satisfactory in the province of Coquimbo, where they obtained the highest returns with Amanda Altamirano, and in the province of Aconcagua, where the party attained an unexpected plurality. In the province of Valparaíso, where the Communists had presented three of their heavyweights, the party came second to the National party, relegating to third place the Christian Democracy, which had enjoyed pluralities in the province since 1961. A significant plurality was obtained in the province of Arauco (63 percent) and a less impressive plurality in the province of Bío-Bío (24 percent). The province of Concepción was a setback for the Communists, considering their 1961 marks. For one, this party lost the advantages it had held in the congressional elections of 1969 and 1965 to the Christian Democracy and then, with fewer votes than the Socialists, it elected only two deputies. The same thing happened in other provinces where Socialists and Communists ran candidates at the same time.

As on other occasions, the Radical party had come to this election divided. While the faction in the opposition elected one senator in the provincial grouping of Atacama-Coquimbo and three deputies (two of them in Greater Santiago), the progovernment Radical party elected five deputies (two of them in the northern provinces and the rest in the agricultural provinces). Apart from this, none of the factions of the old Radical party was still represented in the provinces like Coquimbo, Ñuble, or Chiloé where they had been strong in the past. The MAPU was one of the minor parties that shrunk heavily; from eight deputies it had only two left, one in Linares, the other in Concepción. Having abandoned the Christian Democracy proved also deleterious for the Christian Left; in fact, from its eight candidates—the influential Silva Solar among them—who were considered to have good chances, only one, Luis Maira, was elected in the First District of Santiago.[145] The API fared no better and elected only one deputy in Coquimbo and another in Maule. It can be said unequivocally that all these groups were on the verge of extinction and probably would not have survived one more electoral test. As had happened after the split of *Ibañismo,* these microparties were ready for assimilation by any of the major forces in the political spectrum.

In view of these being the last elections held in democratic Chile, the 1973 congressional elections had remarkable characteristics. Aside from the bias introduced by partisan considerations, the majority of the larger political groups emerged with advantages. The Socialists obtained the leadership of the Popular Unity as they not only enlarged their electoral support in the agricultural provinces but were also able to successfully compete with the Communist party in provinces where there had previously been no contest. Socialist advances in the agricultural provinces of Middle Chile had occurred in phase with a Christian Democratic decline. But not only the Left profited from this decline; a surprising comeback of the Right (National party) in its old bastion, the agricultural provinces, was an indication that the values and norms of the old agrarian society had not vanished from the countryside and that there were still many individuals willing to endorse the conservative postulates of the Right. No doubt, these were agricultural entrepreneurs, small rural proprietors, and peasants favored by the agrarian reform, for whom all the structural changes in the countryside appeared to have been achieved already.

A remarkable trend that showed up in the 1973 congressional elections was the determination with which the aristocratic oligarchy of the country jumped into the political scene. After more than three decades of gradual withdrawal from active politics, the aristocracy threw into the electoral contest the largest and most impressive contingent of its members; Alessandri, Errázuriz, Bulnes, Ochagavía, Pérez de Arce, Phillips, Riesco, Ossa, Monckeberg, and Montt were among the conspicuous families who again, as in the halcyon decades of the early century, reached the Congress. Obviously, these families were trying to defend their threatened interests and political views, but pleas for support drew positive responses from the electorate. One of the points that foreign analysts, who are prone to generalize about Latin America, have failed to recognize is the very distinct character of the Chilean aristocracy. This is not a rich, authoritarian, but pusilanimous higher class that can easily be neutralized (as in Cuba) by populist movements. A traditional predisposition to political combat has made the Chilean aristocracy a formidable political adversary, and this is what the Popular Unity and the Christian Democracy failed to realize when they took for granted that the Right, as a political force, was finished.

For the Christian Democracy there was a slight electoral recovery, when its marks are compared with the presidential election of 1970 and the municipal elections of 1971, although its percentage in 1973 was lower than in 1969. In a strange case of compensation, its electoral reduction in urban places and in the agricultural provinces of Middle Chile was paralleled with an increase of support from the northern and southern provinces, where it had never been very strong.

It cannot be emphasized enough that the 1973 elections were special in that most of the major parties emerged with advantages. Even the Communist party, although it maintained the electoral percentage of 1969 and kept its grip on the northern provinces, was able to make advances in Aconcagua and Bío-Bío where it had never before enjoyed a great response. Obviously, the undecided character of the 1973 elections left each side claiming victory in a political stalemate that heightened polarization and violence in the last six months of President Allende's administration. Under those circumstances of ideological obfuscation and high emotionalism it was difficult to make a sober assessment of the political situation in the country and to prevent the final collapse of democracy. And this state of mind, unfortunately, is the heritage that those troubled times have passed on to the future.

5
The Regionalization of Politics

A purpose of electoral geography is to unveil the spatial patterns of party support and to relate voting behavior to the socioeconomic characteristics of the population.[1] Such a consideration of politics places ideological motivations, at least for the moment, in second place and focuses on the ecological-regional substrata of voting reactions. This approach distinguishes voting behavior patterns, both in time and space, that are not expressed by a global view of the politics of a country. In his pioneer work on the electoral geography of Chile, Ricardo Cruz Coke, who was greatly influenced by the French school, chose to look at electoral returns from the viewpoint of a party's fluctuating support in the provinces of the country.[2]

The approach in this chapter will be different. We will trace the tendencies of the electorate between 1932 and 1973 in each of the sociogeographical regions that were defined in chapter 1. The results of nineteen presidential and congressional elections held in this time span will be analyzed to test constituency strength and to establish variations of popular support. Since presidential elections in Chile were usually entered by party coalitions, the regional variations of returns for these elections were considered on the basis of votes obtained by rightist, center-right, center-left, and leftist candidates. These denominations correspond to the position of the parties included in each alliance within the political spectrum of the country at the time of the election. For example, all candidacies of Salvador Allende are considered as genuine left, whereas the candidacies of Eduardo Frei are typical cases of center-right coalitions. Carlos Ibáñez del Campo's candidacy in 1942 was obviously of rightist character, whereas in 1952 he was backed by predominantly center-left political groups. Candidates from the Radical party were considered to be representatives of the Center-Left. In some elections it is difficult to ascertain whether a centrist candidate appealed more to the Right or to the Left. In these borderline cases the appellation Center correctly defines the ideological position of the candidacy.

The Leftist North

Traditionally the northern provinces of Chile have demonstrated a strong endorsement of leftist parties. This was particularly true from 1932 to 1973, when the Communist party averaged between 31 and 26 percent in the provinces of Tarapacá and Antofagasta, thereby overshadowing support for the Socialist party. In fact, during this period the Socialists seldom exceeded 20 percent in elections that were not contested by the Communists and obtained far less in elections in which both Communists and Socialists nominated candidates. Only in the congressional elections of 1949, when the Communist party was banned from politics, could the Socialist party attain 34 percent of the provincial vote in Antofagasta, and again in 1953, when the Communist party was still underground, could it reach 34 percent in Tarapacá. This shows that the two popular parties were competing for the same sector of the electorate and that generally the winner was the Communist party. The worst showing of Socialists occurred in the second half of the 1940s when the party was severely weakened by internecine struggles. In 1945, when the crisis was at its peak, the Socialists obtained 8 percent of the vote in Tarapacá, whereas the Communists gained a plurality with 31 percent. The changing degrees of support experienced by the Socialist party in the northern provinces results in the highest values of electoral variation from all the parties included in Table 6. It is also interesting that the Communist party, although it could usually rely on adequate support from these provinces, shows the second highest value of variation. Thus, popular support for these two parties could not be taken for granted in any given election, at least not in terms of the absolute number of voters.

In presidential elections the leftism of the northern population is less pronounced (Table 7). Center-left combinations, which generally brought Marxist parties and Radicals together, enjoyed a

Table 6

Average Vote (%) and Standard Deviations (d) of the Major Parties.
Congressional Elections, 1932-1973

Province	Conservative party %	d	Liberal party %	d	Christian Democracy %	d	Radical party %	d	Democratic party %	d	Socialist party %	d	Communist party %	d
Tarapacá	–	–	19	3	21	6	22	7	1	4	18	14	31	12
Antofagasta	4	3	11	4	18	9	24	4	6	5	20	10	26	9
Atacama	12	11	13	8	25	11	32	13	3	5	25	15	17	6
Coquimbo	8	5	27	11	16	10	26	8	1	1	19	7	16	2
Aconcagua	22	8	28	9	22	16	19	6	1	2	9	7	16	10
Valparaíso	22	7	13	8	19	14	16	7	7	5	14	6	13	6
Santiago I	17	7	11	3	18	14	19	6	7	3	13	5	10	4
Santiago II	21	11	10	6	21	16	12	5	3	2	18	9	13	6
Santiago III	20	8	15	6	21	14	14	6	7	6	15	7	12	8
Santiago IV	22	8	15	8	23	9	12	4	6	3	14	6	12	3
O'Higgins	23	8	16	7	16	9	13	5	5	6	13	5	14	3
Colchagua	32	10	23	8	25	11	15	5	–	–	15	11	7	4
Curicó	23	11	20	5	26	10	17	5	1	5	16	11	16	9
Talca	23	6	19	7	14	12	14	4	2	10	13	7	12	7
Maule	22	8	28	7	16	15	25	4	13	8	3	1	–	–
Linares	19	6	23	9	15	12	18	6	9	7	12	9	2	1
Ñuble I	20	5	16	7	21	18	26	4	2	3	9	8	5	4
Ñuble II	22	8	10	4	19	13	30	10	8	6	12	7	7	2
Concepción	12	5	8	4	16	14	19	7	8	6	19	7	21	7
Arauco	9	8	–	–	22	7	30	14	5	7	20	5	30	16
Bío-Bío	19	7	17	8	20	11	27	9	10	5	10	4	13	9
Malleco	10	9	29	12	27	11	27	8	7	5	8	4	4	1
Cautín	15	8	14	5	15	10	19	7	9	8	7	7	6	2
Valdivia	5	2	24	8	16	11	22	5	8	7	17	13	7	2
Osorno	15	6	21	5	18	14	27	8	2	2	13	9	6	11
Llanquihue	23	9	22	7	27	10	21	8	1	1	15	12	5	3
Chiloé	28	5	20	5	14	12	21	4	–	–	13	10	3	6
Aysén	12	8	13	6	25	15	28	7	–	–	16	8	9	5
Magallanes	3	2	3	3	28	18	29	15	–	–	50	9	10	9

277

Table 7
Average Vote (%) and Standard Deviations (d)
of Presidential Coalitions from 1932 to 1970

Province	Right %	d	Center-Right %	d	Center-Left %	d	Left %	d
Tarapacá	23	10	36	20	38	24	26	18
Antofagasta	18	9	39	24	42	28	27	16
Atacama	19	7	36	16	47	23	20	5
Coquimbo	29	7	32	15	39	20	24	17
Aconcagua	36	17	36	11	28	13	24	15
Valparaíso	33	11	43	12	29	16	24	14
Santiago I	32	13	40	15	31	22	20	13
Santiago II	24	10	40	15	30	20	22	17
Santiago III	35	8	34	11	29	20	21	12
Santiago IV	36	9	41	13	30	19	22	13
O'Higgins	35	16	40	17	25	17	22	13
Colchagua	44	21	38	16	15	7	19	15
Curicó	40	14	37	12	25	11	20	15
Talca	36	41	38	12	24	15	10	9
Maule	48	15	35	14	27	10	16	13
Linares	43	17	36	12	23	14	18	15
Ñuble	38	12	39	13	30	14	17	14
Concepción	22	9	35	12	38	25	26	17
Arauco	24	13	20	6	45	25	35	21
Bío-Bío	35	10	38	16	32	16	24	16
Malleco	42	8	41	21	31	14	17	16
Cautín	36	10	42	71	29	17	14	13
Valdivia	34	7	37	17	34	20	20	16
Osorno	36	9	34	15	35	15	18	13
Llanquihue	43	15	40	13	24	8	16	12
Chiloé	36	13	28	17	34	9	16	13
Aysén	33	14	39	16	41	18	19	13
Magallanes	13	6	34	17	45	30	33	18

better response than any other combination. Even center-right candidates received higher returns than leftist candidates. Obviously the averages hide the fact that in his last three candidacies (1958, 1964, and 1970), Salvador Allende never obtained less than 35 percent of the provincial total. These high returns raised very much the average percentage that otherwise would have been abnormally low for provinces of such developed leftist leanings. Remarkable in this context is the fact that the Radical presidential candidates Pedro Aguirre, Juan A. Ríos, and Gabriel González Videla obtained higher vote percentages than Allende ever mustered. Even Eduardo Frei, an undeniably center-right figure, was defeated by Allende in 1964 by only a few percentage points. The degree of leftism in presidential elections definitely fell behind that evinced in congressional elections.

In the northern provinces leftism can be partially explained by the degree of information within urban societies and the activism of powerful worker organizations.[3] In relatively isolated mining settlements the development of the "company state" and the ensuing negative reaction of workers have contributed greatly to the promotion of anticapitalistic ideologies that have not always been endorsed because of their social content but rather as avenues for the expression of resentment.[4] The political ambivalence of the workers of Chuquicamata, especially in the elections of the 1970s, suggests that the expectation of personal benefits rather than ideological conviction may have prompted their overwhelming support for the Left.

The socially progressive attitudes of northerners cannot, however, be totally ascribed to union exposure and political radicalization. The fact that the second strongest party in the North is the Radical, and not the Socialist party, suggests that there exists a strong laicism and a social democratic substratum that has been faithful to the Radical party. Only in the 1970s did this support go over to the National party or to the Popular Unity. Previously the vote for the Radicals had been more constant than for the Socialists or the Communists (Table 6). Moreover, the laicism and social democratic postulates of the Radicals (added, of course, to the appeal of local personalities) may have attracted a considerable number of the Socialist supporters in the troubled times of their party. And during the prohibition of the Communist party, many of its members may have voted for the Radical party, as Ricardo Cruz Coke indicates.[5] The province of Atacama, more than any other northern province, demonstrated a solid backing of the Radicals. There the party achieved an average of 38 percent over forty-one years, and center-left combinations obtained their highest returns.

It may come as a surprise to those who emphasize the leftism of the North that the Christian Democracy reached relatively high percentages and had a faithful constituency there, particularly in the province of Antofagasta, where its lowest returns lay between 5 and 8 percent of the provincial vote. Even the extremely leftist province of Tarapacá supported the Christian Democracy at moderate levels before its halcyon years of the 1960s. Atacama, on the contrary, did not respond to the Christian Democrats in the early years of this survey, but it increased its support after 1957. No wonder, then, that in this province the Christian Democracy has the highest deviation values of all the northern provinces (Table 6).

From the early 1920s the accommodated classes of the North have endorsed the Liberal party, especially when Arturo Alessandri was at the height of his popularity and he was known as "the lion of Tarapacá." Support for the Liberals and later for the National party has not markedly slackened. In fact, they have the smallest deviation values of all parties in the northern provinces. In 1973 the National party even experienced a strong rise in this part of the country. Atacama has been less responsive to rightist parties; before 1961 the Liberals held more than 10 percent of the vote, but since then they have been unable to reach that mark again. The Conservatives have never enjoyed popularity in the North, where they invariably obtained national lows. Their highest return ever was 32 percent of the Atacama vote in 1945.

The Radical-Liberal *Norte Chico*

Coquimbo and Aconcagua, not to exclude the southern portion of Atacama, have voted predominantly for the Liberal and the Radical parties. Liberals show the highest provincial averages for the period between 1932 and 1973 in Coquimbo and Aconcagua, even though their standard deviation for that period is relatively high. The mid-1940s and early-1950s were the best years for the Liberals in Coquimbo, probably due to the appeal of the Zepeda family from the city of Ovalle. In the province of Aconcagua the prestige of the Cerda family may be the basis for the stability of the liberal constituency during the 1930s and 1940s. There is little doubt that the Liberals were the main representatives of the Right in the province of Coquimbo, with the vote for the Conservatives rarely rising above the 10-percent mark (only in 1937 and 1945). Since only the Liberals were carrying the banner

The Regionalization of Politics

for the Right, rightist presidential combinations seldom did well in the *Norte Chico;* in fact, it was there that they experienced their lowest national returns (Table 7). In Aconcagua, closer to metropolitan Chile and increasingly agricultural, Conservatives enjoyed higher returns (though they never surpassed the Liberals) and rightist candidates obtained better electoral responses.

The Radical party (born in the valley of Copiapó, province of Atacama) was the second most successful party in the *Norte Chico* between 1932 and 1973. Its best electoral successes came from Coquimbo in the 1940s (probably due to the personal popularity of Gabriel González Videla) and in the 1930-1940s from the province of Aconcagua. Again the positive response of the electorate appears to have been associated with the prestigious figure of the Radical President Pedro Aguirre Cerda, a native of the province. However, once these glorious years were over, the Radical clientele embraced the growing Christian Democracy and the leftist combination of the FRAP.[6] The *Norte Chico's* support of the Radical party is illustrated by the fact that three Radical presidential candidates who ran for center-left alliances obtained not less than 60 percent of the provincial vote and that this coalition had a low standard deviation. However, the decline of the party during the 1960s and 1970s became very conspicuous in these two provinces.

The decreasing fortune of the Radicals primarily benefited the rising Christian Democracy. In fact, this party, which had had no response from the provinces of the *Norte Chico* during the 1930s and 1940s, soared to electoral highs of 30 and 40 percent during the early 1960s. Since then it has gradually decreased to between 30 and 20 percent. Steady gains of the Christian Democracy took place in the province of Aconcagua, but in Coquimbo it could never achieve a clear electoral triumph.[7] Because of its changing fortune the Christian Democracy has the highest standard deviation of all parties in the *Norte Chico* (Table 6).

Among the parties of the Left the Socialists have traditionally fared better than the Communists, particularly in the mining centers of the province of Coquimbo. The Socialist constituency, miners and industrial proletariat, is among the most steady in the *Norte Chico* in congressional, but not in presidential, elections. However, Salvador Allende gained 45 and 43 percent of the vote in the presidential contests of 1964 and 1970, so that the low average is occasioned by his and other leftist candidates' poor showing in previous elections. The Communist party was stronger than the Socialist in the early 1940s, but its ban from politics in 1948 dealt it a blow from which it was to recover slowly and with difficulty. After 1961 the Communist returns in Coquimbo sluggishly held around 15 percent of the provincial vote. A faster rise was experienced in the province of Aconcagua, where in the 1973 election the party won the popular representation from the Socialists. The expansion of mechanized mining in Aconcagua and the contention of Petras and Zeitlin that mining centers are "diffusion centers of radicalism" among agricultural voters may explain the resurgence of Communism in this agricultural-mining area.[8]

The Capricious Metropolitan Area

Political analysts, well furnished with theoretical principles but with scant knowledge of the geography of the country and the psychology of the Chilean voter, have found the political reactions of metropolitan Chile puzzling, if not aberrant. This area, although uniform in terms of urbanization, economy, and social texture, is very changeable in its political behavior in both space and time. The political leanings of Valparaíso, for example, cannot be equated with Santiago; in the same manner, the four districts of the capital province also at times display remarkable differences.

Traditionalist-Progressive Valparaíso

In spite of the apparent contradiction in the above heading, there is no better characterization of the political behavior of this province. The coexistence of traditionalism and progressivism evidenced by the values on Table 6 (p. 277) shows that all major parties except the Christian Democracy have maintained a steady clientele over the years. Nevertheless, the average percentages indicate that the Conservative party is slightly ahead of the rest and that its returns have been around 22 percent. In only one election did the party experience a smashing defeat: in 1965 its electoral support fell to 5 percent, when a great part of its constituency defected, apparently to the Christian Democracy. The Liberals were not as strong and were also less consistent than their rightist allies; they could seldom reach more than 17 percent of the provincial vote, and their interelectoral variations were also greater.

The rightist leanings of the province of Valparaíso are further demonstrated by the success of center-right or rightist candidates, who enjoyed not only higher provincial percentages but also increased support from the electorate, as the standard deviation values reveal (Table 7).

Between 1932 and 1961, second place in Valparaíso was occupied by the Radical party with percentages close to 20. Only when the Christian Democracy emerged as the dominant political force of the province did the Radicals begin to lose ground. In fact, after 1957 the Radical party never again held more than 18 percent of the provincial electorate. Whenever it established alliances with the Left, the response from the voters of Valparaíso was not enthusiastic; only Juan A. Ríos in 1942 was able to win the province for his center-left coalition. Still more discouraging were the results obtained in that province by leftist candidates. In his four bids for the presidential office Allende never received more than 36 percent of the provincial vote, and in 1970 Valparaíso gave a plurality to Tomic and not to the national winner, Salvador Allende.

Even though the Left showed poorly in presidential elections, the vote in congressional elections for Communists and Socialists was by all standards good. Between 1932 and 1973, Socialists did slightly better than Communists. Their average percentages of popular support and standard deviations (Table 6) are remarkably similar. The Socialists dominated the leftist scene in the 1930s and early 1940s, whereas the Communists led in Valparaíso in the late 1960s. In these two periods the electoral rise of the one party led invariably to the decline of the other, with the Communists enjoying the winning margin during the later years.

The constituency of the Democratic party was also very steady in Valparaíso, where most of the leaders of the unions and artisan associations belonged to that party. Prestigious local figures also enjoyed electoral support and won seats in Congress. Since the municipal elections of 1963 Valparaíso has been a Christian Democratic stronghold and no other party has posed a serious challenge to its dominant position. The growth of the Christian Democracy in that province is attributable to the assimilation of ex-*Ibañista* and radical forces and the support of the increasing contingent of new voters, since, as suggested by Moulian, the other major parties, except for the Radicals, did not suffer serious losses.[9]

The coexistence of progressive and traditionalist forces in Valparaíso can be explained by the geographical heterogeneity of the province. Alongside dynamic urban industrial centers there are areas of intensive agriculture; and while landowners and entrepreneurs support the Right, rural and urban workers endorse the Left. Caught in the center, the middle class divides its loyalties between Radicals and Christian Democrats.

Heterogeneous Santiago

Voting patterns in the province of Santiago are no clearer cut than those in Valparaíso. The reason for this lies in the diverse social composition of each of the four districts. While the First District can be defined as highly urban and middle class and the Fourth District as conspicuously rural, the Second and Third districts are a conglomerate of social groups. Moreover, the Third District, which was a dominantly upper class area in the 1930s and 1940s, became increasingly popular in the 1950s and 1960s. This development brought about greater instability among the constituencies of the Second and Third districts than those of the First and Fourth districts.

In the First District, the core of Greater Santiago, the dominant and most stable party was the Radical party, which was able to keep its clientele at a relatively even level from 1932 until 1961. Thereafter, the national collapse of the Radicals found their clientele changing over to the Christian Democratic and the National parties. This might well be an example of the middle class shifting its electoral preference from one centrist party to another and from there to a rightist party. These leanings of Santiago's First District are further evinced by the high degree of support enjoyed by center-right and rightist presidential candidates, whereas center-left and leftist candidates could never obtain highly positive responses from this electorate (Table 7). The Conservatives received strong support during the forty-one years considered here, but their interelectoral deviation was greater than that of the Liberals, who, although supported by a smaller percentage of the district's electorate, had a more stable constituency. The Christian Democracy made remarkable advances in this district from 1963 to 1965, but relinquished the leadership to the Right in 1967. On the Left, the Socialist party did better than the Communist party, particularly in the 1930s and 1940s; however, after 1961 the Communists assumed the lead. Only in the 1973 congressional elections could the Socialists obtain more votes than their leftist partners and finish third after the Nationals and Christian Democrats.

The Second District Shows a distinct Conservative preference during this forty-year period. However, the 22 overall percentage (Table 6) reflects high party returns in the 1930s and 1940s, and masks record lows of 5 and 3 percent in the mid-1960s. The slacking of the Right was caused by a shift of the electorate to the Christian Democracy, which in 1965 attained 48 percent and in 1973 32 percent of the district's vote. The Radical party has never been strong in the Second District. In its best years it collected 20 percent of the vote in congressional elections. Radical presidential candidates, however, were more fortunate. Aguirre Cerda in 1938, for example, attracted 60 percent of the district's electorate, when he ran as candidate of a center-left coalition. Leftism has been strong in the Second District, but not to the extent of surpassing the center-right forces. Strongest on the Left was the Socialist party with returns as high as 32 percent in 1937 and 1973. The Communists, although more stable in terms of constituency, never enjoyed the popularity of the Socialists. The highest vote obtained by a Communist candidate in the Second District was 21 percent in 1969. In this area of Santiago the electoral advantages of the Socialists worked negatively for the Communists. During the years of the Popular Unity, the Second District was all for Allende who had trailed Frei by 13 percentage points in the presidential election of 1964. The great variation of the Christian Democratic vote in the course of time explains that party's high standard deviation.

Favorable to rightist and center-right parties has been Santiago's Third District where the Conservatives maintained the overall leadership from 1932 to 1973. The Liberals fared better here than in the First or Second districts and this contributed to higher returns for rightist presidential alliances than for any other combination. The Right's best years were the 1930s, although in 1969 and 1970 it was obviously recovering from the doldrums of the mid-1960s. The leaders of the Left in the Third District were once again the Socialists with percentages of over 20 in the 1930s and early 1940s and 26 percent in 1973, which placed them second to the Christian Democrats. The Communists, with half of the vote of the Socialists and more interelectoral deviation, never obtained more than 18 percent in this district. The Christian Democrats, as in other districts of Santiago, gained first place in 1965 and held it till 1973. In presidential elections the Third District favored rightist candidates first and center-right candidates second. Allende never won a plurality here, but Radical presidential candidates—J. A. Ríos and González Videla—with the help of the Left were able to defeat rightist and center-right candidates.

The rural Fourth District of Santiago has commonly backed the Right in congressional as well as in presidential elections. Standard-bearer of rightist predominance was the Conservative party, which in its best years (1932-1949) seldom received less than 30 percent of the district vote. Liberals obtained barely half of the conservative vote, but their constituency was as stable as that of their rightist partners. The rapidly growing Christian Democracy captured votes from the Right and also from the Radicals, and contributed to the decline observed among Nationals and Radicals in the elections of the late 1960s. In the 1973 elections the Christian Democracy was still able to maintain its support among the district electorate at 42 percent, and neither the Right nor the Left could expand their clientele to any extent. Very likely peasants from this rural area of the province of Santiago who had benefited from the agrarian reform were the ones who remained faithful to the Christian Democracy. The Left progressed in the Fourth District during the late 1960s, and it was the Communists who made the fastest advances. In the 1973 congressional elections they received 22 percent of the district vote against 12 percent for the Socialists. This may be considered an indication of the inroads made by Communist activists from Greater Santiago among organized rural workers in the vicinity of the capital city.

As a whole Santiago shows a slight predilection for the parties of the Right,[10] particularly for the Conservative party of the past, although in presidential contests the balance moves more towards center-right candidates and, to a lesser degree, towards center-left candidates. From 1932 to 1973 a candidate of the

Left never obtained a plurality in the province of Santiago. Only Aguirre Cerda, the candidate for the Popular Front in 1938—but a member of the Radical party—convincingly defeated the candidate of the Right in the province of Santiago.[11]

The "Traditionalism" of the Agrarian Provinces

The agrarian provinces of Middle Chile have commonly been considered as strongholds of the Right. This generalization, however, masks decisive fluctuations of support for the Right. For instance, there exist remarkable differences between the political behavior of an agrarian-mining province like O'Higgins and an isolated agrarian province like Maule. Likewise, the voting patterns of agrarian Linares can hardly be compared with those of the more urbanized agrarian province of Talca. Obviously the "traditional homogeneity" needs further examination.

Parties of the Right have enjoyed moderate support and constituency stability in Colchagua, Curicó, Talca and Ñuble I. Less enthusiastic has been the support in O'Higgins, Ñuble II, Linares, and Maule. In the first group of provinces the Conservative party was dominant (a maximum of 45 percent of the Colchagua vote in 1957), but in Maule and Linares (in the second group) the Liberal party proved stronger. It is evident that in the agrarian provinces with longer aristocratic rule and closer to Santiago, the Conservatives were more influential, whereas further south the Liberals (relative newcomers to the countryside) were favored. In presidential elections rightist candidates were repeatedly successful followed by center-right candidates. The Center-Left or Left, with the exception of the last two candidacies of Salvador Allende, had little success (Table 7). Parties of the middle ground were not enthusiastically supported in these provinces, at least until the emergence of the Christian Democracy. Nevertheless, in the two districts of Ñuble, the Radical party held a winning edge over the Conservative and Liberal parties in the period from 1932 to 1969. From 1963 until 1969, the Christian Democracy was overwhelming in all the agricultural provinces of Middle Chile. Its minimum support came from Maule, which during that period preferred the Radical party.[12] In 1973, however, Maule made an impressive turn in favor of the Christian Democracy with 41 percent of the provincial vote. During the 1950s a great part of the electorate in the provinces of Talca and Linares turned towards Ibañez del Campo's populism and remained in center-left positions well into the 1970s. The strength of the Popular Democratic party in the province of Talca is a clear sign of this populist proclivity.

Among the agrarian provinces O'Higgins deserves special consideration. Though slightly conservative over time, this province also shows a persistent leftist leaning. In fact, the Socialist party in the 1930s and 1940s and the Communist party in the 1970s kept the vote for the Left at a relatively high average (considering the traditionalism of the agrarian society) of 20 percent. This is attributable mainly to the radicalism of the El Teniente copper miners,[13] whose consistent support for the Left raised the returns of the whole province considerably in that direction. Their political influence did not, however, go beyond the limits of the municipality in which the mine was located. General theories of leftist diffusion from mining centers into rural municipalities would certainly not apply in the case of El Teniente.

Evident inroads have been established by the Socialist party in the provinces of Curicó and Talca since the early 1950s with levels of support near 25 percent. This growth must be linked to the appeal of prestigious local figures and not to ideological conviction. The appeal of the Naranjo family in Curicó is a case in point. In the late 1960s and early 1970s, the Communists tried to benefit from the success of the Socialists in both provinces, and in 1973 they succeeded in Curicó as they surpassed the provincial vote for the Socialists. Provinces like Linares and Ñuble were impermeable to leftist ideas between 1932 and 1970; in 1973, however, the Socialist party obtained close to one-third of the vote in the two districts of Ñuble.

The dominance of the Right in the agrarian provinces has not been as strong as one might have expected. The activism of centrist and leftist parties and the growing political independence of the peasants, achieved by the introduction of the single ballot and the implementation of the agrarian reform, greatly weakened this political dominance. The National party's upsurge in these provinces in 1973 was due more to personal conviction among the voters than to electoral imposition by the landowners, as had been the case in the past.

Concepción-Arauco: The Leftist Enclave

The peculiarity of being an urban-industrial enclave in a predominantly agricultural region is apparent in the leftist leanings of Concepción and the neighboring coal-mining districts of Arauco. Since 1932 Concepción has demonstrated preference for the Socialist and Communist parties. Although in the 1930s and early 1940s the Socialists gained pluralities in this province, it was the Communists from 1965 to 1973. The lowest returns for both parties coincided with the *Ibañismo* populist wave that caught the Socialists split into antagonistic factions and the Communists banned from active politics. Once this spell was over, the leftist support was stronger than it had been in the late 1930s and early 1940s. The classical thesis that an industrial proletariat in an urban environment is prone to leftist radicalism is applicable in this situation but is the exception rather than the rule in Chile.

In accordance with these leftist leanings, candidates of center-left alliances (Table 7) have fared better in Concepción and Arauco than other combinations. In 1964, the center-right Eduardo Frei came close to Salvador Allende, leader of the Left. Conversely, candidates of the Right have never fared well in either province. In periods of leftist contraction, the progressive electorate of Concepción felt relatively at ease with the social democratic postulates of the Radicals; they show therefore secondary levels of support and also higher deviations than rightist parties (Table 7). Equally, Radical presidential candidates who ran with the support of the Left (Aguirre Cerda, Ríos, González Videla) scored smashing victories over their rightist or center-right opponents.

With its aversion to parties with religious connotations, Concepción was but a moderate supporter of the Christian Democracy. However, in 1965, at the height of the Christian Democratic wave, this party reached its peak (36 percent) at the expense of a severe reduction of the Right. Surprisingly, in 1973 the Christian Democracy again won a plurality over the rejuvenated Communist and Socialist parties. In the late 1940s and early 1950s there was a sound democratic constituency whose influence spilled over into neighboring Ñuble and Arauco, where the Democratic party obtained very high returns (32 percent) in the 1953 congressional elections and was only slightly surpassed by the Radicals. After the *Ibañismo* wave, it almost vanished from these provinces as its clientele moved to the Christian Democracy or toward the Left.

Remarkable in Concepción is the fact that the parties of the Right, Conservative and Liberal, maintained a steady constituency, so that their deviation values are the lowest of all parties. This reveals that in spite of an overwhelming but not very consistent support for the Left, the parties of the Right were able to keep their electoral support relatively constant, while other parties suffered from voter shifts.

Political Regionalism in La Frontera

Unlike countries in Latin America or Europe, Chile did not experience party development with strong regional overtones except in some of the *Frontera* provinces, and there only for short periods of time. Even though in an overall view the provinces of Bío-Bío, Malleco, and Cautín favored the Radical party, in the 1930s and again in the early 1950s these provinces gave overwhelming support to the Agrarian and Agrarian Laborite parties, which were sponsored by the agriculturalists in the region.[14]

The dominance of the Radical party in the *Frontera* provinces was not due so much to the ideological appeal of the party as to the fact that wealthy, anticlerical landowners of that area formed a special interest group within the Radical party. The influence of this group was very important to the ultimate triumph of Juan A. Ríos as a Radical candidate in 1942. The great appeal of the Radicals in these provinces continued well into the late 1960s and even withstood the mounting wave of the Christian Democracy. However, by 1973 they had almost disappeared from the political scene with their position of power being taken over by the Right and the Christian Democracy.

The Liberal party was the predominate force of the Right in the *Frontera* provinces from the 1930s to the 1950s. Its center of strength was the province of Malleco where it received 45 percent of the provincial vote in the 1945 congressional elections. By comparison the Conservatives were never as successful. Apart from high returns in Bío-Bío in 1945, they rarely exceeded 10 percent of the provincial vote in other years. A combination of right-wing Radicals and Liberals resulted in a very strong vote for presidential candidates of the Center-Right and in one of the lowest levels

The Regionalization of Politics

of endorsement of leftist presidential contestants (Table 7). Nor were center-left presidential candidates successful in this part of the country. Some writers have contended that in the periods of the decline of the Radical party its former supporters defected to the National party, particularly in the province of Cautín.[15]

Until 1961 the Christian Democracy was barely in evidence in these provinces; but it quickly grew to be the dominant force of the 1960s and 1970s, though at less impressive levels than in the urban and agrarian provinces of Middle Chile. The province of Cautín was the only one that provided really high returns for the Christian Democracy, and it did so at the expense of Radical votes. A great part of the success of the party in this province was due to the presentation of local candidates, a fact that proves again the strong regional proclivity of the *Frontera* electorate. Also catering to localism, the Democratic party and its splinter groups enjoyed a good level of support. In 1961 these parties received 29 percent of the regional vote, and in the provinces of Bío-Bío and Cautín remnants of the Democratic party were still alive in 1969. As a matter of fact, a PADENA deputy was elected in the province of Cautín as late as 1973.

Leftism was not very successful in these provinces. Still, the Socialist party was able to maintain a stable constituency (Table 6), which was at times not enough to elect a deputy. The Communists had even fewer supporters than the Socialists, but after 1969 they began to grow in numbers and in 1973 surpassed the Socialists in Bío-Bío.[16] In accordance with this trend Guillermo Briones found that, while in the provinces of Malleco and Cautín the leftist vote was much lower than expected from the high percentage of industrial workers, in the province of Bío-Bío the endorsement of the Left was higher than expected.[17] Judging from the returns of the 1973 congressional elections, the upsurge of the Left was far from impressive, notwithstanding the mobilization promoted by the Popular Unity among the urban and rural proletariat of *La Frontera*.

The Center-Right Tendencies of the Provinces of Modern Colonization

In their political preferences the *Frontera* provinces do not differ from their neighbors to the south; Valdivia, Osorno, and Llanquihue have consistently supported the Liberal party (Right) and the Radical party (Center). Both liberal and radical constituencies have maintained even levels of support and stability in the course of the years (Table 6). In presidential elections the preferences of the electorate have gone to rightist and center-right candidates, and leftist candidates have been rejected. Slightly different is the situation of Llanquihue, where the Right was represented by the Conservative rather than by the Liberal party. Llanquihue's preference for the Conservatives is matched by that of Chiloé, its immediate neighbor to the south.

The emergence of the Christian Democracy in these provinces was sudden as it was in the rest of the country, but since it had little effect on the support of the Right and the Radical party, it is to be assumed that its growth was due to an attraction of former *Ibañista* forces that were significant in this region and to a strong endorsement of the Christian Democracy by newly registered voters.[18] Remnants of *Ibañismo* in the province of Valdivia provided a certain level of support for the Democratic and PADENA parties; however, after 1965, it faded away. In the province of Valdivia the Socialists kept the forces of the Left alive from 1932 to 1972. The Socialist party was very strong in Valdivia and Llanquihue during the early 1940s, but weakened considerably in the late 1940s and 1950s. In the province of Osorno, except for a high vote for the Popular Socialists (a party favorable to Ibañez del Campo) in 1953, the Left did not fare well either. In fact in 1957 it almost vanished from the provinces of recent colonization. It was probably the endorsement of the socialist elements that made the Radical party so strong in these provinces.

The 1973 congressional elections gave a plurality to the Socialists in Valdivia and unusually high returns to the Communists in Osorno. This may be an indication of an upsurge of the Left in these provinces where its support had been traditionally low.

Conservative and Radical Chiloé

With more consistency than any other province, including the most traditional provinces of agricultural Middle Chile, Chiloé has voted for the Conservative party and its successor, the National party. But, in another example of political ambivalence, the voters of the province have given the same degree of support to the centrist Radical party. Both parties have in fact similar overall averages and standard deviation values (Table 6). Still more remarkable, lower returns for the one party were not often accompanied by higher returns for the other, indicating that fluctuations among the electorate affected the weaker parties, but not the heavyweights of the province.

In keeping with these trends, rightist candidates in Chiloé have enjoyed a winning edge with a slight advantage over center-left candidates (Table 7). Noteworthy is the fact that radical presidential candidates usually established alliances with the Left and that their high returns therefore stemmed more from the stable radical constituency than from a substantial leftist backing. Actually, leftist presidential contenders, Allende included, seldom obtained more than one-third of the provincial vote.

The stronghold of Conservatives and Radicals on Chiloé's voters is also distinguished by the sluggish growth of the Christian Democracy during the 1960s. In 1965, in their best election ever, the Christian Democrats received no more than 20 percent of the vote. With a strong Right and the Radicals occupying the middle ground, the Christian Democracy had little room for expansion. Only in the last congressional elections in 1973, when the Radical party was in definite contraction, was the Christian Democracy able to raise its percentage to 35 and thus gained its first plurality in that province.

In the same manner, the growth of the Left was retarded by the popularity of the Radical party, which before the 1950's had attracted all the leftist voters of the province. The Socialists, especially the Popular Socialist party headed by Raúl Ampuero, a native of Chiloé, capitalized on the unfulfilled socialistic aspirations of the people and obtained good electoral returns in the 1950s. But they rarely threatened the Radical or Conservative parties. However, when the Radicals weakened in the 1970s the Socialist party support climbed to 32 percent of the provincial vote. Ruralism, traditionalism and dependency have been mentioned as the main reasons for the adherence of Chiloé to the Right. But what about the strong endorsement of the Radical party? It seems that a large number of owner-cultivators, working at subsistence levels, although they longed for social progress, nevertheless opposed the extreme leftist position. For these people, the Radical party was progressive enough. In fact, though the Socialists received good support in the depressed province of Chiloé, the Communists were never able to make progress in the islands.

Socialist Magallanes

Under social and economic conditions very similar to those found in industrial areas of developed nations, the political response of Magallanes was similar to that of the industrial proletariat: endorsement of democratic socialism. In the absence of a landowner class, and with a merchant bourgeoisie not as affluent as that of Middle Chile, there were no bases from which the Right might develop. More in keeping with the political-economic conditions of the province were the bourgeois-democratic postulates of the Radical party, which was supported by the rich and by the middle class. The Left, represented by the Socialist party, attracted the industrial workers of the oil fields and the rural workers of coal mines or of large sheep-raising *estancias* owned by corporations.

In Magallanes the principal opponents in political contests were the Socialist and the Radical parties. The results were usually in favor of the Left, with very high returns in presidential as well as in congressional elections. Whenever the Radicals and the Left formed a presidential alliance, the triumph of their candidates was overwhelming, as shown by their high average percentage (Table 7). Since a slight turn of the Radicals to the right of the political spectrum upset the balance of forces in presidential elections, the second most successful alliances were those between the Radical and other centrist or rightist parties. Only Allende, in 1964 and 1970, could attract enough votes for a genuine leftist coalition. Nevertheless, his low returns in 1952 and 1958 depressed the long-time average of the Left in presidential elections.

The Christian Democracy could not compete successfully with Socialists and Radicals in Magallanes until 1969, when the number of deputies was raised to two. Previously the only deputy seat for this province had been won by the Socialist or Radical parties, the outcome of the election depending very much on the local electorate's perception of how the incumbent representative had performed in the Congress. Finally in 1973, the Christian Democracy, taking advantage of the failing strength of the Radicals, elected its first deputy in Magallanes. The political changes of recent times also had their repercussions in this province of socialist tradition.

Neighboring Aysén, populated like Magallanes by a large number of natives from Chiloé, has displayed the same political patterns as Magallanes. The most consistent party has been the Socialist, but the Christian Democracy became dominant in the late 1960s and until 1973 elected the only deputy for Aysén. In presidential elections the winning margin has gone to center-left alliances, since the Radical party was fairly strong also in this outlying province.

National Survey

In a global perspective of party support several characteristics emerge as relevant in both time and space. Even the long periods of leftist dominance in the North were interrupted by doldrums and drastic shifts in the electorate. The same applies to the Radicals' support for Conservatives in the South, and in the rest of the country support for parties flowed and ebbed with the changing times. Nowhere in Chile could a party claim continuous strong response from the electorate: plurality never meant total deliverance of the electoral body to any particular party.

Furthermore, although a party may have mustered impressive support in one election (e.g., the Radicals in the 1940s and the Christian Democracy in the 1960s), in the next election this backing may have been on the verge of collapse. This has been a conspicuous feature of Chilean politics resulting from the fact that partisan competition has taken place within a framework of freedom of choice and guaranteed impartiality from the party in government. Thus, in spite of the imperfections its pluralistic political system may have had, during the last decades political development has taken place in an atmosphere of greater freedom in Chile than in any other Latin American country.

Electoral responses to party stimuli have depended mainly on personal motivation and local circumstances; ecology has also had an impact, but not the determining one. A relatively low proportion of the electorate appears to have been influenced by ideologies, if one considers as an indication of this the minimum levels of support that have been given to certain parties between 1932 and 1973. Illustrative of this is the not impressively high but steady support enjoyed by the Communist party in the northern provinces, in the metropolitan area, and in Concepción. This party has been able to rely on a constituency that has changed only moderately from one election to the next. By comparison the support for the Socialists has varied more, especially in the northern provinces and in the provinces of recent colonization. The parties of the Right, particularly the Conservative party, have experienced the lowest variations in the traditional agricultural and the *Frontera* provinces, whereas the highest fluctuations of their constituencies have occurred in the North and in the metropolitan area. The control exerted by the rightist parties over the peasantry is the explanation for their low variations in Middle Chile. But this situation began to change after 1958 as a consequence of the emergence of the Christian Democracy and the FRAP.

Among the parties of the middle ground the Christian Democracy has experienced the maximum variations of support at the polls. Its high standard deviations stem from the fact that nowhere in Chile until the late 1950s did this party receive a high percentage of the provincial vote and that its clientele increased only in the mid-1960s, but then it did so very dramatically. The greatest fluctuations of the Christian Democracy have taken place in the traditional agricultural provinces of Middle Chile, in the metropolitan area, and in the South. In the North, contrary to what one might expect, the party has experienced only slight interelectoral changes.

The Radical party, notwithstanding its late electoral contraction, has appeared relatively steady in terms of constituency. Its lowest variations have been experienced in the agricultural provinces of Middle Chile, where it seems to have enjoyed the loyalty of the provincial middle class and of the bureaucracy. The highest fluctuations have occurred, paradoxically, in the province of Atacama, the cradle of the Radical party, and in Concepción, where, in times when the Left was in trouble, the Radical party seemed an acceptable alternative for the leftist voter.

As for the Left, the electoral results of forty-one years have revealed both its regions of strength and its areas of weakness. Without doubt, the Communist and Socialist parties drew their most consistent support from the provinces where the labor force was tightly organized and where the unions' leadership was under the control of one of these parties. This was true in the mining centers of the North, the industrial districts of the province of Concepción, and the southernmost province of Magallanes. The positive relationship between the strength of organized labor and the size of the vote for the Left also shows up in the more recent growth of the Communist and Socialist vote in the agrarian provinces of Middle Chile. However, this development would not have been possible without the massive mobilization and unionization of the peasantry undertaken by the Christian Democrats in the mid-1960s. Assumptions that preferences for the Left are linked with the degree of urbanization of municipalities or provinces are unwarranted. If this correlation does exist in some urban centers, it is due not so much to the radicalization of the urban poor as to the presence of organized workers and to the influence of structural shortcomings on the political responses of the voters.

The electoral fluctuations of the Democratic party have been very high in the metropolitan area, whereas in some agricultural provinces (Talca, Maule, and Cautín) the party has enjoyed a more loyal following. In general terms, the changing fortunes of small or short-lived parties in the political spectrum of the country are very closely related to the demands of groups with interests clearly attached to a specific geographical space, like the Agrarian party, which was the political organ of southern agriculturalists, or the People's National Vanguard, which was an expression of the socialist views of miners in the province of O'Higgins. In other cases the persistence of a certain political group in a province of Chile was based on the personal appeal of men like Rafael Tarud in Talca or Fernando Luengo in *La Frontera* and Cautín.

In a national summary the highest interelectoral variations of all constituencies are found in the metropolitan area of the country. This finding again contradicts the thesis of a positive correlation existing between the degree of urbanization and the leftist vote. Even the Communist party, the party with the steadiest support, experienced its major oscillations in Santiago and Valparaiso. Marked variations of support, added to the high proportion of the national returns represented by the provinces of the metropolitan area, make these the most decisive areas in the country. Thus, to their overall centralism electoral predominance has been added. As it became clear that many presidential and congressional elections were decided by the voters of Santiago and Valparaiso, a mixture of feelings of conformism and resentment towards the metropolitan area grew in the distant provinces. Therefore, the contention that the leftist proclivity of the far North and the extreme South, and the development of regionalist parties in *La Frontera* and recently colonized provinces, rather than being ideologically motivated, were rebellious responses to the overwhelming centralism of the metropolitan area is not to be discarded.

Considering the varied sociogeographical nature of the country, ths analysis of electoral responses in Chile during recent decades makes it evident that, far from a national consensus in politics, substantial spatial disparities have existed. The various regions of the country, the different social groups, and the individual voters reacted to political stimuli in a fashion that was greatly shaped by local conditions and by their perceptions of their place in the nation and in the country's society. Consequently, while regions or provinces supported a certain party or a particular candidate—inspired by their own specific motivations—other regions or provinces disagreed considerably.

It follows that the clains of "overwhelming support" or a "majority mandate" never really held true in the country. National consensus in politics—at least from the point of view of electoral responses—rarely existed. The only party that ever came close to justifying those claims was the Christian Democratic party: in the mid-1960s it claimed pluralities, but not always *majorities*, in more provinces of the country than any other party. Leaving aside all partisan explanations of this predominance, the phenomenon may be explained by the argument that the Christian Democratic doctrine articulated better than any other the heterogeneous demands of the Chilean voters. By comparison, the Right and the Left, even during the happiest days of the Popular Unity government, were unable to achieve national consensus because their political messages were oriented toward particular groups, and not toward the nation as a whole. This reality, which is deeply rooted in the geographical diversity of the country, has been overlooked by ideologists and politicians because it was easier for them to think of the Chileans as a unified and homogeneous population.

A customary emphasis on ideological stimuli rather than on ecological conditions and personal motivations has made the interpretation of many electoral contests contradictory, if not aberrant. This regional study of politics and social groups in Chile has been conceived precisely in order to stress the geographical fundamentals and the social conditions that underlie the act of decision making at the time of an election. From the historical developments outlined in Chapter 4, it is clear that the fortunes of Chilean parties have been very changeable. Political gods in Chile have had fragile feet of clay: momentary favorites have been overturned by a well-informed and politically conscious electorate that was often difficult to satisfy. To take for granted the support of a particular region or a certain social group has repeatedly proven to be a costly electoral mistake, one that has made Chilean politics a very hazardous game. It does not come as a surprise, then, that the road to socialism in Chile has not been as linear as has often been assumed. It has been a winding path that has frequently turned back upon itself.

Notes

Chapter 1

1. Rómulo Santana. "Reseña geográfica de Chile," in Corporación de Fomento de la Producción, eds., *Geografía Económica de Chile. Primer apéndice* (Santiago: Editorial Universitaria, 1966), pp. 6-14.

2. Wolfgang Weischet, *Chile. Seine länderkundliche Individualität und Struktur* (Darmstadt: Wissenschaftliche Buchgesellschaft, 1970), p. 12.

3. Arturo Valenzuela, "Political Participation, Agriculture and Literacy: Communal versus Provincial Voting Patterns in Chile," *Latin American Research Review* 12:1 (1977), pp. 106-109.

4. Armand Mattelart and Manuel A. Garretón, *Integración nacional y marginalidad* (Santiago: Editorial del Pacífico, 1965), pp. 27-37.

5. Armand Mattelart, *Atlas social de las comunas de Chile* (Santiago: Editorial del Pacífico, 1965), pp. 13 ff.

6. Walter Stöhr, "Geographische Aspekte der Planung in Entwicklungsländern. Die Südamerikanische Problematik und das Beispiel Chiles," *Wiener Geographische Schriften* (1967), p. 384.

7. Instituto Nacional de Estadísticas, *Características Generales de la Vivienda, Censo de 1970* (Santiago: Instituto Nacional de Estadísticas, 1974), pp. 38-39.

8. Brian L. Berry, "Relationships between Regional Economic Development and the Urban System: The Case of Chile," *Tijdschrift voor Economische en Sociale Geografie* 60 (September-October 1969), p. 305.

9. Jürgen Bähr and Winfried Golte, "Una regionalización demográfica y económica de Chile," in Wilhelm Lauer, ed., *Land-*

flucht und Verstädterung in Chile (Wiesbaden: Franz Steiner Verlag, 1976), p. 30.
   10. Mattelart, *Atlas social*, p. 20.
   11. Instituto Nacional de Estadísticas, *Población. Resultados definitivos del XIV Censo de Población, 1970: Total país* (Santiago: Instituto Nacional de Estadísticas, 1970), p. 75.
   12. Leland R. Pederson, *The Mining Industry of the North Chico* (Evanston: Northwestern University Studies in Geography, 1966), pp. 262-267.
   13. Mattelart, *Atlas social*, pp. 32-36.
   14. Benjamín Subercaseaux, *Chile o una loca geografía* (Santiago: Ediciones Ercilla, 1954), p. 58.
   15. Departamento de Economía, Universidad de Chile, *Ocupación y desocupación en el Gran Santiago (1974-1975)* (Santiago: Universidad de Chile, 1975), pp. 2-3.
   16. Instituto Nacional de Estadísticas, *Características Generales de la Vivienda*, pp. 38-39.
   17. Jürgen Bähr and Winfried Golte, "Eine bevölkerungs- und wirtschaftsgeographische Gliederung Chiles," *Geoforum* 17 (1974), p. 28.
   18. Roberto Santana and Philippe Grenier, "État et régionalisation en Amérique Latine: le cas du Chili," in Claude Bataillon, ed., *Etat, pouvoir et espace dans le Tiers Monde* (Paris: Presses Universitaires de France, 1977), p. 173.
   19. Instituto Geográfico Militar, *Atlas de la República de Chile* (Santiago: Instituto Geográfico Militar, 1970), pp. 209-210.
   20. Mattelart and Garretón, *Integración nacional y marginalidad*, pp. 47-49; Stöhr, "Geographische Aspekte der Planung in Entwicklungsländern," pp. 386-387.
   21. Mattelart, *Atlas social*, pp. 74, 78, and 86.
   22. Santana and Grenier, "État et régionalisation en Amérique Latine," p. 173.
   23. Mattelart and Garretón, *Integración nacional y marginalidad*, p. 46.
   24. Weischet, *Chile*, pp. 464-470.
   25. Mattelart and Garretón, *Integración nacional y marginalidad*, p. 55.
   26. Raúl Guerrero, "Estructuras agrarias, despoblamiento y trama urbana en La Frontera," *Cuadernos Geográficos del Sur* 1 (1971), p. 71.
   27. Donald MacPhail et al., "Chile's 'Forgotten' Region:

La Montaña," *AAG Program Abstracts, New Orleans 1978* (Baton Rouge: Association of American Geographers, 1978), p. 100.

28. Santana and Grenier, "État et régionalisation en Amérique Latine," pp. 177-179.

29. Winfried Golte, *Das südchilenische Seengebiet* (Bonn: Bonner Geographische Abhandlungen, 1973), pp. 53-67.

30. Weischet, *Chile*, pp. 473-475.

31. Jean-Pierre Blancpain, *Les Allemands au Chili (1816-1945)* (Köln: Böhlau Verlag, 1974), pp. 388-396.

32. Golte, *Südchilenische Seengebiet*, p. 66.

33. Berry, "Regional Economic Development and the Urban System," p. 305; Stöhr, "Geographische Aspekte der Planung," pp. 386-387.

34. Mattelart and Garretón, *Integración nacional y marginalidad*, pp. 51-53.

35. Santana, "Reseña geográfica de Chile," p. 14.

36. Philippe Grenier, "Los problemas de la pesca en la región de Chiloé," *Revista Geográfica de Valparaíso* 3:1-2 (1969), pp. 68-70.

37. Graciela Uribe and Cristina Castillo, "Estrategia para un desarrollo planificado: la microregión de Chiloé insular," *Informaciones Geográficas* 20 (1970), p. 198.

38. Mattelart and Garretón, *Integración nacional y marginalidad*, p. 56.

39. Uribe and Castillo, "Estrategia para un desarrollo planificado," pp. 224-229.

40. Pedro Cunill, *Geografía de Chile* (Santiago: Editorial Universitaria, 1970), p. 167.

41. Jürgen Bähr and Winfried Golte, "Entwicklung und Stand der Agrarkolonisation in Aysén unter dem Einfluss der Verstädterung," in Lauer, ed., *Landflucht und Verstädterung*, pp. 103-116.

42. Mattelart and Garretón, *Integración nacional y marginalidad*, p. 53.

43. Philippe Grenier, "Le pouvoir politique chilien comme agent d'organisation spatiale aux confins chiléno-argentins de la Patagonie," *Actes du XLII Congrès International des Américanistes, Paris, 1976*, pp. 527-536.

44. Mattelart, *Atlas social*, pp. 118-119.

45. Simon Collier, *Ideas and Politics of Chilean Independence, 1808-1833* (Cambridge: Cambridge University Press, 1967), pp. 345-348.

46. Federico Gil, *The Political System of Chile* (Boston: Houghton Mifflin, 1966), pp. 99-100.

47. Wolfgang Prieur, "Die Entwicklung des Verfassungsrechtes in Chile bis 1971," *Jahrbuch des Öffentlichen Rechts der Gegenwart* 20 (1971), p. 550.

48. Ibid., pp. 548-549.

49. Richard B. Gray and Frederick R. Kirwin, "Presidential Succession in Chile: 1817-1966," *Journal of Interamerican Studies* 11:2 (1969), pp. 146-148.

50. Prieur, "Entwicklung des Verfassungsrechtes in Chile," p. 549.

51. The administrative units of the country, provinces, departments, delegations, subdelegations, and communes, were replaced, in June of 1974, by regions, provinces, and communes. Decree Law no. 573 and no. 575, June 1974; Decree no. 1230, October 1975; Decree no. 1317, January 1976. The highest authority of a region is the intendant and of a province the provincial governor, both appointed by the president of the Republic.

52. Luis Galdames, *A History of Chile* (New York: Russell and Russell, 1964), p. 362.

53. Early constitutional documents were the Constitution of 1811, the Constitution Ordinance of 1812, the Constitution of 1818, the Constitution of 1822, the Constitution of 1823, the Constitutional Laws of 1826, and the Constitution of 1833. The complete texts of all these documents are reproduced in Luis Valencia A., *Anales de la República* (Santiago: Imprenta Universitaria, 1951) 1:38-185.

54. Weston H. Agor, *The Chilean Senate* (Austin: University of Texas Press, 1971), pp. 134-135.

55. Prieur, "Entwicklung des Verfassungsrechtes in Chile," p. 547.

56. Weston H. Agor, *Latin American Legislatures: Their Role and Influence* (New York: Praeger Publishers, 1971), pp. 6-14.

57. Dieter Nohlen, "Sozio-Ökonomischer Wandel und Verfassungsreform in Chile 1925-1972," *Verfassung und Rechte in Übersee* 6:1 (1973), p. 67.

58. Gil, *Political System of Chile,* p. 105.

59. Prieur, "Entwicklung des Verfassungsrechtes in Chile," p. 551.

60. Ibid., p. 548.

Chapter 2

1. Alberto Polloni, *Las Fuerzas Armadas de Chile, en la vida nacional* (Santiago: Editorial Andrés Bello, 1972), pp. 235-237.
2. Alberto Edwards, *La fronda aristocrática* (Santiago: Editorial del Pacífico, 1952), p. 198.
3. Atilio Borón, "La evolución del régimen electoral y sus efectos en la representación de los intereses populares: el caso de Chile," *Revista Latinoamericana de Ciencias Políticas* 2:3 (1971), p. 406.
4. *Constitución Política de la República de Chile.* Article 25.
5. Wolfgang Prieur, "Die Entwicklung des Verfassungsrechtes in Chile bis 1971," *Jahrbuch des Öffentlichen Rechts der Gegenwart* 20 (1971), p. 558.
6. "Chile: Agreement on the Rules of the Game," *Latin America* 6:12 (March 1972), pp. 92-93.
7. Ronald H. McDonald, "Apportionment and Party Politics in Santiago, Chile," *Midwest Journal of Political Science* 13:3 (August 1969), pp. 456-459.
8. Ricardo Cruz Coke, *Geografía electoral de Chile* (Santiago: Editorial del Pacífico, 1952), p. 61.
9. Bruce H. Herrick, *Urban Migration and Economic Development in Chile* (Cambridge, Mass.: MIT Press, 1965), pp. 44-45.
10. McDonald, "Apportionment and Party Politics," p. 470.
11. Ignacio Arteaga, *Partido Conservador. XIV Convención Nacional—1947* (Santiago: Imprenta Chile, 1947), pp. 22-30.
12. Sergio Guilisasti, *Partidos políticos chilenos* (Santiago: Editorial Nascimento, 1964), p. 24.
13. Frederick B. Pike, "Aspects of Class Relations in Chile, 1850-1960," *Hispanic American Historical Review* 43:1 (February 1963), p. 17.
14. Germán Urzúa, *Los partidos políticos chilenos* (Santiago: Editorial Jurídica de Chile, 1968), p. 62.
15. René Arriagada and Onofre Jarpa, *Por una política nacional* (Santiago: Ediciones Nueva Política, 1952), pp. 35-38.
16. Paul E. Sigmund, "Christian Democracy in Chile," *Journal of International Affairs* 20:2 (1966), p. 333.
17. Radomiro Tomic, "Chile Faces Human Development," in M. Zañartu and J. J. Kennedy, eds., *The Overall Development of Chile* (Notre Dame: University of Notre Dame Press, 1969), pp. 8-10.

18. Luis Scherz, "The People's Role in the Revolution," in Zañartu and Kennedy, *Overall Development of Chile*, pp. 100-102.
19. Heino Froehling, *Die Spaltung der Christdemokratischen Partei, 1969* (Bonn: Verlag Neue Gesellschaft, 1971), pp. 150-159.
20. Florencio Durán, *El Partido Radical* (Santiago: Editorial Nascimento, 1958), pp. 23-25.
21. Tomás Moulian, *Estudio sobre Chile* (Santiago: Editorial Orbe, 1965), p. 46.
22. Federico Gil, *The Political System of Chile* (Boston: Houghton and Mifflin, 1966), p. 260.
23. Ricardo Donoso, *Alessandri. Agitador y demoledor* (México: Fondo de Cultura Económica, 1955) 2:277-292.
24. Urzúa, *Partidos políticos chilenos,* p. 90.
25. Frederick B. Pike, *Chile and the United States 1880-1962* (Notre Dame: University of Notre Dame Press, 1963), p. 87.
26. James O. Morris, *Elites, Intellectuals and Consensus* (Ithaca: Cornell University Press, 1966), p. 102.
27. Wilhelm Mann, *Chile luchando por nuevas formas de vida* (Santiago: Editorial Ercilla, 1935), p. 107.
28. Gil, *Political System of Chile,* p. 285.
29. Hernán Ramírez, *Origen y formación del Partido Comunista de Chile* (Santiago: Editorial Austral, 1965), p. 124.
30. Guilisasti, *Partidos políticos chilenos,* pp. 257-269.
31. Paul W. Drake, "The Chilean Socialist Party and Coalition Politics, 1932-1946," *Hispanic American Historical Review* 53:4 (November 1973), p. 636.
32. Julio C. Jobet, *El Partido Socialista de Chile* (Santiago: Prensa Latinoamericana, 1971), pp. 24-27.
33. Ernest Halperin, *Nationalism and Communism in Chile* (Cambridge, Mass.: MIT Press, 1965), pp. 93-107.
34. Miles D. Wolpin, *Cuban Foreign Policy and Chilean Politics* (Lexington, Mass.: D.C. Heath, 1972), pp. 151-154.
35. "Qué es el MIR. Documento preparado por el Comité Central del MIR en la Clandestinidad," mimeographed, 20 pp. The ideological substance of the movement is outlined in pages 5 to 11.
36. Urzúa, *Partidos políticos chilenos,* pp. 76-78.
37. Jean-Pierre Blancpain, *Les Allemands au Chili (1816-1945)* (Köln: Böhlau Verlag, 1974), p. 862.
38. Ibid., p. 864.
39. Donoso, *Alessandri,* 2:256-269.

Notes to Chapter 2

40. R. E. Scott, "Political Elites and Political Modernization. The Crisis of Transition," in S. M. Lipset and A. Solari, eds., *Elites in Latin America* (New York: Oxford University Press, 1967). p. 120.

41. Information extracted from the *Diccionario Biográfico de Chile*, 13 edición (Santiago: Empresa Periodística Chile, 1965-1967).

42. Armando Uribe, *The Black Book of American Intervention in Chile* (Boston: Beacon Press, 1974), pp. vii-ix.

43. Frank Bonilla and Myron Glazer, *Student Politics in Chile* (New York: Basic Books, 1970), pp. 10, 63-68.

44. Emilio Willems, *Latin American Culture* (New York: Harper and Row, 1975), pp. 55-59.

45. Scott, "Political Elites," p. 122.

46. Bonilla and Glazer, *Student Politics in Chile*, pp. 55, 64.

47. Scott, "Political Elites," p. 119.

48. Weston H. Agor, *The Chilean Senate* (Austin: University of Texas Press, 1971), pp. 25-27.

49. George McBride, *Chile: Land and Society* (New York: American Geographical Society, 1936), p. 11.

50. Francisco A. Encina, *Nuestra inferioridad económica* (Santiago: Imprenta Universitaria, 1912), pp. 66, 69.

51. Urzúa, *Partidos políticos chilenos*, pp. 126, 148.

52. Agor, *The Chilean Senate*, p. 25.

53. Robert R. Kaufman, *The Politics of Land Reform in Chile, 1950-1970* (Cambridge, Mass.: Harvard University Press, 1972), p. 79.

54. Frederick M. Nunn, *Chilean Politics, 1921-1931* (Albuquerque: University of New Mexico Press, 1970), pp. 10, 174.

55. Frederick M. Nunn, "New Thoughts on Military Intervention in Latin American Politics. The Chilean Case, 1973," *Journal of Latin American Studies* 7:2 (1975), p. 274.

56. Ibid., p. 275.

57. Paul E. Sigmund, *The Overthrow of Allende and the Politics of Chile, 1964-1976* (Pittsburgh: University of Pittsburgh Press, 1977), pp. 85-87.

58. "Chile: Military Alliance," *Latin America* 6:45 (November 1972), p. 353.

59. Arturo Valenzuela, *Political Brokers in Chile* (Durham, N.C.: Duke University Press, 1977), pp. 16-27.

Chapter 3

1. Arnold J. Bauer, *Chilean Rural Society* (Cambridge: Cambridge University Press, 1975), pp. 176-180.
2. Jaime Eyzaguirre, *Historia de Chile* (Santiago: Editorial Zig-Zag, 1973), p. 453.
3. Jaime Eyzaguirre, *Fisonomía histórica de Chile* (Santiago: Editorial del Pacífico, 1965), pp. 62-64.
4. George McBride, *Chile: Land and Society* (New York: American Geographical Society, 1936), p. 10.
5. Bauer, *Chilean Rural Society*, p. 19.
6. César Caviedes, "Die Aconcagua-Mündung, Mittelchile," *Die Erde* 105:3-4 (1974), pp. 217-222.
7. Bauer, *Chilean Rural Society*, p. 49.
8. Mary Lowenthal, "Kinship Politics in the Chilean Independence Movement," *The Hispanic American Historical Review* 56:1 (January 1976), pp. 67-71.
9. Luis Valencia, *Anales de la República*, vols. 1-2 (Santiago: Imprenta Universitaria, 1951); Chile, Cámara de Diputados, *Monografía de la Cámara de Diputados, 1811-1945* (Santiago: Publicaciones de la Cámara de Diputados, 1945), 92 pp.
10. Emilio Willems, "A classe alta chilena," *America Latina* 10:2 (abril-junho 1967), p. 44.
11. Bauer, *Chilean Rural Society*, p. 194.
12. The cosmopolitan society of Valparaíso in the early decades of the nineteenth century has been accurately described by Maria D. Graham, *Journal of a Residence in Chile, during the Year 1822* (New York: Praeger Publishers, 1969); see, also, Roberto Hernandez, *Valparaíso en 1827* (Valparaíso: Imprenta Victoria, 1927).
13. Fernando H. Cardoso, "The Entrepreneurial Elite in Latin America," *America Latina* 10:4 (October-December 1967), pp. 25-28.
14. Frederick B. Pike, "Aspects of Class Relations in Chile, 1850-1960," *Hispanic American Historical Review* 43:1 (February 1963), p. 16.
15. Carl Solberg, *Immigration and Nationalism. Argentina and Chile, 1890-1914* (Austin: University of Texas Press, 1970), pp. 72-77.
16. Nicolás Palacios, *Raza chilena*, vol. 2 (Santiago: Imprenta Universitaria, 1918), pp. 102-107.

17. Solberg, *Immigration and Nationalism*, p. 168.
18. Valencia, *Anales de le República*, 1:469-586.
19. Jean-Pierre Blancpain, *Les allemands au Chili (1816-1945)* (Köln: Böhlau Verlag, 1974), pp. 613-637.
20. Victor C. Dahl, "Yugoslav Immigrant Experiences in Argentina and Chile," *Inter-American Economic Affairs* 28:3 (Winter 1974), pp. 3-26.
21. Solberg, *Immigration and Nationalism*, pp. 69-70.
22. Donald W. Bray, "The Political Emergence of Arab-Chileans, 1952-1958," *Journal of Inter-American Studies* 4:4 (1962), pp. 557-562.
23. Useful in tracing intermarriages among aristocratic and bourgeois families is the information contained in the *Diccionario Biográfico de Chile*, 13 edición (Santiago: Empresa Periodística Chile, 1965-1967).
24. Enrique Bunster, *Chilenos en California* (Santiago: Editorial del Pacífico, 1954), p. 149.
25. Ibid., pp. 121-128.
26. Bauer, *Chilean Rural Society*, pp. 192-195.
27. Markos Mamalakis, *The Growth and Structure of the Chilean Economy* (New Haven: Yale University Press, 1976), pp. 161-163.
28. Cardoso, "Entrepreneurial Elite," p. 42.
29. Maurice Zeitlin and Richard E. Ratcliff, "Research Methods for the Analysis of the Internal Structure of Dominant Classes: The Case of Landlords and Capitalists in Chile," *Latin American Research Review* 10:3 (Fall 1975), p. 54.
30. James Petras, *Politics and Social Forces in Chilean Development* (Berkeley, Los Angeles: University of California Press, 1969), p. 39.
31. María Grossi Ackermann, "Burguesía industrial e ideología de desarrollo en Chile," *Revista Mexicana de Sociología* 33:4 (1971), p. 742.
32. Pike, "Class Relations in Chile," p. 21.
33. Albert Lauterbach, *Managerial Attitudes in Chile* (Santiago: Universidad de Chile, Instituto de Economía, 1961), pp. 60-65.
34. Grossi Ackermann, "Burguesía industrial e ideología de desarrollo," pp. 744-749.
35. Mamalakis, *Chilean Economy*, p. 155.
36. Ricardo Lagos, *La concentración del poder económico. Su teoría. Realidad chilena* (Santiago: Editorial del Pacífico, 1961), pp. 101-163.

37. Maurice Zeitlin, Lynda A. Ewen, and Richard E. Ratcliff, "New Princes for Old? The Large Corporation and the Capitalist Class in Chile," *American Journal of Sociology* 80:1 (July 1974), pp. 103-105.
38. Zeitlin and Ratcliff, "Research Methods," p. 36.
39. Lagos, *Concentración del poder económico,* p. 169.
40. Bray, "Political Emergence of Arab-Chileans," p. 558. Matte, Alfonso, and Allende were contenders of Ibañez del Campo in the presidential contest of 1952.
41. Willems, "A classe alta chilena," p. 48.
42. Eduardo Blanco Amor, *Chile a la vista* (Santiago: Editorial del Pacífico, 1952), pp. 76-78.
43. Tomás Moulian, *Estudio sobre Chile* (Santiago: Editorial Orbe, 1965), p. 70.
44. Ben G. Burnett, *Political Groups in Chile* (Austin: University of Texas Press, 1970), p. 66.
45. Orlandina Oliveira de Muñoz, "Situación de clase y contenidos ideológicos. Análisis de comerciantes y empleados públicos en Santiago," *Revista Mexicana de Sociología* 33:2 (1971), pp. 302-306.
46. Anibal Quijano, "The Urbanization of Latin American Society," in Jorge E. Hardoy, ed., *Urbanization in Latin America. Approaches and Issues* (Garden City, N.Y.: Anchor Press–Doubleday, 1975), pp. 114-117.
47. Ibid., p. 150.
48. Pike, "Class Relations in Chile," pp. 21-23.
49. Oscar Alvarez A., "El problema de la familia en Chile," *Revista Mexicana de Sociología* 20:2 (1958), p. 420.
50. Rodolfo Stavenhagen, "Seven Fallacies about Latin America," in James Petras and Maurice Zeitlin, eds., *Latin America. Reform or Revolution?* (Greenwich, Conn.: Fawcett Publications, 1968), pp. 23-26.
51. Robert C. Williamson, "Social Class, Mobility and Modernism: Chileans and Social Change," *Sociology and Social Research* 56.2 (January 1972), pp. 153, 158-162.
52. Pike, "Class Relations in Chile," pp. 27-28.
53. Oliveira de Muñoz, "Situación de clase y contenidos ideológicos," pp. 314-318.
54. Ricardo Cinta, "Desarrollo económico, urbanización y radicalismo político," *Revista Mexicana de Sociología* 31:3 (1969), p. 646.
55. Carl Martin, *Landeskunde von Chile* (Hamburg: L. Friede-

richsen & Co., 1923), p. 523.

56. Alan Angell, "Chile: The Difficulties of Democratic Reform," *International Journal* 24:3 (1969), p. 519.

57. Kenneth P. Langton and Ronald Rapoport, "Social Structure, Social Content, and Partisan Mobilization. Urban Workers in Chile," *Comparative Political Studies* 8:3 (October 1975), pp. 338-340.

58. Williamson, "Social Class," pp. 161-162.

59. Jorge Ahumada, *En vez de la miseria* (Santiago: Editorial del Pacífico, 1958), p. 53.

60. Pike, "Class Relations in Chile," pp. 27-28.

61. Moulian, *Estudio sobre Chile,* p. 46.

62. Germán Urzúa, *Los partidos políticos chilenos* (Santiago: Editorial Jurídica de Chile, 1968), p. 63.

63. Moulian, *Estudio sobre Chile,* pp. 46-47.

64. Oliveira de Muñoz, "Situación de clase y contenidos ideológicos," pp. 313-318.

65. Angell, "Democratic Reform," p. 521.

66. Urzúa, *Partidos políticos chilenos,* p. 64.

67. Aníbal Pinto, "Desarrollo económico y relaciones sociales en Chile," *Aportes* 20 (abril 1971), p. 11.

68. Víctor Nazar, "El proceso de formación de la clase obrera en Chile," *Revista Mexicana de Sociología* 36:1 (1974), p. 83.

69. James O. Morris, *Elites, Intellectuals, and Consensus* (Ithaca: Cornell University Press, 1966), pp. 72 ff.; and Lauterbach, *Managerial Attitudes,* p. 35.

70. Frederick B. Pike, *Chile and the United States 1880-1962,* p. 109.

71. Nazar, "Proceso de formación de la clase obrera," pp. 85, 90.

72. Average salaries in diverse occupational categories for the years 1964, 1965, 1966, 1967, 1968, 1969, and 1970 are found in O.E.A. Instituto Interamericana de Estadística, *América en Cifras 1972,* vol. 5, Situación Económica: Precios, salarios, consumo y otros aspectos económicos, cuadro 352-05, p. 74.

73. Christian Lalive d'Epinay and Jacques Zylberberg, "Dichotomie sociale et pluralisme culturel: la dispersion politique de la classe ouvrière chilienne," *Cahiers Internationaux de Sociologie* 59 (1975), p. 270.

74. Alain Labrousse, *L'expérience chilienne: réformisme ou révolution?* (Paris: Éditions du Seuil, 1972), pp. 374-376.

75. Instituto Nacional de Estadísticas, *Encuesta continua de*

mano de obra. Resultados del Gran Santiago, abril-junio 1971 (Santiago: Instituto Nacional de Estadísticas, 1971), p. 20.

76. Gerry Foley, "The Workers Move Forward—as Allende Retreats," in Les Evans, ed., *Disaster in Chile* (New York: Pathfinder Press, 1974), pp. 136-141.

77. Christian Lalive d'Epinay and Jacques Zylberberg, "Les réligions au Chili entre l'aliénation et la prise de conscience," *Social Compass* 21:1 (1974), pp. 85-100.

78. Lucy C. Behrman, "Patterns of Religious and Political Attitudes and Activities during Modernization: Santiago, Chile," *Social Science Quarterly* 53:3 (December 1972), pp. 520-533.

79. Eyzaguirre, *Historia de Chile*, p. 594.

80. Alan Angell, *Politics and the Labour Movement in Chile* (London: Oxford University Press, 1972), pp. 20-22.

81. Solberg, *Immigration and Nationalism*, pp. 104-105.

82. Angell, *Politics and the Labour Movement*, pp. 32-35.

83. Burnett, *Political Groups*, pp. 104-105.

84. Angell, *Politics and the Labour Movement*, pp. 112-115.

85. Moulian, *Estudio sobre Chile*, p. 55.

86. Angell, *Politics and the Labour Movement*, p. 119.

87. J. Samuel Valenzuela, "The Chilean Labor Movement: The Institutionalization of Conflict," in Arturo Valenzuela and J. Samuel Valenzuela, eds., *Chile: Politics and Society* (New Brunswick, N.J.: Transaction Books, 1976), pp. 143-144.

88. Henry A. Landsberger, Manuel Barrera, and Angel Toro, "The Chilean Labor Union Leader: A Preliminary Report on his Background and Attitudes," *Industrial and Labor Relations Review* 17:3 (April 1964), p. 410.

89. Atilio Borón, "Movilización política y crisis política en Chile: 1920-1970," *Aportes* 20 (abril 1971), pp. 67-68.

90. Alejandro Portes, "Occupation and Lower Class Political Orientations in Chile," in Valenzuela and Valenzuela, eds., *Chile: Politics and Society*, pp. 211-214.

91. Lalive d'Epinay and Zylberberg, "Dichotomie sociale et pluralisme culturel," p. 263.

92. Brian H. Smith and José L. Rodríguez, "Comparative Working-Class Political Behavior," *American Behavioral Scientist* 18:1 (September 1974), pp. 59-72.

93. Alberto Valdés, "Wages and Schooling of Agricultural Workers in Chile," *Economic Development and Cultural Change* 19:2 (January 1971), pp. 313-315.

94. McBride, *Chile: Land and Society*, p. 148.

95. Gene E. Martin, *La división de la tierra en Chile Central* (Santiago: Instituto de Geografía, Universidad de Chile, 1960), pp. 134-136; Emilio Klein, "Tipos de dependencia y obreros agrícolas en Chile," *Boletín de Estudios Latinoamericanos y del Caribe* 16 (junio 1974), pp. 16-27.

96. George M. Korb, "Communicating with the Chilean Peón," *American Journal of Economics and Sociology* 25:3 (July 1966), p. 284; Wolfgang Weischet, *Agrarreform und Nationalisierung des Bergbaus in Chile* (Darmstadt: Wissenschaftliche Buchgesellschaft, 1974), p. 15; Klein, "Tipos de dependencia y obreros agrícolas," p. 21.

97. Klein, "Tipos de dependencia y obreros agrícolas," p. 22.

98. Solon Barraclough, "Agrarian Reform in Chile," in Dale L. Johnson, ed., *The Chilean Road to Socialism* (Garden City, N.Y.: Anchor Press-Doubleday, 1973), pp. 484-487.

99. Dirección de Estadística y Censos, *IV Censo Nacional Agropecuario. Resumen General del País* (Santiago: Dirección de Estadística y Censos, 1969), p. 10.

100. William J. Smole, *Owner-Cultivatorship in Middle Chile* (Chicago: Department of Geography, University of Chicago, 1963), pp. 150-157.

101. Arturo Valenzuela, *Political Brokers in Chile* (Durham, N.C.: Duke University Press, 1977), pp. 73-84.

102. John R. Stevenson, *The Chilean Popular Front* (Philadelphia: University of Pennsylvania Press, 1942), pp. 83-84.

103. Jeannine Swift, *Agrarian Reform in Chile* (Lexington, Mass.: Heath Lexington Books, 1971), p. 34.

104. Robert R. Kaufman, *The Politics of Land Reform in Chile, 1950-1970* (Cambridge, Mass.: Harvard University Press, 1972), pp. 66-73.

105. David Lehmann, "Political Incorporation versus Political Stability: The Case of the Chilean Agrarian Reform, 1965-70," *Journal of Development Studies* 7:4 (July 1971), pp. 377-383.

106. Almino Affonso, *Trayectoria del movimiento campesino chileno* (Santiago: ICIRA, n.d.), p. 18.

107. Law 15020 defined an *unidad económica* as a parcel of land that can support a peasant family. The size of that unit changes across the country.

108. *Asentamiento* refers to the legal status of expropriated farms on which former tenant-workers were allocated land for

personal and collective use. Individuals did not hold titles of ownership since it was to be decided later if the *asentamiento* was to become individual or collective property.

109. Eduardo Frei, *Sexto mensaje del Presidente de la República don Eduardo Frei M. al inaugurar el período de sesiones ordinarias del Congreso Nacional* (Santiago: Dirección de Informaciones y Radiodifusión de la Presidencia de la República, 1970), p. 61.

110. Kaufman, *Politics of Land Reform,* pp. 137-144.

111. David Lehmann, "Agrarian Reform in Chile, 1965-1972," in David Lehmann, ed., *Agrarian Reform and Agrarian Reformism* (London: Faber and Faber, 1974), p. 97.

112. Weischet, *Agrarreform und Nationalisierung des Bergbaus,* pp. 30-31.

113. Klaus Rother, "Stand, Auswirkungen und Aufgaben der chilenischen Agrarreform," *Erdkunde* 27:4 (Dezember 1973), p. 311.

114. The discrepancy is created by the alleged number of families that received land during the Christian Democratic administration. CORA records from the Frei years mention 29,139 families, whereas CORA information from the Allende years cites only 20,976. This is probably a case of data manipulation for political purposes.

115. Oficina de Planificación, *Informe económico anual* (Santiago: Editorial Universitaria, 1972), pp. 66-69.

116. Lehmann, "Political Incorporation versus Political Stability," pp. 377-378.

117. Labrousse, *L'expérience chilienne,* p. 264.

118. David Thorstad, "A Simmering Crisis in the U.P.," in Evans, ed., *Disaster in Chile,* pp. 99-101.

119. Brian Loveman, "The Transformation of the Chilean Countryside," in Valenzuela and Valenzuela, *Chile: Politics and Society,* p. 263.

120. Régis Debray, *Conversations with Allende* (London: NLB Publishers, 1971), p. 102.

121. Hernán Ramírez, *Origen y formación del Partido Comunista de Chile* (Santiago: Editorial Austral, 1965), pp. 38-46.

122. Morris, *Elites, Intellectuals, and Consensus,* pp. 98-100.

123. Urzúa, *Partidos políticos chilenos,* p. 58.

124. Frank Bonilla and Myron Glazer, *Student Politics in*

Chile (New York: Basic Books, 1970), pp. 183-200.

125. Langton and Rapoport, "Social Structure," pp. 334-339.

126. Sandra Powell, "Political Change in the Chilean Electorate, 1952-1964," *Western Political Quarterly* 23:2 (June 1970), p. 378.

127. Ernesto A. Isuani and Rubén A. Cervini, "Análisis del voto de izquierda en Santiago de Chile: un modelo causal," *Latin American Research Review* 10:3 (Fall 1975), pp. 110-115.

128. Emile Durkheim, *Le suicide* (Paris: Presses Universitaires de France, 1967), pp. 272-286.

129. Carl Stone, "Social Modernization and Left Wing Voting in Chile," *Social and Economic Studies* 20:4 (December 1971), p. 353.

130. Alejandro Portes, "On the Interpretation of Class Consciousness," *American Journal of Sociology* 77:2 (September 1971), pp. 231-243.

131. Alan Angell, "Chile: The Difficulties of Democratic Reform," *International Journal* 23:3 (1969), p. 521.

132. Torcuato di Tella et al., *Huachipato et Lota. Étude sur la conscience ouvrière dans deux entreprises chiliennes* (Paris: Éditions du Centre de la Recherche Scientifique, 1965), pp. 226-227.

133. Moulian, *Estudio sobre Chile*, p. 55.

134. Williamson, "Social Class," pp. 160-161; Powell, "Chilean Electorate," p. 377.

135. Valenzuela, *Political Brokers*, p. 26.

136. Ricardo Cinta, "Desarrollo económico, urbanización y radicalismo político," *Revista Mexicana de Sociología* 31:3 (1969), p. 644.

137. Daniel Lerner, *The Passing Traditional Society: Modernizing the Middle East* (Glencoe: Free Press, 1958), pp. 61-73.

138. Ricardo Cruz Coke, *Geografía electoral de Chile* (Santiago: Editorial del Pacífico, 1952), pp. 109-111.

139. Alejandro Portes and Adreain Ross, "A Model for the Prediction of Leftist Radicalism," *Journal of Political and Military Sociology* 2 (Spring 1974), pp. 36-39.

140. Cinta, "Desarrollo económico," p. 675.

141. William Kornhauser, *The Politics of Mass Society* (Glencoe: Free Press, 1959), p. 150.

142. Guillermo Briones, "Estructura social y estructura política. Un análisis ecológico de la sociología electoral," *Revista Mexicana*

de Sociología 32:6 (1970), pp. 1518-1521.

143. Raymond B. Pratt, "Parties, Neighborhood Associations and the Politization of the Urban Poor in Latin America: An Exploratory Analysis," *Midwest Journal of Political Science* 15:13 (August 1971), pp. 495-497.

144. Daniel Goldrich, "Political Organization and the Politization of the *Poblador*," *Comparative Political Studies* 3:2 (July 1970), pp. 194-196.

145. Portes and Ross, "Leftist Radicalism," p. 37.

146. Howard Handelman, "The Political Mobilization of the Urban Squatter Settlements: Santiago's Recent Experience and its Implications for Urban Research," *Latin American Research Review* 10:2 (Summer 1975), pp. 43-44.

147. Hugo Blanco, "The Workers' Cordones Challenge the Reformists," in Evans, *Disaster in Chile,* pp. 182-185.

148. Franz Vanderschueren, "Political Significance of Neighborhood Committees in the Settlements of Santiago," in Dale L. Johnson, ed., *The Chilean Road to Socialism* (Garden City, N.Y.: Anchor Press–Doubleday, 1973), pp. 280-283.

149. Henry A. Landsberger and Tim McDaniel, "Hypermobilization in Chile: 1970-1973," *World Politics* 28:4 (July 1976), pp. 540-541.

150. Thomas G. Sanders, "The Process of Partisanship in Chile," *American Universities Field Staff Reports* 20:1 (1973), pp. 8-10.

Chapter 4

1. Paul W. Drake, "The Political Responses of the Chilean Upper Class to the Great Depression and to the Threat of Socialism, 1931-33," in Frederic C. Jaher, ed., *The Rich, the Well Born and the Powerful. Elite and Upper Class in History* (Urbana: University of Illinois Press, 1973), pp. 307-308.

2. Ricardo Donoso, *Alessandri. Agitador y demoledor* (México: Fondo de Cultura Económica, 1953) 1:397-401.

3. Frederick M. Nunn, *Chilean Politics 1920-1931. The Honorable Mission of the Armed Forces* (Albuquerque: University of New Mexico Press, 1970), pp. 117-126.

4. Clarence H. Haring, "Presidential Elections in South America," *Foreign Affairs* 10:2 (January 1932), p. 329.

5. John R. Stevenson, *The Chilean Popular Front* (Phila-

delphia: University of Pennsylvania Press, 1942), pp. 51-52.
6. Donoso, *Alessandri*, 2:116.
7. *El Mercurio*, October 31, 1932, pp. 1, 9, 11, 13.
8. Germán Urzúa, *Los partidos políticos chilenos* (Santiago: Editorial Jurídica de Chile, 1968), p. 73.
9. Stevenson, *Chilean Popular Front*, p. 54.
10. Drake, "Political Responses," p. 313.
11. Donoso, *Alessandri*, 2:132-135.
12. Urzúa, *Partidos políticos chilenos*, p. 75.
13. Stevenson, *Chilean Popular Front*, pp. 70-71.
14. Ricardo Cruz Coke, *Geografía electoral de Chile* (Santiago: Editorial del Pacífico, 1952), p. 83.
15. Donoso, *Alessandri*, 2:206-207.
16. Paul W. Drake, "The Chilean Socialist Party and Coalition Politics," *Hispanic American Historical Review* 53:4 (November 1973), pp. 628-629.
17. Donoso, *Alessandri*, 2:256-294.
18. Cruz Coke, *Geografía electoral*, p. 91.
19. Donoso, *Alessandri*, 2:298-300.
20. Clarence H. Haring, "Chile Moves Left," *Foreign Affairs* 17:3 (April 1939), p. 623.
21. Markos Mamalakis and Clark W. Reynolds, *Essays on the Chilean Economy* (Homewood, Ill.: Richard D. Irwin, 1965), pp. 236-240.
22. Stevenson, *Chilean Popular Front*, pp. 97-102.
23. Drake, "Chilean Socialist Party," p. 632.
24. Stevenson, *Chilean Popular Front*, p. 110.
25. Florencio Durán, *El Partido Radical* (Santiago: Editorial Nascimento, 1958), p. 192.
26. Donoso, *Alessandri*, 2:357.
27. Urzúa, *Partidos políticos chilenos*, p. 86.
28. Federico Gil, *The Political System of Chile* (Boston: Houghton Mifflin, 1966), p. 71.
29. George Strawbridge, *Ibañez and Alessandri: The Authoritarian Right and Democratic Left in Twentieth Century Chile* (Buffalo: Council of International Studies, State University of New York at Buffalo, 1971), pp. 25, 37.
30. Durán, *Partido Radical*, pp. 412-415.
31. Ignacio Arteaga, ed., *Partido Conservador. Notas para la historia política del Partido Conservador* (Santiago: Imprenta

Chile, 1947), pp. 35-39.
32. Drake, "Chilean Socialist Party," p. 636.
33. Cruz Coke, *Geografía electoral*, p. 74.
34. Jack R. Thomas, "The Evolution of a Chilean Socialist: Marmaduke Grove," *Hispanic American Historical Review* 47:1 (February 1967), pp. 36-37.
35. Donoso, *Alessandri*, 2:428-433.
36. Serafino Romualdi, "Labor and Democracy in Latin America," *Foreign Affairs* 25:2 (April 1947), p. 487.
37. Alan Angell, *Politics and the Labour Movement in Chile* (London: Oxford University Press, 1972), p. 112.
38. Ibid., pp. 114-115.
39. Robert J. Alexander, *Communism in Latin America* (New Brunswick: Rutgers University Press, 1957), pp. 202-204.
40. Ernst Halperin, *Nationalism and Communism in Chile* (Cambridge, Mass.: MIT Press, 1965), p. 128.
41. Donoso, *Alessandri*, 2:476.
42. Cruz Coke, *Geografía electoral*, p. 71.
43. Markos Mamalakis, *The Growth and Structure of the Chilean Economy* (New Haven: Yale University Press, 1976), pp. 105-107.
44. Donoso, *Alessandri*, 2:502-503.
45. Halperin, *Nationalism and Communism*, pp. 55-57.
46. René Arriagada and Sergio O. Jarpa, *Por una política nacional* (Santiago: Ediciones Nueva Política, 1952), p. 5.
47. Aníbal Pinto, "Desarrollo económico y relaciones sociales en Chile," *Aportes* 20 (abril 1971), p. 24. A recent comprehensive study on populism in Chile is Paul W. Drake, *Socialism and Populism in Chile, 1932-52* (Urbana: University of Illinois Press, 1978).
48. Gil, *Political System of Chile*, p. 74.
49. Francisco J. Moreno, *Legitimacy and Stability in Latin America* (New York: New York University Press, 1969), p. 164.
50. Tomás Moulian, *Estudio sobre Chile* (Santiago: Editorial Orbe, 1965), p. 102.
51. Gil, *Political System of Chile*, p. 79.
52. Alejandro Magnet, *Nuestros vecinos argentinos* (Santiago: Editorial del Pacífico, 1956), pp. 123-137.
53. Donald W. Bray, "Peronism in Chile," *Hispanic American Historical Review* 47:1 (February 1967), pp. 39-41.
54. Frederick M. Nunn, "New Thoughts on Military Interven-

tion in Latin American Politics: The Chilean Case, 1973," *Journal of Latin American Studies* 7:2 (1975), pp. 274-275.

55. Raúl Silva, *Camino al abismo. Lo que no se ha dicho sobre el proceso de la Línea Recta* (Santiago: Editorial Universitaria, 1955), pp. 41-73.

56. William G. Tyler, "An Evaluation of the Klein and Saks Stabilization Program in Chile," *America Latina* 11:1 (March-June 1968), pp. 52-69.

57. Donald W. Bray, "The Political Emergence of Arab-Chileans, 1952-1958," *Journal of Inter-American Studies* 4:4 (October 1962), pp. 557-562.

58. Ernesto Würth, *Ibañez. Caudillo enigmático* (Santiago: Editorial del Pacífico, 1958), p. 326.

59. Nemesio Alvarado, *El turco Tarud. La verdad sobre un tiempo y una historia* (Santiago: Ediciones Territorio, 1970), pp. 181-182.

60. Julio C. Jobet, *El Partido Socialista de Chile* (Santiago: Ediciones Prensa Latinoamericana, 1971), pp. 22-23.

61. Sergio Guilisasti, *Partidos políticos chilenos* (Santiago: Editorial Nascimento, 1964), p. 261.

62. Moreno, *Legitimacy and Stability*, p. 166.

63. James Petras, *Politics and Social Forces in Chilean Development* (Berkeley, Los Angeles: University of California Press, 1969), p. 178.

64. Urzúa, *Partidos políticos chilenos*, p. 96.

65. Gil, *Political System of Chile*, p. 81.

66. Moulian, *Estudio sobre Chile*, pp. 112-115.

67. Mamalakis, *Chilean Economy*, p. 96.

68. Moulian, *Estudio sobre Chile*, pp. 154-155.

69. Paul E. Sigmund, *The Overthrow of Allende and the Politics of Chile, 1964-1976* (Pittsburgh: University of Pittsburgh Press, 1977), p. 29.

70. Moreno, *Legitimacy and Stability*, p. 167.

71. Arturo Valenzuela, "The Scope of the Chilean Party System," *Comparative Politics* 4:2 (January 1972), p. 199.

72. Pinto, "Desarrollo económico y relaciones sociales," p. 31.

73. Radomiro Tomic, "Chile Faces Human Development," in M. Zañartu and J. J. Kennedy, eds., *The Overall Development of Chile* (Notre Dame: University of Notre Dame Press, 1969), pp. 9-10.

74. Régis Debray, *Conversations with Allende* (London: NLB, 1971), pp. 81-82.

75. Orlando Millas, "Christian Democratic Reformism: The Chilean Experiment," *World Marxism Review* 8:11 (November 1965), pp. 65-67.

76. Paul E. Sigmund, "Three Views of Allende's Chile," in A. Valenzuela and J. S. Valenzuela, eds., *Chile: Politics and Society* (New Brunswick, N.J.: Transaction Books, 1976), pp. 129-132.

77. Sergio de Santis, "Chile," *International Socialist Journal* 2:9 (June 1966), p. 336.

78. Miles D. Wolpin, *Cuban Foreign Policy and Chilean Politics* (Lexington: Lexington Books, 1972), p. 136.

79. Federico Gil and Charles J. Parrish, *The Chilean Presidential Election of September 4, 1964* (Washington: Institute for the Comparative Study of Political Systems, 1965), pp. 38-41.

80. Orville G. Cope, "The 1964 Presidential Election in Chile: The Politics of Change and Access," *Inter-American Economic Affairs* 19:4 (Spring 1966), pp. 24-27.

81. Halperin, *Nationalism and Communism*, p. 217.

82. Maurice Zeitlin and James Petras, "The Working-class Vote in Chile: Christian Democracy versus Marxism," *British Journal of Sociology* 21:1 (March 1970), pp. 18-28.

83. Halperin, *Nationalism and Communism*, p. 221; Zeitlin and Petras, "Working-class Vote," p. 24.

84. Sandra Powell, "Political Change in the Chilean Electorate, 1952-1964," *Western Political Quarterly* 23:2 (June 1970), p. 380.

85. Brian H. Smith and José L. Rodríguez, "Comparative Working-class Political Behavior: Chile, France and Italy," *American Behavioral Scientist* 18:1 (September 1974), p. 66.

86. Zeitlin and Petras, "Working-class Vote," p. 27.

87. James Petras and Maurice Zeitlin, "Miners and Agrarian Radicalism," *American Sociological Review* 32:4 (August 1967), p. 580.

88. Sigmund, *Overthrow of Allende*, p. 36.

89. De Santis, "Chile," pp. 355-357.

90. Pinto, "Desarrollo económico y relaciones sociales," pp. 36-37.

91. Moulian, *Estudio sobre Chile*, p. 159; see also *Christian Science Monitor*, March 6, 1965, p. 6.

92. Orville G. Cope, "The 1965 Congressional Election in

Chile: An Analysis," *Journal of Inter-American Studies* 10:2 (April 1968), pp. 265-267.

93. C. J. Parrish, A. Von Lazar, and J. Tapia Videla, *The Chilean Congressional Election of March 7, 1965* (Washington: Institute for the Comparative Study of Political Systems, 1967), p. 37.

94. *Constitución Política de la República de Chile,* Article 50.

95. Robert R. Kaufman, *The Politics of Land Reform in Chile, 1950-1970* (Cambridge, Mass.: Harvard University Press, 1972), p. 90.

96. George W. Grayson, "Chile's Christian Democratic Party: Power, Factions and Ideology," *Review of Politics* 31:2 (April 1969), p. 150.

97. Kaufman, *Politics of Land Reform,* pp. 86-88.

98. Grayson, "Chile's Christian Democratic Party," pp. 150-153.

99. Alain Labrousse, *L'expérience chilienne: réformisme ou révolution?* (Paris: Éditions du Seuil, 1972), pp. 147-149.

100. Pinto, "Desarrollo económico y relaciones sociales," p. 33.

101. Sigmund, *Overthrow of Allende,* p. 57.

102. Michael Francis and Eldon Lanning, "Chile's 1967 Municipal Elections," *Inter-American Economic Affairs* 21:2 (Autumn 1967), pp. 32-34.

103. Kaufman, *Politics of Land Reform,* pp. 130-131.

104. Sigmund, *Overthrow of Allende,* p. 39.

105. James Petras and Allen Young, "Labour and Christian Democracy in Chile," *International Socialist Journal* 3:14 (March-April 1966), pp. 187-195.

106. Angell, *Politics and the Labour Movement,* p. 76.

107. Sigmund, *Overthrow of Allende,* p. 61.

108. *New York Times,* September 2, 1968, p. 11.

109. Grayson, "Chile's Christian Democratic Party," pp. 158-159.

110. Paul E. Sigmund, "Latin American Catholicism's Opening to the Left," *Review of Politics* 35:1 (January 1973), pp. 65-76.

111. Michael J. Francis and Hernán Vera, "Chile: Christian Democracy to Marxism," *Review of Politics* 33:3 (July 1971), pp. 327-328.

112. George W. Grayson, "The Frei Administration and the 1969 Parliamentary Election," *Inter-American Economic Affairs* 23:3 (Winter 1969), pp. 63-65.

113. Charles J. Parrish et al., "Electoral Procedures and Political

Parties in Chile," *Studies in Comparative International Development* 6:12 (1970-1971), p. 264.

114. Monica Thresfall, "Shantytown Dwellers and People's Power," in Philip O'Brien, ed., *Allende's Chile* (New York: Praeger Publishers, 1976), pp. 170-172.

115. Guillermo Briones, "Estructura social y estructura política. Un análisis ecológico de la sociología electoral," *Revista Mexicana de Sociología* 32:6 (1970), p. 1518.

116. Grayson, "Frei Administration," p. 67.

117. Sigmund, *Overthrow of Allende*, p. 78.

118. Michael J. Francis, *The Allende Victory: An Analysis of the 1970 Chilean Presidential Election* (Tucson: University of Arizona Press, 1973), pp. 30-43.

119. Miles D. Wolpin, "Chile's Left: Structural Factors Inhibiting an Electoral Victory in 1970," *Journal of Developing Areas* 3:2 (January 1969), pp. 207-230.

120. Francis and Vera, "Christian Democracy to Marxism," p. 329.

121. Sigmund, *Overthrow of Allende*, pp. 85-87.

122. Ibid., pp. 103-105.

123. Francis, *Allende Victory*, p. 64.

124. Compare James Petras, "Two Views of Allende's Victory," *New Politics*, 8:4 (Fall 1970), pp. 72-76; and Francis, *Allende Victory*, pp. 71-73.

125. Francis, *Allende Victory*, p. 66.

126. Benno Galjart, "Allende y los campesinos: un análisis ecológico de las elecciones de 1970 en Chile," *Boletín de Estudios Latinoamericanos y del Caribe* 16 (junio 1974), pp. 50-66.

127. Petras, "Allende's Victory," pp. 73, 76.

128. Francis, *Allende Victory*, p. 65.

129. Lester A. Sobel, ed., *Chile and Allende* (New York: Facts on File, 1974), p. 34.

130. Sigmund, *Overthrow of Allende*, p. 123.

131. Francis, *Allende Victory*, p. 67.

132. Sigmund, *Overthrow of Allende*, pp. 143-144.

133. A review of opinions on the Allende administration is in Arturo Valenzuela and J. Samuel Valenzuela, "Visions of Chile," *Latin America Research Review* 7:3 (Fall 1975), pp. 155-175.

134. Hugo Zemelman and Patricio León, "Political Opposition to the Government of Allende," *Government and Opposition*

7:3 (Summer 1972), p. 327.
135. Sigmund, *Overthrow of Allende,* p. 149.
136. Paul E. Sigmund, "Catholicism's Opening to the Left," p. 62.
137. "Chile: Time to Rethink," *Latin America* 6:3 (January 21, 1972), p. 23.
138. "Chile: Democracy Continues," *Latin America* 6:6 (February 11, 1972), p. 44.
139. Sigmund, *Overthrow of Allende,* p. 171.
140. Sobel, *Chile and Allende,* pp. 73-77.
141. "La Derecha prepara el enfrentamiento," *Punto Final* 178 (febrero 27, 1973), pp. 8-9.
142. "Chile: Power to the People," *Latin America* 9:19 (February 9, 1973), p. 42.
143. Dieter Nohlen, *Chile. Das sozialistische Experiment* (Hamburg: Hoffman und Campe, 1973), p. 337.
144. Sigmund, *Overthrow of Allende,* p. 200.
145. "Izquierda sacará más senadores y diputados, *Punto Final*

Chapter 5

1. M. A. Busteed, *Geography and Voting Behaviour* (London: Oxford University Press, 1975), pp. 25-39.
2. Ricardo Cruz Coke, *Geografía electoral de Chile* (Santiago: Editorial del Pacífico, 1952), pp. 71-89.
3. James Petras and Maurice Zeitlin, "Miners and Agrarian Radicalism," *American Sociological Review* 32:4 (August 1967), pp. 583-585.
4. J. Douglas Porteous, "The Company State: A Chilean Case Study," *Canadian Geographer* 18:2 (Summer 1973), pp. 119-123.
5. Cruz Coke, *Geografía electoral,* p. 75.
6. Tomás Moulian, *Estudio sobre Chile* (Santiago: Editorial Orbe, 1965), p. 142.
7. Aníbal Pinto et al., *Chile hoy* (México: Siglo Veintiuno Editores, 1970), p. 218.
8. Petras and Zeitlin, "Miners and Agrarian Radicalism," pp. 581-584.
9. Moulian, *Estudio sobre Chile,* p. 136.
10. Pinto, *Chile hoy,* p. 214.

11. German Urzúa, *Los partidos políticos chilenos* (Santiago: Editorial Jurídica de Chile, 1968), p. 83.
12. Moulian, *Estudio sobre Chile*, p. 145.
13. Francisco Zapata, "Action syndicale et comportement politique des mineurs chiliens du Chuquicamata," *Sociologie du Travail* 17:3 (1975), pp. 230-242.
14. Cruz Coke, *Geografía electoral*, p. 89.
15. Pinto, *Chile hoy*, p. 217.
16. Arturo Valenzuela, *Political Brokers in Chile* (Durham, N.C.: Duke University Press, 1977), p. 14.
17. Guillermo Briones, "Estructura social y estructura política (un análisis ecológico de la sociología electoral)," *Revista Mexicana de Sociología* 32:6 (1970), pp. 1520-1521.
18. Moulian, *Estudio sobre Chile*, pp. 142-144.

Bibliography

Abbott, Roger S. "The Role of Contemporary Parties in Chile." *American Political Science Review* 44:2 (1951), pp. 450-463.

Affonso, Almino. *Trayectoria del movimiento campesino chileno.* Santiago: ICIRA, n.d.

Agor, Weston H., ed. *Latin American Legislatures: Their Role and Influence. Analyses for Nine Countries.* New York: Praeger Publishers, 1971.

———. *The Chilean Senate. Internal Distribution of Influence.* Austin: University of Texas Press, 1971.

———. *The Decisional Role of the Senate in the Chilean Political System.* Madison: University of Wisconsin, Land Tenure Center, 1969.

Aguilar, Luis E. "Political Traditions and Perspectives." *Problems of Communism* 20 (May-June 1971):62-69.

Ahumada C., Jorge. *En vez de la miseria.* Santiago: Editorial del Pacífico, 1958.

Alexander, Robert J. *Communism in Latin America.* New Brunswick: Rutgers University Press, 1957.

———. *Latin American Politics and Governments.* New York: Harper and Row, 1965.

———. "Socialism's Uncertain Future." *New Politics* 9:3 (Fall 1971), pp. 12-20.

Almeyda, Clodomiro. *Visión sociológica de Chile.* Santiago: Imprenta Atenea, 1957.

Alvarado, Edesio. *El turco Tarud. La verdad sobre un tiempo y una historia.* Santiago: Ediciones Territorio, 1970.

Alvarez, Oscar. "El problema de la familia en Chile." *Revista Mexicana de Sociología* 20:2 (1958), pp. 413-428.

Ammon, Alf. *Die Christliche Demokratie Chiles. Partei Ideologie. Revolutionäre Bewegung.* Bonn: Friedrich-Ebert-Stiftung, 1971.
Angell, Alan. "Chile: The Difficulties of Democratic Reform." *International Journal* 24:3 (1969), pp. 515-528.
——. "La clase obrera y la política en Chile." *Desarrollo Económico* 9:33 (abril-junio 1969), pp. 33-65.
——. *Politics and the Labour Movement in Chile.* London: Oxford University Press, 1972.
Arriagada, Genaro. *La oligarquía patronal chilena.* Santiago: Ediciones Nueva Universidad, 1970.
Arriagada, René, and Jarpa, Onofre. *Por una política nacional.* Santiago: Ediciones Nueva Política, 1952.
Arteaga U., Ismael, ed. *Partido Conservador. Notas para la historia política del Partido Conservador.* Santiago: Imprenta Chile, 1947.
Ayres, Robert L. "Economic Stagnation and the Emergence of the Political Ideology of Chilean Underdevelopment." *World Politics* 25:1 (October 1972), pp. 34-61.
——. "Electoral Constraints and the Chilean Way to Socialism." *Studies in Comparative International Development* 8:2 (Summer 1973), pp. 128-161.
Bähr, Jürgen. "Bevölkerungsgeographische Untersuchungen im Grossen Norden Chiles." *Erdkunde* 26:4 (Dezember 1972), pp. 283-294.
Bähr, Jürgen, and Golte, Winfried. "Eine bevölkerungs- und wirtschaftsgeographische Gliederung Chiles." *Geoforum* 17 (1974):25-42.
Bataillon, Claude, ed. *État, pouvoir et espace dans le Tiers Monde.* Paris: Presses Universitaires de France, 1977.
Bauer, Arnold J. *Chilean Rural Society. From the Spanish Conquest to 1930.* New York: Cambridge University Press, 1975.
Behrman, Lucy C. "Patterns of Religious and Political Attitudes, and Activities during Modernization: Santiago, Chile." *Social Science Quarterly* 53:3 (December 1972), pp. 520-533.
——. "Political Development and Secularization in Two Chilean Urban Communities." *Comparative Politics* 4:2 (January 1972), pp. 269-280.
Bello C., Emilio. *Recuerdos políticos. La junta de gobierno de 1925: su origen y relación con la reforma del régimen constitucional.* Santiago: Editorial Nascimento, 1954.

Berry, Bryan J. "Relationships between Regional Economic Development and the Urban System. The Case of Chile." *Tijdschrift voor Economische en Sociale Geografie* 60 (September-Oktober 1969):283-307.

Bicheno, H. E. "Anti-parliamentary Themes in Chilean History: 1920-1970." *Government and Opposition* 7:3 (Summer 1972), pp. 531-388.

Biedma, Patricio. "El comportamiento político de la burguesía chilena." *Marxismo y Revolución* 1 (julio-septiembre 1973): 79-90.

Biehl, J., and Fernández, Gonzalo. "The Political Pre-requisites for a Chilean Way." *Government and Opposition* 7:3 (Summer 1972), pp. 305-326.

Blanco Amor, Eduardo. *Chile a la vista.* Santiago: Editorial del Pacífico, 1952.

Blancpain, Jean-Pierre. *Les allemands au Chili (1816-1945).* Köln: Böhlau Verlag, 1974.

Blasier, S. Cole. "Chile. A Communist Battleground." *Political Science Quarterly* 65:3 (September 1950), pp. 353-375.

Boizard, Ricardo. *La Democracia Cristiana en Chile.* Santiago: Editorial Orbe, 1963.

Bonilla, Frank, and Glazer, Myron. *Student Politics in Chile.* New York: Basic Books, 1970.

Borón, Atilio A. "Desarrollo económico y comportamiento político." *Revista Latinoamericana de Ciencias Políticas* 1:2 (junio 1970), pp. 236-287.

———. "La evolución del régimen electoral y sus efectos en la representación de los intereses populares: el caso de Chile." *Revista Latinoamericana de Ciencias Políticas* 2:3 (septiembre 1971), pp. 395-436.

———. "Movilización política y crisis política en Chile: 1920-1970." *Aportes* 20 (abril 1971):41-69.

Bray, Donald W. "Peronism in Chile." *Hispanic American Historical Review* 47:1 (February 1967), pp. 38-49.

———. "The Political Emergence of Arab-Chileans, 1952-1958." *Journal of Inter-American Studies* 4:4 (October 1962), pp. 557-562.

Briones, Guillermo. "Estructura social y estructura política. Un análisis ecológico de la sociología electoral." *Revista Mexicana de Sociología* 32:6 (1970), pp. 1513-1525.

Briones, Guillermo. "La estructura social y la participación política." *Revista de Sociología* 1:1 (1964), pp. 86-106.
Briones, Guillermo, and Waisanen, F. B. "Aspiraciones educacionales, modernización e integración urbana." *America Latina* 10:4 (octubre-diciembre 1967), pp. 3-21.
Bunster, Enrique. *Chilenos en California.* Santiago: Editorial del Pacífico, 1954.
Burnett, Ben G. *Political Groups in Chile. The Dialogue between Order and Change.* Austin: University of Texas Press, 1970.
Burnett, Ben G., and Johnson, Kenneth J. *Political Forces in Latin America. Dimensions of the Quest for Stability.* Belmont: Wadsworth Publishing Co., 1968.
Burr, Robert N. *By Reason or Force. Chile and the Balancing of Power in South America, 1830-1905.* Berkeley–Los Angeles: University of California Press, 1967.
Busteed, M. A. *Geography and Voting Behavior.* London: Oxford University Press, 1975.
Butland, Gilbert. *Chile. An Outline of its Geography, Economics and Politics.* London: Institute of International Affairs, 1951.
Cabezas P., Rubén. *Pensamiento económico de los partidos políticos históricos chilenos.* Santiago: Editorial Universitaria, 1964.
Campbell, John C. "Political Extremes in South America." *Foreign Affairs* 20:3 (April 1942), pp. 516-534.
Cardoso, Fernando H. "The Entrepreneurial Elite in Latin America." *America Latina* 10:4 (December 1967), pp. 3-21.
Carrière, Jean. "Conflict and Cooperation among Sectorial Elites." *Boletín de Estudios Latinoamericanos y del Caribe* 19 (diciembre 1975):16-27.
———. "Landowners and the Rural Unionization Question in Chile: 1920-1948." *Boletín de Estudios Latinoamericanos y del Caribe* (junio 1977):34-52.
Castro, Baltazar. *Me permite una interrupción?* Santiago: Editora Zig Zag, 1962.
Chaney, Elsa M. "Old and New Feminist in Latin America: The Case of Peru and Chile." *Journal of Marriage and the Family* 35:2 (May 1973), pp. 331-343.
Chile. Cámara de Diputados. *Monografía de la Cámara de Diputados. 1811-1945.* Santiago: Publicaciones de la Cámara de Diputados, 1944.
Cinta, Ricardo G. "Desarrollo económico, urbanización y radi-

calismo político." *Revista Mexicana de Sociología* 31:3 (1969), pp. 643-688.
Cockcroft, James D., et al. *Dependence and Underdevelopment.* Garden City, N.Y.: Anchor Books, 1972.
Collier, Simon. *Ideas and Politics of Chilean Independence: 1808-1833.* Cambridge: Cambridge University Press, 1967.
Conning, Arthur M. "Rural-Urban Destination of Migrants and Community Differentiation in Rural Regions of Chile." *The International Migration Review* 6:2 (Summer 1972), pp. 148-157.
Contreras G., Víctor. *Bitácora de la dictadura. Administración de Ibáñez, 1927-1931.* Santiago: Imprenta Cultura, 1942.
Cope, Orville G. "The 1964 Presidential Election in Chile: The Politics of Change and Access." *Inter-American Economic Affairs* 19:4 (Spring 1966), pp. 3-29.
———. "The 1965 Congressional Election in Chile: An Analysis." *Journal of Inter-American Studies* 10:2 (April 1968), pp. 256-276.
Corporación de Fomento de la Producción, ed. *Geografía económica de Chile. Primer Apéndice.* Santiago: Editorial Universitaria, 1966.
Corvalán, Luis. *Chile hoy. La lucha de los comunistas chilenos en las condiciones del gobierno de Frei.* Buenos Aires: Editorial Anteo, 1965.
Cruz Coke, Ricardo. *Geografía electoral de Chile.* Santiago: Editorial del Pacífico, 1952.
Cunill, Pedro. *Geografía de Chile.* Santiago: Editorial Universitaria, 1970.
Dahl, Victor C. "Yugoslav Immigrant Experiences in Argentina and Chile." *Inter-American Economic Affairs* 28:3 (Winter 1974), pp. 3-26.
Daugherty, Charles H., ed. *Chile: Election Factbook.* Washington: Institute for the Comparative Study of Political Systems, 1963.
De Santis, Sergio. "Chile. Part I and Part II." *The International Socialist Journal* 2:9-10 (June, August 1965), pp. 446-468.
Debray, Régis. *Conversations with Allende. Socialism in Chile.* London: NLB, 1971.
Debuyst, F., and Garcés, Joan. "L'option chilienne de 1970. Analyse des trois programmes electoraux." *Contradictions* 1 (1972):139-166; 2 (1972):151-179.
Di Tella, Torcuato, et al. *Huachipato et Lota: étude sur la con-*

science ouvrière dans deux entreprises chiliennes. Paris: Editions du Centre National de la Recherche Scientifique, 1965.

Donoso, Ricardo. *Alessandri. Agitador y demoledor.* Mexico: Fondo de Cultura Económica. Vol. 1, 1953; Vol. 2, 1955.

——. *Las ideas políticas en Chile.* Santiago: Editorial Universitaria, 1967.

Drake, Paul W. *Socialism and Populism in Chile, 1932-52.* Urbana: University of Illinois Press, 1978.

——. "The Chilean Socialist Party and Coalition Politics, 1932-1942." *The Hispanic American Historical Review* 53:4 (November 1973), pp. 619-643.

Durán B., Florencio. *El Partido Radical.* Santiago: Editorial Nascimento, 1958.

Durkheim, Emile. *Le suicide.* Paris: Presses Universitaires de France, 1967.

Edwards, Alberto. *La fronda aristocrática.* Santiago: Editorial del Pacífico, 1952.

Edwards, Alberto, and Frei, Eduardo. *Historia de los partidos políticos chilenos.* Santiago: Editorial del Pacífico, 1949.

Encina, Francisco A. *Nuestra inferioridad económica.* Santiago: Imprenta Universitaria, 1912.

Evans, Les, ed. *Disaster in Chile. Allende's Strategy and Why It Failed.* New York: Pathfinder Press, 1974.

Eyzaguirre, Jaime. *Fisonomía histórica de Chile.* Santiago: Editorial del Pacífico, 1965.

——. *Historia de Chile.* Santiago: Editorial Zig Zag, 1964, 1973.

Fernández, Sergio. *Aspectos de la división del Partido Conservador.* Santiago: n.p., 1950.

Francis, Michael J. *The Allende Victory: An Analysis of the 1970 Chilean Presidential Election.* Tucson: University of Arizona Press, 1973.

Francis, Michael J., and Lanning, Eldon. "Chile's 1967 Municipal Elections." *Inter-American Economic Affairs* 21:2 (Autumn 1967), pp. 23-36.

Francis, Michael J., and Vera G., Hernán. "Chile: Christian Democracy to Marxism." *Review of Politics* 33:3 (July 1971), pp. 323-341.

Frei, Eduardo. *Pensamiento y acción.* Santiago: Editorial del Pacífico, 1956.

Friedman, John, and Lackington, Tomás. "Hyperurbanization and

National Development in Chile: Some Hypotheses." *Urban Affairs Quarterly* 2:4 (June 1967), pp. 3-29.
Froehling, Heino. *Die Spaltung der Christdemokratischen Partei. 1969.* Bonn: Friedrich-Ebert-Stiftung, 1971.
Galdames, Luis. *A History of Chile.* New York: Russell and Russell, 1964.
Galjart, Benno. "Allende y los campesinos: un análisis ecológico de las elecciones presidenciales de 1970 en Chile." *Boletín de Estudios Latinoamericanos y del Caribe* 16 (junio 1974):50-66.
Garcés, Joan. "Las relaciones entre parlamento y presidente en Chile." *Revista del Instituto de Ciencias Sociales* 12-13 (1968-1969):207-225.
———. "Chile 1971. A Revolutionary Government within a Welfare State." *Government and Opposition* 7:3 (Summer 1972), pp. 281-304.
Germana, César. "El estado y las masas marginales en Chile." *Boletín de E.L.A.S.* 6:4 (diciembre 1970), pp. 5-49.
Gil, Federico. *Genesis and Modernization of Political Parties in Chile.* Gainesville: University of Florida Press, 1962.
———. *The Political System of Chile.* Boston: Houghton and Mifflin Company, 1966.
Gil, Federico, and Parrish, Charles J. *The Chilean Presidential Election of September 4, 1964.* Washington: Institute for the Comparative Study of Political Systems, 1965.
Glazer, Myron. "The Professional and Political Attitudes of Chilean Students." *Comparative Education Review* 10:2 (June 1966), pp. 282-295.
Goldrich, Daniel. "Political Organization and the Politization of the *poblador.*" *Comparative Political Studies* 3:2 (July 1970), pp. 176-202.
Goldrich, Daniel; Pratt, Raymond; and Schuller, C. "The Political Integration of Lower-class Urban Settlements in Chile and Peru." *Studies in Comparative International Development* 3:1 (1967-1968), pp. 4-22.
Golte, Winfried. *Das südchilenische Seengebiet. Besiedlung und wirtschaftliche Erschliessung seit dem 18. Jahrhundert.* Bonn: Bonner Geographische Abhandlungen, Ferdinand Dümmlers Verlag, 1973.
Gómez, Sergio. *Los empresarios agrícolas.* Santiago: Instituto de Capacitación e Investigación en Reforma Agraria, 1972.

Gouré, Leon, and Suchlicki, Jaime. "The Allende Regime: Actions and Reactions." *Problems of Communism* 20:3 (May-June 1971), pp. 49-61.

Gray, Richard B., and Kirwin, Frederick R. "Presidential Succession in Chile: 1817-1966." *Journal of Inter-American Studies* 11:1 (January 1969), pp. 144-159.

Grayson, George W. "Chile's Christian Democratic Party: Power, Factions and Ideology." *Review of Politics* 31:2 (April 1969), pp. 147-171.

——. "The Frei Administration and the Parliamentary Elections of 1969." *Inter-American Economic Affairs* 23:2 (Autumn 1969), pp. 49-74.

Grenier, Philippe. "Los problemas de la pesca en la región de Chiloé." *Revista Geográfica de Valparaíso* 3:1-2 (1969), pp. 55-91.

——. "Le pouvoir politique chilien comme agent d'organisation spatiale aux confins chiléno-argentins de la Patagonie." *Actes du XLII Congrès International des Américanistes, Paris 1976.* Vol. 1, pp. 527-536.

Grossi A., María. "Burguesía industrial e ideología de desarrollo en Chile." *Revista Mexicana de Sociología* 33:4 (1971), pp. 729-760.

Guerrero, Raúl. "Estructuras agrarias, despoblamiento y trama urbana en La Frontera." *Cuadernos Geográficos del Sur* 1:1 (1971), pp. 65-75.

Guilisasti T., Sergio. *Partidos políticos chilenos.* Santiago: Editorial Nascimento, 1964.

Guzmán, Jorge H. *Gabriel González Videla. Biografía, análisis crítico de su programa.* Santiago: Imprenta Universo, 1946.

Halperin, Ernst. *Nationalism and Communism in Chile.* Cambridge, Mass.: MIT Press, 1965.

Handelman, Howard. "The Political Mobilization of the Urban Squatter Settlement: Santiago's Recent Experience and Its Implications for Urban Research." *Latin American Research Review* 10:2 (Summer 1975), pp. 35-72.

Hansen, Roy. "Public Orientation to the Military in Chile." *Pacific Sociological Review* 16:2 (June 1973), pp. 192-208.

Hardoy, Jorge, ed. *Urbanization in Latin America. Approaches and Issues.* Garden City, N.Y.: Anchor Press–Doubleday, 1975.

Haring, Clarence H. "Presidential Elections in South America." *Foreign Affairs* 10:2 (January 1932), pp. 327-331.

Haring, Clarence H. "Chile moves left." *Foreign Affairs* 17:3 (April 1939), pp. 618-624.
Hernández, Roberto C. *Valparaíso en 1827. Con un apéndice acerca de la época.* Valparaíso: Imprenta Victoria, 1927.
——. *El roto chileno. Bosquejo histórico de actualidad.* Valparaíso: Imprenta San Rafael, 1929.
Herrick, Bruce H. *Urban Migration and Economic Development in Chile.* Cambridge, Mass.: MIT Press, 1965.
Holmes, Olive. "Chile. Microcosm of modern conflict." *Foreign Policy Reports* 22:9 (September 1946), pp. 106-115.
Huizer, Gerrit. "Comunidades agrícolas. Internal Colonialism and Agrarian Reform in Chile." *America Latina* 11:4 (October-December 1968), pp. 110-127.
Ibañez, Bernardo. *Defensa de la clase obrera.* Santiago: Imprenta Yungay, 1943.
Instituto de Economía. *La migración interna de Chile en el período de 1940-1952.* Santiago: Universidad de Chile, Instituto de Economía, 1959.
——. *Subdivisión de la propiedad agrícola en una región de la zona central de Chile.* Santiago: Universidad de Chile, Instituto de Economía, 1960.
Instituto Geográfico Militar. *Atlas de la República de Chile.* Santiago: Instituto Geográfico Militar, 1970.
Isuani, Ernesto, and Cervini, Rubén A. "Análisis del voto de izquierda en Santiago de Chile; un modelo causal." *Latin American Research Review* 10:3 (Fall 1975), pp. 103-120.
Ize, M. F. "La Democracia Cristiana en Chile. Análisis de una experiencia." *Foro Internacional* 38 (1969):111-135.
Jaher, Frederic, ed. *The Rich, the Well Born and the Powerful. Elite and Upper Class in History.* Urbana: University of Illinois Press, 1973.
Jobet, Julio César. *El Partido Socialista de Chile.* Santiago: Ediciones Prensa Latinoamericana, 1971.
Jobet, Julio César, and Chelén, Alejandro. *Pensamiento teórico y político del Partido Socialista de Chile.* Santiago: Editora Quimantú, 1972.
Johnson, Dale L. "Industrialization, Social Mobility and Class Formation in Chile." *Studies in Comparative International Development* 3:7 (1967-1968), pp. 127-151.
——, ed. *The Chilean Road to Socialism.* Garden City, N.Y.:

Anchor Press–Doubleday, 1973.
———. "The National and Progressive Bourgeoisie in Chile." *Studies in Comparative International Development* 4:4 (1968-1969), pp. 63-86.
Johnson, John J. *Political Change in Latin America. The Emergence of the Middle Sectors.* Stanford: Stanford University Press, 1958.
Joxe, Alain. *Las Fuerzas Armadas en el sistema político chileno.* Santiago: Editorial Universitaria, 1970.
———. "L'équilibre politique chilien." *Politique Etrangère* 32:2 (1967), pp. 173-195.
Kaufman, Robert R. *The Chilean Political Right and Agrarian Reform: Resistance and Moderation.* Washington: Institute for the Comparative Study of Political Systems, 1967.
———. *The Politics of Land Reform in Chile.* Cambridge, Mass.: Harvard University Press, 1972.
Kay, Christopher. "La participación campesina bajo el gobierno de la Unidad Popular en Chile." *Revista Mexicana de Sociología* 36:2 (1974), pp. 279-295.
Klein, Emilio. "Tipos de dependencia y obreros agrícolas en Chile." *Boletín de Estudios Latinoamericanos y del Caribe* 16 (junio 1974):16-27.
Korb, George M. "Communicating with the Chilean Peon." *American Journal of Economics and Sociology* 25:3 (July 1966), pp. 281-296.
Kornhauser, William A. *The Politics of Mass Media.* Glencoe, Ill.: Free Press, 1959.
Labbens, Jean. "Tradition et modernisme: l'université au Chili." *America Latina* 13:1 (janeiro-março 1970), pp. 66-82.
Labrousse, Alain. *L'expérience chilienne: réformisme ou révolution?* Paris: Editions du Seuil, 1972.
Lafferte, Elías. *Vida de un comunista. Páginas autobiográficas.* Santiago: Talleres Gráficos Lautaro, 1957.
Lagos, Ricardo. *La concentración del poder económico. Su teoría, realidad chilena.* Santiago: Editorial del Pacífico, 1961.
Lalive d'Epinay, Christian, and Zylberberg, Jacques. "Dichotomie sociale et pluralisme culturel: la dispersion politique de la classe ouvrière chilienne." *Cahiers Internationaux de Sociologie* 59 (juillet-decembre 1975):255-272.
———. "Les religions au Chili entre l'aliénation et la prise de con-

science." *Social Compass* 21:1 (1974), pp. 85-100.
Landsberger, Henry A. "Do Ideological Differences Have Personal Correlates? A Case Study of Chilean Labor Leaders at the Local Level." *Economic Development and Cultural Change* 16:2 (January 1968), pp. 219-243.
Landsberger, Henry A., and McDaniel, Tim. "Hypermobilization in Chile: 1970-1973." *World Politics* 28:4 (July 1976), pp. 502-541.
Landsberger, Henry A., et al. "The Chilean Labor Union Leader: A Preliminary Report on His Background and Attitudes." *Industrial and Labor Relations Review* 17:3 (April 1964), pp. 399-420.
Langton, Kenneth P., and Rapoport, Ronald. "Social Structure, Social Context, and Partisan Mobilization: Urban Workers in Chile." *Comparative Political Studies* 8:3 (October 1975), pp. 318-344.
Lanning, Eldon. "A Typology of Latin American Political Systems." *Comparative Politics* 6:3 (April 1974), pp. 367-394.
Lauer, Wilhelm, ed. *Landflucht und Verstädterung in Chile. Exodo rural y urbanización en Chile*. Wiesbaden: Franz Steiner Verlag, 1976.
Lauterbach, Albert. *Managerial Attitudes in Chile*. Santiago: Instituto de Economía, Universidad de Chile, 1961.
Lehmann, David, ed. *Agrarian Reform and Agrarian Reformism. Studies of Peru, Chile, China and India*. London: Faber and Faber, 1974.
———. "Peasant Consciousness and Agrarian Reform in Chile." *Archives Européennes de Sociologie* 13:2 (1972), pp. 296-325.
———. "Political Incorporation versus Political Stability: The Case of the Chilean Agrarian Reform, 1965-1970." *The Journal of Development Studies* 7:4 (July 1971), pp. 365-395.
León Echaíz, René. *Evolución histórica de los partidos políticos chilenos*. Buenos Aires: Editorial Francisco de Aguirre, 1971.
Lerner, Daniel. *The Passing of Traditional Society: Modernizing the Middle East*. Glencoe, Ill.: Free Press, 1958.
Lipset, Seymour, and Solari, Aldo, eds. *Elites in Latin America*. New York: Oxford University Press, 1967.
Loewenstein, Karl. "Legislation for the Defense of the State in Chile." *Columbia Law Review* 44:3 (May 1944), pp. 366-407.
Lowenthal, Mary. "Kinship Politics in the Chilean Independence

Movement." *Hispanic American Historical Review* 56:1 (February 1976), pp. 58-80.
Lira M., Eugenio. *La Cámara y los 147 a dieta.* Santiago: Editorial Te Ele, 1968.
MacPhail, Donald D. "Chile: Processes of Social Evolution." *Focus* 24:7-8 (March, April 1974), pp. 1-8, 1-7.
MacPhail, Donald D., et al. "Chile's 'Forgotten' Region: La Montaña." *A.A.G. Program Abstracts, New Orleans,* 1978, p. 100.
Maggi, Gina. *Patria y traición. Confabulación Ibañez-Perón.* Buenos Aires: Ediciones Gure, 1957.
Magnet, Alejandro. *Nuestros vecinos argentinos.* Santiago: Editorial del Pacífico, 1956.
Mamalakis, Markos. *The Growth and Structure of the Chilean Economy. From Independence to Allende.* New Haven: Yale University Press, 1976.
Mamalakis, Markos, and Reynolds, Clark W. *Essays on the Chilean Economy.* Homewood, Ill.: Richard D. Irwin, 1965.
Mann, Wilhelm. *Chile luchando por nuevas formas de vida.* Santiago: Editorial Ercilla, 1935.
Martin, Carl. *Landeskunde von Chile.* Hamburg: L. Friedrichsen and Co., 1923.
Martin, Gene E. *La división de la tierra en Chile Central.* Santiago: Instituto de Geografía, Universidad de Chile, 1960.
Martz, John D. *The Dynamics of Change in Latin American Politics.* Englewood Cliffs: Prentice Hall, 1971.
Mattelart, Armand. *Atlas social de las comunas de Chile.* Santiago: Editorial del Pacífico, 1965.
Mattelart, Armand, and Garretón, Manuel A. *Integración nacional y marginalización. Un ensayo de regionalización social de Chile.* Santiago: Editorial del Pacífico, 1965.
McBride, George. *Chile: Land and Society.* New York: American Geographical Society, 1936.
McCoy, Terry L. "La reforma agraria chilena: un análisis político del cambio estructural." *America Latina* 13:2-3 (abril-setembro 1970), pp. 30-50.
———. "The Seizure of 'Los Cristales': A Case Study of the Marxist Left in Chile." *Inter-American Economic Affairs* 21:1 (Summer 1967), pp. 73-93.
McDonald, Ronald H. "Apportionment and Party Politics in

Santiago, Chile." *Midwest Journal of Political Science* 13:3 (August 1969), pp. 455-470.
Medhurst, Kenneth. "Why Chile?" *Government and Opposition* 7:3 (Summer 1972), pp. 273-280.
Menges, Constantino C. "Public Policy and Organized Business in Chile: A Preliminary Analysis." *Journal of International Affairs* 20:2 (1966), pp. 343-365.
Millas, Orlando. "Christian Democratic Reformism: The Chilean Experiment." *World Marxist Review* 8:11 (November 1965), pp. 65-69.
Molina, Sergio, and Larraín, Hernán. "Democratic Socialism, Not Totalitarian Socialism." *The L.A.D.O.C. Keyhole Series* 13 (September 1975):1-9.
Montero, René. *La verdad sobre Ibañez.* Santiago: Editorial Zig Zag, 1952.
Moran, Theodore H. "The Alliance for Progress and the Foreign Copper Companies and Their Local Conservative Allies in Chile, 1955-1970." *Inter-American Economic Affairs* 25:4 (Spring 1972), pp. 3-37.
Moreno, Francisco J. *Legitimacy and Stability in Latin America: A Study of Chilean Political Culture.* New York: New York University Press, 1969.
Moreno, Francisco J., and Mitrani, Barbara. *Conflict and Violence in Latin American Politics.* New York: Thomas Y. Crowell, 1971.
Morodó, Raúl. *Política y partidos en Chile. Las elecciones de 1965.* Madrid: Ediciones Tauro, 1968.
Morris, James O. *Elites, Intellectuals and Consensus: A Study of the Social Question and the Industrial Relations System in Chile.* Ithaca: Cornell University Press, 1966.
Morris, James O., and Oyaneder, C. *Afiliación y finanzas sindicales en Chile, 1932-1959.* Santiago: Instituto de Organización y Administración, Universidad de Chile, 1962.
Moulian, Tomás. *Estudio sobre Chile.* Santiago: Editorial Orbe, 1965.
Mujal-Leon, E. M. "The Communist Party of Chile, 1969-1973: The Limits of Pluralism." *World Affairs* 136:2 (1973), pp. 132-151.
Nazar, Víctor. "El proceso de formación de la clase obrera chilena." *Revista Mexicana de Sociología* 36:1 (1974), pp. 77-104.
Needler, Martin C. *Latin American Politics in Perspective.* Princeton:

D. Van Nostrand, 1963.
Needler, Martin C., ed. *Political Systems of Latin America.* New York: Van Nostrand Reinhold, 1970.
——. "The Closeness of Elections in Latin America." *Latin American Research Review* 12:1 (1977), pp. 115-121.
——. *Chile. Das sozialistisches Experiment.* Hamburg: Hoffmann and Campe, 1973.
Nohlen, Dieter, and Boye, Otto. "War die Konterrevolution unvermeidlich? Mittelschichten und Militär in Chile," *Verfassung und Recht in Übersee* 7:4 (1974), pp. 369-384.
Nohlen, Dieter. "Die chilenische Christdemokratie nach den 'historischen' Wahlen." *Civitas* 10 (1971):232-262.
——. "Sozio-ökonomischer Wandel und Verfassungsreform in Chile, 1925-1972." *Verfassung und Recht in Übersee* 6:1 (1973), pp. 65-85.
Nunn, Frederick M. *Chilean Politics 1920-1931: The Honorable Mission of the Armed Forces.* Albuquerque: University of New Mexico Press, 1970.
——. "New Thoughts on Military Intervention in Latin American Politics: The Chilean Case, 1973." *Journal of Latin American Studies* 7:2 (1975), pp. 271-304.
O'Brien, Philip, ed. *Allende's Chile.* New York: Praeger Publishers, 1976.
Odell, Peter R., and Preston, David A. *Economics and Societies in Latin America. A Geographical Interpretation.* London: John Wiley and Sons, 1973.
Olavarria B., Arturo. *Chile bajo la Democracia Cristiana.* Santiago: Editorial Nascimento, 1966, 1967, and 1971.
Oliveira de Muñoz, Orlandina. "Situación de clase y contenidos ideológicos. Análisis de comerciantes y empleados públicos." *Revista Mexicana de Sociología* 33:2 (1971), pp. 285-327.
Palacios, Nicolás. *Raza chilena. Libro escrito por un chileno y para los chilenos.* Santiago: Imprenta Universitaria, 1918.
Palma Z., Luis. *Historia del Partido Radical.* Santiago: Editorial Andrés Bello, 1967.
Pardo Z., Miguel. *El sufragio universal en Chile.* Santiago: Universidad de Chile, 1945.
Parrish, Charles J., et al. "Electoral Procedures and Political Parties in Chile." *Studies in Comparative International Development* 6:12 (1970-1971), pp. 255-266.
——. *The Chilean Congressional Election of March 7, 1965.* Wash-

ington: Institute for the Comparative Study of Political Systems, 1967.

Petras, James F. "Chile: Nationalization, Socioeconomic Change and Popular Participation." *Studies in Comparative International Development* 8:1 (1973), pp. 24-51.

——. *Politics and Social Forces in Chilean Development.* Berkeley-Los Angeles: University of California Press, 1969.

——. "Two Views of Allende's Victory." *New Politics* 8:4 (Fall 1970), pp. 73-81.

Petras, James F., and Young, Allen. "Labour and Christian Democracy in Chile." *International Socialist Journal* 3:14 (March-April 1966), pp. 187-195.

Petras, James F., and Zeitlin, Maurice, eds. *Latin America. Reform or Revolution?* Greenwich, Conn.: Fawcett Publications, 1968.

——. "Miners and Agrarian Radicalism." *American Sociological Review* 32:4 (August 1967), pp. 578-586.

Petras, James F., and Zemelman, Hugo. *Peasants in Revolt. A Chilean Case Study, 1965-1971.* Austin: University of Texas Press, 1972.

Pierson, William W., and Gil, Federico. *Governments of Latin America.* New York: McGraw Hill, 1957.

Pike, Frederick B. "Aspects of Class Relations in Chile, 1850-1860." *Hispanic American Historical Review* 43:1 (February 1963), pp. 14-33.

——. *Chile and the United States, 1880-1962.* Notre Dame: University of Notre Dame Press, 1963.

——. "Church and State and Political Development in Chile." *A Journal of Church and State* 10:1 (Winter 1968), pp. 99-113.

Pinto, Aníbal, et al. *Chile hoy.* México: Siglo Veintiuno Editores, 1970.

——. "Desarrollo económico y relaciones sociales en Chile." *Aportes* 20 (abril 1971):6-40.

Polloni, Alberto R. *Las fuerzas armadas de Chile en la vida nacional.* Santiago: Editorial Andrés Bello, 1972.

Porteous, Douglas J. "The Company State: A Chilean Case Study." *Canadian Geographer* 17:2 (Summer 1973), pp. 113-126.

Porter, Charles O., and Alexander, Robert J. *The Struggle for Democracy in Latin America.* New York: Macmillan, 1961.

Portes, Alejandro. "Leftist Radicalism in Chile (A Test of Three Hypotheses)." *Comparative Politics* 2:2 (January 1970), pp. 251-274.

———. "Los grupos marginalizados: nuevo intento de explicación." *Aportes* 18 (octubre 1970):131-147.
Portes, Alejandro. "On the Interpretation of Class Consciousness." *American Journal of Sociology* 77:2 (September 1971), pp. 228-244.
———. "Political Primitivism, Differential Socialization and Lower-class Leftist Radicalism." *American Sociological Review* 36:5 (October 1971), pp. 820-835.
———. "Status Inconsistency and Lower Class Leftist Radicalism." *Sociological Quarterly* 13:3 (Summer 1972), pp. 361-382.
Portes, Alejandro, and Ross, Adreain. "A Model for the Prediction of Leftist Radicalism." *Journal of Political and Military Sociology* 2 (Spring 1974):33-56.
Powell, Sandra. "Political Change in the Chilean Electorate, 1952-1964." *Western Political Quarterly* 23:2 (June 1970), pp. 364-383.
Prado, José M. *Reseña histórica del Partido Liberal.* Santiago: Imprenta Andina, 1963.
Pratt, Raymond B. "Parties, Neighborhood Associations, and the Politization of the Urban Poor in Latin America: An Exploratory Analysis." *Midwest Journal of Political Science* 15:13 (August 1971), pp. 495-524.
Prieur K., Wolfgang. "Die Entwicklung des Verfassungsrechtes in Chile bis 1971." *Jahrbuch des öffentlichen Rechtes der Gegenwart* 20 (1971):535-672.
Quinzio-Figuereido, J. M. "El sistema electoral chileno." *Revista de Estudios Políticos* 186 (1972):297-378.
Raczynski, Dagmar. "Migration, Mobility, and Occupational Achievement: The Case of Santiago, Chile," *The International Migration Review* 6:2 (Summer 1972), pp. 182-198.
———. "Oportunidades educacionales. Origen socioeconómico versus educación en Chile." *Revista Latinoamericana de Sociología* 1 (1974):66-94.
Ramírez N., Hernán. *Origen y formación del Partido Comunista de Chile.* Santiago: Editorial Austral, 1965.
Ratcliff, Richard E. *Kinship, Wealth and Power: Capitalists and Landowners in the Chilean Upper Class.* Madison: Land Tenure Center, University of Wisconsin, 1973.
Reimer, J. "Circulación de las elites en Chile." *Revista Latinoamericana de Ciencias Políticas* 1:2 (1970), pp. 288-332.

Remmer, Karen L. "The Timing, Pace and Sequence of Political Change in Chile, 1891-1925." *Hispanic America Historical Review* 57:2 (May 1977), pp. 205-230.

Rother, Klaus. "Stand, Auswirkungen und Aufgaben der chilenischen Agrarreform." *Erdkunde* 27:4 (Dezember 1973), pp. 307-322.

——. "Zum Fortgang der Agrarreform in Chile." *Erdkunde* 28:4 (Dezember 1974), pp. 312-315.

San Martin, Hernán. *Geografía Humana de Chile.* Santiago: Editora Quimantú, 1972.

Sanders, Thomas G. *The Process of Partisanship in Chile.* New York: American Universities Fieldstaff Reports, 20:1, 1973.

——. *Urban Pressure, Natural Resource Constraints, and Income Redistribution in Chile.* New York: American Universities Fieldstaff Reports, 20:2, 1973.

Sater, William F. *The Heroic Image in Chile.* Berkeley–Los Angeles: University of California Press, 1973.

Sigmund, Paul E. "Allende in Retrospect." *Problems of Communism* 23 (May-June 1974):45-62.

——. "Chile: Two Years of Popular Unity." *Problems of Communism* 21 (November-December 1972):38-51.

——. "Christian Democracy in Chile." *Journal of International Affairs* 20:2 (1966), pp. 332-342.

——. "Latin American Catholicism's Opening to the Left." *Review of Politics* 35:1 (January 1973), pp. 61-76.

——. *The Overthrow of Allende and the Politics of Chile, 1964-1976.* Pittsburgh: University of Pittsburgh Press, 1977.

Silva M., Raúl. *Camino al abismo. Lo que no se ha dicho sobre el proceso de la "Línea Recta."* Santiago: Editorial Universitaria, 1955.

Silvert, Kalman H., and Jutkowitz, Joel M. *Education, Values and the Possibilities for Social Change in Chile.* Philadelphia: ISHI Occasional Papers in Social Change, 1976.

Sinding, Steven W. "The Evolution of Chilean Voting Patterns: A Re-examination of Some Old Assumptions." *Journal of Politics* 34:3 (August 1972), pp. 774-796.

Singleman, Peter. "Campesino Movements and Class Conflict in Latin America. The Functions of Exchange and Power." *Journal of Inter-American Studies and World Affairs* 16:1 (February 1974), pp. 39-72.

Smith, Brian H., and Rodríguez, J. L. "Comparative Working Class Behavior: Chile, France and Italy." *American Behavioral Scientist* 18:1 (September 1974), pp. 59-96.

Smole, William J. *Owner-Cultivatorship in Middle Chile.* Chicago: University of Chicago, Department of Geography, 1963.

Snow, Peter G., ed. *Governments and Politics in Latin America.* New York: Holt, Rinehart and Winston, 1967.

Snyder, Richard C., and Wilson, Hubert H. *Roots of Political Behavior.* New York: American Book Company, 1949.

Soares, Glaucio, and Hamblin, Robert L. "Socio-Economic Variables and Voting for the Radical Left: Chile 1952." *American Political Science Review* 61:4 (December 1967), pp. 1053-1065.

Sobel, Lester A., ed. *Chile and Allende.* New York: Facts on File, 1974.

Solberg, Carl E. *Immigration and Nationalism. Argentina and Chile, 1890-1914.* Austin: University of Texas Press, 1970.

———. "Immigration and Urban Social Problems in Argentina and Chile." *Hispanic American Historical Review* 49:2 (May 1969), pp. 215-232.

Stevenson, John R. *The Chilean Popular Front.* Philadelphia: University of Pennsylvania Press, 1942.

Stöhr, Walter. "Geographische Aspekte der Planung in Entwicklungsländern. Die Südamerikanische Problematik und das Beispiel Chiles." *Wiener Geographische Schriften,* Festschrift Leopold G. Scheidl zum 60. Geburtstag, Teil II, 1967, pp. 377-393.

Stone, Carl. "Social Modernization and Left-Wing Voting in Chile." *Social and Economic Studies* 20:4 (December 1971), pp. 335-361.

Strawbridge, George. *Ibañez and Alessandri: The Authoritarian Right and the Democratic Left in Twentieth Century Chile.* Buffalo: Council on International Studies, State University of New York at Buffalo, 1971.

Subercaseaux, Benjamín. *Chile o una loca geografía.* Santiago: Ediciones Ercilla, 1954.

Swift, Jeannine. *Agrarian Reform in Chile. An Economic Study.* Lexington, Mass.: Heath Lexington Books, 1971.

Thiesenhusen, William C. *Reforma agraria en Chile. Experimento en cuatro fundos de la Iglesia.* Santiago: Instituto de Economía

y Planificación, Universidad de Chile, 1967.
———. "Chile's Experiments in Agrarian Reform. Four Colonization Projects Revisited." *American Journal of Agricultura Economics* 56 (May 1974):323-330.
Thomas, Jack R. "The Evolution of a Chilean Socialist: Marmaduke Grove." *Hispanic American Historical Review* 47:1 (February 1967), pp. 22-37.
———. "The Socialist Republic of Chile." *Journal of Inter-American Studies* 6:2 (February 1964), pp. 203-220.
Tomasek, Robert D., ed. *Latin American Politics. Studies of the Contemporary Scene.* Garden City, N.Y.: Anchor Books-Doubleday, 1970.
Tyler, William G. "An Evaluation of the Klein and Saks Stabilization Program in Chile." *America Latina* 11:1 (janeiro-março 1968), pp. 47-71.
Uribe, Armando. *The Black Book of American Intervention in Chile.* Boston: Beacon Press, 1974.
Uribe, Graciela, and Castillo, Cristina. "Estrategia para un desarrollo planificado: La microregión de Chiloé insular." *Informaciones Geográficas* 20 (1970):185-234.
Urzúa, Germán. *Los partidos políticos chilenos. Las fuerzas políticas. Ensayos de insurgencia política en Chile.* Santiago: Editorial Jurídica de Chile, 1968.
Urzúa, Paul. *La demanda campesina.* Santiago: Ediciones Nueva Universidad, 1969.
Valdés, Alberto. "Wages and Schooling of Agricultural Workers in Chile." *Economic Development and Cultural Change* 19:2 (January 1971), pp. 313-329.
Valencia A., Luis. *Anales de la República.* Santiago: Imprenta Universitaria, 1951.
Valenzuela, Arturo. *Political Brokers in Chile. Local Government in a Centralized Polity.* Durham, N.C.: Duke University Press, 1977.
———. "Political Participation, Agriculture and Literacy: Communal versus Provincial Voting Patterns in Chile." *Latin American Research Review* 12:1 (1977), pp. 105-114.
———. "The Scope of the Chilean Party System." *Comparative Politics* 4:2 (January 1972), pp. 179, 199.
Valenzuela, Arturo, and Valenzuela, J. Samuel, eds. *Chile: Politics and Society.* New Brunswick, N.J.: 1976.
Vekemans, Roger. *Tipología socioeconómica de los países latino-*

americanos. Washington: Pan American Union, Department of Social Affairs, 1963.

Veliz, Claudio. "Obstacle to Reform in Latin America." *World Today* 19:1 (1963), pp. 18-29.

———. "The Chilean Experiment." *Foreign Affairs* 49:3 (April 1971), pp. 442-453.

———, ed. *The Politics of Conformity in Latin America.* London: Oxford University Press, 1967.

Venturino, Agustín. *Sociología chilena con comparaciones argentinas y mejicanas.* Barcelona: Editorial Cervantes, 1929.

Vergara, X. "Coyuntura política e ideologización de la política partidista en Chile." *Revista Mexicana de Sociología* 32:1 (1970), pp. 49-85.

Von Lazar, Arpad, and Kaufman, Robert R., eds. *Reform and Revolution. Readings in Latin American Politics.* Boston: Allyn and Bacon, 1969.

Von Lazar, Arpad, and Quiroz, Luis. "Chilean Christian Democracy: Lessons in the Politics of Reform Management." *Inter-American Economic Affairs* 21:4 (Spring 1968), pp. 51-72.

Wagley, Charles. "The Dilemma of the Latin American Middle Classes." *Proceedings of the Academy of Political Science* 27:4 (May 1964), pp. 2-10.

Waiss, Oscar. *El drama socialista.* Valparaíso: Imprenta Victoria, 1948.

Weatherhead, R., and Maier, J. "Augurio político para la América Latina? La Democracia Cristiana y la victoria de Frei en Chile." *Foro Internacional* 5:18 (1964), pp. 212-224.

Weischet, Wolfgang. *Chile. Seine länderkundliche Individualität und Struktur.* Darmstadt: Wissenschaftliche Buchgesellschaft, 1970.

———. *Agrarreform und Nationalisierung des Bergbaus in Chile.* Darmstadt: Wissenschaftliche Buchgesellschaft, 1974.

Wences, Rosalio. "Electoral Participation and the Occupational Composition of Cabinets and Parliaments." *American Journal of Sociology* 75:2 (September 1969), pp. 181-192.

Willems, Emilio. "A Classe Alta Chilena." *America Latina* 10:2 (abril-junho 1967), pp. 42-54.

———. *Latin American Culture. An Anthropological Synthesis.* New York: Harper and Row, 1975.

Williamson, Robert C. "Social Class, Mobility, and Modernism.

Chileans and Social Change." *Sociology and Social Research* 56:2 (January 1972), pp. 149-163.
Wilson, Samuel. *Occupational Mobility and Social Stratification in Latin American Cities.* Ithaca: Cornell University, Dissertation Series, 1972.
Winn, Peter, and Kay, Cristobal. "Agrarian Reform and Rural Revolution in Chile." *Journal of Latin American Studies* 6:1 (1974), pp. 135-159.
Wismer, Hartmut. *Gewinnbeteiligung, Mitbestimmung und Leistungsentlöhnung in Landwirtschaftlichen Grossbetrieben Mittelchiles im Rahmen der Agrarreform.* Berlin: Institut für Ausländische Landwirtschaft der Universität Berlin, 1972.
Wolpin, Miles D. "Chile's Left: Structural Factors Inhibiting an Electoral Victory in 1970." *Journal of Developing Areas* 3:2 (January 1969), pp. 207-230.
———. "Socialism and System of Transformation in Chile." *Civilisations* 22:2 (1972), pp. 221-231.
———. *Cuban Foreign Policy and Chilean Politics.* Lexington, Mass.: Heath Lexington Books, 1972.
Würth, Ernesto. *Ibañez. Caudillo enigmático.* Santiago: Editorial del Pacífico, 1958.
Young, George F. *Germans in Chile. Immigration and Colonization, 1849-1914.* New York: Center for Migration Studies, 1974.
Zañartu, Mario, and Kennedy, John J., eds. *The Overall Development of Chile.* Notre Dame: University of Notre Dame Press, 1969.
Zapata, Francisco. "Action syndicale et comportement politique des mineurs chiliens du Chuquicamata." *Sociologie du Travail* 17:3 (Septembre 1975), pp. 225-242.
Zeitlin, Maurice. "Determinantes sociales de la democracia política en Chile." *Revista Latinoamericana de Sociología* 2:2 (1966), pp. 223-236.
Zeitlin, Maurice, et al. "New Princes for Old? The Large Corporation and the Capitalist Class in Chile." *American Journal of Sociology* 80:1 (July 1974), pp. 87-123.
Zeitlin, Maurice, and Petras, James. "The Working-class Vote in Chile: Christian Democracy versus Marxism." *British Journal of Sociology* 21:1 (March 1970), pp. 16-29.
Zeitlin, Maurice, and Ratcliff, Richard E. "Research Methods for

the Analysis of the Internal Structure of Dominant Classes: The Case of Landlords and Capitalists in Chile." *Latin American Research Review* 10:3 (Fall 1975), pp. 5-61.

Zemelman, Hugo, and León, Patricio. "Political Opposition to the Government of Allende." *Government and Opposition* 7:3 (Summer 1972), pp. 327-350.

Zemelman, Hugo, and Petras, James. *Proyección de la reforma agraria. El campesinado y su lucha por la tierra.* Santiago: Editorial Quimantú, 1972.

Zylberberg, Jacques. "Rationalité et irrationalité politique: les contradictions de l'Unité Populaire chilienne." *Res Publica* 16:1 (1974), pp. 63-88.

Index

Aconcagua: province, 13, 159, 163, 197, 202, 216, 228, 247, 271, 273, 280, 281, 282; valley, 83, 84
Agrarian Labor party, 58, 188, 190, 194-195, 202, 223, 237, 290
Agrarian party, 58, 163, 171, 174, 176, 180, 181, 188, 290, 297
Agrarian provinces, 17-20, 53, 54, 74, 113, 135, 160, 163, 166, 171, 174, 178, 182, 186, 188, 193, 202, 206, 210, 214, 216, 217, 224, 226, 227, 229, 233, 235, 246, 256, 257, 258, 260, 267, 268, 270, 272, 273, 287-288, 296
Agrarian reform, 136, 138, 139, 142, 144, 219, 230, 236, 238, 242, 252, 256, 257, 259, 265, 272, 286, 288
Aguirre Cerda, Pedro, 64, 112, 139, 162, 165, 166, 169, 173, 176, 279, 281, 285, 287, 289
Aldunate (family), 87, 88
Alessandri (family), 87, 89, 94, 100, 101, 250, 272
Alessandri, Arturo, 32, 61, 67, 68, 92, 101, 157, 158, 159, 160, 161, 162, 165, 166, 173, 176, 181
Alessandri, Fernando, 181, 182
Alessandri, Jorge, 3, 34, 38, 55, 60, 73, 89, 139, 189, 203, 205, 206, 208, 209, 212, 215, 217, 219, 250, 251, 252, 253, 254, 257, 258, 280
Alfonso, Pedro E., 103, 191, 193
Allende, Laura, 236, 270
Allende, Salvador, 2, 3, 34, 35, 36, 42, 55, 56, 60, 62, 65, 69, 73. 75, 76, 85, 103, 141, 142, 144, 153, 155, 177, 185, 191, 193, 194, 197, 203, 205, 206, 217, 218, 221, 222, 224, 226, 230, 231, 251, 252, 253, 254, 256, 258, 259, 260, 261, 263, 264, 270, 273, 275, 278, 281, 283, 286, 287, 289, 294
Allendista Catholic Movement, 222
Allendista Christian Movement, 128
Alliances, 49, 50, 71, 172, 174, 190, 191, 248, 251, 266
Altamirano, Amanda, 264, 271,
Altamirano, Carlos, 65, 90, 110, 251
Ambrosio, Rodrigo, 238
Ampuero, Raúl, 50, 65, 177, 185, 191, 248, 293
Amunátegui (family), 87
Amunátegui, Gregorio, 222
Anarchic: leftism, 148; syndicalism, 130
Anarchy, 35
Anderson, Jack, 264
Anomie, 16, 24, 148, 150, 151
Anticlericalism, 60, 119, 120, 212, 218, 222, 279
Antofagasta: city, 226; province, 12, 65, 134, 135, 138, 152, 182, 188, 224, 270, 276, 280
API. *See* Popular Independent Action
Apportionment, 51-56
Arauco, 24, 27, 188, 193, 206, 213, 235, 244, 246, 247, 254, 257, 266, 267, 271, 289
Argentina, 27, 94, 107, 114
Ariostazo, 75, 198
Aristocracy, 79-91, 95, 104, 191, 272;

Basque, 80, 81, 85, 92; Castilian, 80, 81, 85, 92; Navarran, 80, 85
Armed forces, 34, 43, 46
Asentamiento, 140, 143, 239, 240, 256, 262; defined, 311
Atacama, 10, 12, 52, 53, 134, 178, 216, 229, 233, 246, 254, 270, 271, 279, 280, 296
Aysén, 27, 29-30, 51, 53, 54, 206, 244, 246, 258, 267, 294-295

Balmaceda (family), 87, 88, 90
Balmaceda, José M., 2, 36, 58
Baltra, Alberto, 241, 242, 251
Baltra, Mireya, 236
Barros (family), 87, 88
Barros, Jaime, 77
Barros, Tobías, 203
Bianchi (family), 94
Bianchi, Arturo, 64
Bío-Bío: province, 22, 54, 92, 138, 188, 247, 271, 273, 290, 291; river, 20
Blanche, Bartolomé, 75, 159
Blest (family), 95
Blest, Clotario, 131
Block of the Left, 162
Bloque de Saneamiento Democrático, 204
Bolivia, 11, 135
Bossay, Luis, 205, 206, 208, 228, 244
Bourgeoisie, 13, 83, 91-103, 97, 98, 99, 101, 103, 107, 118, 135, 138, 139, 190, 221, 229, 294; petty, 137
British: families, 92, 93, 95; merchants, 91
Bulnes (family), 84, 87, 272

Cabinet of Social Sensibility, 190
Caja de Colonización Agrícola, 139, 166
Caja del Seguro Social Obligatorio, 129
"Campaign of Terror," 222, 229
Campusano, Julieta, 236
Capataces, 82
Carrera (family), 86
Carrera, María Elena, 236
Castro, Baltazar, 50, 65, 76, 204, 217
Castro, Fidel, 222
Caudillos, 77, 194, 195, 205

Cautín, 22, 138, 142, 143, 152, 214, 235, 246, 290
Cédula única, 47, 204
Center (political), 56, 59, 116, 215, 251, 275
Center-Left, 128, 210, 275, 276, 281, 286, 287, 291
Center-Right, 275, 278, 283, 286, 287, 290
Central Unica de Trabajadores de Chile (CUT), 131, 132, 143, 204, 210, 238, 240, 259
Central Valley, 17, 18, 25, 82, 141
Centralism, 3, 17, 56, 138, 297
Centros de Reforma Agraria (CERA), 142, 143
Cerda (family), 84, 87, 280
Change: political, 118; revolutionary, 221, 243; social, 57, 60, 117, 118, 145, 150, 155, 189, 264; structural, 2, 43, 220, 249, 272
Chelén, Alejandro, 95
Chile: location, 7; regions of, 7-10; synonym of Santiago, 14
Chillán, 18
Chiloé, 26-29, 54, 92, 135, 138, 186, 235, 246, 248, 267, 268, 292-293, 295
Chilotes, 27, 31
China, People's Republic of, 36, 66, 70, 241
Chonchol, Jacques, 36, 94, 140, 141, 238, 242, 251, 259
Christian Democratic party (Christian Democracy), 49, 55, 59, 60, 73, 74, 94, 100, 102, 122, 134, 137, 140, 141, 142, 144, 145, 149, 152, 205, 210, 213, 215, 216, 217, 218, 220, 221, 222, 228, 229, 230, 231, 232, 233, 236, 237, 238, 240, 241, 242, 243, 244, 246, 248, 249, 250, 251, 254, 258, 260, 262, 265, 266, 268, 271, 272, 279, 280, 281, 284, 286, 287, 288, 289, 290, 291, 292, 293, 294, 295, 296; government of the, 221-253; "non-conformists," 238, 242, 251; "officialists," 237, 249; "rebels," 238, 243, 249; "*terceristas*," 238, 243, 249.

Index

See also Falange Nacional
Christian humanism, 59, 116, 120, 220
Christian Left, 51, 122, 262, 271
Christian Peasants Union, 140
Chuquicamata (copper mine), 226, 254, 279
Church, Catholic, 57, 61, 106, 120, 227, 242
Civil servants, 61, 109, 112, 113, 121, 168, 171, 172, 177, 229, 296
Civil War of 1891, 135
Clarín, El, 103, 203
Class consciousness, 149-150
CODE. *See* Confederation of Democracy
Colchagua, 18, 65, 83, 135, 142, 169, 197, 257, 287; by-election of 1972, 262
Colliguay plot, 198
Colonization, 18, 22, 24; recent colonization, 24-26, 54, 166, 174, 182, 186, 191, 195, 197, 206, 212, 216, 235, 239, 246, 257, 267, 291-292, 296
Commandos comunales, 154
"*Comisión de Hombres Buenos*," 199
Comités compesinos, 143
Commune, 37-39
Communism, 63-64, 66
Communist party, 49, 55, 57, 63, 65, 73, 74, 130, 131, 148, 153, 163, 169, 172, 177, 184, 185, 190, 202, 204, 213, 231, 233, 235, 239, 242, 247, 250, 259, 267, 270, 273, 276, 279, 282, 283, 285, 286, 288, 289, 292, 295, 296; prohibition of, 185, 279; reinstatement of, 66, 204 *See also Partido del Trabajo; Partido Obrero Socialista*
Communist Revolutionary Movement, 66
"Company state," 279
Concepción: city, 20, 38, 145, 224; province, 10, 20-22, 52, 53, 54, 134, 163, 169, 171, 202, 212, 213, 216, 233, 246, 247, 254, 257, 266, 267, 268, 270, 271, 289-290, 295, 296
Concha (family), 87, 88, 90
Concha, Malaquías, 145

Conchalí, 16
Confederación de Trabajadores de Chile (CTCH), 131, 184
Confederation of Democracy (CODE), 51, 62, 265, 266, 267, 268
Congregation of the Holy Cross, 69
Congreso pleno, 40, 181, 184, 230, 258, 259
Congress, 33, 39-43, 70, 73, 85, 90, 101, 168, 180, 184, 199, 215, 229, 248, 258, 261; dissolution of, 42, 158
Conservatism, 104, 115, 220
Conservative party, 49, 57, 72, 81, 96, 105, 106, 110, 115, 119, 160, 171, 176, 177, 178, 180, 181, 182, 197, 202, 210, 214, 215, 232, 280, 282, 284, 285, 286, 297, 290, 292, 293; doctrinary, 57; traditionalist, 57, 186; united, 58
Constitution: early, 302; of 1833, 32, 302; of 1925, 31, 32, 33, 39, 43, 51, 161
Constitutional guarantees, 32, 34
Copiapó, 96, 226, 281
Coquimbo: by-election of 1972, 264; city, 13; province, 13, 135, 138, 182, 186, 206, 212, 247, 266, 268, 271, 280, 282
Cordones industriales, 154
Corporation of the Agrarian Reform (CORA), 37, 139, 141, 143, 262
Corvalán, Luis, 242
Correa (family), 83, 84, 87, 88, 90, 100, 101
Cousiño (family), 84, 96
Cousiño, Matías, 96
Cox (family), 96
Coyhaique, 29
Cruz Coke, Eduardo, 177, 181, 182
Cruz Coke, Ricardo, xi, 53, 151, 275, 279
Cuba, 35, 66, 140, 222
Curicó, 83, 85, 135, 182, 256, 287, 288; by-election of 1964, 218, 223
CUT. *See Central Unica de Trabajadores de Chile*
Cvitanic, Jorge, 212

Dávila, Carlos, 158-159

De la Cruz, María, 76, 198
Del Canto, Hernán, 261
Del Río, Sótero, 203
Democratic Alliance, 174
Democratic Front, 215, 216, 217, 218
Democratic party, 62-63, 115, 145, 146, 162, 163, 169, 171, 174, 180, 186, 188, 197, 283, 289, 291, 292, 297
Democratic Party of Chile, 63
Dependence, 18, 23, 136, 137
Depopulation, 27, 52
Deputies, Chamber of, 40, 41, 43, 71, 90, 236, 265
Diario Ilustrado, El, 81
Diez, Sergio, 262, 263
Directorate of Electoral Registry, 47
Dividing number, 49, 163
Durán, Julio, 62, 217, 218, 222, 223, 224, 228, 229
Durkheim, Emile, 147, 148

Eastman (family, 83, 84, 93, 96
Economy, national, 59, 99, 100, 111, 117, 132, 168, 173, 209, 217, 264
Edwards (family), 83, 87, 89, 93, 95, 96, 100
Edwards, Agustín, 96
El Teniente (copper mine), 174, 262, 288
Elections, 1, 46, 47, 157, 275; by-elections: of April 1971, 260; of Coquimbo, 1972, 264; of Curico, 1964, 218, 223; of Linares, 1972, 262-263; of O'Higgins and Colchagua, 1972, 262; of Valparaíso, 1971, 261-262; cartography of, 4-5; congressional, 48, 277: of 1932, 159-161, 163; of 1937, 162-165, 166; of 1941, 64, 169-172, 188; of 1945, 177-180, 182, 188; of 1949, 62, 64, 188, 189, 193, 194, 276; of 1953, 62, 194-197, 289; of 1957, 200-203, 204, 205, 208; of 1961, 210-214; of 1965, 230-236, 293; of 1969, 63, 152, 243-248; of 1973, 53, 60, 62, 63, 265-273, 285, 286, 291, 292, 293; ecological analysis of, 151, 275; electoral fatigue, 48, 251; municipal, 48, 260: of 1935, 162; of 1944, 177, 178; of 1947, 184; of 1950, 189, 191, 193; of 1956, 200; of 1960, 210; of 1963, 216, 283; of 1967, 239-240; of 1971, 259-260, 273; pacts, 49-50; presidential, 48, 275, 278: of 1932, 159-162; of 1938, 166-168; of 1942, 174-176; of 1946, 181-184; of 1952, 191-194 of 1958, 206-209; of 1964, 62, 224-229; of 1970, 253-258, 273; senatorial, 55
Elite groups: economic, 67, 97, 101, 102; managerial, 97, 104; political, 39, 72, 122, 135; social, 81, 85-91, 95; workers', 30, 124
Employees' Union of Chile, 146
Encina, Francisco, 73, 80, 136
Encomenderos, 80
Engels, F., 117
Enríquez, Edgardo and Miguel, 122
Entrepreneurs, 58, 74, 91-93, 58, 100-102, 107, 284
Errázuriz (family), 84, 86, 88, 89, 90, 272
Espartaco, 66
Estancia, 18, 31, 136, 294
Europe, 22, 58, 98, 105, 118, 135, 147
European: colonists, 25, 91, 92, 104; families, 31; liberalism, 61; workers, 123, 130
Expropriation, 141, 142, 259, 262
Extraordinary powers, 34, 40, 161, 184

Faivovich, Angel, 94
Falange Nacional, 57, 58, 59, 131, 165, 168, 171, 174, 180, 181, 182, 185, 188, 197, 203, 213, 237
Farmsteaders, 25
Fascism, 67, 190
FECH. *See* Students Federation of Chile
Federación de Estudiantes Secundarios, 70
Federation of Oil Workers, 134
Female voters, 46, 224, 233, 236, 258
Feminist Party of Chile, 198
Ferrocarril Longitudinal, 18, 85
Fiducia, 107
Figueroa, Emiliano, 158
Firm hand policy, 2, 106, 161, 199, 241, 264

Index

FOCH. *See* Grand Workers Federation of Chile
Foreign relations, 34, 37, 42, 173, 185
France, 91
FRAP. *See* Popular Action Front
Freemasonry, 61, 71, 119, 191
Frei, Eduardo, 3, 35, 36, 42, 55, 56, 60, 69, 73, 85, 95, 102, 140, 141, 142, 152, 188, 199, 203, 205, 206, 208, 217, 218, 222, 223, 224, 226, 227, 228, 230, 232, 236, 239, 240, 241, 243, 249, 268, 275, 279, 289
French minorities, 92, 93
Frente Nacional del Pueblo. See People's National Vanguard
Frödden, Carlos, 75
Fronda aristocrática, La, 81
Front of Revolutionary Workers, 127
Frontera, La, 8, 10, 20, 22-24, 25, 159, 213, 257, 267, 290, 296, 297
Frustration, 117, 118, 127, 128, 147, 148-149
Fuentealba, Renán, 238

Gallo (family), 96, 115
Gana (family), 87, 88, 95
Gandarillas (family), 84, 87, 88
Gandarillas, José, 129
General Confederation of Workers, 130
Germans, 24, 92, 93
Godoy, César, 168
González, Galo, 190
González Madariaga, Exequiel, 198
Gonzalez Videla, Gabriel, 34, 65, 173, 178, 181, 182, 184, 185, 186, 190, 193, 198, 210, 215, 279, 281, 286, 289
González von Marées, Jorge, 67, 68, 76, 171
Government of National Concentration, 185
Grand Workers Federation of Chile (FOCH), 130, 162
Great Britain, 91
Grove, Marmaduke, 64, 75, 76, 158, 159, 160, 161, 162, 165, 168, 177, 186
Guerrilla, 241
Gumucio, Rafael A., 238
Guzmán, Nicomedes, 145

Hacienda, 18, 136
Hales, Alejandro, 95, 203
Herrera, Ariosto, 75
Hidalgo, Manuel, 64, 146
Housing, 11, 16, 21, 28, 31, 153
Huasco, valley, 83
Huerta, Ismael, 76
Huertos, 139
Hypermobilization, 154

Ibañez, Bernardo, 181, 182, 185
Ibañez del Campo, Carlos, 3, 42, 55, 58, 59, 63, 75, 76, 102, 103, 128, 130, 139, 158, 159, 165, 166, 173, 174, 176, 188, 189, 190, 191, 193, 194, 197, 198, 200, 202, 203, 204, 205, 209, 230, 241, 275, 288, 292; legal dictatorship, 158
Ibañismo, 56, 58, 63, 76, 161, 191, 193, 194, 200, 203, 205, 208, 212, 214, 223, 271, 283, 289, 290, 292; Evangelic *Ibañismo,* 128
Iglesia Jóven, 242
Illiteracy, 19, 23, 28
Immigrants, 95, 110
Indians, 20, 23, 24, 25
INDAP. *See Instituto de Desarrollo Agropecuario*
Infante (family), 86, 87, 101
Inflation, 111, 117, 132, 147, 166, 199, 217, 243, 249, 252, 253, 264
Inquilinos, 18, 136, 137
Instituto de Desarrollo Agropecuario (INDAP), 139, 143, 242
Intellectuals, 60, 63, 66, 67, 73, 92, 111, 119, 147, 227, 237
Intendants, 37
Iquique, 11, 63, 226
Irarrázabal (family), 83, 84, 87
Irarrázabal, Manuel J., 38
Italians, 85, 92, 93-94, 95
ITT, corporation, 265

JAP. *See Juntas de Abastecimientos y Precios*
Jacobinism, 115
Jerez, Alberto, 238
Jesuits, 69, 83
Jews, 92, 94
Johnson, Lyndon, 239

"Joined lists," 263
Juntas de Abastecimientos y Precios, 154, 264
Juntas de Beneficencia, 129
Justicialism, 198

Kingship, 85-90, 100, 101, 307
Klein and Saks, consultants, 199, 200
Koch, Osvaldo, 203
Koenig (family), 93

La Compañía, 83
La Serena, 13, 96
Lafferte, Elías, 159, 178
Land seizures, 141
Landowners, 18, 38, 72, 74, 82-85, 86, 97, 138, 189, 235, 238, 256, 284, 288
Larraín (family), 86, 87, 88, 89, 100, 101
Larraín, Jaime, 181
Las Condes, 16, 227
Latifundistas. See Landowners
Latin America, 7, 45, 64, 68, 72, 91, 111, 114, 145, 229, 272, 295
Lavanderos, Jorge, 242
Law for the Permanent Defense of Democracy, 185, 204
Lazo, Carmen, 236
Leaders: labor, 132, 133, 180, 181, 200, 283; political, 2, 38; religious groups, 194
Lebanese. *See* Levantines
Left (political), 12, 21, 53, 56, 57, 63, 114, 133, 134, 145-151, 155, 161, 162, 173, 180, 184, 194, 200, 204, 205, 209, 215, 218, 222, 231, 236, 237, 240, 241, 249, 250, 251, 252, 253, 261, 266, 267, 276, 279, 281, 284, 285, 287, 288, 293, 294, 296; Ultraleft, 154, 155, 220, 221, 241, 263, 265
Leftist Radical party, 51, 263, 265
Leftist Revolutionary Movement (MIR), 66, 110, 122, 127, 143, 148, 153, 241, 263
Legitimacy, 45
Leighton, Bernardo, 93, 230
Lenin, V. I., 118

Letelier (family), 87, 93, 95
Letelier, Valentín, 115
Levantines, 85, 92, 94-95, 104, 203
Liberal party, 32, 49, 58, 97, 105, 111, 115, 119, 161, 163, 171, 176, 178, 181, 184, 186, 197, 202, 210, 212, 215, 232, 280, 282, 284, 285, 286, 287, 290, 291, 292; democratic, 58; progressive, 176, 186; unified, 58
Libertarianism, 148
Liceo, 69, 112-113, 115, 117
Lillo, Baldomero, 145
Linares: by-election of 1972, 262-263; city, 18; province, 18, 142, 188, 202, 216, 257, 262, 263, 270, 271, 287, 288
Línea Recta, 76, 106, 198
Llanquihue: lake, 25; province, 25, 26, 52, 142, 291, 292
Loopholes, constitutional, 33, 261
Lorca, Alfredo, 236
Los Andes, 14
Los Angeles, 23
Lota, 21, 38, 96, 149, 184
Lower class, 74, 120, 121, 145, 147, 162, 230
Luengo, Fernando, 50
Lumpenproletariat, 16, 21
Lyon (family), 93, 95

MacIver (family), 93
MacIver, Enrique, 115
Magallanes, 16, 17, 29-31, 51, 54, 55, 134, 152, 163, 166, 180, 182, 191, 195, 206, 212, 228, 235, 247, 256, 257, 268, 294-295, 296
Magellan, Strait of, 8, 29, 30
Maira, Luis, 69, 70, 238, 271
Male voters, 16, 224, 226, 227, 233, 236, 257, 258, 260, 266
Malleco, 22, 65, 143, 152, 178, 212, 244, 290, 291
Mancomunales, 129, 130
MAPU. *See* Unified Movement of Popular Action
Marcha de la Patria Jóven, 223
Marín, Oscar, 261
Marín Balmaceda, Raúl, 90, 178

Index

Maritain, Jacques, 117
Martínez, Carlos A., 64, 146
Marx, Karl, 117, 147, 159
Marxism, 63, 66-67, 116, 117, 120, 146, 148, 191, 221, 222, 238, 242, 253
Marxist groups, 56, 64, 220
Matta (family), 90, 115
Matte (family), 87, 88, 95, 96, 100
Matte, Arturo, 191, 193, 203
Matte Hurtado, Eugenio, 64, 158, 161
Maule, 19, 20, 27, 52, 83, 138, 197, 214, 244, 246, 257, 271, 287
Mayorazgo, 79
Mayordomo, 82
Media, 3, 14, 23, 31, 153, 199, 222, 223, 252, 253, 258
Medio-pelo, families, 105, 116
Merchants, 91, 107
Mercurio, El, 96
Mery, Hernán, 262
Mery, María Elena, 262, 263
Messianic expectations, 3, 189, 219
Metropolitan area, 14-17, 282, 287, 295, 296, 297
Middle class, 53, 59, 74, 92, 97, 107-114, 120, 154, 162, 229, 230, 232, 240, 249, 253, 265, 284, 296; definition of, 109; political ambivalence, 121; strata, 109-111; values of, 116
Military personnel, 34, 36, 43, 75, 158-159, 198, 253, 259
Miners, 123, 125, 172, 174, 202, 282; coal, 127, 134, 149, 184, 252, 254, 289, 294; copper, 125, 174, 252, 265
Minifundia, 20, 27, 137, 138, 143, 256
Mining: centers, 227, 279; provinces, 12, 54, 122, 123, 166, 178, 184, 213, 217, 223, 239, 247
Ministers of state, 35-37
MIR. *See* Leftist Revolutionary Movement
Mistral, Gabriela, 112
Modernization, 16, 18, 118, 151
Moller (family), 93, 95
Monckeberg (family), 93, 95, 272
Montaña, La, 23
Montero, Carlos, 223

Montero, Juan E., 158
Montt (family), 84, 87, 88, 272
Morandé (family), 83, 93, 95
Moreno, Rafael, 140, 238, 262
Movement of Revolutionary Pobladores, 153
Movement of Support of the Anti-Imperialist Revolution, 66
Movimiento Campesino Revolucionario, 143
"Mummies," 232, 243, 270
Musalem, José, 95
Myth, political, 2

Nación, La, 203
"*Naranjazo,*" 218
Naranjo, Oscar, 218, 221, 288
National Confederation of Unions, 130
National Democratic party (PADENA), 50, 59, 63, 214, 217, 222, 223, 232, 233, 235, 244, 248, 268, 291, 292
National Falange. *See Falange Nacional*
National Montt-Varista party, 97, 117
National party, 58, 105, 240, 243, 244, 246, 251, 252, 253, 260, 262, 265, 267, 268, 270, 279, 280, 284, 288, 291, 292; formation, 58
National Socialist party, 67-68, 161, 163, 168, 171; German, 67
National Society of Agriculture (SNA), 140
Nationalism, 64, 67, 94, 106, 111, 190, 230, 265
Nationalization: of banks, 220; of copper, 219, 226, 230, 236, 237, 238, 259
Neff, Francisco, 75
Neruda, Pablo, 112, 178, 217, 251
New Public Action, 64
Nixon, Richard, 265
Norte Chico, 8, 10, 12, 83, 115, 142, 142, 171, 173, 174, 182, 186, 202, 266, 280, 281
North (area), 8, 10-11, 17, 123, 138, 145, 266, 295, 296; leftism in, 276-280; ports of, 129; urbanization, 11
Northern provinces, 53, 159, 163, 166,

169, 174, 182, 195, 200, 206, 210, 213, 216, 226, 235, 239, 246, 254, 258, 260, 270, 273
Noticias de Ultima Hora, Las, 103
Nuble, 18, 54, 142, 188, 197, 210, 233, 244, 256, 247, 257, 267, 288

Obstructionism, 41, 168, 169, 197, 219, 230, 243, 261
O'Higgins, 18, 19, 65, 83, 137, 142, 213, 228, 233, 256, 267, 287, 288; by-election of 1972, 262
Ojeda, "Pincho," 199
Oligarchy, 67, 74, 109, 118, 138, 169, 229, 242, 265, 272
Olivares, Héctor, 262
Opposition, 36, 41, 42, 43, 168, 184, 185, 190, 197, 198, 210, 215, 217, 219, 229, 230, 231, 236, 239, 252, 261, 263, 265
Order of the Holy Word, 69
Order of the Sacred Heart, 69
Orientals, 92
Osorno, 25, 26, 54, 142, 212, 244, 247, 291, 292
Ossa (family), 84, 87, 272
Ossa Pretot, Sergio, 102
Ovalle (city), 280
Ovalle (family), 87, 90
Owner cultivators, 136, 256, 272, 293
Oyanedel, Abraham, 159

PADENA. *See* National Democratic party
Palacios, Nicolás, 92, 136
Palacios, Pedro, 76
Palestinians. *See* Levantines
Palestro, Mario, 94, 270
Palma, Daniel, 190
Parcelas, 136, 139
Parliamentary Republic, 47, 62, 63
Parra, Abdón, 203
Parra, Bosco, 238, 262
Partido del Trabajo, 66, 68, 202
Partido Democrata, 62, 171, 238
Partido Obrero Socialista, 130, 146
Parties, political, 45, 49, 56-68; decline, 189-190; "historic," 56, 57, 59
Pascal Allende, Andrés, 122
Paternalism, 104, 123, 133, 136, 137
Patria y Libertad, 106

Patrón, 82, 123
Peasants, 18, 135-138, 173, 219, 235, 252, 253, 256, 264, 265, 272, 286
Pekinistas, 66, 77,
Pentecostals, 128
People's Democratic Party, 186, 204, 288
People's National Vanguard, 65, 204, 217, 222
People's Organized Vanguard (VOP), 36, 153
Pérez (family), 86
Pérez Zukovic, Edmundo, 36, 102, 242
Perón, Juan, 198
Personalism, 77, 161, 169, 219
Peru, 11, 135
Petorca (valley), 83, 84
Pinto (family), 86, 87
PIR. *See* Leftist Radical party
Pizarro, Abelardo, 171
Pluralism, 1, 4, 157, 295
Pobladores, 152, 153, 154, 249
Poblete, Orlando, 264
Polarization, 49, 50, 59, 133, 161, 162, 215, 219, 220, 221, 224, 226, 227, 228, 229, 244, 250, 252, 257, 258, 260, 268, 273
Police force, 36
Political establishment, 3, 55, 62, 69, 74, 76, 110, 157, 190, 193, 198, 199, 203, 205, 209, 215, 219
Politicians, 55, 68-77; background, 72-73; "itinerant," 50
Politiquero, 104
Politization, 1, 132, 219, 241, 250
Popular Action Front (FRAP), 62, 65, 204, 205, 206, 208, 210, 214, 216, 217, 222, 223, 230, 231, 232, 235, 240, 243, 248, 281
Popular Front, 97, 131, 139, 146, 162, 165, 166, 168, 169, 172, 176, 188, 189, 270, 287
Popular Independent Action (API), 50, 51, 251, 259, 264, 271
Popular Liberating Alliance, 165, 166, 173
Popular Promotion, 60, 152, 230
Popular Socialist Union (USOPO), 65, 244
Popular Unity (UP), 51, 62, 94, 127,

Index

134, 137, 141, 142, 143, 144, 154, 220, 251, 252, 258, 259, 260, 262, 263, 264, 265, 266, 267, 268, 272, 279, 285; government of, 253-273
Populism, 117, 119, 128, 157, 190, 191, 193, 272, 288
Portales, Diego, 2, 32; idea of state, 57, 80
Prat, Jorge, 199
Prats, Carlos, 36, 76
President of the Republic, 33-35, 55; profile, 35. See also Extraordinary powers
"Priest of Catapilco." See Zamorano, Antonio
Prieto (family), 84, 87, 90
Proletariat, 16, 21, 24, 123, 148, 151, 171, 173, 188, 193, 243, 249, 252, 281, 289, 291
Proudhon, P. J., 117
Providencia, 16, 227
Provinces, administrative units, 8, 10, 37, 302. See also Agrarian provinces; Urban, provinces
Provincianos, 70, 71, 113
Prussia, 91
Puerto Montt, 25, 223
Punta Arenas, 30

Quadragesimo Anno, 59

Rancagua, 14, 19, 83, 262
Ranquil, 24
Ranquil Peasants Union, 140, 143, 256
"Rattling sabres, night of," 157
Recabarren, Luis E., 62, 63, 130, 146
Radical party, 49, 60-62, 71, 73, 99, 102, 119, 122, 131, 152, 160, 161, 162, 163, 168, 171, 172, 173, 174, 176, 177, 178, 181, 186, 188, 189, 195, 202, 204, 205, 210, 218, 231, 323, 235, 239, 240, 241, 244, 247, 248, 249, 251, 259, 262, 263, 267, 268, 271, 276, 279, 280, 281, 283, 284, 285, 287, 289, 290, 291, 292, 293, 294, 295, 296; Democratic party, 62, 176, 265; movement of doctrinary recuperation, 222; Radical Democracy, 62, 251; Radical Doctrinary, 62, 186; socialist, 61
Ramírez, Pedro F., 238
Reformism, 117, 128, 217, 220, 221
Regionalism, 290-291
Regionalization, 7-8, 10, 275-297
Reinoso, Luis, 190
Religion, as background of politics, 127-129, 222, 289
Renca, 16
Republican Militia, 67, 161
Republican Union, 61
Rerum Novarum, 59
"Resistance Societies," 130
"Revolution in Freedom," 60, 223, 238, 243
Revolutionary Marxist Vanguard, 66
Revolutionary Workers Party, 66
Riesco (family), 84, 87, 101, 272
Right (political), 53, 56, 57, 95, 103-107, 114, 171, 172, 173, 177, 178, 181, 182, 188, 193, 205, 209, 210, 212, 215, 218, 220, 230, 232, 240, 248, 250, 261, 272, 281, 284, 285, 286, 287, 289, 293, 294, 295
Ríos, Juan A., 173, 174, 176, 178, 181, 279, 283, 286, 289, 290
Rodríguez, Aniceto, 65
Rodríguez, Luciano, 122
Rodríguez de la Sotta, Héctor, 159, 160
Ross, Gustavo, 162, 163, 165, 176
Rossetti, Juan B., 185
Rousseau, J., 117
Rural: exodus, 13, 18, 28, 112, 123; families, 112, 124
Ruralization, 18, 27, 293

Saint Marie, Darío, 102, 203
San Felipe, 14, 171
Santiago: *Barrio Alto,* 69, 105; Basin of, 17, 74, 83, 84, 85; city, 14, 38, 68, 69, 127, 133, 135, 145, 159, 224, 252, 270, 271; districts: First, 169, 188, 210, 247, 284; Second, 52, 188, 206, 210, 224, 233, 244, 257, 267, 270, 285; Third, 16, 52, 53, 186, 188, 203, 213, 244, 285-286; Fourth, 202, 214, 257, 286; province, 15-17,

54, 55, 120, 134, 138, 142, 159, 160, 163, 171, 174, 191, 202, 206, 214, 223, 224, 246, 247, 253, 254, 257, 268, 284-287, 297
Schaulsohn, Jacobo, 94
Schnake, Oscar, 64, 173
Schneider, René, 259
Schools, 69, 110
Schwarzenberg, Julio, 67
Second World War, 146, 168, 173
Senate, 40, 41, 73, 74, 239, 244
Senatorial districts, 51, 54-55
Sepúlveda, Adonis, 260
Sepúlveda, Claudio, 76
Shantytowns, 153
Sharecroppers, 136, 137, 256
Siglo, El, 185
Silva Solar, Julio, 238, 271
Silva Ulloa, Ramón, 244
Siútico, 105, 116
Social Action Front, 185
Socialismo oriollo, 64
Socialist party, 49, 57, 64, 65, 73, 74, 148, 153, 163, 168, 169, 172, 177, 180, 181, 182, 184, 186, 188, 190, 213, 232, 235, 239, 244, 247, 251, 259, 267, 268, 270, 272, 276, 283, 285, 288, 291, 292, 293, 294, 295, 296; authentic, 65, 177, 180, 181, 186; reunification of, 65, 205
Socialist Democratic party, 50, 259
Socialist Marxist party, 64
Socialist Party of Chile, 185, 197, 202
Socialist Popular party, 50, 65, 185, 188, 190, 191, 197, 199, 202, 204, 248, 292, 293
Socialist Republic of Chile, 158
Socialist Republican party, 61, 162
Socialist Revolutionary Alliance, 64
Socialist Union, 64
Sociedad de Artesanos, 129
Souper, Roberto, 76
South (area), 8, 29-31, 53, 54, 216, 261, 295
Soviet Union, 35, 64, 65, 66, 173, 185
Spaniards, 92, 98
Spanish: colonization, 18, 20, 24; rule, 26, 79, 85, 91

"Statute of Democratic Guarantees," 258
Strikes, 126, 145, 184, 200, 241, 264
Students Federation of Chile, 70
Subercaseaux (family), 83, 89, 93, 95, 96
Syrians. *See* Levantines

Tacnazo, 253
Talca: city, 19, 76; province, 19, 83, 85, 142, 214, 223, 247, 256, 267, 270, 287, 288
Talcahuano, 21
Tarapacá, 12, 138, 186, 197, 216, 235, 247, 254, 266, 276, 280
Tarud, Rafael, 50, 76, 95, 102, 203, 214, 217, 222, 223, 251, 264
Teitelboim, Volodia, 94
Temuco, 23
Teno (valley), 83, 84
Terrorism, 253, 259
Tertiarization, 109
Thayer, William, 93, 240
Tocornal (family), 87, 88
Tohá, José, 36, 95, 103
Tomic, Radomiro, 95, 102, 116, 220, 250, 251, 252, 253, 254, 256, 257, 258, 260, 283
Toro (family), 87, 89
Toro, Víctor, 153
Toro y Zambrano, Mateo, 83
Torres, Isauro, 198
Trade unions, 128-135, 146, 172, 177, 184
Trading companies, 91
Trivelli, Hugo, 36, 94

Ultraleft. *See* Left
Umaña, Pastor, 128
Unemployment, 16, 22, 28, 30, 133, 168
Unified Movement of Popular Action (MAPU), 50, 51, 60, 70, 122, 141, 251, 259, 262, 271
Union of Chilean Peasants, 140
Unions. *See* Trade unions
United States, 35, 70, 91, 103, 173, 239, 265
University, 37, 70, 93, 110, 114, 119, 219, 253; democratization of,

Index

241; reform, 236; of Chile, 35, 69, 146, 239, 252; of Concepción, 66, 146, 239, 252; Catholic University of Chile, 69; Technical State, 252
Urban: marginals, 16, 67, 149, 153, 249, 252; provinces, 53, 113, 136, 152, 159, 160, 166, 178, 180, 186, 191, 194, 195, 203, 206, 208, 214, 215, 235, 239, 244, 248, 249, 254, 260, 267; slums, 153
Urbanism: "excluding," 153; "incorporative," 152
Urbanization, 11, 115, 282; of society, 18, 108-109; and vote for the Left, 151-155
Uribe, Armando, 70
Urmeneta (family), 96
Uruguay, 108
USOPO. *See* Popular Socialist Union

Valdés (family), 100, 101
Valdivia: city, 24; province, 25, 54, 142, 182, 244, 247, 291
Valparaíso: by-election of 1971, 261-262; city, 14, 38, 83, 84, 91, 145, 306; province, 16, 54, 55, 120, 134, 142, 159, 160, 174, 191, 202, 206, 208, 213, 223, 224, 231, 233, 244, 246, 247, 253, 257, 261, 270, 271, 282-284, 297
Vergara (family), 87, 88
Vergara, Colonel, 76

Veto, 33
Vial (family), 87, 88, 100
Viaux, Ambrosio, 75
Viaux, Roberto, 76, 253
Vicuña (family), 95, 101
Villalobos, Alejandro, 153
Viña del Mar, 14, 38, 105, 224, 261
Voters, 46-48, 52, 53; progressive, 151-152. *See also* Female voters; Male voters
"Voters' Revolt," 73, 114, 146
Voting: bribery, 47, 146, 163, 166, 186, 204, 206; working class, 227
Vuscovic, Pedro, 94

War of the Pacific (1879-1884), 145, 146
Wilson, Santiago, 203
Workers, 120, 124, 193, 259, 264, 284, 294; female, 125; industrial, 133; typology, 125-128
Working class, 11, 15, 122-129, 145, 172, 224, 226; consciousness, 128; structure, 124-129

Yarur, Carlos, 103
Yugoslavia, 65, 185
Yugoslavians, 94, 254

Zaldívar, Andrés, 260
Zamorano, Antonio, 76, 128, 206, 208
Zañartu (family), 87, 88
Zañartu, Enrique, 159, 160
Zepeda, Hugo, 178, 280